Realizing Roma Rights

PENNSYLVANIA STUDIES IN HUMAN RIGHTS

Bert B. Lockwood, Jr., Series Editor

A complete list of books in the series is available from the publisher.

Realizing Roma Rights

Edited by

Jacqueline Bhabha, Andrzej Mirga,
and Margareta Matache

PENN

UNIVERSITY OF PENNSYLVANIA PRESS

PHILADELPHIA

Published by
University of Pennsylvania Press
Philadelphia, Pennsylvania 19104-4112
www.upenn.edu/pennpress

Printed in the United States of America
on acid-free paper
10 9 8 7 6 5 4 3 2 1

A Cataloging-in-Publication record is available from the Library of Congress
ISBN 978-0-8122-4899-9

Contents

Realizing Roma Rights: An Introduction

Jacqueline Bhabha

The Roma[1] scholar Ian Hancock opens his classic book *The Pariah Syndrome* with a remarkable quotation from the work of Sam Beck, an American and fellow scholar about his fieldwork in Romania: "Romanians who are in administrative government and political positions of authority, explain the Tsigani [a racial slur for the Roma] situation by referring to America. 'You know,' they say, 'The Tsigani are like your Negroes: foreign, lazy, shiftless, untrustworthy and black.'"[2] Virulent and deep-seated racial hatred is only one of the commonalities linking these two large minorities in the world's richest continents. A recent history of centuries-old slavery and the persistence of dramatic contemporary social and economic disadvantage and marginalization are others.

But alongside the commonalities, there are notable differences. The eminent U.S. civil rights advocate and constitutional law expert Jack Greenberg notes that "for much of their histories, the Roma in Eastern Europe and African Americans traversed similar paths. . . . During World War II . . . their paths forked."[3] He notes the contrast between the development of the civil rights movement and antisegregation legal victories in the United States on the one hand, and the lack of political visibility and concomitant social marginalization and educational segregation of East European Roma on the other. From the perspective of this book, which aims to bring Roma rights issues to the foreground for an international readership interested in contemporary human rights challenges, other differences are also striking and relevant.

A significant difference between the African American and the Roma communities, explored in this book, is the nature of civil society engagement with the communities' respective issues. The American civil rights movement has a long and venerable history, encompassing a broad range of discrete political and social currents to be sure, but eventually generating highly visible and effective national leadership, coherent political and legal demands, and mass mobilization. A huge body of literature reflects this tradition and cumulative experience. By contrast, the Roma movement, in Europe and elsewhere in the world, has not yet established a visible presence as a mass movement. In spite of targeted demands and modest forms of organizing in a range of different countries during the twentieth century, it was only in 1971 that Roma leaders from around the world gathered outside London for the first International Romani Congress, to decide on the symbols of Roma unity and launch concerted legal and political claims.

Another contrast between African American and Roma movements relates to the modality of political organizing. The priorities and the methods advanced by Roma organizations, especially in post-Communist Eastern Europe, were often influenced by external stakeholders. Whereas grassroots activism on African American civil rights was a critical precondition and precursor of constitutional and policy transformations across the United States, advances in the rights and circumstances of the Roma have largely been the result of a different form of activism. Advocates have focused their efforts on legislative and policy reforms, strategic litigation, or access to education and health, with less attention paid to community empowerment and participation. This form of organizing has had some impact. Whereas the 1969 Council of Europe Recommendation on the situation of "Gypsies and Other Travelers in Europe" framed the issue in terms of Roma victimhood and vulnerability, more recent EU member state or commission documents, by contrast, stress the central importance of Roma leadership and active participation in processes of change. Roma activism has forced EU policy makers to engage with the Roma community on more equal terms.[4]

In the United States these developments in the political positioning of the Roma community do not register. The vast majority of Americans, including otherwise well-informed people, know little if anything about the estimated 14 million Roma worldwide, despite a long-standing (if small) Roma presence within the United States. This lack of awareness persists, even with well-publicized recent government-sponsored attacks on Roma settlements in France and Italy, and the proliferation of anti-Roma hate speech, including by representatives of mainstream political parties in Hungary, Romania, and Greece.[5] These situations are discussed in detail in several of the chapters in this volume.

This American knowledge lacuna makes the publication of *Realizing Roma Rights* long overdue. We hope awareness and discussion prompted by the book will stimulate integration of Roma issues into broader social and political debates on ongoing discrimination, stigma, and segregation in the United States, Europe, and elsewhere. Because its focus is cross-regional, and its contributors have diverse backgrounds—national government, the academy, civil society, and international organizations—the book provides insights into a wide range of themes related to Europe's Roma community. Future research needs to target other under-studied Roma populations living all over the world, including Latin America, the United States, and the Middle East.

Realizing Roma Rights explores the dynamics of social exclusion and stigma, the challenges of European and national policy development and implementation, and the history of Roma political and social mobilization. We hope that increased familiarity with Roma rights challenges will stimulate activists and experts who have developed successful strategies for tackling social exclusion in other fields to contribute their insights to advancing the Roma situation.

Part I, "The Long Shadow of Anti-Roma Discrimination," investigates the efficacy of targeted intervention, both from the perspective of impact litigation (Alexandra Oprea) and more broadly across the domains of education, housing, and social violence (Elena Rozzi). Part II, "International and Regional Perspectives," presents the perspectives of government officials (Erika Schlager, David Meyer and Michael Uyehara) involved in Roma rights promotion. The contributors to Part III, "The Longue Durée: The History of Roma Policy as an Element in U.S. Foreign Policy" (Andrzej Mirga, Kálmán Mizsei, and Margareta Matache and Krista Oehlke), switch the focus to European and national institutions themselves and toward the obstacles to Roma inclusion that they have encountered or contributed to. Why is the current impact of vigorous interventions and well-funded innovations targeting Roma exclusion so limited? Exploration of the reasons for this disappointing result lies at the heart of the analysis advanced by the authors in this volume.

Part IV, "The Enduring Challenge of Tackling Anti-Roma Institutional Discrimination and Popular Racism in Contemporary Europe: A

Comparative Analysis," features the work of James A. Goldston and of Will Guy. Part V of this volume is titled "Looking Forward: The Imperative of Roma Community Mobilization and Leadership" (Peter Vermeersch, Teresa Sordé Martí and Fernando Macías, and David Mark). The critical question of Roma political engagement, at the level of leadership within national and European institutions, but also at grassroots level in municipalities, regions, and national forums, resonates across the European Union. It is an urgent continental issue, whether the vantage point is France, Italy, and Spain or, further east, Romania, Czech Republic, and Hungary.

Experts have noted that much European Roma policy, within the European Commission for example, has been prompted not by grassroots demands for justice or inclusion but by pressure from EU member states concerned about Roma migration and its consequences.[6] Related to this, with a few notable early exceptions,[7] current Roma literature has tended to be specialist and technical, focused on particular social challenges or cultural issues but lacking an integrative perspective and, as a result, a broadly based audience interested in questions of human rights and social justice across domains, from gender-related harms to migrant rights, to questions of racial and sexual identity. *Realizing Roma Rights* draws on the recent welcome increase in data (generated by the EU Fundamental Rights Agency, the UN Development Programme, the World Bank, and others) to address the nexus of social exclusion theory and social policy efficacy so central to the human rights advocacy and broader social science fields.

The starting point for discussion of Roma-related issues is the widespread acknowledgment in government, academic, and civil society circles that the Roma population in Europe continues to face disproportionately low access to quality education, health care, and employment within the formal labor market. Examples proliferate: a considerable number of young Roma in Bosnia and Herzegovina, Montenegro, Albania, Moldova, and (to a lesser extent) the former Yugoslav republic of Macedonia have never been to school; in 2011 in Moldova, only 40 percent of Roma reported having medical insurance coverage compared to close to 80 percent of non-Roma; and in Romania, only one in two Roma of working age actually are working.[8]

Several chapters in this book address these issues in detail, highlighting the enduring impact of the long shadow of discrimination and exclusion on quality of life for many within the Roma community. In her chapter, Rozzi presents data showing a decline in the participation of Italian Roma children in schools within the past five years. Italian institutions often ascribe the alarmingly irregular and low participation of Roma children in schools to their culture's "inborn tendency" to dismiss education, a claim that Rozzi deconstructs in her powerful chapter. Probing Roma inclusion policies that have not worked, Matache and Oehlke argue in their chapter that slow and insignificant progress in educational attainment for Roma children is but one small part of a broader contemporary disinterest in implementing equal opportunity principles for Roma. They focus on programs targeting Roma education in Romania as an instance of implementation weakness in the field of education. By concentrating responsibility for Roma educational inclusion within the National Agency for Roma rather than within much more powerful mainstream ministries, they argue, the commitment to raise Roma educational performance has been ghettoized and its impact therefore circumscribed. Skill training and apprenticeship development as well as health care access and provision have suffered from similar weaknesses.

In her chapter, Oprea captures the exclusion and subordination of Roma women, focusing on two interrelated violations of Roma women's reproductive rights. She reminds us that compulsory sterilization of Roma women was widely practiced in the former Czechoslovakia as well as in other countries. Child removal, a more recent phenomenon facing Roma families, became widely evident in 2013 with the high-profile removal of blond children from Roma parents. Oprea suggests these are "only the most visible manifestations of a systemic policy that views Roma mothers as irresponsible and unfit to be parents."

The unsatisfactory Roma situation continues despite an extensive program of European Union programmatic intervention to promote and enhance Roma rights. The antecedents of European attention to the Roma situation are analyzed in chapters by Schlager and by Meyer and Uyehara, long-standing policy experts on minority rights issues. Schlager traces the history of international organization engagement in East European human rights and shows how the denial of citizenship to Roma citizens in the newly formed Czech Republic became an issue for those organizations. Meyer and Uyehara illustrate the process of international engagement with Roma issues through the lens of American engagement. Success in engineering a focus on Roma rights as an important priority for contemporary European policy of course was not tantamount to success in outcomes, they argue, and indeed they concur with the consensus view that the impact of efforts to improve Roma integration and empowerment in the European Union and beyond has been disappointing.

The reasons for the failure of EU Roma policy and the much celebrated Decade of Roma Inclusion that epitomized parts of the policy are the subject of insightful scrutiny in the contributions by Mirga and by Mizsei, two seasoned participants in European Roma policy development. As each demonstrates, the causes of limited impact are multiple and complex and warrant careful study, at both the national and regional level. Some implementation weaknesses are clearly the result of technical deficiencies related to program development, roll out, and evaluation.

Both Mirga and Mizsei provide trenchant analyses of European Roma policy development, its characteristics, and its limitations. Both note the importance of community mobilization as a means of steering and maximizing the impact of technocratic policy development. Mizsei sets himself the task of reconstructing and dissecting the unraveling of Roma integration in European post-Communist market states. He draws on Michael Mann's concept of "the dark side of democracy" to probe a new state of affairs in Eastern Europe that generates mass unemployment and racial attacks against the Roma community.[9] In Hungary, for example, he notes how, within the space of two decades from 1971 to 1993, Roma unemployment skyrocketed from 15 percent to a staggering 72 percent, a fivefold increase. He also observes the impact of newly celebrated "freedom of speech" on the escalation of anti-Roma hate speech. In this challenging context, he argues, European interventions, including the development approach incorporated in the Decade of Roma Inclusion and the establishment of the European Social Fund, fail to counter the post-Soviet dislocation and impoverishment of the Roma community.

Mirga's chapter provides a masterful overview of the development of European Roma policy from the early 1990s to the mid-2000s. As an observer, analyst, and participant in the process, the contributor's vantage point is perhaps unique and certainly compelling. He makes the case that the evolution of Roma policy, focused as it has been on initiatives to target the community's minority status, has resulted in a series of political gains for the Roma community but corresponding losses in the social and economic sphere. Minority status recognition through multifaceted initiatives at the EU level has, he argues, failed to translate into comprehensive and constructive state policies at the domestic level, policies capable of generating social and economic inclusion and opportunity. He concludes pessimistically that greater political visibility and the development of structural funding allocations have so far failed to translate into the profound positive changes needed to turn the tide of exclusion and deprivation.

European policy failure to date is also a result of conceptual failures in targeting stigma and exclusion effectively and ensuring that allocated funds are appropriately distributed and managed. Guy demonstrates in his chapter how the disbursement of EU structural and cohesion funds has been characterized by weak planning and a poor understanding of the drivers of racial hatred. As a result, he argues, hate-filled attitudes and violent attacks have proliferated rather than declined, leading grassroots European Roma coalitions to conclude that most inclusion strategies had not made much difference. Rozzi discusses the situation in Italy, where Roma communities, despite European identity and in some cases long-standing residence, are still considered and treated as "other" or "enemies within," denied cultural legitimacy or authenticity as citizens, and instead visibly excluded in "nomad camps" or illegal settlements, trapped in harsh lives on the margins of legality.

Poor leadership, ethical weaknesses including corruption, and failing national and local administrative structures compound the problem of European Roma policy implementation. For example, as Guy points out, member states receiving European Social Funds, 20 percent of which were meant to be used to support social inclusion initiatives, have not been obliged to declare how much of those funds have been spent. Large unspent resources are known to exist in several of the countries with the highest concentrations of Roma communities.[10] This absence of transparency has continued to stymie efforts to kick-start social regeneration among Roma communities. And yet it has not attracted infringement proceedings by the European Commission (the formal procedures followed if a member state is in breach of EU law) or other measures to compel effective compliance. As a result much of the promise of structural regeneration and inclusion held out by the ambitious Decade programming has disappointed the Decade's architects—including the World Bank and the Open Society Foundations—and others involved in trying to generate significant and enduring progress.

The current Roma situation in Europe offers another set of analytic puzzles and challenges relevant to the relative failure of impact litigation, a favorite tool of contemporary human rights advocates on both sides of the Atlantic. Milestone litigation before the European Court of Human Rights on the forced sterilization of Roma women (discussed by Oprea) and on the discriminatory segregation of Roma children in school (discussed by Goldston) has failed to end the institutional racism at the heart of the court cases or to turn the political and social tide toward effective Roma inclusion. The lack of real impact of the judgments of the European Court of Human

Rights, the world's most robust and far-reaching human rights court, in tackling one of the leading human rights issues within its jurisdiction has perplexed many.

In 2003 a group of European Roma leaders approached Professor Jack Greenberg of Columbia Law School. Greenberg had been the head of the Legal Defense Fund for the NAACP and the lead advocate in the watershed *Brown v. Board of Education* case before the U.S. Supreme Court.[11] This case has been credited with putting to an end the "separate but equal" school policy that was in force across the United States, a policy that upheld the segregation of black schoolchildren in black-only public schools. Roma leaders were interested in learning from Greenberg what the *Brown v. Board* litigation might teach them so that a comparable outcome could be achieved for Roma schoolchildren. Across Europe, tens of thousands of these children are still segregated—as the chapters by Rozzi, Goldston, and Matache and Oehlke document—in different schools, or different classrooms within integrated schools, or different spaces within integrated classrooms, depending on the European country in question.

Greenberg replied that the Roma advocates should note two radical differences between the two sets of litigation and their broader social context. First, in the U.S. situation, *Brown v. Board* was the product of a long process of civil society engagement and activism against racially segregated schools, whereas no such enduring civil society movement was discernible in the case of Europe's Roma community. Second, prior to *Brown v. Board*, school segregation was considered lawful and constitutional but the decision changed that, and as a result, policy and practice changes on the ground followed.[12] In Europe by contrast, the European Convention on Human Rights had, since 1951, prohibited both direct and indirect discrimination. Yet, as Greenberg noted, by 2003, half a century after the convention was signed, "No European or national judicial or administrative organ has ordered the cessation of segregation in any school."[13] Unlike in the United States, European antidiscrimination litigation had not significantly changed the legal framework. It simply declared what was already known to be the law. It followed, argued Greenberg, that litigation alone would not deliver significant gains to the Roma community in the absence of mass mobilization and strong Roma political leadership.

Realizing Roma Rights explores this theme in some detail, analyzing the limitations of legal victories as enduring guarantees of social transformation. The powerful chapter by Goldston probes the similarities and differences between American and European impact litigation, addressing educational segregation and the broader context in which it occurs. Goldston, himself an experienced advocate, notes interesting similarities in the strategic development of antidiscrimination arguments in the courtroom, before going on to probe the significant differences in legal tradition, structure, and impact. He observes how European judicial actors, like American justices before them, have related their antidiscrimination findings to the harsh and multifactorial realities of life for segregated—"discrete and insular"—minorities.[14] This segregation, both sets of judges argue, constitutes a particular circumstance that prevents the community from benefitting from social structures that other communities can and do rely on. Because of this circumstance and others, judicial pronouncements and the legislative measures that sometimes follow have fallen on less fertile soil than other rights-advancing judgments and have not yielded substantial and enduring changes on the ground in either jurisdiction. On the other hand, Goldston shows how U.S. court-ordered remedies have been much more robust in terms of changes in institutional practice than those of their European counterparts. In part this divergence reflects the underlying differences in legal procedure between the two political entities (the European Court of Human Rights cannot change domestic law), and in part it is a consequence of the traditional financial modesty and limited public sphere impact of European human rights remedial awards (the judgment rather than the financial award is considered the main remedy).

Other troubling questions regarding policy failure vis-à-vis Roma rights in Europe arise. It is clear that freedom of movement within the EU, and the 2004 and 2007 eastern expansions of the union to include countries with large Roma populations such as Hungary, the Czech Republic, and then Romania and Bulgaria, have not delivered the gains for the Roma population that they have for other economically disadvantaged European constituencies. Though EU accession played an important role as an engine of social reform in Eastern Europe in the pre-accession phase,[15] it has failed to maintain that stance going forward. As a result, several recently acceded countries, including Romania, as Matache and Oehlke show, evidence retrenchment and complacency with respect to Roma rights, now that the accession process is behind them. Enlargement of course has had a significant impact on Roma mobility in the EU, but here again the result is complex, as Bozzi and Matache and Oehlke note in their chapters.

Mobility, among other factors, has generated political commitments supporting Roma inclusion, especially the EU Framework for National Roma

Integration Strategies up to 2020.[16] The EU Framework and other commitments, such as the *Action Plan on Improving the Situation of Roma and Sinti within the OSCE Area* and the Decade of Roma Inclusion (2005–2015), an international political initiative involving twelve participating states and four observer countries, are also linked to unsuccessful state-led initiatives that have failed to deliver what was promised.[17] In all EU member states, in the past years, with the exception of compulsory schooling, the discrepancies in education between Roma and non-Roma have become even larger.[18] In 2007, for instance, the Romanian government made a commitment to put an end to segregation by adopting a desegregation order, as outlined by Matache and Oehlke. The order promised that starting with the 2007–2008 school year, there would be no separate Roma classes in first and fifth grades. An evaluation conducted after approval of the order showed that 63 percent out of 122 schools continued to form new first and fifth grade classes segregating Roma children.[19]

European Union citizenship has emerged as a weak tool for tackling xenophobic and exclusionary Western European policies toward Roma mobility from Eastern Europe, revealing the fault lines within the concept from the preamble to the Treaty of Rome (the EU founding document) of the "ever closer [European] union" as Roma individuals are deported from one member state to another. A study of the circumstances of Roma migrants commissioned by the Council of Europe and the Organization of Security and Cooperation in Europe (OSCE) concluded that "there exists a massive gap between international and European law, standards and commitments to eliminate racial discrimination on the one hand, and national policies concerning Roma migration on the other."[20]

Paradoxically, mobility has accelerated some negative stereotypes, as both nondiscriminatory practices and xenophobia have been institutionalized across the European Union. Following the collapse of Communism in Europe and the fall of the Berlin Wall in 1989, Roma populations formerly locked into East European states started exercising their newly found freedom of movement. But this has proved a mixed blessing. "Following 1989, old ideas about 'Gypsies' have been dramatically reawakened in Western Europe, in part as a result of the return of Roma migration from Central and Southeastern Europe."[21] The increased visibility of Roma beggars and destitute informal settlements in and around Western European capital cities stands in sharp contrast to the apparently seamless integration of other European migrants moving from south to north or from east to west.

Hostile stereotypes have devastating consequences, as recent European history illustrates again and again. In the case of the Roma, the most immediate is the pervasive experience of personal violence and physical violence. A 2008 seven-country survey conducted by the EU Fundamental Rights Agency, an independent body funded by the European Union, found that approximately one in three Roma surveyed had been targets of violence within the previous year.[22] Small wonder that, in the face of this relentless hostility, many Roma communities retreat into increasingly strong Rom/Gadje [non-Roma] demarcation in their conduct, preferring collective community support and engagement over interaction with majoritarian institutions, be they schools or workplaces.[23] The extensive criminal activity involved in racial attacks does not seem to be matched by vigorous prosecutorial, protection, or prevention strategies, evidencing a concerning dereliction of duty by responsible municipal, regional, or federal bodies. As Guy and Vermeersch note, extreme right and anti-Roma mobilization creates a climate of impunity, exacerbated by economic recession and high unemployment.

Impunity for individual acts of criminal violence is only one fallout from pervasive anti-Roma hate speech. Racial stereotypes justify forms of structural violence, too, where the target community is denied basic and fundamental rights and then blamed for its own destitution. Several chapters in this book illustrate the process whereby Roma communities are denied real access to mainstream institutions and instead forced to carve out precarious living arrangements for themselves. Illiteracy, lack of health care including reproductive health, squalid accommodations, and isolation from the majority community follow. So do tough daily survival strategies that vitiate the ability to maximize opportunity, develop political leadership, or generate community solidarity and mobilization.

But structural violence is not inevitable. In their chapter, Martí and Macías describe an inventive counter-strategy developed in Spain, where racial stereotypes and structural violence are replaced with proactive community outreach, engagement, and participation. The result is a rare success story where mainstream markers of achievement and empowerment become visible over the ashes of exclusion and deprivation.

In general, however, as noted above, the policies adopted by governments, national, regional and local, over the past two decades have shown limited results at the grassroots level. Even well-implemented projects have had only limited impact because of an absence of strong institutional foundations and sustainable structures that outlive the life of creative pilot projects.

Ghettoization and residential segregation exacerbate this problem as institutional weaknesses are concentrated in the areas most populated by disadvantaged communities, including Roma.

A common theme in the Roma literature is the absence of effective Roma political coherence, mobilization, and leadership. A particularly harsh critic is Yaron Matras. He notes:

> It is obvious that the Roma minority in Europe now has a voice, or perhaps many voices, in the processes that shape European policy, and to some extent also the policies of national governments, towards the Roms. But the issue of representation continues to pose some serious challenges . . . none of the Roma associations has a clearly defined constituency or a well-formulated and transparent political mandate. . . . Many Roma non-governmental organizations tend to be . . . run by small circles of friends . . . they usually lack a formal election procedure for officers. . . . There are different perspectives and viewpoints about the future.[24]

In a similar vein, Nicolae Gheorghe, one of the most respected Roma activists and scholars, argues, "Most Roma organizations still operate as 'sects' rather than 'churches,' since they are not part of a broader mass movement . . . there is a dramatically widening gulf between the 'clubs' of Roma political élites—both at national and transnational level—and the communities they are supposed to represent."[25]

These themes resonate with chapters in this book. Both Mark and Vermeersch analyze aspects of Roma activism and political mobilization, noting the challenges raised by malfunctioning democratic processes designed to ensure minority representation and the critical but underutilized role of Roma youth. Mark, for instance, probes the legal frameworks that set the stage for inadequate political representation and participation for Roma communities. Looking at examples from Romania and Hungary, he argues that emerging legislative measures, designed to enhance the representation of minorities, have, paradoxically, compromised free and fair electoral competition for Roma. In Romania, for example, limitations imposed on Roma organizations wishing to register in electoral competitions for parliamentary elections, have eliminated a level playing field for competing organizations and the power of choice for Roma voters. Reflecting on the obstacles that hamper visible and effective participation and mobilization, Vermeersch notes that at present Roma communities lack the necessary organizational capacity, financial means, and symbolic resources to affect change. Amid a new and still emerging institutional context for consultation at the European level, new research is needed that identifies how the Roma can amplify their presence in policy-making debates, voice their claims, and influence policy outcomes.

Despite malformed legislative measures, however, both Mark and Vermeersch contend that within the last decade calls to empower and mobilize Roma communities have emerged at the local level and at the EU level. These have included efforts to put Roma issues on the political agenda as well as vigorous opposition to negative and repressive policies. Vermeersch cites social mobility strategies for young Roma as a promising way forward, particularly through strengthened desegregation efforts and new forms of youth activism.

Martí and Macías by contrast describe the impact of a small-scale educational intervention in Albacete, Spain, directed by the joint leadership of Roma community activists and a socially committed team of university researchers. These contrasting perspectives concur in their vision of the need for well-informed, structured, and responsibly led community political mobilization, the common ground of success for other oppressed and marginalized constituencies—whether racial, sexual, or disabled. Martí and Macías consider how Roma adolescents and young adults can become stakeholders in Roma rights advancement. Part of their analysis involves attention to the challenge of enhancing and solidifying the access to quality education as a necessary instrument of social redistribution and political advancement.

The chapters in this volume probe different strategies for strengthening the rights of the Roma. After decades of violence, stigma, and exclusion, the Roma need targeted measures to discover the potential for positive gain from actions of the majority community. In their chapters, Uyehara and Meyer, as well as Schlager, describe the complex political processes and diplomatic negotiations promoting attention to Roma rights violations, especially in post-Communist Central and Eastern Europe—Uyehara and Meyer from the perspective of the United States State Department and Schlager from the perspective of the OSCE. Schlager examines the importance of political will and deft diplomatic activity in raising the profile of rights violations of marginalized groups such as the Roma in international forums. She juxtaposes the condemnatory intervention of the U.S. Commission on Security and Cooperation in Europe (a stance that eventually led to the mention of the

Roma and their unique social exclusion in the 1990 Copenhagen Document) to the accommodation strategy of the Council of Europe in the early 1990s. Uyehara and Meyer elaborate further on the progression of U.S. "quiet diplomacy" directed at expressing concern about anti-Roma activism and persistent social and economic marginalization. They describe the State Department's dual emphases on the importance of implementing nondiscrimination measures targeting the majority population but at the same time of strengthening the capacity of the minority through educational programs, including the USAID engagement with Roma youth educational programming.

Across a broad span of disciplines, countries, and subject foci, the book delivers an integrated final message. The key work of strengthening implementation capacity and the political clout to deliver it at the grassroots level is still incomplete. It is the responsibility of those engaged in Roma rights realization and in moving forward deliberately and thoroughly, case by case, neighborhood by neighborhood, country by country. We hope that our book contributes to that process, bringing new thinking and renewed political will to a most urgent human rights challenge in one of the richest parts of the world in our time.

PART I

The Long Shadow of Anti-Roma Discrimination

Chapter 1

Roma Children and Enduring Educational Exclusion in Italy

Elena Rozzi

> Even though the school institutions are willing to take care of them
> [Roma], this population actually shows scarce inclination towards
> integration (including the school community) and, consequently,
> the inborn tendency to refuse regular attendance at school in the
> places in which they settle temporarily.
> —Italian Government, *2006 Report to the UN Committee on the*
> *Elimination of Racial Discrimination*

"Nomad" Children in (and Outside) Italian Schools

In Italy, as in many other European countries, available data and estimates
reveal low school enrollment and attendance rates, along with high levels of
illiteracy, among the Roma population. As in the rest of this volume, the term
"Roma" here is used as an umbrella, including also Sinti and Caminanti.
However, the Italian authorities often call these minorities "nomads," even
though they are mostly permanently settled. As I argue in this chapter, this
label, marking a supposed radical difference of Roma people from the
majority population, serves to legitimize discriminatory policies.

Table 1. "Nomad" Children Enrolled in Italian Schools Registered by the
Ministry of Education, 2008–2009 and 2012–2013

School level	Enrolled 2008–2009	Enrolled 2012–2013	Percentage decrease
Kindergarten	2,171	1,906	−12
Elementary school	7,005	6,253	−11
Middle school	3,467	3,215	−7
Secondary school	195	107	−45
Total number of students	12,838	11,481	−11

Source: Based on data from Italian Ministry of Education (MIUR). 2008–2009 data from
Alunni con cittadinanza non italiana: a.s. 2008–2009 (Rome: MIUR, 2009b), 17; 2012–2013 data
from *Gli alunni stranieri nel sistema scolastico italiano:a.s. 2012–13* (Rome: MIUR, 2013), 23.

An estimated 20,000 Roma children below the age of twelve are not enrolled in school.[1] The Ministry of Education reports that there were 11,481
"nomad" students enrolled in Italian schools (only 107 in secondary school) in
2012–2013[2]—a very low number when compared to an estimated population of
36,000 to 39,000 Roma children ages six through fifteen, the ages of compulsory education in Italy.[3] Even though this number of Roma students enrolled
in school is certainly underestimated, the data are alarming.[4] Furthermore, the
situation has not improved, as the total number of "nomad" students enrolled
in Italian schools over the five years from 2008 to 2013 decreased by 11 percent
overall, and by 45 percent at the secondary school level (Table 1).

Moreover, a significant number of enrolled children do not attend school
regularly. While data are not available on Roma students' attendance at the
national level, some data are collected locally. In the course of conducting research in Turin during the 2008–2009 academic year, I found that the proportion of Roma children living in "nomad camps" who regularly attended
elementary and middle schools was extremely low.[5] It must be stressed, however, that the percentage was much higher for Roma students living in general
housing, though lower than the attendance rate of more than 99 percent at
the elementary and middle school level for children in the general population of Turin. According to teachers' observations, most of the Roma students living in general housing finish middle school, while many Roma
children living in camps do not (Figure 1). In Casa della Carità's 2011 national
survey of more than 1,600 Roma individuals, 13 percent of respondents declared that at least one child between ages six and fifteen in their family

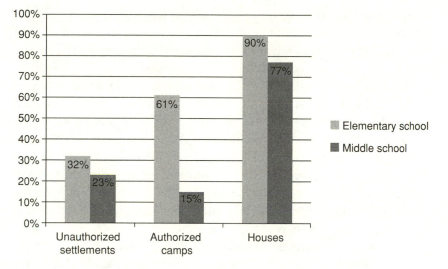

Figure 1. Percentage of Roma children enrolled in and regularly attending elementary and middle schools, by housing type, Turin, 2008–2009. *Source:* Based on unpublished data from the Municipality of Turin.

Table 2. Roma Families with at Least One Child of Compulsory School Age Not Attending School, by Housing Type

Housing type	Number of respondents	Percentage of respondents with school age child not in school
Irregular settlements	227	23
Regular settlements	474	12
In general housing	363	7

Source: Based on data from Fondazione Casa della Carità, *EU-Inclusive: National Report on Labour and Social Inclusion of Roma People in Italy* (Milan: Fondazione Casa della Carità, 2012), 18.

did not attend school, with attendance varying according to housing type (Table 2).

More than a third of the sample (34 percent) lacked any formal education; around a quarter had completed primary education (26 percent); and a third (34 percent) completed middle school. Only 5 percent of the respondents had completed high school, while the percentage of university graduates

in the sample was close to zero (46 percent of the general Italian population have high school diplomas or university degrees). An extremely high
percentage of respondents, 19 percent, were unable to read and write, in contrast to just 1.4 percent of the overall Italian population.[6]

Various measures have been implemented in recent decades to promote the education of Roma children, yet significant results have not been
achieved. Several chapters in this volume, including those by Margareta
Matache and Krista Oehlke and by James A. Goldston, comment on and
explore the limited successes of Roma inclusion strategies in closing the
education gap.[7] The Commission on Culture of the Italian Chamber of Deputies pointed out that "for more than 15 years, the Municipality of Rome has
destined 2.5 million euros per year for the schooling of around 2,000 [Roma]
children, regrettably with results close to zero."[8]

How can this situation be explained? The institutions usually list "nomad"
families' refusal to send their children to school as the main or even the
only reason for low school participation of Roma. The epigraph quotation
for this chapter, drawn from the report submitted by the Italian government
to the UN Committee on the Elimination of Racial Discrimination, accu-
rately reflects this kind of reasoning. First, schools—and more generally,
institutions—are not seen as having any responsibility; rather, they "are willing
to take care of the Roma." Discrimination against Roma children and families in and outside of school is not even mentioned. The problem, according
to the government, is that the Roma population "shows scarce inclination
towards integration (including the school community)." What is more, the
tendency to refuse integration and regular school attendance is interpreted
as an "inborn tendency," somehow related to the nomadic tradition of the
Roma population.[9]

Conversely, Roma rights advocates in Italy often ascribe this minority's low
school attendance and performance to institutional discrimination (including
segregation in "nomad camps" and discriminatory practices in schools), ignoring the influence of some Roma families' attitudes toward school. Eliminating
discrimination and ensuring the housing inclusion of Roma families would,
following this line of reasoning, immediately and automatically lead to full integration of this minority. This position, however, is not only inconsistent with
research evidence, but also does not adequately recognize the agency of the
persons concerned, who are seen as passive victims of discrimination.

In this chapter I argue that low school participation among the Roma
population in Italy is largely the result of institutional policies that segregate

and marginalize this minority in society at large and in schools. Built within a policy framework labeling the Roma as "nomads," these measures are in some cases explicitly aimed at exclusion and control, while in other cases, discrimination is the result of policies supposedly intended to protect the rights of the "nomads." Moreover, the "nomad camps" system, unique in the European context, is hugely expensive: Italy invests millions and millions of euros every year in what is, in fact, a Roma exclusion strategy.

On the other hand, the fact that some Roma families seem to disregard education should not be ignored. Rather, a shift in the interpretation of these attitudes is needed. Adapting the theory of the educational anthropologist John U. Ogbu, I suggest that, rather than as a cultural trait typical of nomadic culture, these attitudes should be viewed as a reaction to pervasive and long-term forms of discrimination by the majority society, a reaction that can be found with similar features in other ethnic minorities subjected to high levels of discrimination.[10]

The opposition between institutional responsibility and Roma families' responsibility is unproductive. Because both play a substantial role in educational outcomes for Roma children, denying the former or the latter impedes a full understanding and tackling of the problem. Rather, the two phenomena must be seen as interrelated factors, since negative attitudes by some Roma families toward school are responses to the discrimination they have suffered.

My analysis will focus on both of these factors: "active" institutional discrimination, particularly the "nomad camps" policy (unique to Italy) and Roma parents' attitudes toward school. I will not analyze the many other factors that also significantly hinder Roma children's school attendance and performance. Most of these factors result from the lack of policies aimed at addressing the marginal socioeconomic conditions of Roma families such as poor living conditions in unauthorized settlements, unemployment, scarce access to health service, the inadequate support by schools for non-Italian-speaking students and children of poorly educated parents, and noninstitutional discrimination (such as racism and harassment by schoolmates).

"Nomad Camps," "Nomad" Students: The Impact of Institutional Discrimination

Italian institutions are largely responsible for the segregation and marginalization of Roma, producing significant obstacles toward Roma children's enjoyment of the right to education. The deliberate housing policy Italy has adopted—the so-called "nomad camps"—is one such example.

A National Roma Exclusion Strategy:
The Policy of "Nomad Camps"

While unauthorized settlements and camps can be found throughout Europe, Italy is the only country where a significant portion of the Roma population lives in camps built and managed by the state institutions, in some cases through the mediation of NGOs.[11] The first "nomad camps" were established by Italian municipalities in the 1970s in order to guarantee the right of "Gypsies" to a nomadic lifestyle.[12] At that time, many Roma families were on the move for reasons mostly linked to economic activities, and they were often prevented from parking and camping by local authorities. In 1973, the Ministry of the Interior asked municipalities to remove these obstacles and build campsites with basic services for the "nomads." In the 1980s and early 1990s, more than half the Italian regions adopted laws that aimed to protect the "Gypsies." The regional laws recognized nomadism as a fundamental cultural trait of the Roma and asked local authorities to build campsites in order to safeguard their right to a nomadic lifestyle.[13]

Today, however, nearly all the Roma families living in camps are permanently settled. The economic activities that required an itinerant lifestyle are no longer profitable. Most importantly, the great majority of the Roma who fled the Balkans in the 1990s or arrived from Romania in the following decade were accustomed to leading a settled lifestyle in their countries of origin. Nonetheless, Italian institutions quickly labeled these newcomers as "nomads," and thus, "nomad camps" were the only housing solution offered.

In 2008, the Italian government declared a "State of Emergency with Regard to Settlements of Nomad Communities." Special commissioners were appointed to carry out measures to tackle the emergency, including the census and fingerprinting of the persons present in authorized camps and unauthorized settlements, removal of the latter, and identification of places to build new authorized camps. The census carried out in Rome identified approximately 7,200 Roma living in camps across the city: 2,220 in seven "authorized camps"; 2,750 in fourteen "tolerated camps"; and an additional 2,200 in eighty "unauthorized camps."[14] The "Nomad Plan" of the Rome municipality, adopted in 2009 by a special commissioner, provided for the transfer of 6,000 of these persons to thirteen new or expanded camps on the outskirts of Rome, beyond the highway around the city. The state of emergency was declared invalid by the Italian Supreme Court in 2011.

As confirmed by many reports and positions taken up by international organizations and NGOs and validated by the available quantitative data analyzed above, the policy of "nomad camps" hinders the social inclusion of the Roma population and has a particularly negative impact on children's education.[15] Common characteristics of unauthorized settlements—poor housing conditions, lack of services, isolation, and concentration of poor and marginalized families—are usually also found in authorized camps.[16] There are only a few advantages to living in an authorized camp: inhabitants are usually provided with some basic services such as water and electricity; they can usually register their residence, thus gaining access to social and health services; and, most importantly, they are more protected from evictions.

In some respects, however, authorized camps are even worse than unauthorized ones. First, authorized camps are often more isolated. To reduce opposition from the majority population, municipalities usually build "nomad camps" in very isolated places on the outskirts of cities, far from schools and other services, poorly served by public transportation, and often on highly congested roads. As a consequence, families who do not own a car cannot transport their children to school, and adolescents cannot travel to school on their own.

To solve the problem of transportation, in recent decades, many municipalities have provided special school buses for Roma children residing in the camps. However, although intended to guarantee the rights of Roma children to education, this policy has generated a number of negative side effects. First of all, the buses often cover long distances, since the children living in a camp are usually scattered among different schools to avoid the "invasion" of "nomad students" into any one particular school. As a result, many Roma children who rely on these special buses arrive at school late and leave early. They miss classes held during the first and last hours of the day, and are prevented from socializing with other pupils outside of school. A Roma girl living in a camp in Rome reports, "Every day I lose almost three hours of school because of the traveling. I should get out at 14.10 but I get out at 12. I go in at 9 in the morning. I almost always skip math because it is held during the first and at the last hour. I don't know anything about math."[17] Moreover, the children brought to school by these special buses—which in the city of Rome are marked with the letter "N" for "nomads"—are identified by their schoolmates and the school staff as the "nomad students," a stigma that frequently negatively impacts the treatment they receive.[18] The distance from the schools and the lack of public transportation also limit the ability of parents to attend school meetings, establish continuous relationships with teachers, and socialize with other parents. Children are also not able to participate in sports or extracurricular activities with their non-Roma peers.

The impact of segregation is particularly strong in situations where the police authorities control access to the camp. A Roma father reports the negative consequences of his family's transfer from a tolerated camp within the city of Rome to an authorized camp built by the municipality on the outskirts of the city, where the family has to coexist with more than one thousand people of different origins:

> We are locked up here and children do not integrate with other children. I am sorry about that, because we want the children to integrate with other children. Not just with the Roma, because in Casilino [the tolerated camp] our children had Italian friends who were coming to our house. Since we moved here they only came once or twice, but then they did not come anymore because they are afraid. . . . Maybe they don't come because they have to show a document at the entrance, maybe because they have to ask the police, maybe because it is too far away. Our children have interrupted their relationship with the Italians. . . . Here we are like dogs, because they move us away from the people. Dogs live in a doghouse and they locked us in [behind] a gate. This place is called "doghouse."[19]

In addition to providing transportation to school, municipalities often fund additional measures, to promote the education of Roma children living in camps. For example, educators accompany children on the bus, monitor children's attendance, and attempt to raise parents' awareness of the importance of education. Once more, these measures are ambiguous. Though geared toward encouraging Roma children's education, these provisions frequently lead to situations where facilitators take the parents' place—hindering the relationship between the students' families and the teachers, rather than fostering it. For instance, quite often parents living in "nomad camps" are not encouraged to visit their children's school; rather, the enrollment procedure is managed by mediators, who also are charged with keeping track of Roma students' report cards and who meet with the Roma students' teachers to discuss learning or behavioral problems.[20]

The Italian National Office on Anti-Racial Discrimination, known as UNAR, has acknowledged in its National Roma Inclusion Strategy that "nomad camps" lead to the social exclusion of Roma and that it is now time to replace this policy.[21] Nonetheless, a number of municipalities continue to invest in maintenance of existing camps or even build new ones. Local authorities often maintain that there are no alternatives. According to them, camps are the only accommodation suited to "nomad culture" and are the cheapest housing solution.

Recent research, however, has documented the astounding cost of the "nomad camp" system. In Rome alone, between 2005 and 2011, at least 69.8 million euros were spent on setting up, running, and maintaining camps, along with an additional 9.3 million euros for education programs addressing enrollment, attendance monitoring, awareness raising, and other related items.[22] An estimated 1.3 million euros per year were also spent on school transport.[23]

As for the unauthorized settlements, some municipalities have carried out an extremely high number of forced evictions, leaving most evicted families homeless and often destroying personal belongings. Between 2007 and 2011, municipal authorities in Milan carried out five hundred evictions, while in Rome between 2009 and 2013, approximately 480 evictions from informal settlements are estimated to have been carried out, at an estimated cost of 7 million euros.[24] Some families have been evicted several times. Evictions are especially devastating for children, who are almost always prevented from continuing to attend school, as a Roma child complains, "Yes I go to school, I am in IV grade and I do well, my classmates, the teacher, everybody treat me fine. I would like to continue this school until junior high school, until I complete all the grades. I would kindly wish that they do not break this camp down anymore, because otherwise because of them, I cannot go to school anymore. . . . My dream is to become a good person, how can I say, like a veterinary or a dancer . . . I don't want that the police to come to evict us again, because otherwise I cannot go to school and my dream cannot come true."[25] The policy of "nomad camps" (including both authorized camps and forced evictions from informal settlements) and the labeling of Roma as "nomad" fulfill a political function. Jean-Pierre Liégeois explains of nomadism in his book *Roma in Europe* that "this element of their supposed identity lies deep in the collective memory and it inspires the settled community's fear of the traveler as unknown, uncontrollable, and dangerous."[26] The radical exclusion, segregation, and control of the Roma thus confirm the stereotype of them as enemy. This projected stereotype can be manipulated by both right- and left-wing politicians, so as to gain popularity, particularly in times of deep economic and political crisis. As Liégeois has pointed out, "Roma/Gypsies are defined not as they are, but rather as sociopolitical necessities dictate they ought to be."[27]

Discrimination in Schools and Self-Fulfilling Prophecies

While housing segregation in Italy is blatant, the country technically does not support segregated schools or classes, unlike many Eastern European countries. In fact, special classes for "nomads," established in the mid-1960s, were abolished in the early 1980s. Today, Roma children are placed in ordinary classes with their non-Roma peers.[28]

Nonetheless, in some schools, Roma children are separated from their classes for hours per week in order to attend "nomad classes," which are special programs meant to support them. Some of the most eminent researchers on the Roma situation in Italy, as well as some Roma parents, argue that these classes are not only ineffective but also prevent Roma children from achieving educational outcomes similar to their peers because they are stigmatized and receive a lower quality education with extremely limited learning objectives.[29] Some Roma children attend these classes for the entire duration of primary school. In some schools, all Roma students are placed in these classes, regardless of their competencies.[30]

Moreover, as reported by Roma students and parents and as documented by researchers conducting participatory observation in schools, teachers in ordinary classes are often less demanding toward "nomad" students, adopting lower learning objectives and more generous evaluation criteria.[31] Sometimes special criteria for the "nomad students," irrespective of their individual situations, are even formally adopted, reinforcing stereotypes held by teachers that all Roma children are disadvantaged, based on their ethnic background. Like the "nomad classes," these measures are ambiguous. On the one hand they are usually intended to take into account the problems that many Roma children do, indeed, face (precarious living conditions, the inability of illiterate parents to support them); on the other hand, these special treatments often become discriminatory practices that prevent equal educational opportunities.

In some schools, "nomad" students are not even assigned homework or allowed to bring their schoolbags home. A Roma fourteen-year-old girl, living in an authorized camp in Turin, reported her experience as follows: "In elementary school the math teacher was good, she gave me assignments to read, to write, everything, but the Italian teacher did not give me anything. . . . I said 'Listen, I come to school, in order to read, to write, to learn, I don't come to look at your face! I want to write and study!' But she only asked me to draw, I didn't like it."[32] A second girl of the same age and living in the same camp indicated, "They didn't give me homework, I told the teacher 'Will you give me homework?' . . . I didn't do the same program as the others, mine was different. Because I had the 'support [program].' The teacher didn't give me anything to do, I sat there and she didn't give me anything to do. So what am I doing at school? It's better that I stay at home."[33]

These policies and practices demotivate Roma children and may lead to self-fulfilling prophecies. If students perceive that their teachers have lower expectations toward them, they may internalize and adapt to the stereotype, lowering their performance. Moreover, the types of behaviors that Roma children have learned in their family are usually stigmatized in the school setting, and they are often forbidden to speak Romani language at school. The education system tends to propose an educational model that competes with the Roma family and community model.[34]

Finally, some schools refuse to enroll "nomad" children, stating they have no places available for additional students, thus reinforcing the feeling by Roma families and students that they are not welcome at school. Discriminatory practices in schools, however, should not be overemphasized. Many school directors and teachers make huge efforts to promote equal opportunities for all their students, including Roma.[35]

"Nomadic" Culture or Reactions to Historic Discrimination?

> I finished middle school, but it's useless! I don't
> force my children to go to school. I tell them: "If you
> want to go, go. If you don't, don't go." In any case
> it's impossible to find a job. As long as I live in a
> camp, they will think that I'm a Gypsy, that I steal. . . .
> If you live in a house maybe they think differently.
> —Interview with Roma father living in an
> authorized camp, unpublished fieldwork, Turin

Roma Parents' Attitudes Toward Schooling

As mentioned at the beginning of this chapter, institutions often attribute low school participation on the part of Roma communities to "nomad" families' refusal of education. Teachers, social workers, and policy makers stress that "nomad" parents do not support their children's academic achievement and even refuse to send their children to school. According to this interpretation, Roma parents apparently want to keep their children out of school because they devalue education, do not trust institutions, and want to protect their children from losing their culture of origin.

Moreover, the refusal of parents to send their children to school is interpreted as a cultural trait typical of Roma and tied closely to their nomadic lifestyle. No matter how many generations have resided in a single place or whether they were forced to move in response to war in their country of origin, Roma are supposed to have an "inborn tendency" to lead a nomadic lifestyle. Even the difficulties that some Roma children face at school are often attributed to the lack of a written culture among nomad populations. The Commission on Culture of the Italian Chamber of Deputies reports that "the Roma child belongs to an oral culture, totally different from the Italian one, and presents cognitive and affective processes different from other children."[36] The "nomad" culture is thought of as a homogeneous, unchangeable, and almost natural reality. This approach is so socially legitimized—and its racist implications are so deeply ignored—that the Italian government adopted it in its *2006 Report to the UN Committee on the Elimination of Racial Discrimination*![37]

The consequences of this interpretation are enormous. It fosters teachers' stereotypes and prejudices against Roma children who are seen, from their first school day and without individual distinctions, as students unable to learn because of their culture. Some schools do not even report Roma children who drop out of school to the competent authorities, allegedly to "respect their culture." That many Roma children do not attend school, even though they are provided with school transportation and other special support measures, is seen as a further demonstration that "nomads" cannot be integrated.

Understandably, in order to reverse these problematic assumptions, Roma rights advocates often overlook the impact of Roma parents' attitudes and behavior, focusing exclusive attention on their socially precarious situation (particularly the segregation and poor living conditions in "nomad camps") as well as on discriminatory practices in schools. This approach, however, obscures the problem. There is an extensive body of research pointing to the relevance of parents' attitudes on school performance of their children. Moreover, research carried out in European countries has shown that Roma parents do not always link scholastic success with economic and social success, a position that can lead them to devalue scholastic achievement. In some cases, parents fear that participation in education could alienate their children from their culture.[38]

These kind of attitudes emerged during my research in Turin, both from the explicit statements of Roma parents and children and from testimonies by teachers and social workers, including some who were highly respectful of Roma families.[39] My research also showed that, in some cases, parents' attitudes may have even more impact on educational achievement than living conditions. For example, some Roma children living in shacks in an unauthorized settlement, lacking access to basic services, attended school more regularly than children who lived in brick houses in an authorized camp with easy access to water and electricity. Both camps were located reasonably close to the schools. According to the teachers I interviewed, the difference between the two groups related mainly to the families' attitudes: the parents living in the unauthorized settlement, who had recently migrated from Romania, seemed to place greater value on education than some of the parents residing in the authorized camp, who had arrived from the former Yugoslavia in the 1990s or who were even born in Italy and had lived their whole life in a "nomad camp."

Moreover, teachers who had taught these parents twenty years earlier reported that in some cases, the parents used to attend school more regularly than their children today. Though the family's living conditions had improved (the parents were brought up in an unauthorized camp without basic services, while their children were born in the authorized camp), the school attendance rate had decreased from one generation to the next. According to the teachers interviewed, some parents, when they were primary school students, even spoke Italian better than their own children two decades later.

Finally, the teachers stressed that non-Roma immigrant students—who also live in marginal socioeconomic conditions and face linguistic problems regularly attend school and usually achieve similar or even better academic results, compared not only with Roma children but also with Italian students with comparable backgrounds. As several researchers have shown, most immigrant parents are as committed to having their children succeed in school as Italian parents of the same social class.[40] In fact, some immigrant parents are even more committed to their children's education than Italian parents. Thus, in promoting the advancement of Roma children's education, the relevance of parents' attitudes should not be ignored. A new approach, which addresses parental attitudes and expectations, is needed.

Ogbu's Cultural-Ecological Theory on Minorities' Education

Studies by John U. Ogbu, an educational anthropologist, on school performance of minorities can make an important contribution in this respect.[41] From his comparative research on differences in school performance among minorities, Ogbu has concluded that divergence in achievement cannot be attributed entirely to cultural and linguistic differences. For example, some of the minorities who perform best in American schools are most distant in culture and language from the majority. In addition, the performance of some minority groups varies in different host countries. For instance, Koreans tend to do well in school in China and the United States—but poorly in Japan. Ogbu also challenges interpretations that link low school achievement by minorities only to social class factors (for example, he presented evidence that African American students perform less well in schools than white students at every social class level) or institutional barriers (such as inadequate curricula and lack of support programs).

Ogbu argues that differences in school performance between minority and dominant group students and between different minorities are caused not only by the treatment of minority groups in society at large and in school, but also by the perceptions of the minorities and how they respond to school due to such treatment (and their perception of it). According to Ogbu, minorities face instrumental discrimination (such as in employment and wages), relational discrimination (such as social and residential segregation), and symbolic discrimination (such as denigration of the minority culture and language). The treatment of minorities in the wider society is reflected in the treatment they receive in school, including the overall educational policies and practices toward these minorities (for example, the policy of school segregation); how minority students are treated in schools and classrooms (such as the level of teacher expectations and teacher-student interaction patterns); and the rewards, or lack thereof, that society gives to minorities for their school credentials, especially through employment and wages.

Ogbu maintains that different minorities perceive and respond to these kinds of treatment in society at large and in schools in different ways, depending on their historic relationship with the dominant group. These perceptions and responses, in turn, affect their attitudes and behavior toward school. Ogbu calls these sociocultural adaptations "community forces." Community forces include (a) beliefs about the instrumental value of education (for example, role of school credentials in getting ahead); (b) relational interpretations of school (for example, degree of trust in schools and school personnel); and (c) symbolic beliefs about school (for example, whether learning school curriculum and the majority language is considered harmful to minority cultural and linguistic identity).

In his research on school performance among minorities in the United States, Ogbu distinguishes between two types of minorities: voluntary (or immigrant) minorities who migrated in hopes of a better future and involuntary (or nonimmigrant) minorities who were brought to the United States as slaves (for example, African Americans) or were conquered (for example, Native Americans). According to his research, the voluntary minorities— after a period of transition needed to overcome language and cultural barriers—for the most part achieved similar or even better academic results compared with the majority. However, the involuntary minorities' school performance is generally lower.

Ogbu explains these differences by focusing on the community forces that are peculiar to each minority type. Individuals belonging to voluntary minorities tend to believe that the discrimination they experience is temporary and may be the result of their foreigner status or because they do not speak English well. They feel strongly that the same strategies that middle-class white Americans employ for success—hard work, following the rules, and getting good grades—will also work for them in school and in the job market. These immigrants generally have an optimistic, pragmatic attitude when they arrive. This leads them to trust white-controlled institutions, like public schools. Moreover, they do not perceive learning standard English and white behaviors as requirements imposed by the dominant group that threaten their group identity. As a consequence, voluntary minority parents are strongly committed to ensuring that their children succeed in school. Their academic expectations for their children are high, and they tend to hold their children, rather than the schools, responsible for their academic performance. Peers also tend to be supportive of success in school, so that voluntary minority students experience minimal peer pressure detrimental to their academic achievement.

Like immigrants, involuntary minorities also believe that hard work and education are necessary to succeed in the United States. However, because they have faced employment discrimination and other barriers for many generations, involuntary minorities have come to believe that discrimination is more or less institutionalized and permanent, and that education and hard work are simply not enough to overcome racism. Family, students, and the community at large are skeptical and ambivalent about the role of education in getting ahead. Moreover, the long history of discrimination which involuntary minorities have faced drives them to distrust white-controlled institutions. Schools are perceived with suspicion because involuntary minorities, with justification, believe that public schools will not educate their children like they educate white children.

Finally, in response to their forced insertion into U.S. society and their subsequent mistreatment, involuntary minorities develop an identity that is defined, to a great extent, by their opposition to white American identity. They interpret their differences in culture and language as markers of their own collective identity to be maintained—not overcome. Certain requirements for success in school—for example, learning standard English, mastering the school curriculum, and exhibiting "good" school behavior—are thus interpreted as ways of imposing white culture on them and depriving them of their identities.

Consequently, involuntary minority parents convey contradictory messages about education to their children. They tell their children to work hard in school; however, their own attitudes and comments reveal their latent mistrust of the school system in terms of its quality and long-term economic potential. These parents tend to hold schools and teachers (rather than their children) accountable for poor academic performance. Parents also tend to regard the school system as a force that negatively separates their children from their family and community. There is considerable evidence that a strong negative peer group influence exists among involuntary minority students, more or less stigmatizing academic success and equating the use of standard English with "acting white." These attitudes and behaviors lead to poor academic performance. This link between parents' mistrust of the school system and academic performance is explored elsewhere in this volume in the context of Spain, by Teresa Sordé Martí and Fernando Macías in their chapter.

As Ogbu has clarified, the characteristics described above merely capture *general* patterns of belief and behavior within different minority groups. His research suggests that some beliefs and behaviors apply to enough members of a minority group to form a visible pattern. However, it should be noted that not all members believe or behave the same way.

Other researchers have questioned several aspects of Ogbu's theory. Some empirical studies have shown that some immigrant groups do not follow the pattern characteristic of voluntary minorities: for example, students from many Latino immigrant groups in the United States have not performed well in school. Attitudes toward education held by second-generation immigrants are often different from those of their parents. Moreover, different patterns can be identified *within* ethnic groups as well as between different minorities.[42] Nonetheless, the core of the theory generally remains unrefuted: differences in school performance, either between varied minority groups or between groups within the same ethnic minority, can at least be partially explained by varied perceptions of and responses to their treatment by the dominant group. Those who perceive their experience of racial discrimination as pervasive tend to devalue education as a vehicle for advancement and develop an oppositional stance toward the majority society's values and rules that is detrimental to their academic success. It must be stressed, however, that this correlation is but one of the many factors that influence school performance, such as the social, economic, and educational status of parents, the family structure, and the characteristics of the school itself (including the quality of education, whether the school practices segregation, etc.).[43]

Adapting Ogbu's Theory to the Situation of Roma Students in Italy

The application of Ogbu's cultural-ecological theory to the Roma and other minorities in Europe might be controversial, as the context is clearly very different from the United States (European countries are not pioneer societies) and no minority group quite fits the category of involuntary minorities. Still, similarities between Ogbu's description of the educational situation of involuntary minorities and that of the Roma in Europe are evident. Though the Roma have not been colonized or brought as slaves to West European countries, they were enslaved in Romania for centuries and were a subordinated, disadvantaged, and discriminated minority everywhere in Europe, including being victimized by the Holocaust.[44]

Ogbu's theory can be useful in interpreting Roma children's low school participation in Italy if we partially adapt the distinction between voluntary and involuntary minorities. To do so, we should consider the following questions: (a) For how many generations has the minority suffered discrimination? (b) How pervasive is this discrimination, referring to both the types of discrimination and their frequency? (c) How institutionalized and formalized are forms of ethnic discrimination? (d) Has the minority also experienced forced assimilation policies?

Minorities subjected to pervasive and institutionalized discrimination and assimilation policies for generations tend to respond to school in the ways analyzed by Ogbu as characteristic of involuntary minorities. In contrast, the responses of those immigrants who were not discriminated against in their country of origin and who experience limited discrimination in the host country are similar to Ogbu's voluntary minorities.

The Roma minority in Italy exemplifies the first type. Roma who have been settled in Italy for centuries and Roma migrants, arriving from the former Yugoslavia and Romania in the last fifty years, have suffered discrimination for countless generations. In Italy, public authorities have enacted anti-Roma legislation since the fifteenth century. Moreover, those who migrated from the Balkans were discriminated minorities in their countries of origin, though the level and type of discrimination varied across the centuries and countries.[45]

The Roma are the most discriminated minority in Italy, especially in the areas of employment, housing, education, access to documentation, and bias displayed in the media and political discourse.[46] They face discrimination on all three of the levels Ogbu identifies: instrumental, relational, and symbolic. They are the only minority that suffers institutional and formalized discrimination based on ethnicity (including the "nomad camp" policy, the "nomad classes" in school, and under the former state of emergency the fingerprinting of Roma in camps, even Italian citizens). Indirect discrimination is also strong (for example, access to public housing requires residence registration, thus disproportionally excluding Roma families). Finally, Roma people have been subjected to forced assimilation policies, particularly by school institutions, more than any non-Roma minority.

The attitudes and behaviors of Roma families toward education, echoing those characteristic of Ogbu's involuntary minorities, should be interpreted as a sociocultural adaptation to the way they have been historically treated by the majority society. First, one can hypothesize that Roma families in Italy are discouraged from investing in education, since they do not believe in its long-term instrumental value. Having faced employment discrimination for many generations, Roma families have come to believe that education, though necessary to get a good job, is not enough for *them*. Roma youth believe that, even if they should manage to achieve a university degree, pervasive discrimination against "Gypsies" would prevent them from being successfully employed (unless they disguise their ethnic identity). Most Roma living in camps seem to have lost all hope that their children will be ever able to get a better job than collecting scrap metal or other marginal economic activities. Even among relatively wealthy Roma families, self-employment is regarded as the only opportunity for economic success. These beliefs, based on their communities' experiences, can largely explain why very few Roma youth in Italy continue to study after completing compulsory education. Disappointment in education, which has proved useless in their personal experience, may also clarify why some Roma parents, who did finish middle school, do not force their children to attend even the compulsory years of school.

Having suffered institutional discrimination, assimilation policies, and denigration of their culture for generations, some Roma families have developed significant mistrust of the school system. In some cases, families fear that their children will lose their culture by attending school. The relevance of these community forces (instrumental, relational, and symbolic beliefs about school) in influencing Roma children's school attendance and performance should be further studied through empirical research.

In contrast, non-Roma immigrants, particularly the first generation, usually have attitudes and behavior resembling those of Ogbu's voluntary minorities. The difference between Roma and non-Roma minorities can be explained by referring to Ogbu's framework. Non-Roma immigrants who belonged to the majority group in their country of origin have not suffered discrimination for generations. In Italy, immigrants are discriminated against, mostly on the private job and housing market, but less pervasively than Roma minorities. Finally, the discriminatory laws and policies these immigrants face are not based on ethnicity, but rather on irregular migration status and nationality: as a consequence, non-Roma immigrants perceive these types of discrimination as temporary and can hope that their children will have a better future.

Adopting Ogbu's view—that Roma parents' and communities' attitudes are shaped by historic and pervasive discrimination and not by "primary" cultural traits[47]—has important implications. First, since these attitudes are the product of a historic interaction, they can *change* in response to alterations in the treatment of the minority group by the majority society. Reducing institutional discrimination will have an impact not only on the structural and institutional obstacles hindering Roma children's education (housing segregation, discriminatory practices by the schools, etc.), but also on obstacles linked to the attitudes of Roma families and communities. Second, teachers, social workers, and policy makers can adopt a self-reflective view, contemplating how they might react if subject to the same kind of discrimination. These approaches might inspire dialogue rather than distance from and contempt toward the "nomads."

Finally, considering social exclusion and discriminatory practices in schools in concert with the dynamics within Roma communities means treating Roma as subjects capable of choice, rather than as passive victims. As Ogbu asserts, "Structural barriers and school factors affect minority school performance; however, minorities are also autonomous human beings who actively interpret and respond to their situation. Minorities are not helpless victims."[48]

From Interpretation to Action

What policy implications can be drawn from the analysis outlined so far in order to increase the school participation and performance of Roma children in Italy? These are difficult times: the deep economic crisis and reduction of welfare policies, paired with rising xenophobic and anti-Roma sentiments in the Italian population, make it very difficult to promote social inclusion policies. Clear and realistic priorities need to be identified.

First, it is crucial to end policies that directly discriminate and marginalize the Roma minority and that foster stereotypes in the majority population. In particular, the policy of "nomad camps" built and managed by local authorities, in cooperation with NGOs, should be immediately stopped, while ensuring adequate and nonsegregated housing to the Roma families living there. Millions of euros might be better spent on inclusion policies. Discriminatory practices against "nomad" students in schools, particularly those that are formalized, should also cease so that Roma children can be treated like their non-Roma peers when they enter school.

Second, as long as pervasive employment discrimination strips education of its instrumental value for Roma families and youth, investment in education alone is unlikely to yield positive dividends. In order to address this problem, inclusion policies should prioritize support in their search for employment for those Roma youth who have finished secondary school or vocational training. The gainful employment of young Roma will improve the living conditions of a number of Roma families in the long-term future. Moreover, these young people can serve as role models for their community at large.

Finally, pedagogical implications can be drawn from Ogbu's cultural-ecological theory.[49] To promote Roma children's attendance and performance, teachers should commit themselves to building trust with these students and their families. Teachers can do this by expecting their Roma students to meet the same high standards that are set for non-Roma and acknowledging that Roma culture is worthy of respect. Furthermore, teachers should show that Roma parents themselves are respected and in fact needed to help their children in succeeding at school. Ogbu clarifies that the teachers should avoid basing expectations about an individual's school performance on group membership: students should be treated as individuals. However, the theory may help educators understand why minority students may behave the way they do when they are following their group's pattern of behavior.[50]

A truly intercultural education, able to accommodate students' cultural variety through flexibility and acceptance, is needed.[51] Trust and personal relationships are crucial in promoting Roma children's education—not because they are unable to recognize the value of institutions due to their premodern culture, but because they have been mistreated by those institutions for generations. The project implemented in the Spanish Roma neighborhood of La Milagrosa, described by Teresa Sordé Marti and Fernando Macias in their chapter in this volume, is an outstanding example of how building relationships based on trust, respect and participation, with Roma students and their parents, may hugely improve children's school attendance and outcomes.

The question of appropriate policies regarding the Roma population is first and foremost a problem of representation; that is, the definition of the object of the policies develops the cognitive framework for interpretation of reality. This in turn lays the groundwork for certain political choices.[52] Thus, only by dismantling the representation of the Roma as "nomads"—who are, by culture or by nature, unable to integrate and who are radically different from "us"—can policies change.

Unfortunately, the low school participation of Roma children often validates the pernicious prevailing stereotypes. The ineffectiveness of measures taken to promote "nomad" children's education—and the comparison with non-Roma immigrant children, who regularly attend school—wrongly imply that the problem lies within "nomad" culture, seen as incompatible with integration into the majority society. This powerful argument influences much more than education policies. As Roma rights advocates, on the one hand, we should stress the impact of the unparalleled discrimination this minority faces, in society and in schools, including the discriminatory side effects of supposedly positive measures. On the other hand, we should support the concept of Roma people as responsible and active subjects, who sometimes reject education as a reaction to the pervasive discrimination suffered for generations and, in particular, to the lack of instrumental value of education for them because of employment discrimination—a reaction that may change, in response to more equal treatment by the majority society.

Chapter 2

Toward the Recognition of Critical Race Theory in Human Rights Law: Roma Women's Reproductive Rights

Alexandra Oprea

A cursory look at Roma health statistics paints a dismal picture. The World Health Organization has affirmed that Roma are "particularly vulnerable to ill health."[1] Diseases such as tuberculosis and iron deficiency abscesses are common.[2] Discrepancies in infant mortality rates among Roma and non-Roma are staggering. In Romania, for example, infant mortality rates for Roma are more than double those of non-Roma (72.8 versus 27.1 per thousand live births).[3] In the UK, the life expectancy of Roma is ten years less than for non-Roma, while in Eastern Europe, it is approximately seventeen years less.[4] Throughout Europe, Roma suffer disproportionately from HIV, tuberculosis, and other diseases.[5] These negative health indicators are exacerbated by a lack of access to health care due to overt and indirect racism experienced in the provision of medical services.[6]

Roma health statistics are difficult to come by, but when available, they are seldom disaggregated by gender, thus creating a nebulous picture of where different sections of the community, including Roma women, stand with regard to health and other social and economic indicators. The scarcity of statistics disaggregated by both race and gender is part of a larger pattern wherein social ills are analyzed using only one axis of exclusion, such as race or gender.[7]

Despite these deficiencies, we know that Roma women suffer from chronic diseases more than their Roma male and non-Roma female counterparts.[8] From representative samples in various Eastern European countries, we also know that Roma women achieve lower educational levels than non-Roma women and Roma men and that unemployment and underemployment rates for Roma women are higher than those for both Roma males and non-Roma women.[9] Critical race theory and the theory of intersectionality in particular have been crucial to quantitatively and qualitatively capturing this subordination of Roma in general and Roma women in particular.[10] This is especially true with regard to Roma women's health and their right to bodily integrity.

This chapter focuses on two interrelated violations of Roma women's reproductive rights: compulsory sterilization and child removal, foregrounding the experience of Roma women who were sterilized. It interrogates traditional human rights, antiracist, and feminist discourses through a critical race theory lens. As such, it aims to construct a more inclusive discourse on reproductive rights and a more robust jurisprudence on discrimination.

Theoretical Lens and Point of Departure

This chapter follows in the intellectual tradition of critical race theory (CRT) and strives to construct a human rights framework borrowed from this tradition.[11] I was first exposed to CRT fourteen years ago under the guidance of Luke Charles Harris and Kimberlé Crenshaw.[12] Developed by legal scholars of color, CRT challenges the construction of racial hierarchy in America and the subordination of people of color. As I read Crenshaw et al.'s groundbreaking *Critical Race Theory: The Key Writings That Formed the Movement* (1996), I remember for the first time feeling a sense of comfort and relief that what I felt and saw was not just "in my head." By interrogating hierarchies that were taken as a given and as "natural" and by exploring the ways the law helped to construct these hierarchies, CRT departed from traditional narratives on race and meritocracy in America. The main tenets of CRT that form the foundation for analyzing rights claims are (1) the focus on institutionalized racism, as opposed to individual acts and intent; (2) the notion that the law can act to legitimize structures of subordination; (3) the belief that there is value in anecdotal evidence, including the narratives of minorities; and (4) that a bottom-up approach and analysis from the perspective of those experiencing intersecting axes of subordination are crucial to achieving justice.[13]

The theory of intersectionality resonated with me. Intersectionality adopts a bottom-up approach to address structural inequality, and encompasses all the CRT tenets just referred to. Developed by black feminist scholar Kimberlé Crenshaw, intersectionality departs from the practice of viewing groups through a unidimensional lens.[14] Instead, it looks at the convergence of different forms of oppression and how they operate to limit the opportunities of individuals in various groups. It still lends itself to an analysis of group-based discrimination, but also considers the various vulnerable groups to which a person might belong.[15]

The theory of intersectionality has been instrumental in understanding the multiple forms of discrimination to which Roma women are routinely subject.[16] Aside from the instances of marginalization mentioned above, intersectionality also helps explain the "unique" position of Roma women—one that coincides neither with that of Roma men nor with that of non-Roma women. As Crenshaw explained in her groundbreaking work, "Black women can experience discrimination in ways that are both similar to and different from those experienced by white women and Black men. Black women sometimes experience discrimination in ways similar to white women's experiences; sometimes they share very similar experiences with Black men. Yet often they experience double-discrimination—the combined effects of practices which discriminate on the basis of race, and on the basis of sex. And sometimes, they experience discrimination as Black women—not the sum of race and sex discrimination, but as Black women."[17] Crenshaw identifies four ways in which women of color experience discrimination: as women; as persons of color; as women and as persons of color; and as women of color. Their representational needs and legal claims vary depending on the type of discrimination faced.

This framework is useful for analyzing the discrimination facing Roma women. As women, they face domestic violence; as Roma, they face police brutality and overrepresentation in the criminal justice system.[18] Because Roma women are subject to the same types of violence faced by the more dominant members of each oppressed group (non-Roma women and Roma men), Roma women are able to represent domestic and human rights claims based on a single axis of exclusion whose coordinates are gender discrimination and race discrimination, respectively.[19] In instances involving discrete claims, theoretically Roma women's experiences would form ideal test cases precisely because they suffer the discriminatory phenomenon suffered by the more dominant group member and do so from an even more subordinate position.

By ideal, I refer to the fact that Roma women experience both race and gender discrimination in addition to—or rather in combination with—other axes of subordination, such as poverty, disability and so forth. This is a bottom-up approach to discrimination analysis.[20] As Mari Matsuda has pointed out, bottom-up analysis relies on the notion that "looking to the bottom—adopting the perspective of those who have seen and felt the falsity of the liberal promise—can assist critical scholars in the task of fathoming the phenomenology of law and defining the elements of justice."[21] This is an effort to deviate from analyzing in the abstract; Matsuda notes that "knowledge of how people experience oppression, or knowledge of the full range of conditions under which they remain oppressed, exposes new problems and possibilities."[22]

Much of law is fashioned not from the bottom up, but from the top down. Crenshaw explains that because gender discrimination claims have been fashioned based on the experiences of white women and race discrimination claims have been fashioned based on the experiences of black men, courts often preclude black women from representing these claims. Sometimes they cannot claim gender discrimination because their race somehow taints this claim. Similarly, they cannot represent a race discrimination claim because their gender interferes.[23]

Although Crenshaw described this problem twenty years ago, the problem persists. For example, a 2011 *Law and Society Review* article examining intersectionality in U.S. employment litigation found that "non-white women are less likely to win their cases than is any other demographic group. Additionally, plaintiffs who make intersectional claims, alleging that they were discriminated against based on more than one ascriptive characteristic, are only half as likely to win their cases as are other plaintiffs."[24]

Another dilemma arises when attempts are made to cross-pollinate these axes of exclusion in political or legal discourse.[25] For example, attempts to draw attention to domestic violence at Roma rights conferences are met with retort ("What does domestic violence have to do with Roma?")[26] or attempts to draw attention to police brutality at women's rights conferences are met with looks of confusion.[27]

The last type of discrimination described by Crenshaw—discrimination that is shared neither with men of color nor with non-Roma women—is the focus of the rest of this chapter. (For ease of reference, I will refer to instances in which minority women experience unique discrimination as sui generis intersectional claims, that is, claims to rights that are based on subordination by interlocking systems of race, gender, and poverty.) Compulsory sterilization is an example of a sui generis intersectional claim. Roma women's experiences mirror neither those of Roma men nor those of dominant white women.[28]

Like Native American and African American women, Roma women have a long history of subordination at the hands of white supremacy.[29] The gendered articulations of this white supremacy have led to the implementation of laws and policies that restrict the reproductive freedom of these women and expand the control of the state/white men over their bodies. Just as the rape of black women by white slave masters was essential to the perpetuation of the system of slavery in the United States, so the rape of Roma women was essential to supporting the system of slavery in the area now known as Romania, where Roma were enslaved for four hundred years.[30] In fact, rape of this sort did not actually constitute a crime. Along with this history, the stereotype of the Roma seductress—Victor Hugo's Esmeralda (in *The Hunchback of Notre Dame*), Bizet's *Carmen*, Cervantes's *La Gitanilla*—reminiscent of the Jezebel trope, kept the rape of a Roma woman from constituting a crime under Romanian law. Ian Hancock points out that, according to the Moldavian Civil code in the 1900s, "if a Gypsy slave should rape a white woman, he would be burnt alive" (Section 28), but if a Romanian should "meet a girl in the road" and "yield to love . . . he shall not be punished at all."[31] The hypersexualized Roma trope pervades postbellum Europe, just as her black counterpart pervades antebellum America, and serves to justify a host of oppressive policies and reproductive violence.[32]

Sexual violence and control over minority women's reproductive capacities have been key parts of the racial projects in Europe as well as in America. Speaking to this intersection, Native American activist and scholar Andrea Smith points out, "The history of sexual violence and genocide among Native women illustrates how gender violence functions as a tool for racism and colonialism among women of color in general."[33] The maintenance of racial hierarchy and domination has entailed control over the ability of minority women to have and keep their children. In furthering these goals, black, Puerto Rican, and Native American women were subject to compulsory sterilization during the neo-eugenics movement of the 1970s in the

United States.[34] The sterilization of Roma women in Eastern Europe parallels this history and serves as an additional example of the global nature of gendered white supremacy.[35]

Similar to the situation for women of color in United States, the characterization of Roma women as wildly fertile and sexually promiscuous is a key component justifying their forced sterilization. These stereotypes are prevalent in various spheres and discourses. It is a stereotype shared by medical professionals, for instance. A Slovakian doctor commented that Roma women "have several partners, are promiscuous, travel a lot, and bring diseases with them from other countries."[36] In 2014, a prominent Romanian politician, Rares Buglea, suggested that ideally a Roma woman should be sterilized after her first child if social workers found that she does not "have the intention [of raising] the child in humane conditions." The same report in which that quote appeared also referenced other racist statements made by Romanian politicians, including Prime Minister Victor Ponta and President Traian Basescu.[37] This thinking comes not only from politicians, but also from less predictable sources and in less obvious terms. Well-intentioned human rights discourse also draws a link between Roma poverty and high birth rates.[38]

By 2003, a pattern of compulsory sterilization of Roma women was documented in reports from countries such as Slovakia; such sterilizations would later form the basis of cases in the European Court of Human Rights.[39] Forced sterilization of Roma women in what was then Czechoslovakia began in the early 1970s. It was estimated that between 1986 and 1987, 70 percent of the women sterilized in that country were Roma. The compulsory and coercive sterilization of Roma women also occurred in other countries.[40] Sometimes the sterilizations were accomplished without the woman's knowledge, and sometimes through blatant force, coercion, or by taking advantage of structural conditions, such as the high illiteracy rate among Roma. Often, the sterilizations were accomplished by relying *both* on the structural vulnerability of Roma women and on coercion and duress. The ability of medical professionals to deploy forceful and coercive tactics was a result of preexisting structures that had already rendered Roma women easy targets, as illustrated in the testimony of one woman, Agáta, twenty-eight, from Svinia: "I was in terrible pain, but I was not given any pills, any injection. Later on, doctors came and brought me to the operating room [for a C-section] and there they gave me anesthesia. When I was falling asleep, a nurse came and took my hand in hers and with it she signed something. I do not know what it was. I could not check because I cannot read, I only know how to sign my name. And, moreover, I was sleepy and tired. When I was released from the hospital, I was only told that I would not have any more children. . . . I was so healthy before, but now I have pain all the time. Lots of infections."[41] Compulsory sterilization in this case is not only a human rights abuse; it is better understood as one manifestation of a broader system of structural abuse. We need a nuanced understanding of historical and contemporary systemic racism against Roma and the gendered dynamics of this subordination to understand compulsory sterilization. It is part of a continuum of violence against Roma women.

Centuries of exclusion from and segregation in educational institutions and discrimination in the workplace, described in detail in several chapters in this volume, laid the groundwork for these reproductive rights violations.[42] For example, in his chapter in this volume, "The Unfulfilled Promise of Educational Opportunity in the United States and Europe," James Goldston analyzes important litigation that challenged school discrimination and segregation, but only generated limited results. Institutionalized racism against Roma in educational institutions, as well as poverty (which render school a luxury for some), reinforce gender roles that emphasize young Roma girls' potential as caregivers and mothers, rather than as students or doctors. Poverty in conjunction with institutionalized racism in educational institutions and with compounding discrimination in the labor market create a reverse incentive structure: sending a girl to school or prioritizing her education become a risky investment, instead of a strategic allocation of resources.[43] The resulting high illiteracy rates of Roma women and the broad exclusion of Roma from medical professions pave the way for various types of medical violence.

Because of the intersectional nature of compulsory sterilization, the practice is often excluded from mainstream feminist debates altogether and is framed unidimensionally in antiracist/Roma rights debates. In terms of the latter, compulsory sterilization is often understood as a racist attack against Roma, stripped of any gendered meaning.[44] Involuntary sterilization of Roma women can be perceived as a genocidal effort against Roma as a whole,[45] but excluding gender from this analysis obscures a key facet: that the other side of the coin is compulsory childbirth. In other words, nationalist/race-centered framing of compulsory and coercive sterilization can easily translate into an underlying discourse concerning a Roma woman's duty to have children in order to keep the race alive. Compulsory childbirth is also reproductive violence, along with the pressure put on Roma women by the Roma patriarchy to bear children (with Roma women's value seen as stemming in part from their ability to bear children and create large families).[46]

While some Roma and human rights discourses ignore the gendered aspect of compulsory sterilization in favor of framing it as an affront to the race,[47] some feminist entities ignore it altogether in their articulation of reproductive rights. The European Women's Lobby (EWL) is a case in point. The bifurcation of race and gender is apparent in the articulation of the organization's overarching goal, "equality between men and women," without mention of equality between women of different races. Reference is made to the Beijing Platform for Action and the UN Convention on the Elimination of All Forms of Discrimination Against Women (CEDAW), without mention of racial discrimination and the Convention on the Elimination of All Forms of Racial Discrimination (CERD).[48] This colorblind ideology carries over into the EWL's discourse on reproductive rights. The lobby's main platform on these rights is a call for increased access to birth control. At a time when the European Court of Human Rights is hearing cases against Slovakia for the compulsory sterilization of Roma women, the EWL repeats claims by the Center for Reproductive Rights, such as, "For too many Slovak women, modern contraceptives remain tragically out of reach."[49] Illustrative of a reproductive rights agenda centered on a white female normativity, this statement does not recognize that "birth control" may mean something different for women from non-dominant races: for them, it may represent a form of violence as opposed to a sign of empowerment.

I do not mean to imply that access to contraceptives is not of relevance to Roma women; it most certainly is. I am merely pointing to a blind spot in feminist discourse in terms of a limited understanding of the raced aspects of "birth control."

According to the report published by the Center for Reproductive Rights, "The government should focus on funding preventative healthcare services that cover all contraceptive methods, including sterilization, to enable women to make free reproductive choices."[50] This framing of sterilization runs contrary to the experiences of many Roma women, whose race renders them vulnerable to the use of sterilization as a means of punishment, rather than empowerment.[51] The colorblind framing of sterilization as a reproductive choice is problematized by Dorothy Roberts, who argues, "The feminist focus on gender and identification of male domination as the source of reproductive repression often overlooks the importance of racism in shaping our understanding of reproductive liberty and the degree of 'choice' that women really have."[52]

Human Rights Jurisprudence and Compulsory Sterilization

While compulsory sterilization has remained unseen in some contexts, it has come to the forefront in human rights discourse and jurisprudence, however problematically. In instances where compulsory sterilization is discussed, gaps in concept and in jurisprudence erase Roma women: that is, their situation is rendered legally invisible.[53]

By looking at how the court frames cases (both Roma "race only" as well as Roma intersectional cases related to race and gender) that come before it, we can better understand how the court conceptualizes rights and what normative notion of social justice it espouses. By examining the types of cases that have been curiously absent from the court's docket, we can perhaps arrive at an understanding of what is considered a legitimate human rights violation. By this, I mean also to implicate NGOs as playing a critical role in terms of selecting cases to bring before the court (via strategic litigation). In other words, jurisprudence and jurisprudential silence work in tandem to shape human rights law and policy. This notion of jurisprudential silence helping to construct human rights discourse borrows from one of the underpinnings of international law: that both acts and omissions, both objections and silence, can be considered to espouse a view.[54] It is important to note here that this criticism is not based on any notion of intent; that is, I do not mean to imply that this exclusion is intentional or motivated by ill will. Rather my contention is that it is attributable to broader doctrinal, structural, and political patterns that are discussed throughout this chapter.

Historically, Roma women have rarely been at the center of human rights discourse and litigation, be it gender-based human rights or race-based human rights.[55] This marginalization is all the more concerning in light of the fact that human rights law was fashioned as a *response* to marginalization.

Human rights developed as a counter to the international law system, which privileges nation-states as the main actors. The impetus behind the development of human rights law was to temper international law's preoccupation with state sovereignty and limit this sovereignty to the extent necessary to protect vulnerable individuals and groups. We now confront a bifurcation in the treatment of civil and political rights on the one hand and economic, social, and cultural rights on the other, a product of the advent of the Cold War and the dissolution of the post–World War II compact that produced the unitary Universal Declaration of Human Rights. This bifurcation diminished the promise of human rights for subordinated groups by deprioritizing structural subordination and material deprivation. The additional division of the human rights regime into women's rights, with CEDAW, and minority rights, with the Convention against Racial Discrimination (CARD), further weakened the promise of human rights by rendering intersectional violations particularly difficult to address.[56] I argue below that these gaps are evident in the compulsory sterilization case law of the European Court of Human Rights and that it is precisely this failure to recognize intersectional marginalization and its structural dimensions that renders justice for Roma women elusive and serves to legitimize systemic subordination.

Between 2009 and 2012, the European Court of Human Rights adjudicated a host of compulsory sterilization cases brought by Roma women against Slovakia.[57] In each instance, the court ruled in favor of the applicants, finding Slovakia liable to the women for violations of the Convention on the Protection of Human Rights and Fundamental Freedoms (the founding document of the European Convention on Human Rights), primarily in relation to Article 3, which prohibits torture, and Article 8, which mandates respect for family life. I focus on *V.C. v. Slovakia* because it set a precedent for the treatment of these claims with respect to Article 14, which prohibits discrimination based on race, gender, and other group markers.[58]

V.C. v. Slovakia has been cited for the principle that laws and practices can disparately impact a certain group, while failing to be discriminatory toward that group.[59] (This stands in contrast to some of the court's earlier rulings.)[60] As discussed below, in effect, the court deemed the compulsory sterilization of Roma women an unfortunate accident.[61] Thus, although the court ruled in favor of the women in all the sterilization cases, these were limited victories that provided a remedy to the individual, but did not delegitimize systemic practices.

In *V.C. v. Slovakia*, a Roma woman who was sterilized alleged a violation of Article 3 (torture), Article 8 (private and family life), and Article 14 (discrimination) of the European Convention on Human Rights. The applicant described having been asked by hospital staff to agree to a sterilization procedure while in labor. While in the birthing position, more than two hours into labor, writhing in pain, she was asked to sign by the words "patient requests sterilization." Under these already coercive circumstances, the hospital staff also falsely represented to her that her life and that of her baby would be in danger, were she to become pregnant again. It was found that her medical chart indicated she was Roma; it was also found that Roma women were placed in separate maternity wards and could not use the same facilities as white women. The court ruled in favor of the applicant on Article 3 and 8, but curiously not on Article 14, which concerns racial and gender discrimination.[62]

By the time of the court's decision, NGOs had already documented a pattern of forced sterilization of Roma women in Slovakia.[63] The applicant presented historical evidence of Communist policy toward Roma, including details relating to the disproportionate number of Roma women sterilized. She showed that in Prešov District, where she resided, 60 percent of the sterilizations performed from 1986 to 1987 had been performed on Roma women, who made up only 7 percent of the population in the district.[64] Other reports corroborated the statistical disparity.[65]

The court was not only presented with evidence showing a widespread pattern of sterilizing Roma women; it was also revealed to the court that Roma women were particularly targeted for sterilization. In other words, the evidence showed not only that a disproportionate number of Roma women had been sterilized, but that sterilizations were the product of a conscious *intent* to target a specific group. Evidence was presented demonstrating that the 1972 sterilization regulation was intentionally deployed to "control the highly unhealthy Roma population" by playing upon Roma women's poverty.[66] A report prepared by the Commission for the Question of Gypsy Inhabitants, with input from health care professionals addressing the reasons behind the low demand for sterilization concluded as follows: "Even a backward Gypsy woman is able to calculate that, from an economic point of view, it is more advantageous for her to give birth every year because she gets significant[ly] more financial resources from the state for the fifth and later descendants . . . for each child, she can get more than the benefit of sterilization. . . . Therefore health workers recommend increasing the grant for sterilization to 5,000 crowns."[67] In addition to this evidence that health care workers considered Roma women backward and in need of incentives to get sterilized, the court was also reminded that the success of medical professionals was sometimes measured by the number of Roma women they convinced to "consent" to be sterilized.[68]

In her arguments to the court, the applicant stressed that her racial background motivated the sterilization. She presented a twofold argument. She claimed (1) that a pattern and practice of discrimination against Roma women existed in Slovakia, and (2) that these broader patterns and racist structures informed the doctors' decision to sterilize her; and she stated that her claim should be "examined in the light of the sterilisation policies and practice existing under the communist regime and also in the context of the widespread intolerance towards the Roma in Slovakia. That climate had influenced the attitudes of the medical personnel. The indication in her medical record that she was of Roma ethnic origin and her treatment as a patient in Prešov Hospital demonstrated the climate in that hospital with regard to Roma patients and the overall context in which her sterilisation had taken place."[69] In addition to her race, she alleged that her gender also played a role. She maintained that she was "subjected to a difference in treatment in connection with her pregnancy. . . . The sterilisation . . . amounted to a form of violence against women."[70] The court, however, refused to find that there had been any discrimination under Article 14, either on race or gender grounds.[71] According to the court, "they . . . displayed gross disregard for her right to autonomy and choice as a patient."[72] The court thus treated V.C. as an individual without any group affiliation.

In order to establish Article 14 discrimination, an applicant must show in her prima facie case that the violations committed by the respondent were either intentional or part of an organized policy. The court here concluded that they were neither.

> The materials before the Court indicate that the practice of sterilisation of women without their prior informed consent affected vulnerable individuals from various ethnic groups. The Court has held that the information available is not sufficient to demonstrate in a convincing manner that the doctors acted in bad faith, with the intention of ill-treating the applicant (see paragraph 119). Similarly, and notwithstanding the fact that the applicant's sterilisation without her informed consent calls for serious criticism, the objective evidence is not sufficiently strong in itself to convince the Court that it was part of an organised policy or that the hospital staff's conduct was intentionally racially motivated (see, mutatis mutandis, *Mižigárová v. Slovakia*, no. 74832/01, §§ 117 and 122, 14 December 2010).[73]

That the court could not find intent with regard to ill treatment of the applicant is less remarkable than that it did not find enough evidence to support a finding of an organized policy based on animus, considering the overwhelming amount of historical, statistical, and anecdotal evidence presented. Its decision disregarded the evidence of structural and institutionalized racism against Roma in Slovakia, the racial history of sterilization in that country, and the manner in which the applicant's treatment reflected the broader policy and stereotypes of Roma women. The court may have arrived at a different decision had it relied less upon intent and more on notions of unconscious bias.[74] Similarly, an understanding of the structural dimensions of Roma women's subordination, especially with regard to illiteracy, social capital, and access to medical professionals of the same race and gender, may have led to a different result.

The court first analyzed the applicant's race discrimination claim. The deployment of a colorblind ideology is noted in references to the conduct not being "racially motivated" and references to "various ethnic groups." (The court did not mention any other ethnic groups in Slovakia that had been subject to disproportionate sterilizations.) Juxtapose this with the Council of Europe Commissioner for Human Rights statement that he was "concerned about what appears to be a widespread negative attitude towards the relatively high birth rate among the Roma as compared with other parts of the population. . . . Such statements, particularly when pronounced by persons of authority, have the potential of further encouraging negative perceptions of the Roma among the non-Roma population. It cannot be excluded that these types of statements may have encouraged improper sterilization practices of Roma women."[75] In light of all the historical evidence, statistical disparity evidence, and the various reports of human rights groups, including Amnesty International and Human Rights Watch, it is unclear what would constitute stronger evidence of a racist organized policy in the court's view. The burden placed upon the applicant by the court's intent doctrine seems insurmountable, even at the prima facie stage. This is especially so in this type of hybrid race-gender case.

Additional hurdles are presented by the applicant's intersectional identity. The court is not doctrinally equipped to understand racial discrimination, much less discrimination based on more than one axis of discrimination.[76] The court's and convention's treatment of race and gender as two separate and unrelated markers makes it difficult for plaintiffs who do not fit simply into just one category or the other.[77] The fact that Roma men were not subjected to sterilizations also impacted the court's ability to see the race discrimination in V.C.'s claim. Specifically, if only Roma women were targeted—and not all Roma, how "organized" could the policy have been? How racial could it have been if it only targeted women? I do not mean to imply that if both Roma men and women were sterilized, the court would find that a prima facie racial discrimination case was established, as the court has shown itself to be reluctant to do so even in instances where the plaintiffs are Roma men.[78] My point, rather, is that there are substantial limitations imposed by the intent doctrine adopted by the court, since in some sense, Roma women are not considered "Roma."

It is also worth noting that the court did not analyze the applicant's gender discrimination claim, where she claimed that the sterilization amounted to an act of "violence against women." Yet it mentioned that "*women* from various ethnic groups" are subjected to this procedure. It thus could have found that the applicant established a prima facie sex discrimination claim. Instead the court ignored this claim and immediately dove into the racial aspect. This is in large part due to the previously discussed conceptualization of gender claims through the experiences of white women. The court did not find this to be an instance of sex discrimination in part because white women were not harmed. In other words, the applicant's race tainted her gender claim.

The outcomes of the compulsory sterilization cases thus represent limited victories. They are progress because, for once, Roma women were placed at the center of human rights legal discourse and individual women obtained redress. But they are limited, piecemeal approaches to justice, based only on the impact on the individual. The outcome of these cases render Roma women legally invisible by failing to take into account their sui generis discrimination claim, as well as by failing to recognize the claim as an instance of both race and gender discrimination under Article 14. An infringement on Roma women's reproductive rights is an instance of race discrimination, an instance of gender discrimination, and an instance of intersectional discrimination.

Another Type of Interference with Reproductive Rights: Child Removal

While compulsory sterilization has garnered some attention in the European Court of Human Rights, the placement of Roma children into state custody has yet to do so. The removal of Roma children is as much an infringement on Roma women's reproductive rights as is compulsory sterilization. The issue of child removal became most pronounced in 2013 with the high profile removal of blond children from Roma parents. The case of Maria in Greece, as well as the recent cases in Ireland and Italy, all illustrate egregious disregard for Roma parental rights.[79] But these are only the most visible manifestations of a systemic policy that views Roma mothers, like black mothers, as "welfare queens," hypersexual, irresponsible, and unfit to be parents.[80] Ascribed maternal deficiencies informed by stereotypical ideas of Roma women combine with poverty and cultural bias to produce an institutionalized preference for the removal of Roma children and the limitation on Roma women's reproductive rights.

The removal of Roma children has historical precedent. During Communism, the removal of Roma children formed part and parcel of many Eastern European reform initiatives. Roma children were placed in residential facilities as part of a "rescue and remove" plan for children living in poverty, born out of wedlock, or born into families where a person had been incarcerated or had a drug or alcohol addiction.[81] Exact statistics concerning the percentage of Roma children in state custody are difficult to ascertain due to prohibitions on collection of racial data in many European countries, but the disparity is undeniable. It is estimated that anywhere from 30 percent to 90 percent of children in state custody are Roma, while Roma make up 3 percent to 12 percent of the general population.[82]

Racism triggers the initial scrutiny of child welfare workers. This is an issue both of direct discrimination and structural marginalization. It involves direct racism in that authorities single out discrepancies in skin color between brown-skinned Roma parents and light-skinned children—indeed, newspapers and airwaves were saturated with images of brown-skinned Roma parents and a blond, light-skinned child in each instance referenced above. This type of discrimination is characteristic of a racial ideology that is informed by notions of racial purity and the same binary schema of shortcuts that is used in the law enforcement arena to determine criminality: racial profiling.[83] These simplifying markers, racial heuristics if you will, are unidirectional; that is, suspicion is not evenly distributed but instead always thrust upon the brown (or black) receiver/object. Just as skin color generates suspicion of criminal misconduct in the racial profiling context of policing, skin color in this context triggers a suspicion of criminal conduct masked as a concern for child welfare. The assumption that light-skinned children with brown-skinned Roma parents are stolen relies upon the historically persistent image of Roma as child thieves, an image readily available to generate hysteria. I term this approach a racial profiling model of child welfare.[84]

There is also a structural component to this racial profiling. Because they live in segregated areas, in Roma ghettos, Roma families become easy prey. Once scrutiny of the state is attracted, cultural bias and factors of poverty color the way in which the family is perceived. A social worker in Bulgaria points out the bias among her staff in terms of their preference for removing Roma children from their Roma ghetto–based homes: "the staff believe that it is better [for the child] in an institution than in the Roma ghetto. I simply know social workers who [want to remove the child], when they enter in a gypsy house and see the misery there—the baby eating a bread crust and boza [fermented watery sugary drink] . . . in this sense the institutions offer better conditions."[85]

A seldom recognized yet integral component of this machinery is the distorted image of Roma women that lies at the heart of removal policy and justifies these perverse interventions. Roma women are portrayed as sexually promiscuous, animalistically fertile, and in the words of Romanian politician Rares Buglea, responsible for "uncontrolled birth rates."[86] Stereotypes regarding promiscuity and hysteria about high birth rates easily translate into sterilization policies. These stereotypes also encourage the notion that Roma women are unfit mothers. This is the implication in a 2014 World Bank program on gender and Bulgarian Roma, for instance.[87] There are numerous direct and indirect references to "the terrible Gypsy mother."[88] For instance, consider the following statement by Buglea: "I know that I will be harshly criticized by the false humanists, but I continue to support the sterilization of Roma women, if after their first birth it is proven by social investigation that they have no conditions and no intention to raise their first child in conditions that are at least minimally humane."[89] He later recanted his statement, saying,

> I apologize if through unfortunate wording I left the impression that I was referring only to a particular ethnicity, and not, as I meant and still want to maintain, I refer to all irresponsible mothers in Romania. I apologize to the members of this ethnic group if they felt offended. Indeed, on Facebook . . . I was referring to some Roma mothers

because of the percentage of these cases, we must admit that this is where we come across such cases more often. But however, I do not refer to the whole ethnicity, I mean any mother who after a birth or two, is found not to have any love and care and concern for those children. I was just proposing some solution to stop this uncontrolled birth rate.[90]

The bad Gypsy mother stereotype builds on a familiar trope that paints the Roma woman as an aggressive, shameless exploiter.[91] I refer to this as the Evil Gypsy Woman/Witch trope, popularized in cartoons, comics and Hollywood horror films as an ugly, usually old, conniving, curse-casting b*tch, such as the Ganush character in Raimi's *Drag Me to Hell* film or the character in the "Treehouse of Horror" episode of *The Simpsons* television show. She also appears in a string of news articles and crime shows on Roma women victimizing or poisoning elderly men.[92] She is involved in the occult, is sometimes a fortune-teller or psychic, and always amoral.[93] She is a take on the Sapphire trope, which portrays black women as domineering, angry, and emasculating.[94] This formulation allows for the easy justification of restrictions on her right to parent. Whereas mothers are usually thought of as nurturers, Roma mothers are thought of as victimizers, not a source of protection for their children, but rather someone from whom their children need protection.

Roma women are widely thought to use their children as a source of income.[95] That is, if a poor Roma woman has several children and is on welfare, she is not looked upon with sympathy. She is not seen as having to withstand the burden of providing for five children in an environment rife with discrimination and structural marginalization. Her problematic access to birth control and her subjection to patriarchal practices are not considered. Race and gender imagery harking back to slavery paint her not as a victim—a label that continues to elude Roma women—but as irresponsible.[96] Universal imagery of "Gypsies" as charlatans turns the Roma's ability to survive centuries of persecution and material deprivation into a "gift for conning."[97] Roma women are commonly believed to exploit their children by birthing them for the sole purpose of collecting state subsidies and forcing them to beg or wash car windows.[98] A particularly egregious example of the demonization of Roma women was the statement by a mayor in Hungary who suggested that Roma women purposely maim their children to receive state support, a new twist on the "welfare queen" stereotype.[99]

Conclusion

Restrictions on Roma women's rights to be mothers (through child removal and sterilization) have coincided not only with an expansion of "fortress Europe" but also an expansion of the carceral state. Here I am referring to barriers to to Romas' ability to establish residency in Western Europe, despite their being EU citizens. Interference with Roma women's reproductive rights has taken place alongside efforts to curtail the movement of Roma across borders and otherwise deprive them of their liberty. Two meanings of confinement are particularly relevant in this context: confinement to country of "origin" and confinement in the commonly used sense of incarceration.

Because antiracist/Roma rights politics and feminist politics are both constructed based upon the experiences of the dominant members in each group (Roma men and white women), the political concerns specific to Roma women are neglected. Feminist discourse, antiracist discourse, and liberal human rights discourse all fail to capture the subordination of Roma women in general and in the sphere of reproductive rights in particular. Human rights law must contend with unconscious bias and the structural subordination of Roma women, with particular attention to how stereotypes of Roma women influence policies, practices, and the law. It is crucial that we explore how these tropes intersect with broader policies such as those on migration and crime and how they reinforce one another and reproduce structures of domination. At the same time, it is important to understand how the law—even human rights law that denounces certain practices—functions to legitimize other systems of subordination. Adopting a critical race theory approach brings us closer to realizing the emancipatory potential of human rights.

PART II

The Longue Durée: The History of
Roma Policy as an Element in U.S.
Foreign Policy

Chapter 3

Policy and Practice: A Case Study of U.S. Foreign Policy Regarding the Situation of Roma in Europe

Erika Schlager

This chapter examines the role of the United States in advancing policies relating to Roma issues in Europe as viewed from the vantage point of the U.S. Commission on Security and Cooperation in Europe. The U.S. Commission on Security and Cooperation in Europe, also known as the Helsinki Commission, is an independent U.S. government agency created by Congress in 1976 to monitor and encourage compliance with the Helsinki Final Act and other commitments adopted by the participating states of the Organization for Security and Cooperation in Europe (OSCE). The Helsinki Commission works closely with the Department of State on matters related to the OSCE, explained in fuller detail later in this chapter.[1]

Relative to parliamentary systems, the U.S. Congress has a strong role in shaping foreign policy. In the 1970s, Congress elevated human rights as an explicit factor in the conduct of relations with foreign governments, exemplified by the establishment of a congressional mandate requiring the Department of State to submit to Congress annual country reports on human rights practices, the passage of the 1974 Jackson-Vanik Act (which de jure tied trade relations to respect for the right to emigrate and de facto tied trade to other human rights issues), and the establishment of the Helsinki

Commission. Members were motivated by various concerns, including U.S. financial and other support for dictatorships. In addition, religious and ethnic NGOs and human rights groups such as Helsinki Watch (later called Human Rights Watch) looked to Congress to advance human rights as a consideration among other competing foreign policy objectives. While Congress's tools were intended to promote human rights, they were also intended to serve as a form of legislative oversight on the executive branch in the conduct of foreign policy.

In the early 1990s, Helsinki Watch issued a series of reports putting a spotlight on human rights violations experienced by Roma in Bulgaria, Czechoslovakia, Hungary, and Romania. In 1991, the Project on Ethnic Relations was founded to address emerging interethnic conflicts in Central and Southern Europe. Although not a human rights organization, it became an active voice in raising awareness of the situation of Roma in Europe, lobbied for the first congressional hearing on the situation of Roma, actively engaged Department of State interlocutors, and participated in OSCE meetings related to Roma.[2]

The denial of citizenship to Roma by the newly independent Czech Republic in 1993 serves as a case study in this chapter, illuminating both the evolution of U.S. engagement as well as the role of various international organizations on this issue, including the Organization on Security and Cooperation in Europe (OSCE), Council of Europe (CoE), and United Nations High Commissioner for Refugees (UNHCR).

The OSCE is a pan-European security forum, originally founded in 1975 as a tool for addressing issues relating to Cold War divisions. In its foundational document, the Helsinki Final Act (negotiated and signed in Helsinki, Finland), the NATO countries, the Warsaw Pact countries, and neutral and nonaligned countries committed themselves to ten fundamental principles guiding relations among states, including respect for human rights, and an ongoing process of review.[3] The original thirty-five participating states, including the United States, Canada, most of Europe, and the Soviet Union, have expanded to fifty-seven states, largely through the breakup of the Union of Soviet Socialist Republics, the Czechoslovak Socialist Republic, and finally the Yugoslav Socialist Federal Republic, rather than the addition of new geography. Its body of consensus-based commitments has grown to include significant human rights provisions. The Council of Europe was founded by ten countries in 1949 as one of the first expressions of post–World War II democratic Europe's integration. According to its founding treaty, membership is limited to European countries that share a commitment to the rule of law and fundamental human rights. In 1950, the CoE member states adopted the European Convention on Human Rights, which remains the foundation for the preeminent supranational system for the adjudication of international human rights claims. In the period discussed in this chapter, the rapidity with which the Council of Europe admitted post-Communist countries as new members led some to express concern that CoE human rights standards were being eroded.[4] The Council of Europe has grown from ten to forty-seven member states today. Finally, the UNHCR was founded to help with the refugee crisis that followed World War II. It is an organ of the United Nations that works around the globe. The scope of its work has expanded to include internally displaced persons and some engagement on matters of statelessness. In his chapter in this volume, Andrzej Mirga illustrates in detail the ways in which, during the 1990s to the mid-2000s, the OSCE and Council of Europe, as well as the UN, became central platforms for Roma issues.[5]

In the early 1990s, the countries of Europe where Roma are the most numerous were just emerging from decades of Communist repression. Their governments were struggling with the transition to democracy, the change from command to market economies, and accountability for past crimes. The irreversibility of the move toward democracy was not a given. Yugoslavia, a country with one of Europe's largest Roma populations, had started the descent into ethnic conflict that ultimately led to genocide in Bosnia-Herzegovina. The chapter in this volume by Kálmán Mizsei chronicles other aspects of "the dark side" of Eastern Europe's transition to democracy, especially its effects on the increased marginalization of Roma.[6]

At issue in the Czech Republic was one of the most important human rights questions in this first post-Communist decade: in essence, could a newly independent state deny citizenship—the right to have rights—to citizens of the former federal state based on their ethnic identity? In the OSCE region, where in the space of a few years there were suddenly twenty-one newly independent states, the answer to this question was profoundly important not only to Roma, but millions of others as well.

1990 Copenhagen Document: First Recognition of Roma Human Rights Issues

U.S. policies relating specifically to Roma begin with the 1990 Copenhagen Document.[7] In 1990, thirty-five countries met in Copenhagen for the second of three planned meetings of a "Conference on the Human Dimension," organized within the framework of what was then known as the Helsinki process (essentially follow-up and review of the implementation of the Helsinki agreement, formally called the Conference for Security and Cooperation in Europe, renamed in 1994 the Organization on Security and Cooperation in Europe). While the first of the three meetings, held in Paris in 1989, concluded without any agreement, the Copenhagen meeting ended with the adoption of a watershed agreement on human rights and democracy. It included the first reference to Roma in an international human rights agreement, and the United States played a key role in achieving the adoption of this text.

The Copenhagen meeting took place at a moment when changes in Europe were accelerating at breakneck speed. On June 4, 1989, seats for part of the Polish parliament were freely contested, paving the way for the historic election of a non-Communist prime minister. The first—and last—free elections were held in the German Democratic Republic (East Germany) on March 18, 1990. Free elections were held in Hungary on March 24, 1990, and in Czechoslovakia on June 8 and 9, just as the Copenhagen meeting started. Representatives of the Baltic states had come to Copenhagen seeking to become OSCE participating states as part of their efforts to reestablish their independence.[8] In short, it was a moment of extraordinary transformation when long-desired aspirations for freedom might be realized.

At the same time, the irreversibility of democratic and human rights improvements was by no means guaranteed, and the changes were far from complete. Accordingly, there was a strong sense that the month-long meeting in Copenhagen represented a window of opportunity to reach ready agreement on a broad range of commitments relating to human rights, democracy, and the rule of law before the window of opportunity slammed shut. In contrast to the mood of the Paris meeting the year before,[9] ambitions in Copenhagen were high and countries tabled proposals on democracy and the rule of law, rights of minorities, conflict prevention, and human rights monitoring. The United States focused first and foremost on its proposal for free and fair elections.

It is safe to say that none of the delegates arrived in Copenhagen with plans to negotiate language on Roma human rights. Nevertheless, several factors put Roma issues on the negotiating table. First, the Copenhagen meeting was held at a time when the situation in Romania was on the front pages, and Roma were part of that unfolding drama. While Poland, Hungary, and Czechoslovakia held elections marking the incremental and peaceful transition from Communism, in Romania, power struggles led to instability and violence. The summary trial and execution of Nicolae Ceausescu in December 1989 was followed by a series of attacks by miners that were part of the post-Ceausescu power struggle. In May 1990, just before the Copenhagen meeting, Romania held presidential and parliamentary elections (neither free nor fair), and the new regime promptly summoned the miners again in mid-June to "defend" the newly installed government from demonstrators. The rampaging miners had many targets: protesters, publishing houses . . . and Roma.[10] Meanwhile, tens of thousands of Romanian nationals, both ethnic Romanians and ethnic Roma, started to flee Romania for the Federal Republic of Germany.

The United States was keenly attentive to developments in Romania, where Ceausescu's brutal minority policies had been a long-standing concern. Moreover, congressional delegations organized by the U.S. Helsinki Commission visited Bucharest in May and then participated in the Copenhagen meeting in June, both reinforcing with the Department of State congressional concerns regarding the human rights situation in unstable Romania and pressing the Romanian delegation directly on human rights issues. The cochairman of the Helsinki Commission, Congressman Steny Hoyer, specifically expressed concern to Romanian delegation head Ion Chelebeu that Roma had been scapegoated in the aftermath of violence in Tirgu Mures and Bucharest.[11]

Second, an unprecedented civil society conference was held in Copenhagen parallel to the formal meeting of participating states. Throughout the month, NGOs held their own events to focus on specific human rights concerns and lobby governments to address those issues in the document being negotiated. One of those NGO activists was Nicolae Gheorghe, an unstoppable force from Romania who would ultimately leave an indelible mark on the OSCE's work on Roma human rights issues. In Copenhagen, Gheorghe advocated for a proposal submitted by the International Romani Union, urging the participating states to protect the human rights of Roma.

As it happened, minority rights—in OSCE-speak, "the rights of persons belonging to national minorities"—was also one of the clusters of issues being negotiated in four working groups in Copenhagen.[12] The specific opening to include Roma issues came in the form of a *joint* proposal submitted by the

Federal Republic of Germany and the German Democratic Republic (the very fact that West Germany and East Germany submitted a proposal together was evidence of the tectonic shifts underway) on combatting "prejudices that lead to violence, totalitarianism, racial hatred, anti-Semitism and the persecution of religious and ideological dissidents."[13]

In fact, there had been a long-standing effort at the United Nations by the United States and others to secure the adoption of a resolution on the problem of anti-Semitism, but Moscow had consistently blocked this effort. At Copenhagen, the Helsinki Commission urged the head of the U.S. delegation, veteran negotiator Max Kampelman, to seize the opportunity to reach agreement on a condemnation of anti-Semitism.[14] As the negotiations proceeded, the Helsinki Commission supported Roma civil society calls to acknowledge the human rights problems experienced by Roma.

Ambassador Kampelman worked to negotiate the text on anti-Semitism, and he successfully secured a specific reference to Roma in the paragraph on anti-Semitism, overcoming initial German reluctance. He also gave prominence to Roma issues by raising the issue of discrimination against Roma in a plenary statement on June 22.[15] Significantly, Kampelman took ownership of the resulting text in Washington. When testifying before Congress about the important achievements reflected in the final Copenhagen Document, he observed that the situation of Roma was "a disgrace, really, and ought to be dealt with" and argued that quiet complicity on the part of governments was one reason he had pushed so hard for the inclusion of explicit references to anti-Semitism and the problems faced by Roma.[16]

The Copenhagen Document was the first international agreement to recognize the human rights problems faced by Roma.[17] As David Meyer and Michael Uyehara suggest in their chapter in this volume,[18] over the next two decades, this document exemplified the forward-leaning approach of the OSCE: the OSCE made Roma human rights issues a standing part of its human rights agenda, hired Roma as civil servants both at the Office for Democratic Institutions and Human Rights in Warsaw as well as on field missions, elaborated an action plan (2003) as a guide for governments and the OSCE's own institutions, and reported on the situation of Roma through its field missions, the High Commissioner on National Minorities, and the Office for Democratic Institutions and Human Rights. The Copenhagen Document was the foundation on which those actions were built, and the United States helped lay that cornerstone.

The Denial of Citizenship: Human Rights Take a Holiday

If the 1990 Copenhagen meeting reflected the ability of the United States to hold up the mantle of leadership and advance principles, the U.S. embassy in Prague in 1994 and 1995 represented the triumph of short-sighted political expediency over the defense of human rights. While events in Romania strongly informed the U.S. approach to Roma issues in Copenhagen, developments in the Czech Republic both shaped and illustrated Washington's engagement with Roma issues for much of Europe's first post-Communist decade.

The Czech Republic has a relatively small Roma population (estimated at two to three hundred thousand out of roughly ten million). Nevertheless, Roma in this country have experienced a remarkable scope of human rights abuse: high-profile racially motivated murders, forced displacement, surges in refugees, sterilization without informed consent, school segregation, controversies relating to the archives and memorial sites of the World War II genocide, and the building of ghetto walls to enclose them (to give an incomplete list). In his chapter in this volume, Will Guy elaborates on the rampant violence, hate mongering, and discrimination Roma confront in the Czech Republic, particularly after enlargements to the European Union.[19]

At the same time, perhaps counterintuitively, the Czech Republic also played an active role in negotiations on the OSCE toolbox relating to Roma, including advancing a proposal for an OSCE commissioner on Roma in the late 1990s. As a consequence, the Czech Republic has often brought into sharp contrast the differences between practice at home and policy abroad.

One of the most illuminating issues to arise in the Czech Republic was the denial of citizenship—the right to have rights—to Roma after the breakup of Czechoslovakia. Although briefly raised by a CSCE mission in 1993,[20] the NGO Tolerance Foundation provided extensive and unimpeachable reporting on the significant number of Roma left stateless by the Czech citizenship law.[21] From its founding in 1918 until 1968, only Czechoslovak citizenship was recognized in Czechoslovakia. During World War II, most Roma in the Nazi-occupied Czech lands (basically the geographic area that is now the Czech Republic) were murdered or perished at Auschwitz. Most Roma in the Tiso-led Slovak puppet state (temporarily spun off from Czechoslovakia at the behest of the Nazis) suffered persecution, but survived. In the postwar period, some Czechoslovak Roma from Slovakia moved to the Czech lands to fill labor shortages created by the mass expulsion of Sudeten Germans. After the 1968 Soviet invasion of Czechoslovakia, the policy of so-called "normalization" included a nominal form of federalism and the creation of Czech and Slovak "republics" with lowercase-r republic citizenship. In practice, this regional citizenship had no legal consequences at all. Yet when the newly independent Czech Republic crafted its citizenship law, it tied Czech Republic citizenship to the earlier "Czech republic" citizenship as a means of excluding Roma whose parents or grandparents had moved from the Slovak region of Czechoslovakia to the Czech lands.[22] In essence, although the Czech law was neutral on its face as to race or ethnicity, tens of thousands of former Czechoslovak citizens who were permanent residents of the Czech Republic were rendered de facto or de jure stateless.[23] Not all of the Czech Republic's Roma were excluded from citizenship, but all of those excluded were Roma.

The OSCE held its first specialized human rights meeting focused on the situation of Roma in 1994, at which time representatives of the Council of Europe, the UNHCR, the OSCE, and EU all voiced concern about the discriminatory nature of the Czech citizenship law. During this early period, Czech officials largely responded to emerging international criticism with general denials. But that changed when the Department of State issued its annual *Country Report on Human Rights* for the calendar year 1994 (released at the beginning of 1995).[24] The Czech government had decided it was time to go on the offensive. In an unusually high-level and public response, Prime Minister Vaclav Klaus attacked the State Department's report, stating, "I must say that I don't believe my eyes what is written there."[25] The annual State Department *Country Reports on Human Rights Practices* do not typically elicit a reaction from the head of government. For the U.S. embassy in Prague, this was especially inconvenient, coming a few months before a scheduled meeting in Washington between Prime Minister Klaus and President Bill Clinton.

Of course, what was at issue was not just citizenship for Roma in the Czech Republic, but the question of how the international community would articulate the standard for citizenship in newly independent states, synthesizing complex law and norms regarding human rights, refugees, and state succession in the Balkans or in the multiethnic regions of the former Soviet Union.[26] The vehemence of the Czech reaction to the State Department's report, when it came, should have been recognized as an indication of the depth of anti-Roma bigotry in the Czech Republic.

But the U.S. embassy in Prague failed to grasp the real significance of the Czech government's harsh reaction and myopically ignored the implications for statelessness and interethnic conflict in the region that might result if other countries followed the Czech model. Instead of pressing the Czech government to change its discriminatory citizenship law, the U.S. embassy sought to deflect Czech government criticism of its *Country Report* at an alternate target. The embassy claimed it was a September 1994 U.S. Helsinki Commission's report—issued nearly half a year before the department's *Country Report*—that prompted the Czech government's sharp response to the State Department publication. First Secretary Cameron Munter (later U.S. ambassador to Pakistan) dismissed the commission's concerns about the Czech citizenship law by blaming Roma themselves, writing, "The problem for many Roma, in my experience, stems from different attitudes toward bureaucratic demands rather than being trapped in the very precise legal status of 'statelessness.'"[27] In other words, the embassy argued that the problem was not that Roma were left stateless, but that they did not understand how bureaucracies worked.

Moreover, in response to Czech pressure, the department watered down its *Country Reports on Human Rights on the Czech Republic* and began to include "exculpatory" additions designed to cast the Czech Republic in a more favorable light. For example, while the 1994 report states that the "rate of expulsion is growing," reports for 1995, 1996, and 1997 emphasized that the number was simply unknown. Reports for 1995 and 1996 stated that fears of mass deportation were "exaggerated." The 1996 report implied this was not an important issue for "local" Roma leaders (who, according to the same report, were focused on racially motivated violence). Reports for 1996 and 1997 claimed that Roma were to blame for not getting citizenship due to their "negligence or ignorance"—ignoring the fact that most former Czechoslovak citizens in the Czech Republic were not required to apply for citizenship at all, but simply deemed citizens.[28]

Members of Congress, meanwhile, continued to raise the Czech citizenship issue in meetings with Czech government officials and members of the Czech parliament and pressed the Department of State to do likewise.[29] At the OSCE Parliamentary Assembly, members of the Helsinki Commission congressional delegation introduced resolutions on nondiscriminatory citizenship norms in the context of state succession and urged increased OSCE efforts to combat discrimination and intolerance against Roma.[30] Improvements in the Department of State's approach and reporting came with the departure of Ambassador Adrian Basora and the arrival of Ambassador Jenonne Walker at the embassy in Prague in late August 1995.

Still, citizenship denials continued, contributing to the economic, social, and political marginalization of the Roma minority and the Romas' general stigmatization as "others."[31] Of those denied citizenship, only a fraction were expelled from the Czech Republic (and generally sent to Slovakia, whether they considered themselves Slovak nationals or not). But the threat of a larger wave of expulsions was ever present. In 1997, the Prague-based Czech Helsinki Committee reported that abandoned babies in the Czech Republic were deemed by the Czech government to be Slovak citizens (apparently on the theory that Czechs could not possibly abandon children). Such children, the number of which was estimated to be fourteen hundred, would be permitted to stay in Czech orphanages while minors, but would be expelled upon reaching their eighteenth birthday. This report provoked a particularly sharp exchange between members of the U.S. Helsinki Commission and the Czech ambassador at a hearing in Washington on NATO expansion.[32]

The UNHCR also pressed the Czech government on the issue of citizenship.[33] As the international community's body tasked with managing refugee crises (and already grappling with consequences of ethnic cleansing in the Balkans), the UNHCR was deeply concerned by the prospect of large numbers of newly stateless Roma. Although many UNHCR recommendations to Prague were confidential, it was hoped that a public report simultaneously prepared by the Council of Europe would provide much needed leverage against the law. It did not.

Instead, when the Council of Europe issued a long-awaited report on the Czech citizenship law in April 1996, it was a disaster. While mildly critical, the report largely whitewashed or ignored many of the law's shortcomings and contradicted published UNHCR interpretations of law. Most shocking was an erroneous assertion regarding the international nondiscrimination law in the context of state succession: "It should be noted that in the context of nationality and state succession, the question of discrimination has been discussed. It is legitimate to make distinctions on the basis of language and, in so far as this denotes a better ability for integration in a country, *on the basis of ethnic origin in giving citizenship to new citizens of a State, also in case of dissolution of a previous State.* Such distinctions are not considered as discrimination and accepted under general principles of nationality law" (emphasis added).[34] In other words, even if the Czech citizenship law had included an *explicit* denial of citizenship for Roma based on their ethnicity, the Council of Europe experts were claiming that would be acceptable. In any case, the report's recommendations, if implemented, would not have meaningfully remedied the problems it weakly acknowledged. The report suggested changes to make the Czech law *less* harsh or *less* discriminatory—in other words, to make the Czech law only *less* in violation of international commitments. With the CoE report in hand, the Czech Parliament passed superficial window-dressing changes to the law that, it stated, addressed the concerns of the Council of Europe.[35] No additional changes, they insisted, would be made.

The single most problematic feature of the Czech citizenship law that entered into force on January 1, 1993, was the establishment of a pool of individuals who (1) previously had Czechoslovak citizenship, and (2) were permanent residents of the Czech Republic, but (3) would be excluded from automatically getting Czech citizenship. The criteria used to establish that pool, reflecting particular features of Czechoslovak history, was designed to exclude Roma. Instead of automatically receiving Czech citizenship, this singular pool of former Czechoslovaks would have to complete a burdensome application process. After the 1996 amendment, that basic feature remained entirely intact. The amendment purported to ameliorate the application process by enabling the Ministry of Interior to grant a waiver confirming that the applicant had a clean criminal record and by easing the process to document permanent residency. Critics argued that the requirement of a clean criminal record (whether waived or not) was itself a violation of the international prohibition on ex post facto criminal penalties. They claimed that local officials routinely turned down Roma applicants even when they met the criteria of the amended law and that the application procedure lacked sufficient forms of appeal or oversight. Those especially disadvantaged included orphans or children in foster care, persons incarcerated in Czech prisons, and others living on the margins of society who had difficulty navigating the sometimes Kafkaesque Czech bureaucracy.

As characterized by one senior American official at the time, the CoE report "cut the floor out from under" efforts to persuade the Czechs to make serious revisions to the law. Civil society advocates were crestfallen. The general feeling was that no more could be done.

Publicly, the Helsinki Commission emphasized the strongest parts of the CoE report.[36]

Privately, commission leaders wrote to Deputy Secretary General Peter Leurprecht to criticize the report's deeply flawed analysis. Moreover, the

Helsinki Commission also signaled that the battle for a nondiscriminatory Czech law was not over: while they welcomed acknowledgment of the law's need for revision, they argued that the 1996 amendment to the law "fails to address its most oppressive effect . . . we urge the leaders of the Czech Republic to undertake a fuller review of their citizenship law and bring it into conformity with the Czech Republic's international human rights commitments. In particular, this must mean granting citizenship to all long-term residents of the Czech Republic who previously held Czechoslovak citizenship."[37]

Although the April 1996 report of experts was a missed opportunity for the Council of Europe to articulate nondiscriminatory standards of citizenship for newly independent states, it was not the only or last opportunity. The Council of Europe addressed fundamentally similar issues through two other avenues: a declaration by the CoE European Commission on Democracy Through Law (ECDL, commonly known as the Venice Commission, the Council of Europe's advisory body on constitutional matters) adopted in September 1996 and a new treaty on citizenship negotiated by CoE member states and opened for signature in November 1997. The complex legal framework of the Czech Republic's citizenship law, intended to mask its inherently discriminatory features, was incompatible with both the declaration and the treaty.[38]

The denial of citizenship was actually symptomatic of the profound prejudice against Roma that manifested itself in a host of ways in the Czech lands. Throughout the first post-Communist decade, the number of violent attacks against Roma climbed year after year. The steady exodus of Czech Roma to Canada and the UK had created bilateral friction between Prague and those countries. NGO reports on school segregation, the sterilization of Roma women without informed consent (detailed in Alexandra Oprea's chapter in this volume),[39] and discrimination in employment, public services, and public places mounted. The U.S. Department of State's *Country Report on Human Rights in the Czech Republic* for 1999 acknowledged, finally, that the number of de facto stateless persons was estimated between 10,000 and 20,000. The economic and social marginalization of Roma was on a deep downward spiral.

In some ways, however, 1997 was a turning point. That fall, there had been a dramatic increase in the number of Czech Roma seeking asylum in Canada. The same year, a wave of bank failures reached the Czech National Bank. The twin developments cracked the positive international image of the Czech Republic tied to Vaclav Havel's human rights presidency on the one hand and the Thatcherite economic reform trumpeted by Prime Minister Vaclav Klaus on the other. Then, in early 1999, the city of Usti nad Labem built a ghetto wall to segregate Roma residents from ethnic Czechs, generating broad and unfavorable international press coverage.

Against a backdrop of growing international concern regarding the persecution of Roma in the Czech Republic, Prague amended the citizenship law in July 1999 by allowing former Czechoslovak citizens who were permanent residents as of December 31, 1992, and who had maintained permanent residency in the Czech Republic after that time, to obtain citizenship by declaration. From a human rights or humanitarian perspective, the 1999 amendments were not perfect. For example, persons who had discontinued their permanent residency to seek asylum in another country would not be eligible. Nevertheless, the amendment made it possible for tens of thousands of previously excluded Roma to secure citizenship.

Multiple factors most likely contributed to this change. First, notwithstanding the initial hesitation within the Department of State and the Council of Europe to push hard for citizenship reform, by 1997 key international stakeholders were by and large all on the same page. The 1996 Czech amendment had failed to placate critics who, if anything, were progressively louder and more united in their call for extending citizenship to all those who were permanent residents of the Czech Republic in 1993. It is also possible that this criticism was more worrisome to officials in Prague as the Czech Republic sought to advance its case for EU accession, even if the European Union did not play a direct or significant role in addressing the denial of citizenship.[40] Finally, a political shift in the Czech Republic put in place a government willing to implement these called-for reforms, an essential ingredient for change.[41]

From Copenhagen to Istanbul

Although it may seem counterintuitive in light of the situation of Roma in the Czech Republic, in 1998 the Czech government proposed that the OSCE Ministerial Council appoint a "High Commissioner for Roma" to coordinate OSCE efforts related to Roma issues. The mandate would be constructed along the lines of the OSCE High Commissioner on National Minorities.[42] The OSCE had previously established a "Contact Point for Roma and Sinti Issues" at its Office for Democratic Institutions and Human Rights in 1994, but the Contact Point essentially acted as a clearinghouse with no additional resources. The 1998 Czech proposal was based, in any case, on the (mis-guided) premise that, since Roma did not fall within the scope of the OSCE's concept of "national minorities," they required a separate institutional mechanism.

Why did officials in Prague propose in 1998 the creation of an OSCE office that would potentially put the spotlight on shortcomings in their own country? There were (at least) two factors. First, some government officials (former Communist-era human rights activists) believed that international instruments could be constructive tools for putting pressure on more recalcitrant elements in the government. Second, other government officials (indeed, the more recalcitrant elements) suggested that since Roma were a transnational diaspora, it should be up to one of the complaining international organizations to "fix" the "Roma problem." At one meeting organized by the Council of Europe in Prague in 1998, this view provoked a sharp rebuke from Dutch parliamentarian and leading voice on Roma human rights issues Josephine Verspaget, who reminded her Czech government colleague that the implementation of international obligations and commitments falls first and foremost to the states.

The United States was not keen on the proposal for a Commissioner on Roma for several reasons. The Czech proposal was built around several flawed premises, including misunderstandings about both the possibilities and limitations of the mandate of the High Commissioner on National Minorities. Washington was also skeptical about the benefits of establishing additional human rights bureaucracies and concerned that the establishment of a plethora of specialized organs dealing with Roma, religion, gender, and other compartmentalized human rights issues might actually weaken human rights advocacy.[43] There was already, in addition to the High Commissioner on National Minorities, an OSCE Representative on Freedom of the Media, and NGOs had advocated creating other additional offices on other specific human rights issues. The Helsinki Commission argued that the credibility of the Czech Republic, as the author of this proposal, was inherently compromised—if the Czechs wanted to be taken seriously as advocates for Roma within the OSCE, they should fix their citizenship law and fulfill their unmet pledge to transfer copies of the Lety concentration camp archives to the U.S. Holocaust Memorial Museum.[44]

At the 1998 Oslo ministerial council, the participating states adopted a decision that was nominally intended to strengthen the OSCE's capabilities for addressing issues relating to Roma.[45] Members of the Helsinki Commission leadership, however, strongly criticized the reality gap between events on the ground and Oslo's result, noting that

> a decision "on the enhancement of the OSCE's capabilities regarding Roma and Sinti issues" and vague language on "developing synergies" among international bureaucracies was substituted for a real and meaningful policy statement. The ministerial decision regarding Roma and Sinti does not use the words "human rights" even once. . . . Rather than underscoring the importance of Romani human rights concerns, the weakly worded decision on Roma adopted in Oslo may have been the product of an effort by those states with the worst records and the least willingness to deal openly and honestly with Roma and Sinti issues to deflect international attention from their inaction and toward a bureaucratic mechanism that plainly lacks the authority and power to adopt and implement effective solutions to the underlying problems.[46]

A better text emerged a year later, at the 1999 Istanbul Summit. There, the OSCE heads of state and government "deplore violence and other manifestations of racism and discrimination against minorities, including the Roma and Sinti [and] commit ourselves to ensure that laws and policies fully respect the rights of Roma and Sinti and, where necessary, to promote antidiscrimination legislation to this effect."[47] The reference to antidiscrimination legislation was specifically intended to reinforce the European Union "Racial Equality Directive."[48]

The successive negotiations helped set the stage for heighted attention to Roma issues by OSCE institutions. In 1999, Nicolae Gheorghe (the Roma NGO activist who had been instrumental in the Copenhagen results) was appointed by the OSCE's Office for Democratic Institutions and Human Rights as its first Roma civil servant. In 2000, the High Commissioner on National Minorities issued a comprehensive report on the situation of Roma in the OSCE region. In 2001, under the Romanian chairmanship of the OSCE, the participating states began work on an action plan that was adopted in 2003.[49] The action plan serves as a set of guidelines for recommended action by the participating states and also establishes a framework for OSCE engagement on Roma issues. There have been two OSCE follow up reports, in 2008 and 2013, on implementation of the action plan by the OSCE participating states.

Together, the agreements in Copenhagen and Istanbul bracketed Europe's first post-Communist decade. Throughout this period, the OSCE served as an important multilateral venue for the United States to raise concerns about the situation of Roma, particularly through regular meetings convened to review the implementation of human rights commitments and weekly meetings of the OSCE Permanent Council in Vienna. The United States also supported OSCE institutional engagement on Roma issues through OSCE field missions in the Balkans, the reporting of the OSCE High Commissioner on National Minorities, and the Office for Democratic Institutions and Human Rights. The OSCE gave the United States a platform in Europe to address concerns about Roma that complemented its bilateral dialogues on human rights and, at times, reinforced the Council of Europe and the European Union.

Has U.S. engagement had a meaningful impact? The path into the "but for" world of counterfactual histories is always uncertain. That said, a few observations are in order. First, but for congressional engagement on Roma issues (read: pressure from the U.S. Helsinki Commission), State Department engagement would have evolved more slowly and weakly. Second, but for what eventually became robust advocacy, the 1996 amendment to the Czech citizenship law might have been the last, leaving tens of thousands of people in the heart of Europe in stateless limbo. When civil society activists and representatives of international organizations despaired that efforts to get meaningful changes to the law would be futile, the resolute commitment of Washington to a nondiscriminatory principle of citizenship provided critical political will.

Although the U.S. reaction to developments in the Czech Republic provides an interesting case study regarding the evolution of U.S. policy and the relationship between U.S. and European approaches, the Balkans would provide multiple additional and equally illuminating chapters. The U.S. role in Dayton or Kosovo may be well known; less well known is the resettlement of Bosnian Roma refugees in Missouri or the heroic action of U.S. ambassador Christopher Hill, who, at considerable personal risk, prevented a mob from lynching Roma in a refugee camp in Macedonia.[50] U.S. engagement on the lead-contaminated camp in Mitrovica would require another chapter altogether. Across the board, one might reasonably ask: what could the United States have done faster, sooner, and better?

Unfortunately, the situation of Roma in Europe has deteriorated in many ways over the past twenty-five years. As other chapters in this volume show, the causes for this deterioration are many—but are ultimately rooted in a racism that is both broad and deep. Indeed, the battle to achieve a nondiscriminatory citizenship law in the Czech Republic presaged the struggle to ensure that the citizenship rights of Roma across the member states of the European Union, including freedom of movement, are protected. That battle is still being waged.

Chapter 4

The U.S. Department of State and International Efforts to Promote the Human Rights of Roma

David Meyer and Michael Uyehara

On March 24, 2009, U.S. secretary of state Hillary Clinton made waves in the world of advocacy for the human rights of Roma, as the first U.S. secretary of state to honor International Roma Day. In a video statement released to commemorate that day, celebrated April 8, she stated, "The United States is committed to protecting and promoting the human rights of Roma."[1] She touched on her personal experience from years before as first lady, visiting Roma communities and working on their behalf as part of the U.S. Helsinki Commission. She noted the systematic discrimination Roma face across Europe, but also drew attention to the intangible cultural heritage of Roma. She highlighted the responsibility of governments to ensure that members of minority communities have the tools and opportunities they need to succeed as productive and responsible members of society. Three years later in Sofia, Bulgaria, Secretary Clinton announced that the United States would become an official observer to the Decade of Roma Inclusion, a European initiative to promote the inclusion and integration of Roma (discussed in Kálmán Mizsei's chapter in this volume),[2] and asserted that for the Obama administration ensuring respect for the human rights of Roma "is a stated foreign policy priority."[3] These statements did not reflect a new policy, but signaled the special attention the U.S. government was paying to the plight of Europe's most marginalized minority and increased diplomatic efforts to combat ongoing anti-Roma prejudice, discrimination, and violence.

Promoting freedom and democracy and protecting human rights around the world are central to U.S. foreign policy and tied to the core U.S. national interest of building a peaceful, prosperous global community. Tolerance, non-discrimination, protection of vulnerable groups, and inclusion of marginalized communities are part of this general policy, and inclusion and integration of Roma occupy a significant place in this agenda. The U.S. Department of State has played a leading role in U.S. government efforts to secure rights for Roma, drawing on international law, multilateral agreements and institutions, and U.S. interests. It has also drawn on the expertise of Roma Americans, who have been described as "hidden Americans."[4]

This chapter will lay out the State Department's policy framework and how it forms part of a regional diplomatic emphasis on protecting the human rights of Roma, discuss the core challenges in countering discrimination against Roma, and describe some of the ways the State Department has responded to these challenges.

Roma Americans

During World War II, the Nazi regime targeted Roma for genocide based solely on their ethnic identity. Apart from Jews, Roma were the only ethnic group in Europe marked for total extermination. Experts estimate that between 500,000[5] and 1.5 million[6] Roma were exterminated during the war, the most violent expression of a long history of anti-Roma discrimination. Recognition and commemoration of this act of genocide are still inadequate. As part of worldwide efforts to build public awareness and remembrance on August 1, 2014, U.S. secretary of state John Kerry commemorated the Roma victims of the World War II genocide and stated, "We must condemn all prejudice wherever it springs up, because we know that words of hatred too often become acts of hatred. Teaching about Roma experiences during the Holocaust is critical in combating prejudice."[7]

Deeply rooted societal prejudices continue today, and some governments, international organizations, and human rights organizations have begun to acknowledge and systematically address the gravity of discrimination against Roma persons.

Systematic historical discrimination led some Roma to seek a better life abroad, and many came to the United States seeking economic opportunity and a more tolerant society. According to Roma American professor Ian Hancock of the University of Texas Austin, however,

> Unlike the situation in Europe, where Gypsies [*sic*] are much in evidence, Roma in the United States have been called the "hidden Americans" because they remain by choice largely invisible. There are two reasons for this: first, the United States is made up of minority groups of all complexions, and so it is easy for Gypsies to present themselves as American Indians, Hispanics, or southern Europeans, and they usually do this rather than identify themselves as Gypsies. Second, most Americans know very little about actual Roma but a great deal about the Hollywood "gypsy" (with a small "g"), and since people fitting the romantic gypsy image are not actually encountered in real life, the real population goes unnoticed.[8]

According to the U.S. Smithsonian Institution, Roma immigrants arrived in the United States as part of larger waves of immigration from various parts of Europe beginning in the nineteenth century. These included Rom from Serbia, Russia, and Austria-Hungary, Ludar from the Balkans, and Romnichals from the United Kingdom.[9] Many Roma families who immigrated to the United States had experienced the horrors of World War II and Nazi genocide policies.

Today's descendants of Roma in the United States, estimated to number one million, continue to make diverse contributions to American culture and society.[10] A small group of Roma Americans have become activists for the broader Roma community, especially in Europe, and have played a role in spurring and shaping U.S. policy on Roma issues. The U.S. Department of State benefits from the activism and expertise of many Roma Americans (and many Roma) in the development of specific tools and actions to respond to the situation of the rights of Roma in Europe.

Several Roma Americans have served as experts on official U.S. delegations to meetings and conferences held by the Organization for Security and Cooperation in Europe (OSCE). At a November 2013 OSCE Supplementary Human Dimension Meeting on Roma issues, Roma American Nathan Mick delivered the U.S. delegation's intervention and participated in working sessions on improving respect for the rights of Roma. Dr. Ethel Brooks, also a Roma American, served as a moderator at this same event; she also spoke at the UN Holocaust Commemoration in New York in 2013 in commemoration of the Roma genocide during World War II.[11] In January 2016, President Obama named Dr. Brooks to serve on the Holocaust Memorial Council, making her the only Roma American on the council since President Clinton appointed Dr. Ian Hancock, cited above, in 1997.[12] The State Department's public diplomacy programs have benefited from several Roma American speakers including Dr. Hancock who have, over the years, traveled to several European countries with support from U.S. embassies in order to discuss Roma issues and human rights with European citizens. The State Department's Bureau of Democracy, Human Rights, and Labor leads a regular meeting of a Roma working group, which gathers experts on Roma issues based in the Washington, D.C., area, including Roma Americans, to exchange information and discuss policy priorities for promoting Roma inclusion across Europe.

Policy Framework

The values captured in the Universal Declaration of Human Rights and in other international and regional commitments are consistent with the values upon which the United States was founded centuries ago and remain the bedrock of the U.S. promotion of human rights globally.

The State Department's policy on Roma today is firmly based on the evolution of human rights obligations and commitments across the European continent and the growth in importance of human rights in U.S. foreign policy. The approach exists within the framework of both a State Department tasked with incorporating human rights into U.S. diplomacy and a European system where human rights can be raised as an issue in diplomatic relations and where the rights of Roma are deemed an issue of particular concern. This framework interacts with European institutions and regional organizations increasingly compelled to address Roma issues and a growing number of Roma and other civil society organizations rallying for equal opportunities in social, civic, and political spheres.

The State Department's focus on human rights gained momentum in 1975, when increased congressional attention led the Department to establish a Coordinator for Humanitarian Affairs. In 1977, Congress established the Bureau of Human Rights and Humanitarian Affairs, which would eventually become the Bureau of Democracy, Human Rights, and Labor (DRL), led by an assistant secretary of state. The specific responsibilities of the bureau have expanded over the years, but the mission remains the same: to lead U.S.

efforts to promote democracy, protect human rights and international religious freedom, and advance labor rights globally.

The importance of human rights in the State Department's mission was reaffirmed in its 2010 Quadrennial Diplomacy and Development Review (QDDR), *Leading Through Civilian Power*. The review stated, "We will ensure our efforts are advancing freedom, equality, and human rights for all vulnerable and marginalized peoples. And we will ensure the dignity of all people by promoting equal treatment, equal rights, and helping vulnerable peoples meet their basic needs in times of difficulty."[13] It also quoted the 2010 U.S. National Security Strategy and noted, "Advancing human rights and democracy is a key priority that reflects American values and promotes our security."[14] Through the QDDR, the U.S. Department of State underscored the importance of human rights in U.S. foreign policy and positioned itself to play a strengthened role in protecting the rights of Roma.

The Organization for Security and Cooperation in Europe

During the Cold War, in 1975, the Helsinki Final Act of the Conference on Security and Co-operation in Europe (CSCE), described in detail in the chapter in this volume by Erika Schlager, laid the groundwork for what would become the Organization for Security and Cooperation in Europe. It included specific language on respect for human rights, stating that "participating States will respect human rights and fundamental freedoms, including the freedom of thought, conscience, religion or belief, for all without distinction as to race, sex, language or religion."[15] While not binding under international law, these political commitments bolstered human rights and democratic activism across Europe, including in the Eastern bloc. President Gerald Ford's signature on the act heralded the rise of human rights as an increasingly important component of U.S. foreign policy. In the 1990s, the United States and other CSCE participating states seized the historic opportunity presented by the end of the Cold War to enhance and further elaborate evolving international norms regarding commitments to human rights and fundamental freedoms.

Sustained focus on the enduring marginalization of Roma individuals is a pillar of current State Department Roma policy and the driver of former Secretary Clinton's decision to prioritize the issue. Buried deep in the 1990 Copenhagen Document, the outcome document of the second Conference on the Human Dimension of the CSCE, is a hard-fought victory for Roma activists: "The participating States clearly and unequivocally condemn to-talitarianism, racial and ethnic hatred, anti-Semitism, xenophobia and dis-crimination against anyone as well as persecution on religious and ideological grounds. *In this context, they also recognize the particular problems of Roma (gypsies)*" (emphasis added).[16] This one sentence was an important acknow-ledgment by OSCE participating states that Roma persons face a unique form of societal discrimination that necessitates specific government action to combat injustices (for further discussion including the U.S. role in the inclu-sion of this phrase, see the chapter in this volume by Erika Schlager).[17]

Just over one year after agreement was reached on the Copenhagen Doc-ument, the Document of the Moscow Meeting of the Conference on the Human Dimension of the CSCE would provide another pillar for the State Department's approach: "The participating States emphasize that issues re-lating to human rights, fundamental freedoms, democracy and the rule of law are of international concern, as respect for these rights and freedoms constitutes one of the foundations of the international order. They categori-cally and irrevocably declare that the commitments undertaken in the field of the human dimension of the CSCE are matters of direct and legitimate concern to all participating States and do not belong exclusively to the inter-nal affairs of the State concerned."[18] This statement, reaffirmed by the OSCE participating states in Astana in 2010, confirmed that respect for human rights is not just a domestic issue for governments but a legitimate area of concern in diplomatic relations.

As an OSCE participating state, the United States strongly supports the OSCE's long-term efforts to promote Roma inclusion, especially the imple-mentation of the 2003 *Action Plan on Improving the Situation of Roma and Sinti Within the OSCE Area*.[19] At the November 2013 Supplementary Human Dimension Meeting in Vienna, the OSCE participating states agreed that it was critical to implement this action plan through better monitoring and as-sessment of the strategies, policies, and measures regarding Roma and Sinti integration. In December 2013 at the OSCE Ministerial Meeting in Kyiv, the United States helped shepherd participating states to consensus on a Minis-terial Decision on Roma and Sinti that specifically highlighted the need to focus inclusion efforts on Roma women and youth. The United States played a leading role in negotiating the text of the decision, which called on partici-pating states to "take active measures to support the empowerment of Roma and Sinti women" and particularly noted the need to promote "equal access for Roma and Sinti women to employment" opportunities. Participating states noted that Roma women and girls were particularly vulnerable to domestic violence, early marriages, and human trafficking because of their systematic socioeconomic marginalization and exclusion.[20] The United States will continue to work with the OSCE and governments across Europe to combat these vulnerabilities and promote the human rights of Roma and Sinti men, women, and youth.

In 2012, the United States provided significant funding for the OSCE's largest Roma-related project to date: Best Practices for Roma Integration, a two-year regional capacity-building program, which concluded in 2014, provided legal assistance and access to individual identity documents; improved living and housing conditions for Roma communities; raised public awareness of Roma issues; and promoted participation and visibility of Roma communities in public life.[21] The project was carried out in seven Balkan countries and was cofinanced by the European Union. The United States hopes that this project will open the door for further collaboration between the OSCE and the European Union on Roma issues.

The Council of Europe

The Council of Europe (CoE) took special steps beyond their other efforts for Roma inclusion to focus attention on the situation of the Roma by convening a CoE High-Level Meeting on Roma in Strasbourg on October 20, 2010. Representatives of the forty-seven Council of Europe countries, the European Union, and the Roma community gathered to adopt the "Strasbourg Declaration" that included guiding principles and priorities in three areas: nondiscrimination and citizenship, including women's and children's rights; social inclusion such as in education, housing, and health care; and empowerment and better access to justice, particularly through international cooperation.[22] As a result of the High-Level Meeting, the council also adopted the "Strasbourg Initiatives," proposals by the council's secretary-general for concrete actions to be implemented by national governments, as well as local and regional authorities, with an immediate and measurable impact. The council's Commissioner for Human Rights also reports regularly on the situation of the Roma.

The Council of Europe addresses the human rights of Roma through several other policy and institutional mechanisms. In addition to the essential European Convention on Human Rights, the council's authority rests on its role in monitoring and preserving member states' obligations arising from other regional agreements. Among the relevant agreements are the Framework Convention for the Protection of National Minorities, legally binding on the thirty-nine council member states that have ratified it, and the European Charter for Regional or Minority Languages. The European Social Charter, which applies to forty-three of the council's forty-seven member states, also protects the human rights of Roma. The European Commission against Racism and Intolerance (ECRI) is composed of forty-seven government-appointed members who are recognized experts on antiracist policy. The ECRI has autonomous status within the council and, among its general recommendations, released one in 1998 on "combating anti-Gypsyism [sic] and discrimination against Roma."[23]

The U.S. ambassador to France is also the U.S. Permanent Observer to the Council of Europe. The U.S. consul general in Strasbourg is the Deputy Permanent Observer. The consul general frequently attends, speaks at, and reports on sessions of the Committee of Ministers Deputies, the council's decision-making body (although he or she cannot vote), and attends plenary sessions of the Parliamentary Assembly of the Council of Europe. In addition, the United States has signed a number of conventions promulgated by the council, such as the Criminal Law Convention on Corruption, and participates as a member or observer in several bodies subordinate to the council. Most significantly, the United States joined the European Commission for Democracy through Law, commonly known as the Venice Commission, in April 2013. As a full member, the U.S. delegate was able to participate in a review of the response to the landmark Sejdic-Finci European Court of Human Rights case, for example. In the case based on complaints brought by a Jewish Bosnian citizen and a Roma Bosnian citizen, the court determined Bosnia and Herzegovina must remove the ethnic limitations on parliamentary and presidential candidates in its post–civil war constitution.[24]

The European Union

The European Union plays an important role on Roma issues within two broad competencies: internal and external. Internally, the European Union recognizes the joint responsibility of European institutions and individual member states to address the challenges of Roma integration. In 2011, the European Commission announced *An EU Framework for National Roma Integration Strategies by 2020.*[25] Each member state was required to produce a Roma strategy delineating a set of policy measures for achieving Roma integration. The European Commission's Directorate General for Justice is specifically charged with overseeing the EU's broader work on Roma issues. Externally, the European Union now requires aspirant member states to also produce Roma integration strategies as a component of their accession process and demonstrate commitment to Roma inclusion. The European Union has spent millions of euros on programs in potential member states to strengthen Roma inclusion.

The United States works actively with European Union institutions through the U.S. Mission to the European Union in Brussels. On human rights issues in particular, biannual Human Rights Consultations between the European Union and the United States provide opportunities for the two sides to discuss areas of concern for both the United States and the European Union. During 2013 and 2014 Human Rights Consultations, Roma issues were included in the agenda at the U.S. request, demonstrating the importance the United States places on holding frank discussions on these issues even with our closest allies.

The State Department's Roma Policy Priorities

For the State Department, discrimination is more than a "Roma issue." It is a direct challenge to a government's responsibility to promote and protect the human rights of all people within its borders. The real measure of the effectiveness of State Department policy is whether it results in an improvement in the daily life of Roma.

As the chapters in this volume highlight, discrimination against Roma is widespread, whether it is manifested as school segregation, walls constructed to divide Roma communities from their neighbors, or a lack of identity documents that limit political participation and access to social services. Discrimination is often rooted in negative societal attitudes toward Roma that reinforce anti-Roma rhetoric and actions. Extremist-led anti-Roma demonstrations across Europe during 2013 unfortunately indicate that populist rhetoric still finds supporters. Even some mainstream European officials speak about the "Roma problem" or use stereotypical characterizations of Roma as "lazy" people with "incompatible lifestyles" who need to be led "back to the world of labor." Government-endorsed anti-Roma rhetoric and intolerance is not acceptable in a Europe that has worked hard for nearly seventy years to build its unity based on the principles of democracy and respect for human rights.

Importantly, there is much work to be done to ensure the full civic and political participation of the Roma population to guarantee that they have a say in their countries' futures. On a policy level, recommendations include promoting Roma participation in political parties, especially in mainstream political parties. Roma civic education and activism must also be promoted, which can be accomplished through strengthening Roma civil society organizations. Instances of State Department engagement in this area include assistance programs sponsored by the Bureau of Democracy, Human Rights, and Labor that support Roma civil society activists and organizations.

More specifically, Roma women are especially marginalized in many cases, and much must be done to build up the effective and equal participation of Roma women in public and political life. Policy recommendations to address their full participation in society include encouraging equal access for Roma women to employment, internships, and mentoring opportunities and targeting special measures, where appropriate, aimed at promoting equal access to and participation in education for Roma girls at all levels. As an example of State Department engagement in this area, in March 2014, U.S. ambassador to Montenegro Sue K. Brown presented the Ambassador's Active Citizenship Award to Fana Delija, coordinator for the Center for Roma Initiatives. The award was given in recognition of Ms. Delija's positive impact on the status of Egyptian and Roma women in Montenegro, achieved through her civic activism.

Roma are also particularly vulnerable to human trafficking, due in part to poverty and multigenerational social exclusion, including lack of access to a variety of social services and employment. Many Roma victims are hesitant to seek assistance from the authorities out of fear of unjust prosecution. To address Roma victims of human trafficking, governments should promote full and effective participation of Roma communities and organizations in anti-trafficking mechanisms, including anti-trafficking law enforcement and victim identification groups. Moreover, trafficking prevention campaigns and efforts should be targeted to Roma communities, particularly those that are segregated and socially excluded. Access to preventative and protective services should also be improved; governments might build public awareness campaigns for communities and law enforcement, along with the necessary adequate shelters and rehabilitative programs, including vocational assistance. The State Department engages on this issue through the Office to Monitor and Combat Trafficking in Persons.

In several countries—for instance, in the Czech Republic, Slovakia, and Hungary, as Will Guy's chapter in this volume describes[26]—unsettling incidents of anti-Roma violence and protests led by extremists, and sometimes encouraged or tacitly supported by mainstream politicians, continue to stoke anti-Roma sentiments. The State Department is concerned about the prospect of inter-ethnic tensions arising from marginalization. Therefore, on the policy level, governments should speak out immediately and forcefully against cases of anti-Roma rhetoric, demonstrations, or violence. It is critical for governments to demonstrate that all forms of intolerance are unacceptable in modern Europe. Governments should also ensure that law enforcement officers are trained in working with minority communities and respond properly to hate crimes and racially motivated crimes. This might include the creation of mediator positions for ethnic minorities to better liaise with law enforcement.

Examples of State Department engagement in this area include work done through the U.S. embassy in Budapest. At the International Law Enforcement Academy in Budapest, the U.S. government has provided training and assistance to police to help them more effectively investigate and prosecute crimes against Roma. In addition, following a string of murders of Roma in Hungary in 2009, the Hungarian government asked for investigative support from the Federal Bureau of Investigation, which the U.S. government provided. In 2013, four individuals were convicted for these murders, with three of the perpetrators receiving life sentences without the possibility of parole.

Roma Policy in Action: Policy Making, Advocacy, and Embassy Action

The U.S. Department of State is tasked with transforming this policy framework into action to combat the above-mentioned challenges of Roma exclusion. Through bilateral and multilateral diplomacy and programming assistance, the State Department spearheads U.S. government efforts to promote the human rights of Roma across Europe. The department seeks to promote a strong, effective Roma civil society capable of self-advocacy, while encouraging governments to create an environment that fosters opportunity and provides effective protection for victims of violence and discrimination. First and foremost, that means engaging directly with Roma communities themselves.

In Washington, the State Department's Bureau of Democracy, Human Rights, and Labor plays the lead role in formulating and overseeing U.S. Roma policy. The bureau works closely with U.S. embassies, a range of State Department bureaus, and other U.S. agencies to coordinate policy objectives and efforts.

At the ground level, U.S. Roma policy is carried out by the men and women, both American and non-American, who work at U.S. embassies and consulates around the world. One of the most basic tools at the State Department's disposal to promote nondiscrimination and tolerance is inclusion through example. U.S. embassies invite Roma organizations and communities to embassy events, host cultural events that showcase the rich heritage of Roma, and visit Roma communities. This sends a powerful signal to host governments that the United States values diversity and views Roma organizations, leaders, and people as active agents in securing their own rights. On many occasions, Roma organizations have confided that displays of solidarity and concern shown to them by U.S. diplomats led to increased respect from local governments, resulted in serious consultations with ministers, or otherwise provided opportunities to have their voices heard. For example, in 2013 the U.S. embassy in Kyiv, Ukraine, worked closely with Roma organizations and local human rights groups to guarantee Roma had a say in the drafting of the government's national Roma strategy by helping convene a discussion between Roma activists and government officials.

As another recent example of U.S. embassy engagement, in 2013 the U.S. embassy in Prague concluded the pilot year of a groundbreaking program that assists Czech Roma youth in finding internship and employment opportunities. The U.S. embassy partnered with the American Chamber of Commerce in the Czech Republic and the Open Society Foundations to provide training in job hunting and interviewing to Roma youth and helped place them in paid internships where they could build their work experience and professional résumés.

U.S. diplomats and officials also speak out publicly and privately to condemn discriminatory practices, hate speech, and hate crimes targeting Roma persons as well as members of other vulnerable groups, such as Jews; Muslims; lesbian, gay, bisexual, and transgender individuals; persons with disabilities; and recent migrants. This is seen in various ways, including, as just one example, in July 2013 the U.S. mission to the OSCE expressed U.S. government concern about several anti-Roma marches and incidents across the OSCE area "that highlight the need for decisive, broad-based action by participating

States to address both the causes and manifestations of anti-Roma senti-ment."[27] Private conversations with government officials, sometimes called "quiet diplomacy," often go unnoticed by external observers, but U.S. am-bassadors and diplomats consistently and firmly reiterate U.S. concerns about anti-Roma rhetoric and the need for implementation of Roma inclu-sion policies. The United States believes that these public and private state-ments can make a difference by pressing governments to fulfill their human rights obligations and commitments.

Perhaps the U.S. Department of State's best known human rights products are the annual *Country Reports on Human Rights Practices*. These public reports include details on the status of human rights in Roma communities, sending an important signal to governments and Roma citizens alike about U.S. awareness and concern. These reports are closely read by governments and NGOs around the world and have historically been important reference points for Roma activists and organizations as they press their governments for reforms and a greater voice in their countries' future. The reports also demonstrate that the United States remains deeply engaged on human rights challenges facing our closest allies and partners. Drawing attention to Roma issues and the negative effects of Roma exclusion on European countries strengthens our strategic relationships in the long term, since improving re-spect for human rights makes countries more democratic and prosperous. These reports help keep governments accountable for their actions and provide opportunities for the United States and our European partners to have a meaningful dialogue on respect for human rights and democratic norms in our own countries.

The State Department does not only focus on the negatives, but also seeks to implement a range of public diplomacy resources to promote tolerance, celebrate Roma culture, and support Roma activists. Annual U.S. embassy- or consulate-sponsored celebrations of International Roma Day, on and around April 8, are emblematic of this. U.S. missions organize events or un-dertake outreach activities that promote awareness of the human rights of Roma and highlight positive Roma contributions to the host country. Such activities have included organizing presentations on Roma culture or on the challenges faced by Roma, public statements or press interviews on the im-portance of promoting greater Roma participation in host country society and institutions, promoting "good news" stories of prominent or successful Roma in the country, or organizing concerts or exhibits that promote Roma culture or the national contributions of Roma. Embassies coordinate these events and activities with local and regional Roma NGOs and engage on the issue of Roma human rights through social media platforms and other public diplomacy resources.

For example, in April 2014, U.S. ambassador to Bulgaria Marcie B. Ries hosted the opening of the photo exhibition "Together Hand in Hand in One Society" at the American Corner in Sofia to celebrate International Roma Day. The photos in the exhibit came from the Integro Association, a respected Roma organization from Razgrad, Bulgaria, which had trained high school students in civic journalism and then held a photo competition among them. In her remarks, Ambassador Ries pointed out the importance of tolerance and integration of minorities in Bulgarian society. She said that integration requires active participation from Roma communities and young leaders who are in a position to effect change in societal attitudes, as well as shared responsibility of all Bulgarians to work to change societal attitudes, challenge prejudices, and encourage tolerance. As another example, in 2015, the U.S. embassy in Slovakia sponsored a wide variety of events for International Roma Day including an interethnic soccer game, a shadowing day for Roma students with the embassy chargé d'affaires, a visit to an integrated school, a photo exhibition, and the release of a multilingual children's book that included the Romani language.

U.S. missions also participate in commemoration of the genocide of Roma during World War II. In 2012, U.S. Special Envoy for Holocaust Issues Douglas Davidson traveled to Berlin to join U.S. ambassador to Germany Patrick Murphy at the unveiling of the Memorial for the Sinti and Roma of Europe Murdered under the National Socialist Regime (Nazism). The completion of this monument represented an important step in recognition of the immense suffering of the Roma people during World War II.

Programming Assistance and Broad Engagement

The State Department also supports Roma inclusion by funding various programs and international efforts. Through the Human Rights and Democracy Fund, the Bureau of Democracy, Human Rights, and Labor has supported Roma-focused programs since 2007. Implemented in countries throughout Eastern Europe and the Balkans, these programs have fostered interethnic dialogue and civic engagements among Roma and non-Roma youth, provided legal services and public education to Roma communities, and trained Roma civic leaders to effectively engage in local, national, and regional advocacy.[28] Recent bureau programming built the capacity of Roma civil society organizations, strengthened the advocacy skills of Roma youth, and provided them with regional networking opportunities.[29]

The International Visitor Leadership Program, the State Department's flagship professional exchange program, brings current and emerging leaders to experience the United States and connect with American colleagues. U.S. missions across Europe send Roma leaders and activists to take part in this program and learn about U.S. experiences with civil rights, antidiscrimination, and civic activism. As just one example, in 2013 a group of Roma activists from the Czech Republic and Slovakia visited several U.S. cities as part of the program. Their visit was chronicled through dispatches for the Roma news website Romea.cz, reflecting on the group's experience and the lessons that activists in both the United States and Europe can learn from each other in promoting nondiscrimination and social inclusion for minorities. In one dispatch, for example, David Beňák drew parallels between the experiences of Native Americans in the United States and Roma in Europe.[30]

U.S. Agency for International Development (USAID) assistance projects across Central and South Eastern Europe directly and indirectly contribute to improving the well-being of Roma communities. Perhaps the best example of USAID's success in promoting Roma inclusion was the $4.5 million Roma youth education program in Macedonia. From 2004 through 2014, USAID's Roma Education Project assisted over 2,500 Roma students at all education levels from preschool to university and markedly improved access, retention, and academic achievement of participating Roma children. The project also trained 453 primary school teachers in interactive and inclusive learning methodology, as well as fostered active participation of parents in the schools' decision-making bodies. This comprehensive approach to inclusion has been recognized as a best practice throughout Europe. As a result of excellent project results, in 2009 the Government of Macedonia assumed scholarship and mentorship assistance for all Roma secondary school students. As of the end of 2014, USAID provided 298 scholarships and the Macedonian government 420.[31]

The breadth of the State Department's efforts on Roma inclusion is further evidenced by the diversity of specialized offices that work directly or indirectly on Roma issues. The United States, through the Bureau of Population, Refugees, and Migration, has pledged $10 million to the Balkans Regional Housing Program, an international effort to provide durable housing solutions for up to 74,000 of the most vulnerable refugees and displaced persons from the Yugoslav Wars. These vulnerable displaced persons include many Roma families. In addition, the State Department's Office to Monitor and Combat Trafficking in Persons produces an annual report, *Trafficking in Persons* (TIP). The TIP report includes assessments of individual countries; its profiles of European countries particularly address the specific vulnerabilities of Roma to becoming victims of trafficking and monitor incidents of the exploitation of Roma.[32] The office works closely with other governments to improve methods and strategies to combat the trafficking of all marginalized groups, including Roma.

Domestic and International Partners

The State Department also works closely with the United States Congress on Roma issues, particularly the U.S. Commission on Security and Cooperation in Europe, or the Helsinki Commission. It benefits from Congressional interest in Roma issues, which is demonstrated, for example, by the 2012 congressional hearing "The Escalation of Violence Against Roma in Europe." Close coordination is on full display on U.S. delegations to OSCE meetings, especially the annual Human Dimension Implementation Meeting, where the State Department and Helsinki Commission collaborate to deliver strong messages on Roma issues and engage with Roma civil society and partner governments on the importance of addressing Roma inclusion.

Another critical element of the U.S. strategy is cooperation with a range of international and intergovernmental organizations, including the European Union, the Council of Europe, the United Nations, the World Bank, and the OSCE, to support policies and programs for Roma and other disadvantaged communities. Many of these relationships and partnerships were described earlier in this chapter.

State Department participation in the Decade of Roma Inclusion initiative, which the United States joined as an official observer in 2012, was another facet of a broad effort to partner with civil society and governments to promote Roma inclusion and to combat racism and prejudice against Roma in Europe. In June 2013, Deputy Assistant Secretary of State Phillip Reeker attended the Decade steering committee meeting in Zagreb, where he delivered a strong statement of U.S. support for the Decade's objectives, saying that the United States would continue its support until the Decade's "work is done." The fact that these remarks were delivered in Croatia, which would soon officially accede to the European Union as its twenty-eighth member, highlighted the importance of promoting Roma inclusion as a pillar of the EU's work to build more prosperous and just societies, not just in long-standing democracies, but in aspirant members as well. The State Department continues to engage frequently on Roma issues with European Union institutions, which assumed important new coordinating responsibilities with the adoption of the EU Framework for National Roma Integration Strategies.

In sum, the U.S. Department of State utilizes a wide range of tools and resources to engage actively with governments on issues affecting Roma communities, maintain close connections with Roma civil society organizations and communities, sponsor outreach activities and programs to promote tolerance and celebrate Roma culture, and help Roma leaders engage with their governments. The responsibility for improving respect for the human rights of Roma in Europe rests first and foremost with European governments. The United States believes that it has a role to play, however, and will work to strengthen the ongoing efforts noted here and continue to develop new strategies and tools to assist our partners in overcoming these challenges.

Policy Future

The challenge of securing human rights and fundamental freedoms for all Roma individuals remains a major obstacle to the goal of a free, whole, and peaceful Europe. The U.S. Department of State will continue its work to help address this issue. Above all, the United States will stay engaged and work to place Roma voices first in the debate over the proper policies to foster their inclusion and well-being. Addressing systematic discrimination against Roma and promoting the Roma voice in deciding their future will remain an overarching priority of U.S. human rights policy in Europe.

The worldwide economic crisis has had a major impact on Europe, but governments have an opportunity to use the recovery to listen to Roma communities and build inclusive societies. The fate of the European human rights and democracy project described in this chapter (and throughout this book), including the European Union, Council of Europe, and Organization for Security and Cooperation in Europe, will also be a decisive factor in how governments work to address these challenges.

The continued implementation of U.S. Roma policy will require finding the best path that is driven by Roma voices and choices, reflective of U.S. interests, and effective in achieving the envisioned results. As Secretary of State John Kerry stated on the occasion of International Roma Day 2016,

> On behalf of President Obama and the people of the United States, I extend my best wishes to all Roma on International Roma Day.
>
> On April 8, we celebrate the rich cultural heritage of Roma people everywhere, and the contributions that Roma make to our societies, including the over one million Americans of Romani descent.
>
> It is also a day to reflect on the exclusion many Roma face in their daily lives and to recommit to effectively remedy discrimination. Unfortunately, segregated schools, extremist anti-Roma rhetoric and violence, and marginalization from political and economic life continue to prevent many Roma children from reaching their full potential.
>
> We are resolved that Romani children deserve the same educational opportunities as their peers, Romani families deserve to live their lives free from the fear of violence, and all Romani individuals deserve the opportunity to provide for their families and have their voices heard by their government.
>
> To commemorate this day, the United States reaffirms our commitment to the inclusion and equal treatment of all Roma people, wherever they call home.[33]

Advancing Roma inclusion is and will remain an important part of the U.S. goal of promoting human rights in Europe and around the world.

PART III

Taking Stock of European Public Policy: The Impact of Roma Inclusion Strategies

Chapter 5

A Critical Analysis of Roma Policy and Praxis: The Romanian Case

Margareta Matache and Krista Oehlke

The early 2000s held promise as the start of an age of great social change for Roma. A broad range of actors from government and civil society had partnered to develop policies to advance a Roma agenda. The Romanian government's 2001 Roma Strategy is a case in point. Considered progressive, the strategy was the country's first post-Communist government initiative explicitly oriented toward Roma inclusion. More generally in the early 2000s, Romania's government institutions seemed more open to partnership with civil society. In preparation for the country's joining the EU in 2007, antidiscrimination legislation was enacted[1] as well as a ministerial notification forbidding school segregation.[2] With good institutional backing, the Roma activists' hopes for robust social change seemed justified. At the same time, targeted policies like these proliferated beyond Romania and throughout the European Union (EU).

However, what originally appeared to be an era of promise for Roma yielded poor results and disappointment. While some initiatives proved successful in particular contexts, overall positive change throughout the European Roma community was limited. As the European Commission (EC) rightly noted in 2008, "Although the European institutions, Member States and candidate countries as well as civil society have addressed these problems since the beginning of the 1990s, there is a widely shared assumption that the living and working conditions of Roma have not much improved over the last two decades."[3] Even more, in 2014, at the third Roma Summit held in Brussels, Jose Manuel Barroso, then president of the European Commission, while acknowledging the progress of the member states toward developing Roma policies, noted, "Now it is essential to focus on the full implementation of these policies, combining legal and financial measures, in order to make a real difference on the ground. Implementation is key for the success of our policies."[4] In particular, after EU accession, member states from Central and Eastern Europe have fallen back on their earlier promises and demonstrated less commitment to achieving Roma inclusion. Their compliance with EU requests for policy reform and monitoring of impact has been poor.

Romania provides a useful case study for analyzing this process. Over the past twenty-five years, a promising set of programs and policies set the stage for what was anticipated to instill notable positive social change for Roma. Romania's post-socialist governments adopted targeted programs, such as affirmative action in education and optional classes in the Romani language, and targeted national policies, such as the 2001 Roma Strategy. The Romanian government's commitment to Roma rights promotion has included participation in international initiatives, such as the Organization for Security and Cooperation in Europe (OSCE), the Decade of Roma Inclusion, and more recently, the EU's creation of a framework for national Roma integration strategies. However, the impact of these policies and initiatives has been minimal.

Using the Romanian political landscape as an example, this chapter provides a critical analysis of the enforcement of post-2000 Roma policies more broadly. Romania is particularly interesting. A relatively new member of the European Union, Romania is not only home to one of its largest Roma populations, but is also the driver of many contemporary controversies in European policies and politics because of its limited success in achieving progress for Roma. The movement of Romanian Roma across the European Union has also increased the visibility of policy failure in Romania and motivated EU decision makers to make new commitments to advance Roma inclusion, with the hope of reducing Roma mobility from Eastern to Western Europe.[5]

This chapter considers the different dynamics and impacts of universal and targeted policies, proposes tools for assessing policy impact, and discusses the major players involved in policy development and implementation. It suggests why the social inclusion and antidiscrimination policies of the Romanian government, particularly those reported in its 2001 *Governmental Strategy for Improving the Roma Situation*, have yet to benefit many members of the Roma community.[6] We analyze the following key policy arenas and gaps: the enforcement and monitoring of policy formulation, the fragmentary nature of some policies, the pitfalls of universal and targeted policies, and finally, divisions among key networks of advocates, institutional actors, donors, and local communities. We analyze these patterns by looking at outcome variables, specifically in education.

The resulting analysis is multifaceted. It includes a discussion of the need for adequate resources, monitoring mechanisms and benchmarks, and it suggests sustained Roma-related interest and expertise at the governmental institutions level. Accordingly, the chapter concludes with a call for increased governmental accountability and a greater Roma presence in decision-making processes from the bottom to the top.

Roma Education in Romania: An Indicator of Limited Progress

Advancing educational attainment for Roma has been the key priority of most players involved in Roma issues. But the discrepancies between Roma and non-Roma in terms of participation and school performance remain huge. According to a 2011 European Union Agency for Fundamental Rights survey conducted in eleven EU countries, a much greater proportion of Roma children of compulsory school age (14 percent) than non-Roma living nearby (3 percent) fail to attend school at all. Furthermore, just 10 percent of Roma aged twenty-five to sixty-four completed secondary school compared to 73 percent of the general population.[7] Correspondingly, the participation of Roma in tertiary education remains extremely low. According to the UNDP/World Bank/EC Regional Roma Survey 2011 survey, only 1 percent of young Roma ages twenty-six to thirty-two have completed university.[8] In contrast, overall in the EU, the level of university graduates of the general population ages thirty to thirty-four goes up to 36.9 percent.[9] Understandably these worrying figures translate into poor outcomes for Roma in the long run, as those lacking an education are later unable to compete on equal ground in the job market. As the European Commission notes in its 2014 assessment report, referring generally to the EU countries, "beyond compulsory schooling, enrollment differences between Roma and non-Roma has become even larger."[10]

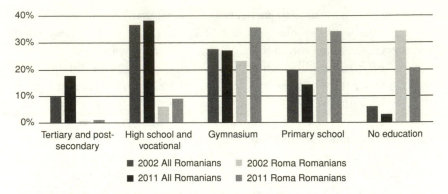

Figure 2. Highest level of education attained for Roma, comparing figures from 2002 and 2011. Graphics and census data analysis by Gabriel Kreindler. *Source:* Based on data from The National Institute of Statistics, Population and Housing Census, 2002 and 2011.

The gaps between the educational participation of Roma and non-Roma increase as levels of education increase. As the graph in Figure 2 shows, in Romania, primary schooling is disproportionately the highest educational level that Roma children achieved in both 2002 and 2011 census data (data is on those above ten years of age, and for Roma, for those who self-identify as such). Roma enrollment in tertiary school rose from 0.2 percent in 2002 to 0.7 percent in 2011, while enrollment in high school rose from 2.3 percent in 2002 to 4.87 percent in 2011. Though the percentage of Roma attending university doubly increased, the difference is an insufficient shift, a growth from 684 students to 3,397 students. In addition, other studies show that from 1998 to 2012, the enrolment of Roma males to college remained around 1 percent and the participation of Roma females between 1998 and 2012 in university increased from 0.7 percent to just 1.6 percent.[11]

These findings contrast with Romania's overall population. During the same decade, the proportion of all Romanians who completed some forms of tertiary and post-secondary education increased from 10 percent to 17.6 percent. The proportion of Romanian students who complete secondary education remained nearly constant, increasing from 36.7 percent to 38.2 percent.[12]

The segregation of Roma children in schools also persists. Though a specific focus of the government, desegregation measures put in place by the Ministry of Education and several Roma rights organizations have produced lackluster results. In 2003, desegregation measures were included in a PHARE 2003 EU and Ministry of Education program, Access to Education for Disadvantaged Groups.[13] A 2009 evaluation showed that 80 percent of the schools participating in the desegregation component of the project still failed to desegregate Roma children in schools and classes.[14] As other chapters in this volume explain in detail, litigation has confirmed this "tradition" of forming "social and educational segregated classes."[15] Evidence presented in *Romani CRISS v. Ionita Asan* showed that children enrolled in first and fifth grades were separated on ethnic and social grounds, despite the school's claim that children belonging to disadvantaged groups were randomly assigned to classes. Predominately Roma classrooms were badly equipped compared to the other classes.[16] Though the 2007 desegregation order clearly outlaws segregation, other cases of segregation continue to be identified across the country.

The huge gap between Roma children and the general population raises urgent questions about the process of European social change in this field. Data from other countries suggest that greater progress is possible. For instance, in Hungary the enrollment rate of Roma children in preschool has risen to 79 percent, and during the past decade in Finland, the participation of Roma children in pre-primary school increased from 2 to 60 percent.[17]

In Romania, an absence of significant progress in education is part of a broader contemporary disinterest in enforcing non-discrimination and equality for Roma. After Romania became a member of the European Union, many instances of institutional discrimination continued to be documented. In 2011, the mayor of Baia Mare built a fifty-meter-long, 2.2-meter-high wall to separate the Roma community from the non-Roma neighborhood.[18] In the same year, Romani CRISS, a local NGO, challenged the regular practice of Marie Curie Hospital in Bucharest of separating Roma children into different wards than other children.[19] In 2013, the municipality of Eforie forcibly evicted one hundred Roma, including fifty children. The vice-mayor warned that if the Roma of Eforie did not leave their homes, they would be killed.[20] Although activists had hoped for robust change in Roma communities as a result of Romania's accession to the European Union, sustained improvements and effective nondiscrimination actions are still lacking.

Policy Formulation Breakdowns

Many factors explain the minimal impact of targeted policies on Roma education, a complexity that is compounded by the myriad actors involved.

Donald S. Van Meter and Carl E. Van Horn suggest that in order to assess outcome performance of public policies, policy makers should distinguish between policy implementation, impact, and program performance. They argue that clearly defined standards to measure success, adequate resources, inter-organizational relationships, and the response of the implementers are essential for successful policy implementation.[21] The 2001 *Governmental Strategy for Improving the Roma Situation* failed to define standards and provide adequate resources for measuring them, which certainly contributed to the lack of the anticipated social change. The 2001 Strategy did not include methods for enforcement, evaluation, and monitoring; it lacked a statement of clear intended results and resource allocations, including an estimated budget for the implementation of all actions. In many ways, the 2001 Strategy was crafted more like a wish list of social inclusion objectives and activities, with the addition of institutions responsible and deadlines.[22]

Moreover, in its policy formulation, the 2001 Strategy did not outline the anticipated impacts of policy. While it laid out *actions* to achieve goals and indicators (such as the number of awareness raising campaigns organized on education), it did not set out clear policy *goals* nor prescribe measurable *results* (such as decrease dropout rates to a certain percentage). Though the *Strategy* aimed to increase access to quality schooling and preschooling, it failed to set precise goals and expected results so that such an increase could be measured.

Policy formulation also did not adequately plan for resources. The 2001 Strategy's plan of action for 2001–2004 lacked indicators and budgets; the 2006–2008 plan did include indicators and sources of funding for each action (such as local financial sources; the budget of the Prefect Office), but it still did not include budget estimates.[23] In 2006, the European Commission expressed its concern over the slow implementation of the 2001 Strategy, noting a lack of adequate resources for implementation and limited participation capacity of Roma themselves and the institutions responsible for Roma issues in the decision-making process.[24]

Despite central, regional, and local mechanisms to coordinate and implement the 2001 Strategy, the absence of resource allocations in relevant Ministries and verifiable indicators and results has impeded progress. An external midterm evaluation in 2005 confirmed that implementation was ineffective at the county and local level but no notable improvements followed in the updated 2006–2008 implementation plan.[25]

Finally, the 2001 Strategy was not systematically charted nor well measured, ultimately impinging on its implementation and results. Nevertheless, considering the still juvenile Romanian democracy at the time, gaps and limitations were to a certain extent anticipated. In addition, the Roma movement was equipped with a limited number of policy experts able and willing to criticize policy proposals and strongly advocate for more qualitative policy design. However, basic elements which are required of any policy proposal were severely lacking, and this discrepancy is clearly linked to the limited level of commitment and political will at the level of governmental institutions.

Looking forward, the recently adopted EU Roma Framework shows some possible trails for failure in Romania as well. Its national correspondent in Romania, the *Strategy for the Inclusion of the Romanian Citizens Belonging to Roma Minority for the period 2012–2020* (henceforth *Strategy for Inclusion 2012–2020*), contained many of the weaknesses of the 2001 Strategy.[26] As with the 2001 Strategy, the 2012 Strategy for Roma did not respect the standards and the elements that meet the criteria of a public policy document, as it is described by *The Strategy for a Better Regulation on the Level of the Central Public Administration 2008–2013*.[27] As the European Commission pointed out in its 2012 assessment of the *Strategy for Inclusion 2012–2020*, "The strategy does not reflect an integrated approach. The strategy would benefit from a clear prioritisation, a closer link between general and specific objectives, directions for actions and actual measures proposed, detailed description of clear targets, responsibilities, budget allocations, as well as of a robust monitoring and evaluation system."[28]

Civil society participation in the consultation process for the *Strategy for Inclusion 2012–2020* was also weak, and NGOs argued that the document did not advance new solutions when compared with the 2001 Strategy and developing initiatives, nor did it set out specific targets and budget lines to achieve them. Roma NGOs and scholars in Europe made similar critiques about the Roma strategies adopted by other EU governments.[29] While there was enough political pressure from the European Commission to push governments to approve the Roma strategies, there was not enough political will on behalf of the governments to adopt high-quality, nonpatronizing policies for the Roma population.

Nevertheless, in 2015, based on the European Commission's recommendations and critics, the Romania Government revised the *Strategy for Inclusion*

2012–2020 and approved the *Strategy for the Inclusion of the Romanian Citizens Belonging to Roma Minority for the period 2015–2020* (henceforth *Strategy for Inclusion 2015–2020*).[30] To its credit, the *Strategy for Inclusion 2015–2020* is inclusive of indicators and expected results and factors in budgetary allocations for 2015–2016 as well as a monitoring and evaluation mechanism. However, NGOs find that some areas of intervention embedded within the strategy are substandard. For instance, Romani CRISS argues that the "housing section" is the weak: "To reach the minimum threshold, the Governments should at the very least . . . revise the indicators and allocate financial resources in order to reach at the very least one thousand homes built per year until 2020."[31] By comparison, the "employment section" fails to address antidiscrimination. Even more, budgetary allocations for this section are vague and insufficient, and there is potential risk for the government to designate an insufficient national financial commitment and rely primarily on European funds. As the UN Rapporteur on extreme poverty and human rights also pointed out in his end-of-mission statement on Romania in 2015,[32] a weak financial commitment on the part of Romania might be further exacerbated by the new placement of the National Contact Point, responsible for governmental Roma programs, from the Ministry of Labor, Family and Social Protection to the Ministry of European Funds.

Breakdowns in the Policy Implementation Process

Policy formulation has not been the only shortcoming of Roma inclusion strategy. At least three other key factors have contributed to inclusion breakdowns: (1) the failure to adopt an inter-sectorial methodology in policy design leading to isolated targeted actions, (2) across the board implementation weaknesses, and (3) insensitivity to minority issues in universal policies. Gaps in these three arenas mutually reinforce each other, leading to minimal results and impacts at the grassroots level.

Isolated Targeted Policy Measures: Affirmative Action Programs

Many post-2000 Roma inclusion policies have taken piecemeal approaches. Although the 2001 Strategy promoted the direct involvement of Roma advocates in the policymaking process and had an appreciation of social science data on Roma marginalization, it failed to successfully integrate its objectives and actions. The second objective of the 2001 Strategy—"supporting the development of an intellectual and economic Roma elite"[33]—exemplifies this lack of cohesion. Aside from reserved seats designated for Roma students at university level, no measures were designed to encourage the development of Roma "elite" and their contribution in policy making. Even with a full array of educational programs, this objective would have posed a serious challenge for institutions, NGOs, and donors in a context where the educational system was, to start with, unwelcoming to Roma children.

The adoption of an affirmative action program for Roma (mentioned above) is an example of fragmented policy making, in which actions focus on one or a few specific programs, lack a multilevel, multi-sectorial approach, and avoid tackling other pieces of the same "policy puzzle." Beginning in the 1990s, several Romanian universities began instituting affirmative action programs for Roma. Later, these programs were launched in high schools at the national level. Between 2000 and 2006, 10,300 students were enrolled in secondary and vocational education on subsidized placements for Roma, and 1,420 students benefited from these placements in universities.[34] However, more placements were available than applications submitted: long before they reached high school or university age, a significant percentage of Roma youth were prevented from benefiting from affirmative action programs. Years of limited preschool access, learning in hostile overall school environments, and living in poverty with pressure to engage in housework were and are some of the inhibiting factors. Affirmative action programs were not adequately equipped to address these obstacles. A Roma child raised in a poor village, having never attended kindergarten or high quality schooling, would not be given the opportunity to access the affirmative action program. A child placed in a segregated and, consequently poor quality classroom or school, unable to read and write after finishing primary school, would also not have this opportunity. Neither would children who had to work growing up and eventually dropped out of school. Despite its good intentions, the affirmative action program has failed to deliver for many marginalized Roma.

According to a Roma Education Fund/Gallup study of the impact of the affirmative action program, "Beneficiaries having access to the reserved places in high-schools are more often young people coming from families with a higher education level and from relatively small households and from families with one or at most two children."[35] The beneficiaries of vocational schools were poorer than those of high school and universities. The affirmative measures program is one of the few sustained Roma-targeted programs, and it certainly has contributed to an increase in the number of Roma students at high school and university level. However, without support from other programs to address participation and quality of education in kindergarten and primary school, affirmative action on its own could not give a real chance to the poorest of the poor or to the most marginalized among the marginalized Roma.

Finally, the relevance and rationale of the program was not adequately represented as a reparatory justice action or as a necessary measure to account for and redeem centuries of state sponsored injustices (e.g. slavery, the Holocaust). Rather, the program was understood as merely a "privilege" or an "additional right" or as "positive discrimination" for Roma youth.

Non-implementation of Approved Policy Measures or Actions

Several policy measures were approved but not implemented. The National Strategy for Early Childhood Education developed in 2005 and amended in 2010 aimed that 70 percent of Roma children between three and six years of age should be enrolled in kindergarten initially by 2010, and after the amendments by 2013/2015.[36] It also promised the allocation of appropriate resources for buses to transport children from their isolated communities to kindergarten classrooms. But in 2011, the number of Roma children enrolled in pre-school was still estimated at 37 percent,[37] and not much has been done to increase these enrollments over the following years. Most Roma children in isolated communities continue to lack transportation facilities. In many communities, NGOs and the Ministry of Education still substitute a few weeks of summer programs for Roma children for kindergarten prior to their enrollment in school; by maintaining this parallel, economical, low-quality, short-term system, the institutions exclude Roma children from exercising their right to preschool education.

The 2001 Strategy stipulated the release of annual implementation reports under the responsibility of an inter-ministerial government committee.[38] The document also required the Ministry of Health to publish annual reports on the health status of the Roma population; the Ministry of Justice and other institutions were required to publish reports concerning human rights situations as well. However, no such thematic reports were issued.

As mentioned, in 2007, the Ministry of Education adopted a ministerial order that forbade segregation. The Desegregation Order clearly specifies that creating separate classes by placing all late enrolled students in the same class can lead to segregation (Article 5, Annex to 1540/2007 Order).[39] The order, starting with the 2007–2008 school year, prohibited the establishment or continuation of separate Roma classes. One year after the approval of the order, a Romani CRISS study confirmed that seventy-seven schools (63 percent) of 122 schools investigated had formed new first and fifth grade classes that segregated Roma children.[40] As the study concludes, "[f]or the majority of segregated schools, the residential isolation of Roma communities is not the factor that determines school segregation." According to a 2014 World Bank report, 24 percent of Roma children enrolled in primary school are placed in classes with a majority of Roma children.[41] To date, the government has initiated a program to remedy the consequences of school segregation on many generations of the Roma children and youth. Who, if any, will be held accountable for the permanence of segregation? And if state institutions don't remedy the situation, which international human rights body should take the lead to ensure that Roma children deprived from the right to quality and equal education benefit from remedies?

These are just a few of the many instances that show a clear mismatch between objectives and their realization and highlight the need for better implementation in the future. EU officials relied on the government's apparent commitment to Roma inclusion and failed to apply EU standards for policies: targeted, implementable, and proportionate to needs.[42] State accountability in relation to implementation of these policies was missed at local, national, and European levels.

Universal Policies and Measures Insensitive to Roma Needs

The 2001 Strategy failed to mainstream Roma needs within broadly based social structures. Instead, Roma issues were effectively ghettoized within targeted Roma-only institutions. The *coordination* role of the National Agency for Roma in the 2001 Strategy was repeatedly mistakenly considered a predominantly implementation role. This reduced the active engagement of relevant mainstream ministries and institutions in addressing Roma problems in their own planning.[43] The National Agency for Roma had become the main implementer. Lacking political power, it was unable to influence players more central to governmental hierarchy and thus failed to coordinate other ministries and make them accountable for Roma-related issues.

Romania has included several minority rights measures in its universal policies since the 1990s. For instance, the constitution guaranteed the rights of the country's minority groups to representation in parliament, even if the minority organization did not pass the minimum threshold of 5 percent of the votes. However, as David Mark details in his chapter in this volume, this right has been translated into unfair rules, leading, paradoxically, to the hindrance of a fair electoral competition for minority votes.

Other laws continue to ignore the specific needs and interests of minority groups. For example, the 2011 Educational Law does not include the desegregation measures articulated in the targeted Desegregation Order approved by the Ministry of Education in 2007, despite persistent NGO advocacy on this topic. Including the critical issue of segregation into mainstream education documents was not considered a priority.

The bilingual system in Romania is an example of a universal policy that is not fully sensitive to minority rights and needs. Although more than 8 percent of the Romanian population is Roma, and a large number of Roma speak Romani, the bilingual education system is primarily directed at intensive learning of foreign languages (English, French) in bilingual schools;[44] but a similar model has not been provided for Romani. The Roma organization Amare Rromentza piloted bilingual kindergartens, using bilingual education primarily to help Roma children learn Romanian, the official language.[45] Although the Ministry of Education supported the initiative, it was not widely expanded nor was it part of universal public policy. For young Roma children who use mainly Romani at home and do not speak Romanian fluently in their early years, bilingual education, at least during kindergarten, could have contributed to a fairer start in school. A targeted ministerial program offers Roma children the opportunity to enroll in optional Romani language and history classes, taught three to four hours a week. There are also isolated cases of classes fully taught in Romani that students can enroll in.[46]

Though mainstream school curricula are insensitive to minority rights and needs, optional classes partially fill the gap. While national history textbooks do not reflect Roma history in Romania, the Ministry of Education has supported alternative Roma history and tradition books, for minority children who choose to learn Roma history. However, this approach prevents the majority population from learning Roma history, thus perpetuating prejudice against Roma and continuing low self-esteem among Roma children.

The Romanian government has thus been slow to include Roma issues in universal policies and equalize opportunities for all children. Roma must rely on limited targeted programs, addressing the urgent or special problems of Roma children: summer kindergartens, health mediators and school mediators, and affirmative action for high school and university. Education policies designed primarily with majority children in mind can only benefit the whole community if they comprehensively take into account the particularities of minorities and disadvantaged groups.[47] In the absence of such universal and integrative policy development, the status quo of educational discrepancies between Roma and non-Roma children over the last quarter century persists.

Policy Networks: Advocates and Their Dialogue with Institutions, Donors, and Local Communities

International organizations, Romanian institutions, Romanian politicians, private donors, and civil society alike have planned and implemented policies and projects to reduce disparities between Roma and non-Roma, especially in the area of education. Where their interests have aligned, these actors have partnered. But these players have also contested each other's roles. Donors and international organizations have competed for influence over Roma affairs, and misaligned goals and incentives have created steep obstacles for the Roma movement.

Roma NGOs have traditionally occupied a relatively powerless position, and their weak mobilization has affected their advocacy efforts and power to negotiate with the government. Roma NGOs have been able to put Roma issues on the public agenda, but usually only when the government had a related issue on the agenda or when institutions needed the legitimacy of the NGOs. NGOs have taken advantage of this momentum, but have still secured only minimal leverage in setting the agenda. The 2001 Strategy highlighted the lack of experience of Roma civil society in policy related matters. NGOs used their limited leverage to advance a Roma strategy for the first time, but they lacked the experience to follow through or achieve enduring gains.

The Roma movement also lacked political power and leverage. State representatives have been unwilling to acknowledge the role of Roma organizations, scholars, and parties and accept them as real partners. Instead politicians have on occasion blamed Roma organizations and parties for failures on Roma-related issues. Mainstream institutions and their representatives, as well as opinion makers and leaders, have sometimes criticized Roma NGOs and politicians for not fulfilling their responsibility to solve the problems of their own "constituencies."[48] But the "Roma responsibility" mentality has weakened the efforts of state institutions to address Roma inclusion and encouraged them to leave this responsibility to Roma institutions, NGOs, and leaders.

In turn, the NGOs' priorities have often been driven by donors' agendas and instructions, perspectives that have impacted their dialogue and interactions with Roma communities. The limited and short-term funding NGOs have received and subsequently implemented have generated frustration and disappointment in the communities. Securing funds to work with Roma children on a one-year project and abandoning them when the project funding runs out placed NGOs in a compromised situation vis-à-vis their beneficiary communities, as the community needs were not adequately sustained. Strategies such as these are evidence of unsatisfactory NGO-donor consultation and dramatic deficits in accountability and transparency.

Discussion of inclusion failures often degenerates into a blame game. The international community has routinely critiqued countries and their governments' inability to protect the rights of their Roma citizens. National politicians point to the failures of Roma people and Roma NGOs in achieving inclusion goals, in the face of generous support policies.[49] Donors criticize grantees for lack of results or systemic change in Roma inclusion. Roma NGOs question governmental investment in Roma inclusion, as well as EU bodies' limited involvement in insisting on government accountability. The blame game for failures of Roma inclusion goes even further, beyond relevant organizations to society as a whole. Teachers point to Roma children and parents when explaining the failure in education; mayors blame the Roma to justify building walls that separate communities.

But the blame game is counterproductive for Roma as well as for governments, the European Union, and general society. A serious evaluation of policies, programs, and measures is necessary and so is an understanding of the different roles and responsibilities of each player involved in Roma inclusion. And as governments are accountable for policy failures and successes, achieving Roma inclusion should be conceived of as its responsibility. In addition, the European Union should enforce its overarching role, to monitor and keep accountable its member states. Roma scholars and advocates themselves should work to build on past failures to develop a more empirically grounded, systematic, and inclusive policy agenda moving forward.

Nevertheless, a new wave of Roma scholars and activists have started to challenge the inclusion agenda that states have delivered to the Roma over the past few decades and look more critically to the Gadje/non-Roma studies on Roma, which had served for policy development for years. There is also an increased and coordinated effort of Roma voices who question and publically discuss the trajectories and the implementation of Roma policies and laws at the local, national, and European level. Much of this inquiry, including a stocktaking of the upsurge in discrimination and economic and social oppression also referenced in this book, and the enduring linkage between ethnicity, class, and racial power will have to be carried forward through systematic, joint dialogue among Roma scholars.

The steady growth of what we call a potential "Critical Romani Studies in Law, Policy and Research Design (RomaniCrit)" is therefore needed. As critical race theorists through the decades have shown how racism has continued to persist despite its condemnation through state policies and norms, in the case of the Roma, scholars and advocates have examined the roots and trajectories of Roma-non Roma discrepancies, rights, and privileges. As argued in the introduction to this volume, African American voices emerged to address breakdowns in state laws. In step with their predecessors, Romani advocates and scholars should convene to examine the limited impact of state policies and laws for Roma and demand a shift in discourse and actions toward Roma inclusion, anti-assimilation and "anti-subordination." A growing number of scholars and advocates have already started to engage in a movement geared to securing a more prominent Roma voice in law and policy design and implementation and in Roma-related studies. We hope this positive momentum will drive a new era for a visible and influential RomaniCrit.

Discussion

This chapter has advanced an analysis of post-2000 European Roma policy, with a focus on educational policies in Romania. While there have been political steps toward formulating a Roma-targeted policy advanced by the European Union, limited knowledge has been invested in drafting the policy and complying with general policy-making standards. Goals, clear re-source allocations, an estimated budget for the implementation of all measures, and an evaluation and monitoring system have been largely absent in the 2001 Roma Strategy and the *Strategy for Inclusion 2012–2020*; and although the *Strategy for Inclusion 2015–2020* shows some progress in addressing these limitations, especially in relation to indicators and monitoring mechanisms, or to budgetary allocations, as we showed, there are still significant gaps in its formulation. Overall, policy makers in Romania have not followed the elements and stages required to achieve results in Roma related policies. In the formulation of Roma policy, the guiding force has been EU pressure, instead of the needs of Romania's Roma communities.

These gaps as well as the lack of political will at the level of the government are reflected in the limited results achieved to date. In addition, the fragmentary approach in implementation taken by the Romanian government led to insignificant results of its flagship programs. For instance, the affirmative action program will be more beneficial if institutions take early and solid action to increase the participation and the quality of education at kindergarten and involve the Roma families closely in the process. It will bring additional added value if represented as it is: a reparatory justice measure for state-sponsored injustices against Roma.

Throughout Europe, governments neglected to assess policy impacts and undertake formal evaluations of educational policy for Roma children. A systematic link between policy objectives and evaluative follow-through will enable governments to consistently assess and revise their policies and build sustainable programs that deliver inclusion and educational advancement. As this chapter has shown, policies to date have not reduced disparities, and often times, their exclusive focus on poverty has exaggerated the stigmatization of the Roma community. The lacunae between policy commitments and outcomes have generated frustration among Roma advocates and scholars, especially since the hopes of an era of significant social change have proved largely false.

We have argued that major players in the Roma inclusion process have failed. In the case of Roma education in Romania, policy failure has resulted from a complex combination of factors. They include government superficiality in complying with EU regulations (the main engine of most Roma policies); institutional limitations and biases in making effective Roma policies; a lack of consideration for the realities and needs of Roma children, the country's historical context, or the relations between Roma and non-Roma; a lack of political power and mobilization of Roma activists; a short-term donor focus on limited and unsustainable interventions; and EU reluctance to monitor and keep member states accountable for their policies and measures.

In many instances, Roma scholars and advocates embraced biased initiatives proposed by the states or scholars. Though these initiatives were poised to "integrate" Roma, a paternalistic discourse was imposed instead. For the most part, and in the past twenty-five years, these top-down policies and approaches have failed.

Past policy failures should inform future action. The Romanian *Strategy for Inclusion 2015–2020* may be a good start, but its limitations on housing and employment, among other areas, need to be addressed in its revision. If genuine results are sought, all stakeholders must participate in the redesign and implementation of the new strategy. Generating appropriate Roma policies, programs, and actions requires the appointment of competent experts to manage Roma institutional portfolios. Real progress will also demand the development of carefully researched policies based on needs and Roma community demands, regular and careful evaluation and actual implementation of planned actions. A human rights-based approach, which tackles the bias and prejudice of the non-Roma population, is imperative. To keep state institutions accountable, rigorous annual external monitoring should become a priority for Roma organizations and private donors.

The momentum of the Roma movement in the early post-Communist decades was concentrated more on policy adoption and less on creating strong links with constituencies. However, as institutions move toward the local implementation of their policies, NGOs need to focus on strengthening their links with Roma individuals and communities to build sustainable and representative partnerships.

Mainstream society can also play an essential role in achieving inclusion. Policies and measures should be designed to overcome stigma and prejudice toward the Roma community and curb the Roma under-privilege and opportunity gap. A minority group cannot advance toward inclusion without the respect and acceptance of the overall population.

Lastly, a critical law, policy, and research perspective should be powerfully advanced by Roma leaders and scholars themselves, one that bolsters the confidence Roma have lost and fights back against assimilationist, dominant laws and policies. Ultimately, a shift in discourse and action, which seriously considers laws and policies against the backdrop of oppression and domination, should galvanize Roma mobilization and participation. A cohesive

RomaniCrit, backed by cogent claims and a lucid agenda, should relentlessly address current obstacles for social change and the impact of entrenched power structures on Roma, as well as monitor and discuss Roma studies, policies, and laws in the public fora. Through questioning individuals and institutions alike, as well as contesting policies that do not work, RomaniCrit should participate in the development of a stronger European movement willing to keep institutions and community organizations accountable.

Chapter 6

Roma Policy in Europe: Results and Challenges

Andrzej Mirga

Since the early 1990s, European policy makers, scholars, experts, Roma representatives, and civil society activists have engaged in discussions about strategies for addressing the harsh social and economic conditions under which Roma communities live. A growing awareness of targeted anti-Roma human rights violations, discrimination, and hate speech has added urgency to these discussions, illustrated by a proliferation of disturbing international and national headlines about Roma migrants depicted as criminals imposing intolerable burdens on receiving states. Major intergovernmental organizations, such as the Organization for Security and Cooperation in Europe (OSCE), the Council of Europe (CoE), and the United Nations and its various agencies, have actively participated in Roma policy making, at times competing with each other for leadership of Roma issues in Europe. In the course of this process, a European Roma policy has emerged.[1]

Since the mid-2000s, the European Union has become a major stakeholder in advancing the integration of Roma in the EU space and beyond. With the 2004 EU enlargement adding several Central European countries to the EU, the center of gravity of Roma policy gradually shifted toward Brussels and its institutions. After the 2007 enlargement (including the addition of Bulgaria and Romania), European Roma policy was further consolidated within EU institutions. This phase of policy formation coincided with the structural funds programming period of 2007–2013, which designated significant budget allocations for social inclusion and integration measures in favor of disadvantaged populations, including Roma. With the 2007 enlargement, some 70 percent of the 10 to 12 million Roma in Europe now live within the EU space.[2] The responsibility of meeting the needs of the vast majority of European Roma provided a stimulus for EU Roma policy development.

European Roma after the Transition from Communism

State programs, formulated to advance Roma integration, are not a new development. In post–World War II Europe, governments of Communist countries pursued policies to assimilate Roma, and in Western Europe, governments tried to accommodate the needs of traveling Roma or "the Gypsy population."[3] However, the situation radically changed after the fall of Communism and the ensuing transition period.[4]

Since the dissolution of Communism, Roma have experienced a paradoxical form of change. With greater freedom for ethnic and political mobilization, they have made political gains, but they have lost out socially and economically. Politically, their ethnic minority status has been confirmed and recognized, but socially, they have been subject to rapid and massive deprivation.[5]

This deprivation has been the outcome of a neoliberal turn that most post-Communist regimes have pursued in their social and economic policies.[6] As some sociologists have noted, this turn has led to the formation of a Roma underclass, subject to extreme social exclusion, discrimination, and victimization.[7] For policy makers, it has become apparent that the specific and complex problems facing the Roma community cannot be solved within the terms of a general minority policy. Rather, a comprehensive and progressive policy is needed, targeted toward the Roma.[8] Thus, since the early 1990s, the international community and civil rights organizations have called for a "constructive" and comprehensive policy, focused on the specific needs and situation of Roma.[9]

Starting in the early 1990s, international organizations such as the OSCE, Council of Europe, and United Nations became central platforms for Roma issues.[10] In addition to assisting and monitoring government action, they have encouraged, facilitated, and supported the design and adoption of governmental programs for Roma integration. More recently, the EU has helped to fund several of these organizations' new Roma projects.[11]

Treaty bodies within the UN and the Council of Europe have shown growing interest in monitoring the Roma situation, as have various non-treaty monitoring bodies within international organizations.[12] Moreover, Roma and non-Roma advocacy groups have been instrumental in bringing Roma cases to the European Court of Human Rights (ECtHR) in Strasbourg. As other chapters in this book note, the number of admissible cases has increased in recent years, as have judgments in favor of the Roma applicants.[13]

Roma policy in Europe is the result of this multisectoral set of efforts targeting national government policy. Hungary was among the first countries to engage with this process by adopting a "Governmental Decree on the Most Urgent Tasks Concerning the Gypsy Community" in 1995.[14] By the time of the 2004 EU enlargement, most Central European post-communist countries had Roma integration policies in place.[15]

Enlargements, Emergence, and Consolidation of EU Roma Policy

The European Union and the European Commission (its administrative arm) were only marginally engaged in Roma issues until the 2004 enlargement brought Central European countries with substantial Roma populations into the Union.[16] Since then, the European Union has developed its own commitments and policy documents, mirroring those adopted by other key organizations, such as the OSCE and the Council of Europe.[17] The aims, focus, and areas identified for support and assistance to member states on Roma did not differ from other organizations' recommendations or political commitments, although the 2000 Race Equality Directive has been thought to improve the Roma situation within the European Union.[18] In 2005, the Open Society Foundations, the World Bank, and several governments launched the Decade of Roma Inclusion, adding an additional layer to the complex structure of initiatives and commitments of Roma policy in Europe already in place.[19]

The 2004 and 2007 EU enlargement, especially the 2007 enlargement (bringing Bulgaria and Romania into the EU), have been of paramount significance for EU Roma policy formulation and consolidation. Growing numbers of Roma took advantage of their new European freedom of movement to travel to cities in "old" EU countries, often causing tensions with the majority population. EU institutions increasingly faced pressure, from governments and from civil society organizations, to provide leadership and propose solutions to escalating Roma-related challenges.[20]

The 2007 enlargement coincided with the period of new structural funds programming between 2007 and 2013. (Structural funds are available for regions whose GDP per capital is below 75 percent of the EU average and are meant to stimulate economic development.) The *Presidency Conclusions of 14 December 2007* called on "Member States and the Union to use all means to improve [Roma] . . . inclusion." The council also requested that the commission "examine existing policies and instruments and to report to the Council on progress achieved before the end of June 2008."[21] While use of structural funds was being negotiated, the commission pressed to have Roma needs incorporated into programmatic documents, such as the National Strategic Reference Frameworks and Operational Programmes.[22] At the same time the commission reiterated that the core issues of Roma inclusion—education, employment, public health, housing and infrastructure, and the fight against poverty—were primarily the responsibility of member states.[23] In the words of the commission, success would require "the political will and capacity of Member State Governments to allocate budgets and support projects which are multidimensional (taking the whole reality of Roma life into consideration) and clearly targeted on the Roma (though *not ethnically exclusive*, that is, allowing for participation of other persons in similar situations regardless of their ethnicity)" (emphasis added).[24]

The 2008 economic and financial crisis, which erupted in the United States and expanded to Europe and throughout the world, was another key development driving the consolidation of EU Roma policy. The commission recognized that the crisis exacerbated preexisting structural problems facing Roma inclusion.[25] Its first response to this challenge was to place a specific focus on Roma in the context of the 2000 Lisbon Strategy (a new strategic goal for the Union that aimed to stimulate employment, economic reform and social cohesion as part of a knowledge-based economy).[26] Then, in September 2010, concerned with the situation of Roma in France (which had worsened during 2010), the commission established a Roma Task Force to evaluate the use of structural funds by member states for Roma integration.[27] The commission also initiated bilateral high-level discussions to encourage national governments to make better use of the structural funds available.[28]

Despite these interventions, the unfolding economic crisis led to substantial political gains among extreme right and populist groups who sought public support by blaming the hardship of the crisis on minorities, immigrants, and Roma.[29] The most critical situation occurred in Hungary, where in a series of attacks against Roma, six people were killed and dozens were injured over the course of 2008 and the first half of 2009.[30] As other chapters in this volume note in greater detail, other developments have also placed Hungary at the forefront of anti-Roma activity. The Jobbik, a far-right, racist party mobilizing people against Roma, has scored electoral gains in both general and European Parliament elections there.[31] Instances of violent attacks against Roma, coinciding with extreme-right orchestrated marches against them, have also been recorded in the Czech Republic, Bulgaria, and Slovakia.[32]

EU antidiscrimination frameworks and binding decisions have not helped lessen routine scapegoating of Roma minorities in a number of member states—a dangerous trend that has been on the rise.[33] In Italy in 2008, an influx of Roma resulted in the declaration of "a state of emergency" in three regions.[34] In France in 2010, a policy of evictions and "voluntary return" of Roma EU citizens from Romania and Bulgaria caused serious tensions between France and the commission, as well as between France, Romania, and Bulgaria.[35] The latter crisis raised the contentious question, "Whose citizens, whose responsibility?"[36] Paradoxically, the dispute over Romanian and Bulgarian Roma in France resulted, in researcher Sergio Carrera's words, in a "distinctive paradigm shift at EU level from the priority given to enforcing EU free movement and nondiscrimination law, towards the promotion of EU (soft) policy coordination of member states' policies on the (re)integration of Roma, now also mixed with a discourse on inclusion and reinsertion."[37] As a result, on May 19, 2011, the Council of the European Union adopted *Council Conclusions on an EU Framework for National Roma Integration Strategies up to 2020*.[38] In June 2011 the European Council officially called for rapid implementation of the Framework on National Roma Strategies.[39]

The decisions have articulated Brussels' concerns with member states' lack of visible progress in social inclusion and integration of the Roma population. Little has been achieved despite repeated urging from the commission that member state governments make better use of the substantial resources available through structural funds.[40] For many stakeholders, including members of civil society, high hopes associated with EU Roma policy implementation during the 2007–2013 programming period have vanished.[41]

The *Council Conclusions on an EU Framework* committed all member states to the development of policy measures designed to systematically tackle anti-Roma socioeconomic exclusion and discrimination throughout the European Union. By the end of 2011, member states were required to finalize their respective National Roma Integration Strategies, intended to incorporate Roma social inclusion within the broader framework of national social inclusion policies. This policy envisioned the establishment of National Contact Points within each member state government, whose responsibility it would be to lead the process, share lessons learned, monitor progress, and regularly update the commission.[42] The European Commission has built on this policy, by communicating regularly on these measures with governments.[43] It has monitored their programmatic strategy documents, as well as the responses of civil society members to national developments.[44]

In critical reviews of the framework document, leading members of civil society have noted the failure to include a well-defined child-centered approach or measures for ending segregation in education. They have noted that the framework had weak provisions for combating racism and discrimination, and that it failed to address the gender inequality faced by Roma women. Finally, civil society leaders have also criticized the failure to define mechanisms for better use of structural funds for Roma inclusion, including disaggregated data collection to monitor progress.[45] Despite these substantial criticisms, it remains the case that in a short time span, the European Union passed from "agnosticism" on minority issues, including the Roma minority, to the elaboration and adoption of a full-scale EU Roma policy.[46] Within this timeframe, the EU also invested in learning about other international organizations' experience in implementing Roma-related policies and measures,[47] studying examples of good practices and possible models supporting and scaling programs among various Roma communities.[48]

Roma Policy Implementation: Reviews and Assessments

The international community, including the European Union, has clearly shown substantial interest in encouraging governments to more effectively implement various Roma policies. This interest has been motivated both by concerns regarding the level of human rights violations and discrimination faced by this minority but also by concerns about Roma migration to Western European cities.[49] The latter concern, widely exploited and exaggerated by mainstream media, has increased societal anti-Roma feelings and benefited populist and extreme right movements in several countries in Europe.[50]

Intergovernmental and civil society organizations have made concerted efforts to help Central and Southern European governments, where most Roma live, to implement measures targeting Roma integration.[51] Less assistance had been offered to Western European governments until the Roma migration crisis (such as in Italy in 2008).[52] However, consolidation of EU Roma policy has changed the situation. Following the *Council Conclusions on an EU Framework*, almost all member states have developed similar programs.[53]

In a 2008 assessment of the situation of Roma in Europe, OSCE's Office for Democratic Institutions and Human Rights (ODIHR) described the complexity of Roma policy in Europe, detailing the stakeholders and initiatives, along with the progress made to that point.[54] The report observed that significant gaps remained unchallenged and that Roma communities remained separated from mainstream society in their ability to access to quality housing, education, employment, public services, and justice. While governments had adopted programs and strategies to tackle Roma problems, the report noted, many integrative efforts had failed due to the lack of a proactive approach at national, regional, and local levels. The report traced the slow pace of change to several causes, but particularly to insufficient political will and lackluster engagement in program implementation by government and local authorities—both, exacerbated by inadequate financial, institutional, and human resources. It found that "Despite rather large numbers of international and national Roma-related initiatives, in proportion to resources invested, these have not alleviated the continuing social and economic inequalities, marginalization, racism, and discrimination faced by Roma and Sinti."[55] The report concluded that, despite many efforts, no *breakthrough* has been reached in the situation of Roma in Europe.[56]

About eighteen months later, the commission arrived at similar conclusions in its staff working document, *Roma in Europe: Progress Report 2008–2010*. While it recognized that "existing instruments and policies" were "in principle appropriate and suitable for the inclusion of Roma," it also noted "an implementation gap" at all levels.[57] Concurring with the OSCE ODIHR findings, the commission document attributed the limited impact of the policies adopted to a "lack of political will and a lack of strong partnerships and coordination mechanisms . . . [and] a lack of capacities and knowledge at the local level to implement instruments and to change the concrete living conditions of Roma communities."[58]

The international community was strikingly united in voicing similar concerns about the minimal progress in realizing Roma social inclusion during this period. At a 2010 High-Level CoE conference in Strasbourg, intergovernmental organizations all called for a renewal of Roma commitments and improved Roma policy implementation. In his speech at that conference, the ODIHR director, Ambassador Janez Lenarcic, stressed the need for action on implementation: "We have a plethora of state commitments that can be remobilized. . . . We must, at this point, send a strong message to both state authorities and Roma communities. Too often we have seen that programmes and priorities at government levels are subject to adaptation, others remain short-lived and unsustainable. Let us confirm unequivocally that we commit to the fundamental rights of Roma and that we shall work, as a priority, towards the implementation of existing commitments."[59] Civil society and other international community representatives also pointed to the financial implications of inaction, noting the lost revenue and significant welfare costs generated by economically inactive Roma populations.[60]

In November 2013, the ODIHR published its second assessment report on the Roma, covering the period between 2008 and 2013. The report noted the overall increase in Roma-related funding but highlighted the marked differences among states, especially in the amounts of funding allocated and the priorities for intervention.[61] Some progress was evident in education for Hungary, Poland, and Serbia; in housing for Spain, Poland, Slovenia, and Croatia; in health, with Roma health mediator programs in Bulgaria, former Republic of Macedonia, Romania, Serbia, and Slovakia; and in some specific areas in education, including early education programs, which twenty-one governments reported supporting; Roma school mediators, which fourteen governments reported providing; and scholarships for Roma children, which fourteen governments reported providing.[62] However, the report concluded that these positive developments were outweighed by dangerous trends such as forced Roma migration, escalating anti-Roma rhetoric and violent incidents, accelerating evictions, and growing populist and extreme-right movements.[63]

The commission issued its own evaluation report a few months later, in connection with the third EU Roma Summit of April 2014 in Brussels. In contrast to the pessimistic overall conclusion of the ODIHR assessment, the *Report on the Implementation of the EU Framework for National Roma Integration Strategies* recognized that "three years after adoption of the EU Framework, progress, although still slow, is beginning to take shape."[64] The commission used a 2011 survey on the circumstances of Roma, conducted by the EU Fundamental Rights Agency (FRA), as a "starting point from which progress [was] measured." The report stressed that the 2011 EU framework set up a "long-term process" that required "sustained political commitment of all stakeholders" and "political leadership." It highlighted the EU's *Council Recommendation on Effective Roma Integration Measures in the Member States* as the "first ever legal instrument on Roma" and the EU Framework for National Roma Integration strategies as the "first . . . comprehensive and evidence-based framework" and "first time ever coordinated effort of member States to close the gap between Roma and non-Roma."[65]

At the same time, the report criticized the scant use of funds allocated for Roma integration. It pointed out that "in the 2007–2013 period, the potential use of EU funds [had] not yet been exploited to support Roma integration." According to the commission, the reasons for this failure included difficulties in finding and integrating national co-financing, overly complex administrative structures combined with a lack of administrative capacity and expertise, and lastly, poor cooperation between authorities and the Roma community.[66]

The commission concluded that creating a "tangible change in the situation of Roma" would only be possible if member states "demonstrate[d] political will and determination" and "honor[ed] the commitments' adopted under the Framework."[67] In short, the commission reiterated views expressed on many previous occasions by other international stakeholders.

Moving Forward: Overcoming Obstacles That Hamper Implementation of Roma Policy

My review of the historical record above leads me to conclude that the commission has not yet resolved the dilemmas hampering effective Roma policy implementation. These dilemmas now include controversies over the collection and use of data on the Roma, the relative merits of targeted as opposed to mainstreamed policy approaches, discussion over strategies for local level or grassroots Roma policy implementation, and finally the roles and responsibilities of Roma themselves.

Data collection has been viewed by most stakeholders as key to ensuring effective Roma policy design, evaluation, and monitoring of progress. For many, the absence of data has meant the inability to register progress or lack thereof.[68] This problem, also raised in the 2013 ODIHR report, has not yet been solved, despite the useful introduction of survey data gathered by the Fundamental Rights Agency in 2011 to provide a baseline against which future progress can be measured.[69]

While the commission claimed its Roma policy has been "evidence-based,"[70] it also recognized that "Member States are not obliged to report on EU funding for Roma or other ethnic minorities. Some even do not allow the collection of ethnic data for constitutional reasons."[71] Nevertheless, the commission continues to assess "Member States' National Roma Strategies implementation on the basis of data submitted by national governments."[72] Relying on data submitted by governments weakens the "robust" monitoring and evaluation mechanism at the state level requested by the EU Framework on National Roma Integration strategies. In addition, while most participating states monitor spending or program beneficiaries, they very rarely collect data to assess program outcomes.[73]

Inadequate funding is another commonly cited cause of ineffective Roma policy implementation.[74] In the second half of the 1990s, governments of Central and Eastern European countries supplemented very limited national funding earmarked for Roma policies with limited amounts of outside donor funding.[75] In the pre-accession period, some EU funding for Roma was earmarked under the PHARE support programme, the EU's main financial instrument for accession of the Central and Eastern European countries.[76]

After the 2004 and 2007 enlargements and the consolidation of the EU Roma policy, a much larger share of EU structural funds became available for Roma policy implementation.[77] However, these funds were earmarked for the broad category of "disadvantaged communities," of which the Roma were only one.[78] Actual allocation of funding towards Roma programs therefore depended on a political willingness to appropriate mainstream funds and general social inclusion funds for Roma purposes.[79]

From the point of view of the commission, therefore, the main issue has not been a lack of funds, but rather a lack of political commitment to use those funds for Roma policy implementation.[80] For implementers of EU-funded programs, such as state agencies, local administration, civil society groups, or Roma organizations, accessing those funds has been a major challenge. In short, funds theoretically available for Roma inclusion did not effectively contribute towards such inclusion.[81]

The international community and civil society have often stressed the the need to engage local authorities in implementation of Roma policy, for example, as in OSCE's original action plan for Roma of 2003.[82] They have explained this emphasis by pointing to insufficient funding, lack of coordination between central governments and/or ministries and local administrations, and above all, the lack of interest or political will on the part of local authorities.[83] In countries with centralized Communist regimes in the past, central authorities were in charge of Roma policy. Though some elements of this heritage have continued after the transition, decentralization reforms have altered the locus of Roma policy significantly.[84] The bulk of available funds from central government budgets, from the donor community, or from structural funds have been directed to local administrations as the main implementers of Roma policy (see, for example, developments in Poland, Hungary, the Czech Republic and Slovakia).[85] Over time civil society—in Romania, for example—has become increasingly involved in implementing Roma policy measures. In some "old" EU member states, highly decentralized, civil society actors have for decades been charged with this task—the Fundación Secretariado Gitano in Spain is a case in point.[86] But, as noted earlier, following the advent of the economic crisis, these decentralization strategies have had to contend with disturbing increases in grassroots pressures to exclude and segregate Roma communities. As a result, the number of Roma isolated or excluded in ghettoized communities has not diminished. Neither has de facto segregation in education or housing.[87]

In sum, the international community, together with the European Union and members of civil society, have tried to overcome the lack of political will for Roma integration on the part of local authorities and majority populations.[88] As noted above, the commission has prioritized this area of work and has asked "authorities to develop local action plans or strategies, or sets of local policy measures within wider social inclusion policies, which could include baselines, benchmarks and measurable objectives for Roma integration as well as appropriate funding."[89] Similarly, civil society has been developing initiatives to support the implementation of Roma policy at the local level by offering assistance in accessing structural funds through such programs as EURoma network, OSF's Making the Most of EU Funds for Roma, and its extension, Mayors Making the Most of EU Funds for Roma Inclusion (MERI).[90] But these positive and well-intentioned efforts have not turned the tide.

Finally, many stakeholders have insisted on more vigorous Roma participation—arguing that "nothing without Roma" has the capability to succeed. And indeed, formally, Roma advocates have been consulted, at local, national, and international levels. Whether this access to policy makers and decision makers has been meaningful is debatable. The dilemma is obvious: to participate effectively, especially at the grassroots level, Roma must significantly bolster their human capital, particularly their educational level.[91] Without progress in the area of education, Roma will continue to act as "passive recipients" of social services rather than "active citizens."[92] Enlarging the circle of the Roma middle-class or educated elite is a prerequisite for such a change.

With the consolidation of EU Roma policy, accompanied by increased funding for Roma programs and projects, more implementers and service providers—including local authorities and international organizations—compete for that funding. However, one effect of discrimination, as mentioned above, has been less availability of educated Roma to run such programs. Thus, unfortunately, because of weak educational, organizational, and financial capacity, Roma implementers have been losers in this competition. As a result, much of the funding is channeled to many different intermediaries who provide assistance and services to Roma communities, including consultations, expertise, research and reporting, multiple and small scale projects. But this growing number of implementers has not generated profound changes for the community or ensured tangible outcomes on the ground.

Given the complexities and history I have outlined in this chapter, I would argue that there is no alternative to the central role of the European Union and member states in the development of EU Roma policy. However, some major rethinking is needed to guarantee that adopted Roma policy measures are implemented more effectively than they have been to date. This rethinking requires an unequivocal assurance from governments in receipt of EU funds that they will generate and sustain the political will necessary to ensure that policy instruments and financial resources earmarked for the Roma generate concrete outcomes. Most significantly, recipient governments must ensure the engagement of Roma themselves as active agents of change rather than passive recipients of help.

Chapter 7

Reconstructing Roma Integration in Central and Eastern Europe: Addressing the Failures of the Last Quarter Century

Kálmán Mizsei

The Paradox of Democratic Transformation and Deepening Discrimination

Contrary to popular perception in Central and Eastern Europe, achieving Roma integration is not an impossible task. Paradoxically, most Central and Eastern European countries in their Communist period made significant strides in Roma integration, but this progress unraveled immediately after these same countries became liberated from their Communist regimes. Though the passing of Soviet socialism should not be mourned, serious policy thinking is needed to probe how to reverse the Roma segregation and social exclusion reimposed in this period of liberal democracy in Central and Eastern Europe. This chapter reconstructs and analyzes the unraveling of Roma integration in European post-Communist market states and suggests that what was partially and distortedly achieved under Soviet socialism should surely be achievable within the free politics of Central and Eastern Europe.

I define integration as (1) an improvement in access to public services and work opportunities, and (2) society's adoption of a nondiscriminatory stance toward the minority population. In what follows, I refer to Hungarian studies of employment and public services that document the reversal of integrationist trends. My definition of integration leaves out the issue of political representation of Roma for two reasons. First, I view actual economic and social equality as the primary issue; the road toward this equality is varied. Second, forms of political representation may vary widely in each country, depending on many factors. In his chapter in this volume, "Leading by Example: Roma in European Politics Beyond 2014," David Mark discusses political representation and participation of Roma in much greater detail, drawing examples from Romania and Hungary.

Michael Mann describes ethnic cleansing as a phenomenon characteristic of modernity and a trait of the "dark side of democracy."[1] Democratization, he says, is an inevitable effect of modernization but so are adverse consequences, such as ethnic intolerance in response to a growing multiethnic population. Unfortunately, the last quarter century has seen a resurgence of this dark side of democracy in post-Communist Central and Eastern Europe, a process that caught liberal advocates of the rule of law, capitalism, and democracy by surprise. Three socialist federations disintegrated in the process of the collapse of socialism,[2] and were replaced by ethnically based nation-states. These nation states produced ethnic strife, and, in the case of Yugoslavia, a succession of ethnically fueled civil wars culminating in ethnic cleansing itself.[3]

While Roma were rarely victims of post-Yugoslav ethnic cleansing—with the exception of Kosovo where Roma suffered at the hands of formerly cleansed returning Kosovar nationals[4]—they have been victims of the much broader process of post-Soviet Europe's transition to a market economy and democracy. While discrimination against Roma has not reached the point of ethnic cleansing in most cases, Mann's study is still useful because some of the strategies he describes are mimicked by the intolerant environments of post-Soviet Central and Eastern Europe. And the risk remains that, as intolerance continues to grow, anti-Roma episodes will increase and eventually qualify as instances of ethnic cleansing.

This chapter focuses more on the experience of the countries that were part of the Soviet bloc and now are in the European Union—Bulgaria, Czech Republic, Hungary, Romania, and Slovakia and less on the post-Yugoslav and Albanian cases. A rich area for further exploration would be why in the area of much ethnic cleansing after the failure of socialism—Yugoslavia—

there seems to be less anti-Roma conflict than in the new EU member states that could, theoretically, invest much more into solving the problem. An in-depth comparative perspective among the Roma situations in post-Communist countries is much needed.

In countries with large Roma populations, the transition from socialism to a market democracy has led to Roma suffering. The nature of this suffer-ing has depended on the type of transition in question. It has included phys-ical ethnic cleansing in post-conflict situations such as Kosovo (as mentioned above) and social and geographic marginalization in more peaceful contexts such as those in Hungary and Slovakia. In the latter situations, Roma segre-gation was initially a result not of ethnic policies but rather of *economic* tran-sition. Roma who had been employed under the previous socialist regime found themselves suddenly unemployed in the early 1990s.[5] In their socio-logical research, Kemény and Havas found that in Hungary in 1971, over 85 percent of Roma men were employed (comparable to the rate of non-Roma men), while by 1993, only 28 percent held jobs. While racial prejudice un-doubtedly played a role, so too did the stagnant skill profile of the Roma after five decades of Soviet socialism. Appropriate for work in the state-owned heavy industry sector, their skill set did not change to meet the demands of the newly emerging, more technically demanding industries with compa-nies that were typically competitive, foreign owned, and embedded in inter-national markets.

This situation, to some extent an unintended consequence of radical economic reforms, was aggravated by characteristics of the emerging post-socialist democratic politics that Mann refers to as the dark side of democracy's infant phase. Roma became scapegoats for the hardship and dislocation of a society in the process of economic transition. In Kosovo and Bosnia, large numbers of Roma were chased away from their homes, many of them forced to settle in refugee camps. In many other post-Communist countries, the proliferation of discrimination was more gradual, as socialist international-ism was replaced with national renewal. The "Roma threat" became an all too convenient rallying cry for populist politicians trying to gain traction in the political marketplace. After so many years of censorship, any call to limit hate speech and insulting public political talk was construed as decadent Western political correctness or an effort to limit freedom of thought. Even in the best governed countries of the region, such as the Czech Republic, legal strategies, including those based on international law, only had a limited impact. In the well-known Roma discrimination case at the European Court of Human Rights (ECtHR), *D.H. and Others v. the Czech Republic*, discussed in detail in the chapter in this volume by James A. Goldston, the applicant complained about school segregation in Ostrava.[6] After a long process, the Court Grand Chamber finally ruled against the local government's practice of school segregation.[7] However now, fourteen years after the case was launched, the unlawful practices still continue, multiplied across other schools in the region. Legal efforts alone, without the backing of affirmative developmental efforts in practice, are not sufficient to reverse the impact of segregation.

As democracy has emerged, so newly gained freedoms and reduced levels of fear have contributed to the birth of an organized and energetic *civil society*.[8] But, once again paradoxically, the impact of increased freedom has been multi-faceted; it has allowed ordinary citizens to articulate a broad range of claims not permissible under state socialist rule. Among them have been demands by some that their children not attend class with Roma children.[9] After the transition from a socialist seller's labor market to a buyer's free market, small and large businesses started to discriminate in their hiring practices against Roma, a group they perceived as "people who steal," and a less reliable workforce. The advent of democracy has not immediately brought with it an inclusive or tolerant public culture. Moreover, in decentralized post-socialist democratic politics, the fight for public resources increasingly has left Roma in disenfranchised positions. When it has come to making decisions about local infrastructure investment and other questions of resource allocation, Roma have been nowhere as competitive as the mainstream populations in their respective cities and villages. In fact, a reverse process has taken place: Roma have gradually been crowded out of the work place, have had increasingly lower school attendance, and have faced deteriorating housing conditions.

Roma exclusion has continued and indeed, after the 2008 international economic crisis, hostility from the majority society has intensified. In his edited volume *The Gypsy "Menace"* (2012), Michael Stewart documents an acceleration of harassment against Roma during the crisis period in Central and Eastern Europe, including murderous attacks on Roma houses as well as, for the first time in history, the dramatic growth of political parties such as the Hungarian Jobbik with an "anti-Gypsy agenda" as the centerpiece of their political ideology.[10] Will Guy devotes a section of his chapter in this volume to the Hungarian context and details escalating attacks on Roma following the 2004 and 2007 phases of European Union (EU) enlargement.[11]

Evolving European Union Engagement

Concurrent with this process, a strong human rights activism has emerged with a focus on the Roma population. It has relied on two great traditions. First and foremost, it has been formed by the opposition to socialism in the 1970s and 1980s—that opposition itself a product of human rights concerns and agendas—predominantly in Poland, Hungary, and to an extent, Czechoslovakia. Poland did not have significant numbers of Roma to make the issue of Roma human rights there one of great political and policy concern. However, Hungary, the Czech Republic, and the Slovak Republic did. In Hungary, a strong anti-poverty and pro-Roma human rights movement emerged in the 1980s, coinciding with the development of a strong, largely liberal oppositional current.[12] This movement was strengthened by the active involvement of the Open Society Institute (OSI), first in Hungary and later in the rest of the region. The second tradition, the American civil rights movement, with much U.S. success already behind it, has informed the ethos of American activists supporting Roma.[13] While the newly renamed Open Society Foundations (OSF, previously known as OSI) contributed to the growth of Roma human rights organizations, other significant players emerged soon after the collapse of socialism. The most prestigious among these has been Romani CRISS, established by Nicolae Gheorghe in Romania in 1993, barely three years after the collapse of Ceausescu's dictatorship.

Just as "anti-Gypsy" intolerance has intensified in Central and Southeastern Europe, so has anti-Roma political activity grown in Western Europe, even though a much smaller number and proportion of Roma (some of them recent irregular migrants from Eastern Europe) live in that part of the continent. The traditionally strong bastion of human rights, France, engaged in symbolic anti-Roma action when President Sarkozy, in the summer of 2010, spectacularly and unlawfully ordered the expulsion of Roma who were illegally in France, a move designed to placate the segment of the electorate calling for radical anti-immigrant measures.[14] Sarkozy's act, however, generated unintended consequences. Civil society reaction inspired Viviane Reding, then EU Vice-President and Commissioner for Justice, to voice her concern about the French expulsions.[15] This high-level EU statement marked the first time any governmental structure of significant power, even in

Western Europe with its democratic traditions, had seriously engaged with a concrete case of Roma human rights violation in post-World War II history. The row between Reding and the French government drew the attention not only of European Union institutions but also of the broader public, even though Reding had to eventually retreat because of France's general political strength within the Union.

The European Union has slowly but steadily increased its engagement with Roma rights issues over the last few years. The long-term impact of this engagement has yet to be seen. This is to be expected, given the complexity of EU decision making, based as it is on the cooperation of independent states willing to subordinate limited parts of their sovereignty for the common cause, while attentively protecting their remaining national prerogatives. For instance, education is a national prerogative in the European Union as is employment policy. This political reality places severe limits on the scope of action of the European Commission or the European Parliament, institutions that, despite the demands of some critics, are not the equivalents of national governments or national parliaments.

Despite these limitations, the European Commission's 2010 communication *The Social and Economic Integration of the Roma in Europe* demonstrates that international organizations are willing to taking a stand on equal rights for Roma in Europe, building on earlier statements by the Council of Europe (CoE) and the Office for Democratic Institutions and Human Rights of the Organization of Security and Cooperation in Europe (OSCE).[16]

The Decade of Roma Inclusion: A Precursor to Deeper EU Engagement

The European Union did not only use its muscle to make countries respect European human rights standards; as Andrzej Mirga notes in his contribution to this volume, EU enlargement provided more public funds to spend on improving the social and economic situation of Roma.[17] International organizations mirrored this developmental approach. For example, while at the United Nations Development Programme (UNDP) as Regional Director for Europe and the Commonwealth of Independent States (CIS), I initiated a comparative study on the social situation of Roma living in poverty in Bulgaria, the Czech Republic, Hungary, Romania, and Slovakia—countries that, in two consecutive waves of accession in 2004 and in 2007, joined the European Union. Published in 2002, the study put its faith in targeted governmental action as a way to alleviate Roma disenfranchisement, although it was better at describing the situation than at generating workable policy recommendations.[18] One positive outcome of the publication was its impact on World Bank president James Wolfensohn, who together with Open Society Foundations founder and chairman George Soros initiated the Decade of Roma Inclusion (the Decade). A high-level conference, "Roma in an Expanding Europe: Challenges for the Future," launched the Decade of Roma Inclusion in Budapest on June 30 and July 1, 2003.[19] Hungarian prime minister Péter Medgyessy convened the conference, in which eight governments participated, thus providing a robust start for an intergovernmental structure with the additional design element of strong participation from NGOs.

With that governance design and the goal of making a difference in education, employment, housing, and health, the Decade was predicated on governments' taking principal responsibility for the fate of their Roma citizens. The initiative put its faith in a fundamentally *developmental* process, with George Soros's Open Society Foundations and Roma NGOs driving the Decade's human rights approach. This approach was also designed to better secure Roma "ownership" of the process, which in reality meant co-ownership with governments. The Decade aimed to address traditional areas of domestic government engagement with Roma—housing, education, employment, and health—by offering an intergovernmental resource to facilitate cross-country learning. This approach created opportunities for both peer pressure and positive encouragement from frontrunners to laggards.

After the Sarkozy crisis in France described earlier, the European Union took stronger action on Roma integration in Europe: in April 2011, the European Commission published *An EU Framework for National Roma Integration Strategies up to 2020* (henceforth *EU Framework for National Roma Integration*), which the Council of the European Union reinforced in its May *Council Conclusions*.[20] The Decade was a precursor to the EU engagement through the *EU Framework for National Roma Integration* in more than one way. For example, the areas defined by the *EU Framework for National Roma Integration* were identical to those defined by the Decade, clear evidence that the Decade had set the stage for enlightened engagement by a much better resourced actor, the European Union: education, employment, housing and health.

To complete a fairly complex picture, the new EU member states— Bulgaria, Czech Republic, Hungary, Romania, and Slovakia—all shared an increasingly hostile public attitude toward Roma while both rights-based Roma NGOs and international and intergovernmental organizations became increasingly vocal in stressing the need for government actions to integrate Roma successfully. The 2008 economic crisis worsened the situation of a significant constituency within the majority population, fueling further anti-Roma sentiment. At the time of this publication, changes on the ground are impossible to assess precisely given the lack of comparative data. However, any improvements that have occurred have not been commensurate to present needs, particularly those resulting from the tremendous dislocation experienced by Roma in the 1990s. The empirical research program on Roma in the region—the integrated household survey conducted by UNDP, World Bank, and EU Fundamental Rights Agency, with the support of the European Commission and the Open Society Institute in Budapest—unfortunately does not yet enable us to make reliable conclusions about progress over time, across the region as a whole or in individual countries.[21]

The intergovernmental model of the Decade has yielded modest results over the course of its ten years. Governments appear to have used the bi-annual International Steering Committee meetings to highlight their projects "for the Roma," without any serious assessment of the *policy* value of the funds spent. The impact of most of the Roma NGOs has also been minimal. Rather than using the meetings to move governments toward a strategic approach toward Roma integration, they have often vented their frustration with the situation of Roma in their countries and often grandstanded to show radicalism without a real strategic purpose. The professional quality of discussions, as well as that of the national "Decade Watch" documents, has been substandard and has declined over time. Sectoral workshops have sometimes resulted in more interesting discussions, but their impact has been mostly inconsequential, lacking any real feedback mechanism into national or international policies. Still, the Decade meetings have established a practice of Roma civil society representatives consulting with governmental officials, even if representatives of the governments have, over the years, become of lower and lower status.[22] The Decade also lost relevance for some of the participating countries because as they joined the EU, these countries began to pay more attention to the "stronger external master" given the EU's financial significance and its ability to shame countries flouting rules. The weaker the governance of a country, the more this applied.

One exciting outcome of the Decade initiative has been the Roma Education Fund (REF), originally meant to be co-sponsored by the World Bank and George Soros. REF was intended as a laboratory for policies designed to narrow the educational disadvantage of Roma children.[23] However, it has not fully realized its potential. After Wolfensohn's presidency came to an end, the World Bank's engagement in REF decisively weakened. Instead of matching Soros' investment as expected, its contributions have remained minimal, and though funding sources have since somewhat diversified, they still remain inadequate. While REF's demonstration effect is noteworthy—as it is the only international fund of its kind adapted for a specific professional purpose in the area of Roma inclusion—it has not yet fulfilled its ambitious goals. Governments have shown little interest in learning from these rich empirical experiences of work designed to shape Roma educational policies: thus, REF has also struggled to maximize the political impact of the evidence generated by its field projects.

In a pioneering study, the World Bank has assessed the economic losses caused by Roma exclusion.[24] Building on this start, a detailed policy paper would be useful. Such a document might monetize the required investment (now that we have the first estimate from the World Bank about the potential monetary benefits from full Roma inclusion) and provide a clear, detailed, and practical roadmap differentiating between the countries of the region. Economic clarity in the articulation of necessary affirmative measures for Roma in different educational levels from primary to tertiary could provide a vital contribution to the argument to invest adequately in Roma education with the ambition of full emancipation.

EU Structural Funds in the Service of Roma Integration

Recognizing the crucial importance of the European Union for Roma, George Soros also initiated a fund in 2006 whose main purpose was to catalyze the use of available EU funds for the benefit of Roma by new EU member states as well as EU candidate countries in the Western Balkans. This was the genesis of "Making the Most of EU Funds for Roma (MtM)," which I chaired from its inception through 2013.[25] Analytically, the period before publication of the European Commission's *An EU Framework for National Roma Integration* can be distinguished from the subsequent period. the *Framework* was reinforced by *Conclusions* of the Council of the European Union,

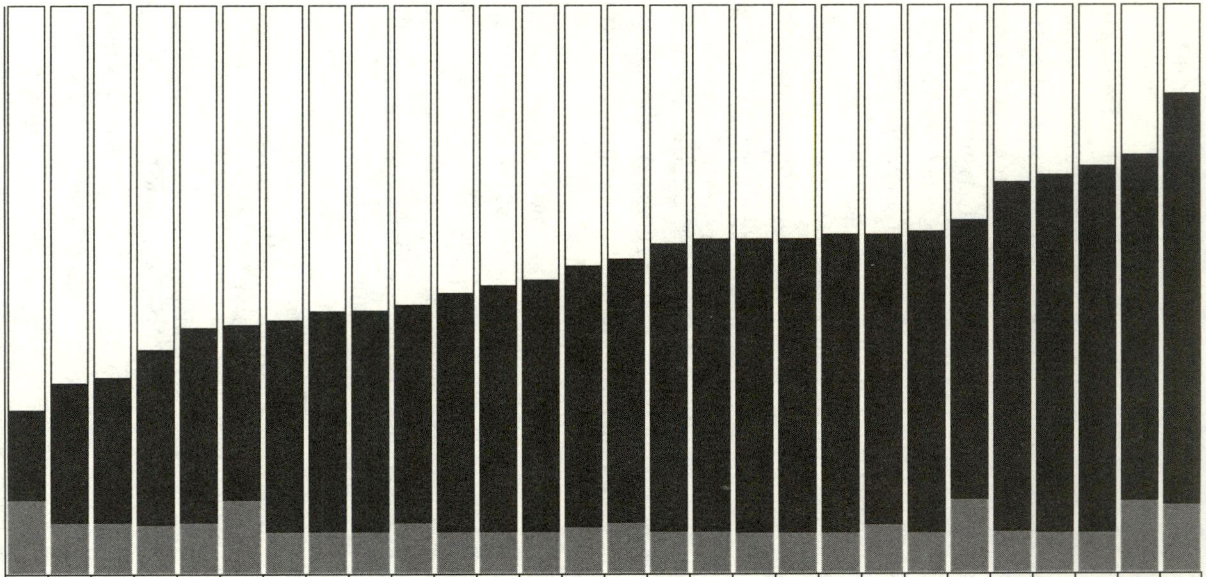

Figure 3. European Social Fund (ESF) 2007–2013 advances and interim payments to EU member states as a percentage of ESF envelope in each country, April 30, 2013. *Source:* EU Directorate-Generale: Employment, Social Affairs, and Inclusion, Brussels, 2013.

	RO	BG	MT	CZ	SK	HU	FR	NL	GR	CY	DK	LU	IT	EU-27	SI	UK	FI	DE	ES	SE	PL	BE	LT	AT	IE	PT	EE	LV
☐ unclaimed	71.3	66.6	65.4	60.6	56.7	56.1	55.5	53.9	53.6	52.6	50.9	49.5	48.4	46.0	44.7	41.9	41.3	41.2	41.2	40.6	40.3	40.0	38.4	31.3	30.0	28.4	26.5	15.6
■ interim	15.7	24.4	25.6	30.4	34.3	30.9	37.0	38.6	38.9	38.4	41.6	43.0	44.1	45.6	46.3	50.6	51.2	51.3	51.3	51.9	51.0	52.5	48.6	61.2	62.5	64.4	60.5	72.2
▨ advances	13.0	9.0	9.0	9.0	9.0	13.0	7.5	7.5	7.5	9.0	7.5	7.5	7.5	8.4	9.0	7.5	7.5	7.5	7.5	7.5	8.7	7.5	13.0	7.5	7.5	7.1	13.0	12.3

a high-level political act, suggesting responsibility for serious subsequent follow up by member states.[26]

As Figure 3 shows, the countries with the lowest level of European Social Fund expenditure, compared to allocation—in the final year of the seven-year EU funding cycle of 2007–2013—were those with the largest concentration of Roma. Since these countries are also amongst the very poorest in the EU, EU social inclusion funds can have a disproportionately significant role there than in countries with a higher per capita GDP (gross domestic product). However, in Romania, Bulgaria, Hungary, and Slovakia, the utilization of EU funds is at its lowest. The use of EU funds for poverty alleviation is also disproportionately low. Consequently, a portion of these funds have been wasted, and another portion remains unused. Even if, at the end of the cycle, the use of funds accelerates and countries take advantage of a certain grace period, thanks to special rules and extension authorization, funds spent in haste without careful planning are even less likely to generate positive outcomes.

There is no methodologically reliable analysis on the use of EU funds to promote Roma inclusion. And yet, it is known that there are at least two major ways funds can benefit socially excluded Roma. The first is direct infrastructural or social funding for Roma parts of settlements and for Roma people. Second, programs may indirectly benefit Roma by addressing particular geographic areas where many of them live (as in the case of the Hungarian "Most Disadvantaged Micro-regions Program") or aspects of poverty, such as lack of employment, since poverty affects them disproportionately.[27] Still, scattered evidence shows that relative to the crucial social importance of the issue, spending on areas important to Roma has so far generally been trivial, and even when assigned to a relevant area, often disbursed on other, unrelated programs. Evaluation culture is flimsy at best when it comes to Roma-related projects. For example, the European Union generally only looks at fulfillment of administrative rules in project implementation and fails to look at impact—in this East European post-socialist environment of weak governance, a particularly unsatisfactory practice.

Some argue that EU-funded projects are detrimental to the Roma cause. This is particularly the case—it is claimed—where Roma NGOs shift from their original human rights mission to EU projects, and compete with each other when their comparative advantage is not compelling.[28] Also, where EU budget rules allow much higher salaries for project personnel than the national environment would justify, public resentment develops, detrimentally affecting programs. These factors can also adversely affect the public standing of the Roma NGO movement, especially in biased environments where distorted public opinion holds that the state "spends too much on the lazy Roma."

Conclusions

My experience with the "Making the Most of EU Funds for the Roma" suggests that responsible government authorities must considerably improve their technical capacities to allocate funds.[29] This is particularly true in Romania, one of the poorest EU members, at the same time with the largest number of Roma. Government officials are often preoccupied by aspects of EU fund *use* other than their real value. Strategies for fund allocation, as well as mechanisms for fund use, should be subject to informed public discussions at the national—strategic—level as well as within relevant government sectors and grass-roots communities themselves. How much should be spent from the EU funds on poverty alleviation, Roma inclusion, school desegregation, and public housing solutions? These and similar foundational questions are very rarely asked on policy-making levels and virtually never subject to public debates.

Different segments of the Roma poverty conundrum need to be approached at different governance levels. Whereas local governments typically deal less with employment issues, they have greater power over issues related to schooling, school desegregation, and public housing. Governments in the region have been thinking perilously little about the question of how to incentivize and oblige local governments to desegregate and reduce poverty among Roma, even though the one of the names for EU funds—cohesion funds—implies that this equalizing effort should be applied not only at the level of the European Union but also within countries. Thus, even if national programs are construed with appropriate goals in mind, they need enabling regulations and other mechanisms. Without those, fund disbursement depends entirely on local goodwill and power relations. Even the best formulated programs, such as those in Hungary targeting the most depressed micro-regions, face difficulties in achieving their target, as the independent program evaluation of it shows.[30]

Both development and Roma circles debate whether EU funds should be dedicated directly to Roma or to more general social inclusion and antipoverty purposes that would be of indirect benefit to Roma. Some advocates demand Roma-specific operational programs. Proponents of these "pure" programs argue that if this approach is not taken too little will be spent on Roma. However, others suggest that governments that only dedicate rather modest funds to the Roma feel justified in doing this because Roma can draw on other funds, such as sectoral funds. Roma integration is far too important and complex a *national* issue to be limited to modestly funded Roma programs. Therefore, the best approach combines many professional approaches in housing, infrastructure, education, health, and employment—with some funds explicitly (and, in the spirit of EU funds, not exclusively) targeting Roma and some targeting the needy more generally. In addition, particularly disadvantaged micro-regions should also be targeted, as in the Hungarian program. Finally, Roma exclusion and Roma cultural issues will need specific attention, an issue addressed by Matache and Oehlke, in their chapter, "A Critical Analysis of Roma Policy and Praxis: The Romanian Case."

National governments in Central and Eastern Europe should have every reason to address the Roma inclusion challenge as a very high strategic priority. Placing Roma inclusion high on the agenda would address the Roma plight and counter anti-Roma majority sentiments particularly rampant in Hungary, Slovakia, Romania, Bulgaria, Serbia, and to some extent Macedonia, where ethnically driven disruptions have reached high levels. Such social disruptions have already occurred on many occasions, most visibly during the clashes in Bulgaria at the end of 2011.[31]

As well, appropriate state education of the Roma population would improve future employment rates overall for countries with rapid population aging and, in many instances, decline—as the age profile of Roma is much younger than that of the majority population. For this reason, and in the hope that the European Commission has learned how to encourage governments in the region to spend more (and more effectively) on Roma, many hoped that the national instruments and institutions for the new Multiannual Financial Framework (MFF) for 2014–2020 (the next budget period for EU funding) would reflect richly on the experiences of the national governments and the EC in the previous seven-year period. Some anticipated that the goals of the *EU Framework for National Roma Integration* would be fully built into the Partnership Agreements—the key agreements between member states and the European Commission over funds use in the MFF—as well as into concrete operational programs. These hopes were largely disappointed. Governments did not make serious efforts to take stock of previous low spending or the reasons for it. Nor were institutional mechanisms established to learn from best practices—domestically or in a broader international perspective—with the aim of scaling them up.

These shortcomings occurred despite the fact that the *EU Framework for National Roma Integration*, adopted in 2011, called on EU member states to create space for additional Roma programs still in the EU programming period that ended in 2013. Given the picture presented in Figure 1, this should not have been difficult—unspent money was available. However, among the new EU member states, only Hungary tried to answer the European Commission's call to design additional Roma-related programs. The other new member states did not design any significant programs to address the Roma issue in response to the EU Framework strategy.

Even in the case of Hungary, NGOs criticized the *spirit* of the government programs for not being explicitly anti-segregationist; indeed, in some cases it seemed they had the opposite stance. Most recently, one of the NGOs, the Chance for Children Foundation, won a court case against municipal authorities for reopening a Greek Catholic church school in a predominantly Roma area. The NGO determined that this was a separatist move, since the children from the area had previously attended a school with non-Roma children. The municipal authorities, with the help of the church, had thus reversed an earlier pro-integration step and reinstated a situation of school segregation. Unfortunately, the court's positive ruling was reversed by the Curia, Hungary's Supreme Court, in April 2015.[32]

It is too early to say whether the European Union will be more successful in inserting a meaningful Roma integration and social inclusion component into the 2014–2020 operational programs than it has been in the past. Certainly the European Commission is pressuring governments to do this, but, at the moment, the outcome is unclear.

A quarter of a century after Roma segregation in Europe resurfaced as a major public issue, questions about how to reverse this dangerous trend remain as open as ever. One major question is whether the Roma plight is best addressed as an individual or as an ethnic group human rights issue—given that many Roma are well integrated into the majority community and reject ethnic collective human rights methods. Another issue relates to the appropriate balance between grass-roots community mobilization and hard-nosed professional development advocacy. Clearly Roma integration and social inclusion advocacy must be based on skilled budgetary projections and well-informed, professional policy proposals. Political action needs to come from

Roma communities, including those that are particularly marginalized and disenfranchised, as well as from powerful political constituencies, such as the leadership of the European Union. Input from the national political leadership is, alas, often a weak link in the chain. None of the new EU member states, and only a few Balkan countries, have parties in power or near power that could promote a rights-respecting attitude and show positive leadership in tackling Roma segregation and social decline. And yet, ironically, this approach would benefit the majority community as much as it disenfranchised Roma. For any prospect of success in advancing this agenda, both grass-roots and institutional leadership and advocacy are essential.

PART IV

The Enduring Challenge of Tackling
Anti-Roma Institutional
Discrimination and Popular Racism
in Contemporary Europe:
A Comparative Analysis

Chapter 8

Anti-Roma Violence, Hate Speech, and Discrimination in the New Europe: Czech Republic, Slovakia, and Hungary

Will Guy

Modern Roots of Anti-Roma Hostility

Anti-Roma antagonism is nothing new. Hostility against Roma has existed since the very early days of Roma arrival in Europe. Despite having lived in Europe for more than six centuries, Roma have generally been viewed as dark-skinned aliens. As several chapters in this book confirm,[1] recent upsurges of aggression and hate speech in Western Europe have mostly been prompted by influxes of Roma migrants related to the 2004 and 2007 phases of European Union enlargement. Anti-Roma violence in Italy, France, and the United Kingdom has included state-sanctioned razing of clusters of temporary dwellings (rendering their occupants homeless) and attempts to deport nonindigenous Roma migrants. (Elena Rozzi's chapter in this volume illustrates the repercussions of these grave instances in Italy.) Though Roma made up a very small percentage of those migrating to Western Europe both before and after the economic crisis of 2008, their arrival from Central and Eastern European (CEE) countries to EU states, whether as asylum seekers prior to EU enlargement or later as economic migrants, generated wholly disproportionate and uniformly hostile coverage in the popular media.[2] This chapter concentrates on events since 1989, in three CEE countries where physical assaults on Roma have manifested on a greater, more murderous scale than in Western Europe. Though by no means confined to the Czech Republic, Slovakia, and Hungary, targeted crime against Roma is on the rise in these countries.

Following the collapse of Communist rule in 1989, people living in areas characterized by obsolete heavy industry or labor-intensive agriculture became victims of structural change. These populations suffered widespread unemployment as rust belt industries shut down and agriculture became privatized in the rapid transition to a market economy. Among these workers and their families, the Roma people were some of those hardest hit. Decades of structural discrimination in the areas of education and employment had left them unable to benefit from opportunities in the market economy. Often the first to lose their jobs and the last to be reemployed, many Roma breadwinners became dependent on state benefits. Some sought work in the informal economy at minimal wages, while, as the media widely reported, others turned to crime.[3]

The plight of the Roma reinforced popular prejudices painting them as inherently criminal and lazy, parasites who were unwilling to work and content to live on petty theft and welfare support to the detriment of their non-Roma fellow citizens. Roma were sometimes accused of deliberately having many children to maximize their income from child benefits. It was no coincidence that anti-Roma feelings were strong—and extremist demonstrations, prevalent—in areas where general unemployment was high. During times of generalized economic insecurity, Roma have commonly been viewed as an undeserving drain on limited state resources.[4]

Of course anti-Roma hostility had also existed during the four decades of Communist rule following the Second World War, when many believed that Roma had been unfairly favored by the authorities. At a time when public funding had been diverted from housing and consumer goods in order to establish the heavy industries central to the Soviet economic model, programs to rehouse Roma from their previous overcrowded and unsanitary living conditions created particular resentment. While fear of the totalitarian regimes curbed more overt anti-Roma discrimination, once those repressive powers were removed, citizens felt able to voice their opinions freely and act on them. Resulting sporadic racist attacks and vilification by extremists were soon accompanied by growing residential, social, and educational segregation.

This account focuses on the European Union as the key political body ultimately responsible for providing a framework for Roma integration in Europe, rather than other involved supranational organizations. However, as Andrzej Mirga and other contributors acknowledge in their chapters in this volume, the United Nations, the Organization for Security and Co-operation in Europe (OSCE), with its Office for Democratic Institutions and Human Rights (ODIHR), and the Council of Europe (CoE) as well as several international NGOs, have all addressed the increase in anti-Roma hate crimes and hate speech in their commitments and recommendations.

EU Enlargement and Its Aftermath

To ensure their political and economic security, many countries newly liberated from the Soviet bloc joined NATO and the European Union. To earn EU membership, specific criteria had to be satisfied including "stability of institutions guaranteeing democracy, the rule of law, human rights and respect for and protection of minorities."[5] To help applicants meet these requirements, the European Commission cofinanced programs aimed at improving the living conditions, employment, education, health, and, not least, the safety of marginalized Roma. At the same time, all CEE countries were bound by commitments and recommendations made by organizations they had joined such as the OSCE, the Council of Europe, and the UN. For example, the CoE's *Framework Convention for the Protection of National Minorities* required all signatories "to promote, in all areas of economic, social, political and cultural life, full and effective equality" for minorities.[6]

The European Union also strengthened its safeguards protecting racial and ethnic minorities by adopting the Race Equality Directive in 2000—an EU-wide law empowering the commission to take action against direct and indirect discrimination and harassment.[7] As it pertains to Roma, this measure authorized legal action both in cases of discrimination, most importantly in the areas of education, housing, and employment, as well as in cases of physical and verbal abuse. The EU commitment to nondiscrimination and equality was further affirmed the same year by the adoption of the Charter of Fundamental Rights,[8] eventually incorporated into EU law by the 2009 Lisbon Treaty.[9]

Though their domestic programs to benefit Roma had achieved little significant change, the Czech Republic, Slovakia, and Hungary were still among the ten new countries admitted to the European Union in 2004. As part of the accession process, these countries had been required to transpose EU antidiscrimination law into their domestic laws, measures which in principle offered Roma greater protection. Furthermore, as EU member states, these countries now had access to greater financial resources to improve the situation of their Roma citizens in the form of structural and cohesion funds. These resources—around a third of the EU's budget—were intended to reduce development disparities between regions and member states by financing training to boost employment, infrastructure improvements, rural development, education reform, better access to health care services and, since 2009, housing initiatives for marginalized communities. In his chapter, Andrzej Mirga examines the impact of these funds.[10]

In 2007 Bulgaria and Romania also became EU members. This EU enlargement led to highly publicized clashes between Roma migrants from these countries—the poorest in the European Union—and local security forces in Italy and France, acting on government instructions to expel them. In response to these events, the Council of the EU, the EU's most powerful body, and a coalition of international and national NGOs, including the grassroots, umbrella network for European Roma (European Roma Grassroots Organisations Network, ERGO), put intense pressure on the commission to take action.[11] Eventually, in 2011, the commission introduced *An EU Framework for National Roma Integration Strategies up to 2020*, which required all member states to produce a set of integrated policy measure.[12] These measures were designed to strengthen efforts toward Roma inclusion by 2020, by improving access to education, employment, health care, and housing. Important though these measures were, they did not grapple with the need to build political will in each country to promote inclusion: the commission insisted that its role was supervisory and that ultimate responsibility for successful inclusion rested with the member states.

In the meantime, take-up of structural funds for Roma by CEE countries remained low. A 2009 report on progress noted that "Slovakia received by far the worst ranking, followed by the Czech Republic and Hungary."[13] Monitoring was also carried out by the OSCE, which in its 2003 Action Plan had recommended that participating states should act to combat racism and discrimination and improve the conditions of their Roma populations, especially in the area of equal access to education.[14] Its first progress assessment in 2008 emphasized the need for participating states to increase their efforts. Despite these encouragements, the inclusion strategies did not make much of an impact on the situation of Roma. In 2013, the European Roma Policy

Coalition concluded, "The majority of these strategies were weak, not implemented, and failed to deliver inclusion, with systematic and ongoing racism and discrimination [continuing] against Roma within the EU."[15]

The commission, as the EU's executive arm responsible for policy implementation, sought to persuade member states to replicate examples of good practice. International and national NGOs, including Roma and pro-Roma NGOs, continued to raise the alarm about the mounting levels of violence and discrimination against Roma. Amnesty International published a chilling report listing serious attacks on Roma in Hungary in 2008 and 2009 and criticizing the authorities' failure to acknowledge that these crimes were racially motivated.[16] The critical state of affairs in Hungary prompted OSCE ODIHR to organize a field assessment visit in 2009.[17]

Contrary to expectations, CEE national strategy plans paid relatively little attention to violence against Roma. A series of violent anti-Roma demonstrations across the region led by far-right groups, coupled with slow progress in realizing National Roma Inclusion Strategies, highlighted the need for effective countermeasures. Attempts were made in the Czech Republic, Slovakia, and Hungary to ban extremist organizations with mixed results. The response of the authorities to demonstrations and violent attacks has been inconsistent.

The Czech government has monitored extremism in annual reports, and police have protected Roma from far-right demonstrations.[18] Although some successful prosecutions were brought against hate crimes in all three countries, in Hungary, where eighty-four cases of "violence against members of a community" were investigated between 2005 and 2009, "only one case was indicted and made it to the court." Likewise in the same period for "'incitement against a community' only one case reached courts annually."[19] Meanwhile in 2014, in line with its 2003 Action Plan, OSCE ODIHR organized meetings "to prevent police abuse and violence against Roma and Sinti people and to improve trust and confidence in the police among Roma and Sinti people."[20] Its follow-up 2009 Action Plan renewed calls for promoting tolerance and combating prejudice. However, its subsequent assessment in 2013 reported that, in spite of some positive developments, the period since 2009 had been "dominated by negative trends, including a disturbing number of hate crimes against Roma, the use of extremist anti-Roma rhetoric, and continuing reports of police ill-treatment."[21]

The deteriorating situation was further exposed by research from the European Union Agency of Fundamental Rights (FRA), an agency charged with providing expert advice to EU institutions and member states and ensuring protection of the basic rights of people living in the European Union. FRA published a report based on "the first EU-wide survey to ask 23,500 individuals with an ethnic and minority background about their experiences of discrimination and criminal victimization in everyday life" during the previous twelve months.[22] According to the report, Roma and sub-Saharan Africans constituted the highest percentage of those reporting assaults, threats, and serious harassment with a perceived racist motive. Roma in CEE countries featured prominently.

In December 2013, the Council of the European Union issued a stern recommendation "on effective Roma integration measures in the member states," prefaced by a list of EU treaties prohibiting discrimination on ethnic, gender, or social grounds. The section on antidiscrimination called for adoption of the following measures: desegregation, avoidance of illegal forced evictions, protection of women and children, and combating prejudice including "anti-Roma rhetoric and hate speech." It also referred member states to examine the case law of the European Court of Human Rights in order to check the legality of their current procedures.[23] In the same year, the commission sent country-specific recommendations with concern for their treatment of Roma to five member states—Bulgaria, the Czech Republic, Hungary, Romania, and Slovakia.

In short, after EU enlargements, much official attention was placed on strengthening safeguards protecting racial and ethnic minorities. However, programs to benefit Roma achieved little significant change and take-up of structural funds for Roma by CEE countries remained low. Despite the importance of these measures, the problem of political will to promote inclusion has continued to be a difficulty.

Forms of Extremism

Since 1989, overt expressions of anti-Roma extremism—including traumatizing physical attacks on Roma and demonstrations by neo-fascist groups—have occurred regularly in the CEE region. From 2000 on, far-right paramilitary groups, linked to extremist political parties, have also organized repeated demonstrations. These have usually been organized in neighborhoods already experiencing conflict between Roma and non-Roma communities, with the paramilitaries claiming to defend the non-Roma community against "gypsy criminality" in the face of alleged government failure to take effective action.

Hate speech has been widespread, underpinning and provoking both violence and discriminatory acts. "Gypsies to the gas chambers" has been a frequent chant at demonstrations, a threat that harks back to the extermination of an estimated half million Roma in Nazi concentration camps.[24] While hate speech is overtly and blatantly racist, coded statements conveying similar meanings in more insidious ways have also proliferated. The extreme right has spoken openly of Roma as congenital parasites but, more worryingly, mainstream politicians at the national and local level, as well as the media, have conveyed similar messages, in implicit but readily understandable form. Politicians have taken advantage of space created by existing racist discourse, particularly at election times to turn the Roma into convenient scapegoats responsible for growing social inequality.[25] While it is extremists who have made the headlines, influential politicians, judges, police forces, and much of the general population continue to hold similar views. Public opinion polls have consistently shown that Roma are the most despised group of all. Despite a slight decrease in the prevalence of negative opinions between 1991 and 2009, the proportion of those with unfavorable views of Roma was still at discouraging levels in 2009: 84 percent in Czech Republic, 78 percent in Slovakia, and 69 percent in Hungary.[26]

Physical Assaults

Assaults on Roma began soon after the rigid controls of Communist regimes were replaced by the permissive freedoms of embryonic democracies. Between the end of 1989 and May 1995, an estimated twenty-seven Roma died as a result of racist attacks in the Czech lands alone, while similar fatalities occurred in Slovakia.[27] In more recent years, the Czech Republic, Hungary, and Slovakia have seen some of the worst cases of anti-Roma violence, including fatalities and serious injuries, attacks on children, and the use of guns, knives, firebombs, and hand grenades.[28] The gruesome nature of some of the murders, along with subsequent messages of support from some in the majority population, underscores the vehemence of ongoing anti-Roma hatred.

In 2008 and 2009 four Hungarians, motivated by what they saw as failure by the state to suppress "Gypsy crime," committed twenty attacks before they were apprehended.[29] This group murdered six Roma in their homes, including a five-year-old child, and seriously injured five others. On some of these occasions, they set fire to Roma houses with Molotov cocktails and then shot the fleeing occupants. For months, police rejected the hypothesis that these were linked racist assaults, even though the methods of attack were similar. When the assailants eventually came to trial, the charges initially made no mention of racist motives.

In 2010 in Slovakia, an unemployed army reservist shot and killed six members of a Roma family, including a twelve-year-old boy, before turning his gun on himself. Soon afterward, graffiti were scrawled at the site of the shooting. The graffiti praised and thanked him for his deed.[30]

In 2012 in the Czech Republic, a Roma man looking for scrap metal was shot in the head with a crossbow. His killer was sentenced to ten years imprisonment for manslaughter, his plea of self-defense having been rejected—not helped by his statement that "if the people he believed were thieves had been 'white,' he would definitely not have behaved as he did."[31] He also expressed his appreciation for public support from a demonstration organized by the ultra-right Workers Social Justice Party (Dělnická Strana Sociální Spravedlnosti, DSSS) and a petition by residents of his neighborhood stating that "in his situation they would have done exactly the same thing."[32]

These vignettes exemplify the current spate of murderous attacks on Roma. As disturbing as the attacks themselves is the fact that sections of the majority population responded not with outrage but with overt support for the killers. Reflecting on the 2010 shootings by the army reservist, a Slovak Roma activist commented bitterly: "To me the reaction of . . . society has been worse than the killings themselves. Rather than focusing on the killer the message has been: the shooting was bad but these Roma he killed were bad too."[33]

Ultra-Right Parties and Paramilitary Groups

After 1989, ultra-right groups emerged at different times with varying success in CEE countries.[34] While anti-Roma discourse was sometimes the most prominent plank in their electoral platforms, right-wing extremists have also been hostile to Jews, immigrants, and indigenous ethnic minorities. Ultra-right political parties, dating from the early 1990s, were later followed by more aggressively militant anti-Roma parties and civic organizations. Some had associated paramilitary wings displaying explicitly neo-Nazi emblems and uniforms. Explaining the appearance of this phenomenon across the

CEE region, Merin Abbass argues that "Especially in hard times of financial and economic crisis, right-wing extremists seek to benefit from people's insecurity and fear and to exploit them for their own political aims."[35] These parties have had some success at the ballot box; however, in spite of their populist rhetoric, most have remained marginal—at least in parliamentary representation.

Basing his reflections on Slovakia but arguing a broad applicability, Tomáš Nociar identified a common feature of many CEE extremist organizations. They "operate[d] on the border between constitutional conformity and right-wing extremism" and sometimes exploit legal confusions.[36] Attempts by the state to ban such parties and organizations often result in the prompt emergence of relabeled, but functionally identical bodies. Undoubtedly nationalist sentiments expressed by some within the ranks of government and the judiciary have played their part in subverting the political resolve to persevere with legal challenges.

In Hungary, uniquely, an extremist party has become so well established that it can no longer be described as marginal.[37] With the support of one in five Hungarian voters following the 2014 election, Jobbik became the main opposition party. Here the boundaries between right-wing extremism and mainstream "center-right" politics have become so blurred that the two groups could almost be said to have merged. The presence of racists in governing Czech and Slovak coalitions has made no equivalent impact.

Czech Republic

The Worker's Party, inspired by National Socialist principles (that is, Nazism), has proclaimed the inherent criminality of certain ethnic minorities, especially Roma and Vietnamese. A center-right Czech government tried and failed to ban the party in 2009, having neglected to present sufficient evidence of "its antidemocratic aims, xenophobic, racist, and chauvinist program, and involvement with the violent actions of banned neo-Nazi groups." The following year, the Supreme Administrative Court upheld a more carefully prepared ban by a new caretaker technocrat government. In response, the party simply resurrected itself as the Workers' Party for Social Justice (DSSS) and retained many of the same aims and programs.[38]

Electoral marginality has not meant that these parties lack influence. Though it only won 1.14 percent of the votes in the 2010 parliamentary elections, the DSSS party has gained publicity by staging confrontational marches in localities with Roma inhabitants. A regular feature of DSSS activism, these marches aim not only to intimidate Roma, but also to provoke clashes with the security forces, enabling DSSS "defenders" in local Czech communities to win sympathy as victims of police brutality. Popular support for these marches has grown, prompting the Romea civic association to write an open letter appealing for dialogue in 2013 to non-extremist participants in these demonstrations.[39]

Slovakia

The most significant nationalist player in Slovakia has not been a political party but a civic organization. Slovak Solidarity (Slovenská Pospolitosť Národná Strana, Slovak Solidarity-National Party, henceforth SP) raised its public profile from 2003 onward when its members began to wear uniforms. The government countered this initiative, provoking a series of clashes between SP members and the police. These incidents "culminated in a ban being imposed on [this party] . . . in March 2006 because of its antidemocratic character." A further attempt in 2008 to close down the parent SP civil organization failed and "served only to mobilize its members and sympathizers."[40]

In 2009, following a series of high-profile marches led by Marián Kotleba to protest against alleged "gypsy crime," the SP founded a new political party, called the People's Party—Our Slovakia (Ľudová Strana Naše Slovensko, ĽSNS). Although the ĽSNS only gained 1.33 percent of the votes in the 2010 parliamentary elections, in November 2013 Kotleba was unexpectedly elected governor of the Banská Bystrica region, an area with high unemployment and low wages. His manifesto vowed to fight "unfair favoritism of Gypsy parasites."[41] Political analysts tried to explain the shock defeat of the ruling party's front-runner by suggesting that Kotleba's success "was fuelled partly by anti-Roma sentiments and partly by the legitimization of nationalist discourse by [current premier] Robert Fico's first government," in the words of a writer for the *Slovak Spectator*.[42] This coalition had included ultra-nationalist Ján Slota, who recommended dealing with Roma "with a long whip in a small yard."[43] The *Slovak Spectator* article added that Kotleba had "frequently organized and participated in anti-Roma demonstrations or marches commemorating the Nazi-allied wartime Slovak state" and "has been detained and charged repeatedly for crimes including racial defamation."[44] One populist strategy he adopted was attempting to demolish a Roma settlement built illegally on land that a supporter had gifted Kotleba so that he could claim ownership rights as justification for the destruction.[45]

Hungary

Until 2009, Hungary had a Social Democrat (SD) government and was regarded as the most progressive CEE country for promoting initiatives targeting Roma integration. Following the secretly taped admission by the SD prime minister that he had lied about the dire state of the economy during the 2006 electoral campaign, the center-right Fidesz party won 53 percent of the popular vote in 2010. The previously marginal ultra-right Movement for a Better Hungary (Jobbik Magyarországért Mozgalom, henceforth Jobbik) won 17 percent—only 2 percent less than the previous SD governing party. In the 2014 election, Fidesz retained its two-thirds majority, while Jobbik strengthened its position gaining 21 percent of the votes. Although this was less than the 25 percent won by the center-left alliance, the partners in that coalition separated into their own factions after the election, making Jobbik the second largest Hungarian party.[46]

In 2010 Jobbik's electoral platform was predominantly anti-Roma, and combatting "Roma criminality" became its main message. Jobbik argued they were the only party that dared speak the truth about the Roma situation. But in increasingly difficult economic circumstances, Fidesz, too, became more overtly nationalistic and anti-Roma, taking advantage of the ideological space Jobbik had created to convey messages echoing Jobbik rhetoric, particularly concerning Roma criminality. Confident of its strength, Jobbik "played down its anti-Semitism and anti-Roma rhetoric" in the 2014 election.[47]

In addition to its members of the Hungarian National Assembly and three seats in the European Parliament, there were four Jobbik mayors, one of whom—in a discussion on "the possible outcome of an unavoidable civil war"—named Jews and Gypsies as "the races which have to be ground up as soon as possible."[48] The party's main support came from non-Roma in areas with a significant Roma presence, particularly in eastern Hungary.

In May 2007, Jobbik formed a uniformed paramilitary wing, the Hungarian Guard (Magyar Gárda), with Jobbik's leader, Gábor Vona, serving as its head. As in the Czech Republic and Slovakia, extremist groups—with the support of Jobbik—organized marches and demonstrations to intimidate local Roma inhabitants in places where there had allegedly been incidents between ethnic groups. In 2008 and 2009, court rulings ordered the dissolution of the Hungarian Guard for "violating [other citizens'] . . . right to dignity and equality" but in response a similar organization—the New Hungarian

Guard (Új Magyar Gárda) —was soon established and continued holding events. Gábor Vona even appeared in parliament wearing its uniform—only slightly altered—with impunity.[49]

In each of the three countries, the political complexion of the party in power has been a factor influencing the strength of government political will to combat anti-Roma extremism. In the Czech Republic and Hungary, Social Democrat-led governments have been relatively willing to promote Roma inclusion, though, as Pap has noted, Hungarian politicians of all colors have undoubtedly been influenced by widespread voter anti-Roma antipathy.[50] Thus, though 80 percent of Jobbik voters believe, not surprisingly, that "criminality is in the blood of Gypsies," this view is also held by 59 percent of supporters of other parties.[51]

By contrast in Slovakia, parties regarded as left-wing have been in coalition with nationalists and populists and have been less favorable to Roma inclusion.

Hate Speech and Discrimination in Mainstream Politics

All CEE region states joining the European Union had to adopt antidiscrimination legislation as a condition of entry. The 2008 Framework Decision on Racism and Xenophobia made incitement to racism an EU-wide crime punishable by up to three years' imprisonment.[52] Nevertheless, there was little effective action against right-wing extremist organizations: although neo-Nazis were subject to surveillance, governments tolerated, and at times even defended, radical nationalists.[53]

Leading politicians often implied anti-Roma opinions in discreet ways, but occasionally they spoke out frankly, lending credence to the extremist statements of ultra-right representatives. Racism has been particularly damaging at the local level, where local authorities and mayors have been allowed to assume a leading role in discriminatory acts against Roma communities. Some local authorities have tried to hide the presence of Roma inhabitants by building containing walls between the Roma and majority populations; others have sought to rid themselves of Roma altogether by transferring them to remote areas predominantly inhabited by Roma—in reality, ghettos.

While NGOs have worked to reduce the social exclusion of Roma communities and provide humanitarian aid, they have been powerless to prevent the pressures of gentrification driving the evictions or the exploitation of

Roma tenants in neo-liberal economies, where provision of public housing is not a priority. Intergovernmental organizations (such as the United Nations High Commissioner for Refugees and the United Nations Development Programme [UNDP]) and Roma and pro-Roma networks have responded by documenting these developments and trying to influence governments to oppose them.

Czech Republic

The center-right Czech prime minister from 2010 to June 2013, Petr Nečas, attributed recent economic difficulties to the welfare dependency of "scroungers"—an unambiguous reference that was not lost on the public at large. In fact Eurostat figures suggested that the relatively prosperous Czech Republic was only spending about half the EU average per head on unemployment and disability-related benefits. As one of his first acts after taking power in 2010, Nečas abolished the post of minister for human rights and minorities as "a 'luxury' the country could not afford."[54]

A Czech mayor, Jiří Čunek, was elected to the senate with an overwhelming majority after having evicted Roma families from the town center and rehoused them in portacabins.[55] He characterized his actions as "the removal of an ulcer." Čunek then became leader of the Christian Democratic Party and deputy prime minister in a center-right coalition government, but later resigned after accusations that he had accepted a bribe and had fraudulently claimed social welfare support.[56] In 2012, he was reelected to the Senate and implausibly—having built a political career on racially abusing Roma—elected chair of the Senate Subcommittee on Human Rights and Equal Opportunities.[57]

The notorious Matiční Street wall was erected by a North Bohemian local authority, which made the familiar claim that the barrier was protecting other residents from noise and refuse emanating from the Roma inhabitants of an adjacent apartment block. After an outburst of protest from international and domestic organizations, the council complied with the Czech parliament's order to demolish the barrier. Rather than emulating this local authority's example and attracting unwelcome publicity in the process, other Czech councils have preferred to adopt the alternative strategy of discreet "ethnic cleansing." Roma families with rent arrears have been evicted from city centers to peripheral areas already afflicted by multiple deprivation, raising still further the risk of inter-ethnic tensions.[58]

Slovakia

In Slovakia, some politicians have warned that the majority population was in danger of being swamped by rapidly rising Roma numbers. During his 2002 election campaign, the current Slovak prime minister, Róbert Fico, promised to "actively control the irresponsible growth in the birth rate of the Romany population."[59] Justifying a reduction in family allowances, he reportedly claimed that "The Roma found out that it was profitable to have children due to family allowances. We cannot turn a blind eye to this. . . . If we let it be as it is now, I can guarantee that in ten years we will have one million Roma here."[60] This poisonous rhetoric was consistent with the initiative taken by some Slovak medical staff to sterilize Roma women without their consent or knowledge. The European Court of Human Rights condemned this "inhuman" conduct (referred to as a form of genocide by some) in 2011.[61] Nevertheless, similar sterilizations have taken place in the Czech Republic and Hungary.[62] In her chapter in this volume, Andrea Oprea discusses this pattern of compulsory sterilization as an example of contemporary systemic racism against Roma.[63]

In 2004, the year Slovakia introduced its antidiscrimination act, a new cap on child benefits, deliberately targeted at Roma, halved the income of large families. Roma demonstrated in fourteen towns, holding banners proclaiming "We want to work, not to be beggars," while some also took food from shops. The government mobilized over two thousand police and soldiers to restore order with water cannon, cattle-prods, and truncheons.[64]

By mid-2013, fourteen containing walls had been erected in Slovakia.[65] The most substantial case of ghettoization was the demolition of the Roma quarter in Košice, Slovakia's second largest city, as well as the removal of its inhabitants to bleak concrete blocks in the Luník IX district. The former mayor, Rudolf Schuster—later president of Slovakia—was responsible. A subsequent Košice mayor concluded, "If you know for a fact that a certain group of people is criminal and intolerable, of course you will not want them for neighbors. Besides, Roma don't pay the rent."[66] As the CoE's Human Rights commissioner noted "racist and notably anti-Roma discourse, sometimes of a distinctively aggressive nature, is still common among mainstream politicians in Slovakia."[67]

Hungary

Evictions have taken place in Hungary too, particularly in Budapest, targeting poor people in general in addition to the Roma community in particular. Hate speech in Hungarian mainstream discourse has been especially striking. For example, in July 2012, an unemployed Roma was arrested as the suspected murderer of a female police psychologist. Gábor Vona, Jobbik party leader and leader of the opposition, then demanded the death penalty, reportedly asserting that 90 percent of all murderers are "Gypsies," while 100 percent of all victims are Hungarians.[68] Two months later, Fidesz, the party in power, discussed reintroduction of the death penalty, which would have contravened both the Hungarian Constitution and EU law. The police chief of Miskolc (a former center for heavy industry, with Hungary's largest Roma population) had expressed similar prejudices, stating that all burglaries in December and January 2009 had been committed by people of "Gypsy origin." He was removed from his post but "quickly reinstated after thousands demonstrated publicly to support him." Later that year, a police trade union allied itself to Jobbik, and its secretary-general stood as a Jobbik candidate in the European elections.[69]

On New Year's Eve, 2012, two Hungarian youths were stabbed. Although only one of the assailants was Roma, a founding member of Fidesz and close friend of Prime Minister Orban, Zsolt Bayer, wrote in a newspaper linked to government, as Lydia Gall reported: "A significant part of the Roma are unfit for coexistence. They are not fit to live among people. These Roma are animals, and they behave like animals. . . . These animals shouldn't be allowed to exist. In no way. That needs to be solved—immediately and regardless of the method." Neither Fidesz nor the prime minister condemned Bayer or suggested he should be expelled from the party, though the deputy prime minister voiced his opposition to the statements made. Meanwhile the newspaper supported the author's right to free speech.[70]

Jews as well as Roma have found themselves the target of racist language. Bayer had earlier referred to Jews "as stinking excrement called something like Cohen."[71] In November 2012, a Jobbik member and vice chairman of parliament's foreign affairs committee asked for a list of Jews in parliament and government as they might "present a national security risk to Hungary."[72]

Countering Anti-Roma Violence, Hate Speech, and Discrimination

The European Commission's 2014 progress report admitted that "Thirteen years after the EU's landmark antidiscrimination directives were adopted in

2000, discrimination against Roma is still widespread."[73] The report drew attention to the 2013 recommendation of the Council of the EU mentioned earlier. The recommendation suggested that in future the EU would take firm action to enforce its antidiscrimination laws. However, this strong stance had been qualified by the proviso that Roma integration measures should be carried out "while fully respecting the principle of subsidiarity and the Member States' primary responsibility in this area."[74]

Member states are also now required to earmark 20 percent of their European Social Fund (ESF) budget until 2020 for social inclusion, although they have no obligation to declare how much funding they have used. Meanwhile, doubts remain both about take-up and the extent to which Roma would be effectively targeted, "taking into account the fact that data collection on ethnic grounds can be a sensitive issue and acknowledging that Member States should choose their own monitoring methods."[75] A UNDP report on ESF usage in Slovakia concluded that although Roma were declared as beneficiaries, the extent to which they had actually benefited from ESF funding could not be measured.[76]

Lack of political will can be compounded by other factors such as poor organization and planning. The commission's progress report argued that "Roma-specific problems are generally not due to gaps in legislation, but rather to its implementation."[77] The accompanying EC Staff Working Document commented sharply on Romania's shortcomings: "Implementation and mainstreaming of many legally adopted policies and programs in the field of social inclusion have been delayed, due to a lack of implementation capacity and funding and the absence of strong commitment by public authorities."[78] A 2014 Amnesty International report expressed deep skepticism. It noted that although the commission was responsible for ensuring compliance with EU laws, it had "to date failed to take clear and decisive action to address discrimination and violence against Roma in member states," in spite of the availability of infringement procedures as a legal tool.[79] While atmospheric pollution had triggered EU legal proceedings, violations of fundamental human rights, such as hate crimes, had not. Roma citizens of the European Union were the losers—but so too were their countries.

At the national level, CEE member states that have signed up to pursue the goal of Roma inclusion, have failed to achieve firm all-party agreements to pursue integration policies irrespective of election results. Spain, for example, had managed this and consequently was able to implement projects eradicating shantytowns by rehousing Roma among the wider population as well as job creation schemes, in spite of severe recession marked by high levels of house repossession and unemployment. By contrast, the technocratic Czech government's planned reform of the much criticized practice of placing Roma children in special schools for those with learning difficulties was blocked by its center-right successor. During this period, an OSCE ODIHR field assessment of educational provision for Roma children in the Czech Republic called on the government to end their marginalization and segregation by taking positive steps to implement the 2010 National Action Plan for Inclusive Education.[80] The report also pointed out that OSCE participants, including the Czech Republic, had committed themselves to introduce school desegregation programs as advocated in the 2003 OSCE Action Plan.

A report from the EU Agency of Fundamental Rights has rightly noted that small, local initiatives can be as important as large scale ones, "precisely because they are small and develop valuable integrated micro-level strategies that work at the level of real people rather than more abstract notions of 'Roma.'"[81] Furthermore, key areas like housing are the competence of municipalities in most member states. Networks such as the European Alliance of Cities and Regions for Roma Inclusion have partnered with the Dosta! campaign to bring non-Roma closer to Roma citizens, offering prizes for instances of best practice. Successful, long-established CEE projects, where close cooperation between supportive local authorities and Roma representatives has been a crucial factor, have included:

- *Ostrava* (Czech Republic), where flooding in 1997 prompted an NGO initiative to rehouse Roma and non-Roma victims together. Future tenants participated in the planning and construction work in the move from temporary containers to purpose-built rental accommodation. This project developed into a professional organization providing social and community services for various socially excluded groups, including Roma.[82]
- *Šumiac* (Slovakia), where the local council made a positive decision that Slovak villagers and Roma inhabitants had mutual interests in a joint future. Consequently, the mayor welcomed participation in Slovakia's first Roma infrastructure program as an opportunity both to provide better water for the whole population and to encourage Roma to move into the main village. Accompanying projects resulted in a shared community center and non-segregated education.[83]

- *Hódmezővásárhely* (Hungary), where an equal opportunity plan included desegregating education by busing, which resulted in improved educational outcomes overall. The plan also involved the replacement of Roma settlements with newly built public housing for low-income families, including Roma; job creation schemes; and vocational education.[84]

These are exceptions, however, and a number of CEE Roma have considered migration to the West as their best hope, provoking hostile reactions in much of the popular media. Nevertheless, some local authorities and institutions in Western Europe have adopted a positive approach to Roma migrants, understanding that most have come to find work and escape the poverty and racism of their homelands. While French national governments have deported Roma migrants, several local authorities, such as Bobigny near Paris, have tried to protect and rehouse them. Meanwhile, Spain has adopted the most inclusive approach of all, simply requiring migrant EU citizens to register and prove their identity in order to gain "an unconditional right to residence."[85] Unfortunately, little media attention has been paid to studies showing how Czech and Slovak Roma children, formerly in special schools but later integrated in mainstream schools in the UK, soon caught up with their non-Roma peers.[86]

In spite of positive local initiatives, the only effective way to reduce fear and tensions in areas of multiple deprivation in CEE countries would be to directly attack their fundamental causes through systemic reform such as sustained programs of regional development. The World Bank argued that an "emphasis on inclusion policies would complement rights-based approaches by tackling the economic and social barriers that Roma face."[87] European structural funds, if effectively utilized, should result in training and jobs for both young non-Roma and Roma, offering both groups a future without the imperative of emigration to more prosperous regions in their homelands or abroad to Western Europe. Such long-term funding would also underpin inclusive initiatives, including provision of public housing. These measures would need to be accompanied by intercultural education in schools and media campaigns, featuring national and local politicians and Roma NGOs, demonstrating that Roma are a valuable resource. Failing this, if the same minimal rate of progress continues, there will be a real and growing danger of civil strife.[88]

C h a p t e r   9

The Unfulfilled Promise of Educational Opportunity in the United States and Europe: From *Brown v. Board* to *D.H.* and Beyond

James A. Goldston

In both the United States and Europe, the legal struggle of certain disadvantaged groups for educational opportunity has been central to the broader quest for equal justice. Segregated and inferior education—of African Americans in the United States and of Roma in Europe—has been a major cause of life-long inequalities in economic advancement and social welfare. For many, respective efforts to end discrimination and segregation in schools were intended not just to improve opportunities for members of specific populations but also, by expanding legal protection for the most vulnerable, to consolidate the rule of law and human rights for all.

In neither the United States nor Europe has the promise of equal treatment been realized. But the nature, duration, and impact of litigation to challenge school discrimination and segregation on either side of the Atlantic have been starkly different. The effort to contest, end, and reverse the effects of racial segregation in schools has a longer history and a more extensive, if far from perfect, record of impact in the United States than in Europe—both in respect of the levels of educational segregation and the nature of public discourse and acceptance. However, on both sides of the Atlantic, far more is needed to translate the gains of jurisprudence (even if partial and transient) into the reality of educational opportunity for all.

I begin here by recounting the legal campaign against racial segregation of African Americans and the mixed impact of *Brown v. Board of Education* and its progeny.[1] I then describe more recent judicial developments addressing segregation in European schools, which have yet to yield a discernible change in the situation of Roma children. In the third section, I highlight some of the most salient factors that may begin to underlie the different outcomes to date of these two major examples of cause litigation. I conclude the chapter with a brief summary of steps required to build upon recent jurisprudential advances in bringing about more equal schooling for Roma. (Another chapter in this volume, "Toward the Recognition of Critical Race Theory in Human Rights Law: Romani Women's Reproductive Rights" by Alexandra Oprea, explores the limited outcomes of impact litigation for Roma women.)

Desegregation in the United States: Civil Rights for African Americans

The U.S. narrative centers on *Brown v. Board of Education*, which is perhaps the paradigmatic example of strategic litigation to pursue social change. During the first half of the twentieth century, racial segregation in university, secondary, and primary education was the law in numerous states, principally though not exclusively in the old Confederacy. A concerted legal campaign launched by the NAACP began to yield change in the mid-1930s when the Court of Appeals of Maryland in 1936 ordered desegregation of the University of Maryland Law School, followed by the U.S. Supreme Court in 1938 of the Law School at the University of Missouri.[2] In 1950, the Supreme Court struck down laws in Oklahoma and Texas, which had mandated racially segregated graduate education.[3]

The crowning achievement in this campaign, *Brown* outlawed racial segregation in primary schools and overturned a fifty-eight-year-old precedent suggesting that segregated schools could be "separate but equal."[4] Interpretations of *Brown* and its legacy are far from uniform, and they have varied over time. But even those deeply critical of the limited progress litigation has had in desegregating U.S. schools acknowledge *Brown*'s power in galvanizing a national conversation about race relations and the place of race in American public life.

With respect to the problem most directly concerned—educational segregation—*Brown*'s record is mixed at best. In the first decade after *Brown*, the decision was met with massive resistance in the South—a systematic effort, organized at the highest levels of state governments, to defy *Brown*'s command. As a result, little progress was made in desegregating schools during this time. Scholars Gary Orfield and Chungmei Lee have observed that "serious desegregation of the black South only came after Congress and the Johnson Administration acted powerfully under the 1964 Civil Rights Act."[5]

It took fourteen years for the Supreme Court to make clear, in *Green v. County School Board*,[6] that freedom of choice plans which allowed students to choose where to attend school were insufficient to eliminate segregation. Two years later, *Swann v. Charlotte-Mecklenburg Board of Education*,[7] told state and local governments to take proactive steps, which could include busing, to integrate schools. Even so, desegregation in many cities occurred only in the 1970s. Even this was limited outside the South, in part because the Supreme Court began to move away from vigorous integration, starting with its ruling in 1974 in *Milliken v. Bradley*, which held that court-ordered busing across school district lines was not permissible without clear evidence of an intent to discriminate on grounds of race in the drawing of district lines.[8]

From the mid-1960s through the late 1980s, notwithstanding the Supreme Court's caution, federal government support for integration brought about increased integration. By the late 1980s, the high point of desegregation, 44 percent of black students nationwide attended majority white schools, and they enjoyed increasing graduation rates and a narrowing achievement gap.[9]

However, the early 1990s marked a distinct retrenchment in Supreme Court jurisprudence,[10] which has continued over the past two decades amid increasingly aggressive social and political resistance to race-conscious remedies for segregation. As a result, during this time the United States has experienced steady resegregation of both black and Latino students.[11] National levels of exposure in public schools of black students to white students have returned to those of the late 1960s, and Latinos have likewise experienced intensifying levels of isolation from other ethnic groups.[12] Although the seventeen states of the old South that had legalized segregation at the time of Brown are "still far less segregated than in the 1950s," Orfield and Lee note, "the country's rapidly growing population of Latino and black students is more segregated than they have been since the 1960s and [society is] going backward faster in the areas where integration was most far-reaching."[13] On the historic ruling's fiftieth anniversary, it was noted, "While *Brown* condemned segregated public schools as 'inherently unequal,' public schools today persist in remaining racially unbalanced in many large metropolitan areas."[14]

As a result of the 2007 Supreme Court decision striking down even voluntary desegregation by school districts (in which Chief Justice Roberts, joined by three other justices, famously declared, "The way to stop discrimination on the basis of race is to stop discriminating on the basis of race"),[15] "School desegregation . . . has . . . been radically constrained."[16] In a despairing note, Orfield and Lee conclude, "Nearly 40 years after the assassination of Dr. Martin Luther King, Jr., we have now lost almost all the progress made in the decades after his death in desegregating our schools."[17]

If *Brown* has yet to end segregation in schools, what of its other impacts? Particularly in the first quarter century after *Brown* was decided, many assessments viewed the case and its achievements as momentous—not so much for its effect on students, but rather for its reverberations throughout American politics and society. Richard Kluger's 1976 landmark study of *Brown* was emblematic of this tendency, concluding, "Probably no case ever to come before the nation's highest tribunal affected more directly the minds, hearts and daily lives of so many Americans. . . . The decision marked the turning point in America's willingness to face the consequences of centuries of racial discrimination."[18] According to Kluger, *Brown* "meant that black rights had suddenly been reborn under a new law. Blacks' value as human beings had been changed overnight by the declaration of the nation's highest court. At a stroke, the Justices had severed the remaining cords of de facto slavery. The Negro could no longer be fastened with the status of official pariah."[19]

Kluger was not alone. Another leading commentator observed, "*Brown* may be the most important political, social and legal event in America's twentieth-century history. Its greatness lay in the enormity of the injustice it condemned, in the entrenched sentiment it challenged, in the immensity of law it both created and overthrew."[20] Editors of a leading law review suggested, "No modern case has had a greater impact either on our day-to-day lives or on the structure of our government."[21]

Subsequent assessments have been less categorical. Some scholars have argued that, in fact, given the many other historical trends underway in the 1950s and 1960s, the litigation that led to *Brown* made little difference in respect of discrimination and segregation. For example, Michael Klarman suggests, "From a long-range perspective, racial change in America was inevitable owing to a variety of deep-seated social, political and economic forces."[22] More generally, Gerald Rosenberg observes that "courts had virtually no effect on ending discrimination in the key fields of education, voting, transportation, accommodation and public places, housing. Courageous and praiseworthy decisions were rendered, and nothing changed."[23] Additional commentary has suggested that the field of race discrimination is not alone in having suffered a political and legal backlash in recent years.[24]

Still other observers suggest that, even sixty years after *Brown* was decided, its full effects have yet to be revealed. In Martha Minow's view, over the span of time, "*Brown v. Board of Education* may have more influence on racial justice outside the context of schooling, more influence on schooling outside the context of racial integration, and more significance to law outside of both race and schooling."[25]

Even those who contend that *Brown II* (the ruling on remedies for segregation) and its use of the "all deliberate speed" formula for implementation "removed much of the force of its decision," and that "the important goal of full equality in education . . . was compromised from the beginning and that fifty years after *Brown* there is little left to celebrate," note that *Brown* "marked a critical effort by the Supreme Court to send to the country a strong message: that legalized racial inequality in America would no longer be tolerated."[26] It seems hard to dispute that, whatever the shortcomings of *Brown* and the legal campaign against racial segregation in the schools, "millions of Americans" were "impacted profoundly by the end of legal segregation" which *Brown* ordered.[27] Outside U.S. borders, Richard Goldstone, retired Justice of the South African Constitutional Court, and his law clerk, have written that *Brown* demonstrated "the ability of courts to promote human rights and [of] lawyers to effect social change."[28]

The Challenge to Discrimination Against Roma Children in Europe

In Europe, by contrast, litigation and associated advocacy aimed at challenging discrimination against, and segregation of, Roma children in schools have had far less time to generate impact to date—either on the state of Roma education or the broader discourse around the place of Roma in European societies. As several chapters in this volume confirm, in much of Europe, the pervasive denial of access to quality education has been a continuing obstacle for Roma.[29] Because they or their parents lack proof of identity or any means of transport from isolated ghettos, in some countries many Roma do not attend school at all.[30] In other countries, Roma are segregated into Roma-only schools of lower quality because educational placement simply reproduces preexisting patterns of residential segregation. "Roma-only" classes in some schools reflect often arbitrary and erroneous assessments of language or behavior, or outright racial prejudice. Finally, in a number of countries, many Roma children are streamed for psychological tests, deemed unfit for "normal" education, and shunted into "special" remedial schools and classes for those deemed to suffer from one or another form of developmental, educational, psychological, emotional, social, or other disability. Throughout Europe, Roma children attend school less often than others, remain for shorter periods, and are regularly provided education of substandard quality.

Although Roma live and suffer discrimination in virtually all countries in Europe, in Central and Eastern Europe, where most Roma reside, discrimination and segregation in schools have been most pronounced. The current situation reflects a centuries-long history of oppression. Indeed, in Wallachia and Moldavia, which encompassed much of what is modern-day Romania, Roma were enslaved for hundreds of years.[31]

Prior to the Communist era, Roma children received public education in limited numbers. In a significant number of Communist countries after 1945, education was one of the means by which Roma were assimilated pursuant to an official ideology which aspired to formal equality but avoided acknowledgement or discussion of ethnic difference.

In the Czech Republic, to take one example, it has been reported that these policies lowered the number of Roma with no schooling from 26 percent (men) and 36 percent (women) in 1970 to 3 percent in 1980.[32] Although this effort increased literacy for some, it was often carried out through various forms of segregation, which isolated Roma and ensured that most did not graduate from secondary school. A report for the European Union points out the prevalence of this practice: "Segregation has characterised the education of many Romani children since the 1950s. Discrimination and residential segregation have led to the segregation of Romani children in Roma-only standard schools and classes and in schools for children with mental disabilities."[33] In 1963, the Czech Ministry of Education published instructions concerning the by then widespread placement of "gypsies" (cikáni) into special schools for children with mental disabilities. The Ministry instructed local schools that children without an identified mental disability should not be placed into special schools, while incorrectly placed children should be transferred to regular elementary schools.[34] Yet the mis-assignment of Roma continued. By 1989, Roma accounted for approximately 1.4 percent of the total population,[35] but 40 percent of all pupils at special schools for the mentally disabled.[36] At the time, Roma children were twenty-eight times more likely to be placed into special schools.[37]

Following the end of Communism, ethnic segregation has not materially diminished in most countries of Central and Eastern Europe. In Hungary, for example, an analysis for the United Nations Development Programme (UNDP) found that "the rising autonomy of schools to accept or dismiss students, hand in hand with the introduction of freedom to choose schools, have strengthened educational segregation. The shifting of competencies from the national to regional and local levels gave widened space for institutional discrimination against the Roma, with their overrepresentation in special schools and classes being one of the most debated results."[38]

Data are scarce. A number of factors—including widespread misunderstanding of the requirements of European data protection law, reluctance among many Roma to identify themselves as Roma, and concern grounded in history about the misuse of ethnic data—have perversely reinforced the self-interest of governments who would prefer not to know, or make known, the extent of discrimination and segregation. As studies in recent years have shown, however, Roma children suffer significant educational disadvantages and outcomes compared to other children.[39]

Legal challenges to Roma educational segregation—many of them successful at least in the courtroom—have been brought in at least seven countries. The European Court of Human Rights has condemned discrimination against Roma in access to education in six separate cases—one each from Croatia, the Czech Republic and Hungary, and three from Greece.[40] Domestic courts and/or administrative bodies in Bulgaria, Romania, and Slovakia have also found in favor of Roma students denied equal educational opportunity. All told, as of April 2014, there have been more than thirty cases brought before European courts and/or administrative organs attacking Roma school segregation.[41]

After decades in which de facto Roma segregation in schools throughout Central and Eastern Europe went unnoticed by the courts, this recent comparative flurry of judicial action is welcome. In doctrinal terms, the European Court's first judgment condemning discrimination against Roma in education—in the case of *D.H. v. Czech Republic*—was pathbreaking.[42] The court went out of its way to note that, though its decision was legally binding only on the Czech Republic, the problem of discrimination against Roma in education is of European scope.[43] It is thus all the more important that the ruling advanced non-discrimination jurisprudence under the European Convention on Human Rights in critical ways.

The *D.H.* judgment clarified for the first time that the prohibition against discrimination, contained in Article 14 of the European Convention for Human Rights, applies not only to specific acts, but to systemic practices.[44]

The court did not, as the United Nations Committee on the Elimination of all Forms of Racial Discrimination had, condemn the situation of Roma school assignment as segregation per se.[45] Instead, and perhaps in view of the fact that the European Convention does not mention segregation, the court found that the patterns of overrepresentation of Roma children in "special schools" gave rise to a "strong presumption of indirect discrimination," for which no objective justification existed.[46] However, the court went out of its way to express concern that the discriminatory system of assignment, not only relegated Roma children to "more basic" classes, but "cause[d]" their "segregation": "The Court accepts that the Government's decision to retain the special-school system was motivated by the desire to find a solution for children with special educational needs. However, it shares the disquiet of the other Council of Europe institutions who have expressed concerns about the more basic curriculum followed in these schools *and, in particular, the segregation the system causes* (emphasis added)."[47] The court further brought its interpretation of the prohibition against discrimination in Article 14 in line with European Union law including the Racial Equality Directive,[48] such that, after *D.H.*: (1) Article 14 is seen to bar the indirect discrimination of a general policy or measure which, though couched in neutral terms, generates disproportionately prejudicial effects; (2) intent to discriminate is not an essential element of a claim of discrimination; (3) while they are not required, statistics can be used to establish discrimination; and (4) where an applicant alleging indirect discrimination establishes a rebuttable presumption that the effect of a measure or practice is discriminatory, the burden then shifts to the respondent state to show that the difference in treatment is not discriminatory.

Subsequent cases reaffirmed, and in some ways extended, these principles. In *Oršuš*, where only Roma children were placed in separate primary school classes due to insufficient command of Croatian language, the absence of discriminatory intent did not relieve the state of an obligation to offer an objective justification or a legitimate aim. The court found that neither could be shown, because the system in place lacked adequate legal safeguards such as a clear basis for placing students in special language classes, proper tests, or a program for addressing the special needs of language learners.[49]

In *Horváth and Kiss v. Hungary*, the court followed *D.H.* in finding that, absent an objective and reasonable justification, the overrepresentation due to misdiagnosis of Roma children in special primary schools for persons with "mental disabilities" constituted "indirect discrimination."[50] But the court in *Horváth and Kiss v. Hungary* went further to make explicit that, where members of certain groups have "suffered past discrimination in education with continuing effects, structural deficiencies call for the implementation of positive measures . . . to assist the applicants . . . in following the school curriculum."[51] The court observed that "the misplacement of Roma children in special schools has a long history across Europe."[52] In such circumstances, "the State has specific positive obligations to avoid the perpetuation of past discrimination or discriminative practices disguised in allegedly neutral tests."[53]

In similar fashion, the court in *Lavida and Others v. Greece* found Greece in breach of the non-discrimination guarantee of the Convention, where the relevant authorities had been aware of the existence of racial segregation of Roma children in a school in question, and the need to correct it, and had, without an objective justification, decided "against effective anti-segregation measures."[54]

Each of these cases rested this unprecedented foray into anti-discrimination principles on what the court termed "the vulnerable position of Roma/Gypsies," which "means that special consideration should be given to their needs and their different lifestyle both in the relevant regulatory framework and in reaching decisions in particular cases . . . as a result of their turbulent history and constant uprooting the Roma have become a specific type of disadvantaged and vulnerable minority . . . they therefore require special protection."[55] This rationale (perhaps unintentionally) echoed the famous footnote 4 of the U.S. Supreme Court judgment on *Carolene Products* in its call for special consideration for oppressed minorities. The footnote describes the role of the court as supporting democratic processes, focusing its "more searching judicial inquiry" (in some cases, strict scrutiny) to areas that interfere with those processes, particularly legislation animated by "prejudice against discrete and insular minorities . . . which tends seriously to curtail the operation of those political processes ordinarily to be relied upon to protect minorities."[56] This laid the foundation for the searching inquiry given to *Brown* and other cases. As David Strauss points out, "A good case can be made—and has been made—that *Carolene Products* was the theory of the Supreme Court of the United States under Earl Warren, from the mid-1950s until the late 1960s. The most famous Warren Court decision, of course, was *Brown v. Board of Education*."[57]

At the same time the Strasbourg court was generating these doctrinal advances, Europe's political bodies significantly extended legislative protection against discrimination on grounds of racial or ethnic origin. Examples include:

- from the European Union: the previously mentioned Racial Equality Directive, implements the principle of equal treatment between persons irrespective of racial or ethnic origin; the Charter of Fundamental Rights, Chapter III of which contains various provisions guaranteeing equality and non-discrimination, including Article 21 (prohibiting "Any discrimination based on any ground such as . . . race, colour, ethnic or social origin . . . membership of a national minority");
- from the Council of Europe: Protocol No. 12, an addition to the European Convention on Human Rights extending the nondiscrimination of Article 14 to all legal rights.[58]

These bodies also adopted a series of policy declarations underscoring the extent of discrimination against Roma and the importance of combatting it.[59]

Nonetheless, the situation of Roma education has yet to improve markedly. Court decisions have been inadequately publicized or enforced. In many cases, they have met with indifference or outright resistance.

In *Sampanis and Others v. Greece* (2008), the European court found that denying Roma children from the Psari camp enrollment in primary school in the town of Aspropygros and then placing them in special classes in an annex to the main building—in an environment colored by "racist incidents in the school instigated by the parents of non-Roma children"—amounted to discrimination.[60] Four years later, in *Sampani and Others v. Greece* (2012), a case in the same town with some of the same children,[61] the court noted that there had been no significant changes to the situation that had given rise to the *Sampanis and Others* judgment. Between 2008 and 2010, the school had continued to be attended exclusively by Roma pupils, despite the 2008 finding that this constituted unlawful discrimination.[62]

Not only had there not been implementation, but the mayor of Aspropyrgos, where the school in both *Sampanis* and *Sampani* was located, had rejected a plan to merge two schools to bring about racial integration. In a letter, the mayor reasoned that, since "Gypsies have chosen to live in dumps which they themselves have created" and to "engage in illegal activities," they could not expect "to share the same classrooms as the other pupils of Aspropyrgos."[63]

Perversely, the Committee of Ministers, the Council of Europe's executive body responsible for supervising execution of the court's judgments, had decided in September 2011 to close its examination of the *Sampanis and Others* (2008) case, having found that nearly all of the Roma applicants' children had been enrolled in the school at issue, and that the government had taken satisfactory general measures concerning the admission of Roma children.[64] NGOs continued to maintain that, contrary to the Committee of Ministers' finding, segregation of Roma continued unabated, with resistance by local authorities and non-Roma parents preventing school integration.[65] And despite the finding of discrimination by the authorities in *Lavida* (also in Greece), reports as of late 2013 indicated that the school system there remained segregated, with almost all Roma students attending one school.[66]

In both Bulgaria and Romania, litigation at the domestic level has resulted in findings of discrimination, but these have yielded, at best, uneven results. In 2005, the Sofia District court found that the Bulgarian Ministry of Education, the Sofia Municipality, and School Number 103 impermissibly discriminated against Roma children by taking insufficient measures to ensure that Roma children enjoyed an integrated education.[67] However, while the Bulgarian government has made some efforts to improve equality of access to education, segregation remains persistent.[68] As of 2009, "Roma children with no specific disability continue[d] to be placed in special schools" and "rehabilitation establishments also ha[d] a disproportionate number of Roma children."[69] Bulgaria's *National Roma Integration Strategy for 2012–2020* pledged to integrate Roma children into ethnically mixed schools and improve the quality of schools in predominately Roma communities.[70] It remains to be seen whether policies taken pursuant to these goals will be effective in the face of local resistance to integration.[71]

In Romania, the National Council for Combating Discrimination (NCCD) has on at least one occasion requested that a school end segregation of Roma and non-Roma children (in litigation brought by the NGO Romani

CRISS in 2008, in which the NCCD found that the separation of Roma children in the Josika Mjiklos primary school in Atid into a separate class from non-Roma constituted discrimination).[72] In other cases, local courts have awarded compensation to parents of Roma victims of school discrimination or ordered the NCCD to reopen investigation of alleged school discrimination. For example in 2010, the Craiova Court of Appeal awarded damages to a Roma family whose child was prevented by a teacher from attending class; in 2009, the same court had ordered the NCCD to reopen an investigation of alleged discrimination against Roma based on their ethnically imbalanced distribution in primary school classes.[73] In 2007, the Ministry of Education prohibited all forms of segregation in education.[74] Notwithstanding these judicial and administrative actions, Roma children continue to be placed in segregated classes (a 2011 report found that 65 percent of Roma primary school students learn in classes where they are equal in number to or outnumber non-Roma students) and disproportionately assigned to special schools intended for children with learning disabilities.[75] In 2010, the Council of Europe's Commissioner for Human Rights found that about 50 percent of Roma children in Romania did not even attend school.[76] According to the Council of Europe's oversight body for minority protection, "A considerable number of Roma children continue to fail at school and drop out at an early stage, or remain outside the education system. Cases of Roma children being placed in schools for children with disabilities, in separate schools or in separate classrooms continue to be reported. In recent years, a number of decisions of the National Council for Combating Discrimination have found this conduct to be of a discriminatory nature. However, the impact of these decisions remains limited."[77]

In the Czech Republic, despite vigorous and regular monitoring by the Council of Europe's Committee of Ministers, limited awareness of the *D.H.* judgment, coupled with fierce resistance to its implications by administrators and teachers of practical (formerly special) schools, has resulted in little change in the situation of Roma children. In late 2012, the Committee of Ministers warned that, "according to the statistics presented [by the Government], the overall percentage of Roma students educated in programmes for pupils with 'a slight mental disability' remains disproportionately high even if a slight decrease in this percentage is recorded."[78] Earlier that year, the Office for Democratic Institutions and Human Rights (another international group) similarly noted that "the steps taken by the Czech Government have not "put an end" to the practice the European Court of Human Rights ruled a violation of the Convention; Roma children are still overrepresented in segregated educational arrangements for children with special educational needs. Plans for reforming the education system . . . have, at best, been only partially implemented."[79] According to a 2012 report by the Czech Ombudsperson, while the level of incorrect placements had declined modestly, Roma children were still disproportionately represented in schools offering a limited curriculum, with Roma making up 35 percent of students enrolled in the practical schools (though Roma are less than 5 percent of the Czech population).[80] As of the end of 2013, the government's National Action Plan on Inclusive Education— ostensibly designed to implement the *D.H.* judgment—had no budget or other means for it to be put into effect. In April 2013, the Czech government affirmed that it had no intention of abolishing the system of practical schools with limited curricula, to which many Roma children are assigned.[81] In April 2015, Marcel Chládek, the Czech Minister of Education, declared: "I absolutely reject that the Czech system discriminates against Roma."[82] Meanwhile, nongovernmental initiatives, including within Roma communities, continued to push for progress in integrating Roma children in mainstream schools.[83]

If the situation remains bleak in many countries, there have been some positive signs. *D.H.* gave impetus to advocates for reform by clearly naming a problem—discrimination—that could no longer be ignored. *D.H.* further prompted the government to strengthen informed consent provisions for parents, and remove some of the most egregious manifestations of cultural bias from diagnostic tools used to assess students. Following the *Oršuš* judgment in 2010, the directors of the primary schools whose practices were found wanting by the European Court of Human Rights asked the authorities of Medimjurje county, where the Roma applicants lived, and the Croatian Ministry of Education, to introduce three-year, free-of-charge preschool programs for Roma children to help overcome language barriers.[84] As of September 2013, many Roma children in Medimurje County were attending ethnically integrated kindergartens and preschools.[85] Integration programs have so far addressed only preschool, kindergarten, and primary school.[86] A year earlier, in an unusual display of political support for desegregation, the Minister of Education publicly discouraged Croat parents from protesting the integration process.[87] It may be more than coincidence that this period constituted Croatia's final moment of intensive scrutiny as a candidate for European Union accession.

The judgment in *Horváth and Kiss* gave further impetus in Hungary to reforms of the system of special education which had been set in motion several years before, after the *D.H.* judgment. Among other steps, the committees in charge of educational assessments have adopted a more ethnically neutral method of determining which children to assign to special needs schools.[88] Observers suggest that budgetary impetus—the desire to cut spending by decreasing the number of children with special needs or by educating such children in integrated settings—has proved at least as potent a force for change as principled commitment to non-discrimination.[89] Moreover, in Hungary special education teachers and administrators have mounted less political resistance to desegregation than in the Czech Republic.

With more than half a dozen domestic court cases in the past five years, Hungary has seen more litigation challenging Roma discrimination in schools than any other country. Nonetheless, as recently as April 2015, Hungary's highest court, the Curia, rejected a challenge to the ethnic segregation of a church-run separate school for Roma children.[90] As in other parts of the region, the government of Hungary collects limited ethnic data with which to assess current levels of Roma segregation in special needs schools. Academic and civil society monitors indicate that Roma students continue to suffer high levels of segregation, in part due to their relative lack of mobility and limited opportunity to attend their school of choice due to geography.[91]

In short, overall, despite some change in some places,[92] the situation of Roma segregation in Europe has not markedly improved over the past decade. In Hungary, where the national average for secondary school attendance is 80 percent, only 15 percent of Roma pupils complete secondary school. Only 2 percent of Roma commence higher education and a mere 0.5 percent obtain a degree.[93] A 2011 survey suggests that only about 30 percent of Roma in the Czech Republic complete secondary education, compared with 80 percent of non-Roma.[94] In 2015, the World Bank wrote about Roma in Eastern Europe, "The odds of graduating secondary school are 29 percent at the highest, and much lower in some of the countries in the region, especially among girls"; similar statistics apply to Central Europe.[95] Indeed, in surveys of eleven European Union countries conducted in 2011, only 15 percent of young Roma adults had completed upper-secondary general or vocational education.[96]

If the effects on desegregation of judicial decisions in Europe have been modest at best, their impact on public discourse and attitudes has been equally limited. To be sure, some of the Roma parents who have gone to court to vindicate the rights of their children have found meaning in the simple act of official acknowledgement—by a body such as the European Court of

Human Rights—that those rights were breached and that their children are entitled to better treatment.[97] However, it is not clear how many Roma beyond the applicants in these cases and their immediate family and local community members know much about, let alone feel empowered by them. Nor have judgments condemning discrimination against Roma in schools substantially ameliorated the biased attitudes of many non-Roma or increased the political or social costs of expressing them. To the contrary, some surveys suggest little change in historically persistent anti-Roma attitudes. For example, a 2013 report on a multi-country survey of attitudes towards minorities in the European Union concluded, "Across Europe, we find that Roma were considered the least desirable neighbor, followed by homosexuals and then Muslims."[98] In another example, in March 2014, a Hungarian county judge denying prosecutors' request to dissolve a paramilitary organization which targeted Roma is reported to have said, "the Roma as a category should not be characterized primarily on the basis of race, but rather as a group separated from the majority by its disregard of the traditional values cherished by the majority. They follow a work-shy existence, they don't respect private property and accepted morality."[99]

However, other observers suggest that, at least within the Czech Republic, the *D.H.* judgment helped place the issue of Roma segregation topic on the public agenda. For example, young Roma rappers have created a song and accompanying video with the message that Roma are too smart to be confined to practical schools.[100] As a result of *D.H.*, some have said it is no longer possible for the authorities to deny that discrimination and segregation exist: "The silence which had persisted until 2007, when the authorities regularly denied any discrimination, has ended."[101]

The Sources of Disparate Impacts in Different Places

It would be impossible, given the limits of space, to examine all the myriad factors that might explain the differences in the impact of legal action on the educational segregation of Roma in Europe and African Americans in the United States. Nonetheless, several seem particularly important to note.

First, the underlying rules of legal procedure and decades of legal custom significantly limit the power of continental European courts to order remedies that apply to persons beyond the individual plaintiffs in a case, or to prescribe with any specificity the actions that government officials must take to comply with a judicial ruling. While much of the litigation challenging segregation in the United States has been pursued through class actions, the European Court of Human Rights—and, indeed, most national courts in continental Europe (with the exception of Hungary)[102]—may entertain only the claims of individual victims who come before the court.

Furthermore, the remedies for segregation ordered by the U.S. Supreme Court, though criticized by some as inadequate, were far more robust than those issued by European courts. In *Brown II*, the Supreme Court ordered district courts to issue "such orders and decrees . . . as are necessary and proper to admit to public schools on a racially nondiscriminatory basis with *all deliberate speed* the parties to these cases" (emphasis added).[103] In *Green v. County School Board*, the court ordered the school board at issue "to formulate a new plan and . . . fashion steps which promise realistically to convert promptly to a system without a 'white' school and a 'Negro' school, but just schools."[104] These directions to government agents—which grew increasingly specific and commanding over time—reflected the reality that, unlike most European courts, U.S. courts hearing challenges were exercising equitable powers to repair constitutional violations. As the Supreme Court in *Swann* observed: "If school authorities fail in their affirmative obligations under these holdings, judicial authority may be invoked. Once a right and a violation have been shown, the scope of a district court's equitable powers to remedy past wrongs is broad, for breadth and flexibility are inherent in equitable remedies."[105] By contrast, the European Court of Human Rights has the power to issue a declaration that government conduct is in breach of the European Convention of Human Rights, as well as to award just compensation for harm suffered. But generally the Court does not do more. Even in *D.H.*, the case in which the Court condemned a nationwide practice of segregation, the Court limited itself to ordering payment of the modest sum of 4,000 euros to each of the 18 applicants. It did not order any further remedial measures.

European Court judgments are binding on the parties before them, under the European Convention by which the signatory countries "undertake to abide by the final judgment of the court in any case to which they are parties."[106] Yet states enjoy considerable freedom, subject to the supervision of the Committee of Ministers, in choosing the most appropriate means to execute them.[107] Thus, the court generally does not suggest which specific individual or collective measures should be taken to implement judgments. Precisely because the European Court is a supranational mechanism:

States Parties enjoy a margin of appreciation in how they apply and implement the Convention, depending on the circumstances of the case and the rights and freedoms engaged. This reflects that the Convention system is subsidiary to the safeguarding of human rights at national level and that national authorities are in principle better placed than an international court to evaluate local needs and conditions. The margin of appreciation goes hand in hand with supervision under the Convention system. In this respect, the role of the Court is to review whether decisions taken by national authorities are compatible with the Convention, having due regard to the State's margin of appreciation.[108]

Although the European Convention requires that states afford victims an "effective remedy" for violation of human rights, and the EU Racial Equality Directive demands remedies that are "effective, proportionate and dissuasive," in few if any of the more than two dozen European cases that have been decided, have the courts affirmatively ordered the local authorities to desegregate a school found to have unlawfully separated Roma from non-Roma students.[109] Desegregation may not always the most desirable remedy for the kinds of discrimination which Roma children suffer in many schools.[110] But what European courts have provided to date—little or no redress at all—is surely insufficient.

This legal distinction between a national court like the U.S. Supreme Court and a supranational tribunal like the European Court of Human Rights reflects, and in turn, fosters an underlying cultural difference in impact. The legitimacy of a national court created at the founding of a republic through democratic constitutional means is different from that of a supranational body whose existence is owed to a treaty among governments. The U.S. Supreme Court commands popular respect for, and adherence to, its rulings in a manner that, notwithstanding its authority among elements of the bar and human rights advocates, the European Court of Human Rights has yet to win. When the Supreme Court issued its decision in *Brown* on May 17, 1954, citizens across the United States listened to summaries on the radio and read front-page accounts in major newspapers and magazines.[111] While judgments of the Strasbourg Court have certainly drawn attention and even provoked controversy in individual countries,[112] they rarely attract notice beyond the individual governments litigating a case, except in legal and academic circles. The very notion of a European public space (rather than a series of national conversations) is itself contested.

To be sure, the different impacts of the rulings of U.S. and continental European courts reflect as well the distinctive relationship between law and politics in each context. It is banal yet true to observe that in the United States, law has played a central role in political life—from the debates over the Constitution at the nation's founding to the varying, but decisive, place of the Supreme Court as, at times, an obstacle and, at other times, an enabler of change.[113] U.S. courts have long been an arena for social contest—from the Scopes monkey trial to the Pentagon Papers. Without exaggerating the point, in Europe, legal progress, particularly in the field of non-discrimination, has been more visibly achieved through the adoption of legislative rules than court judgments.[114]

Of course, law has contributed significantly to political change in many other contexts outside the United States. To take one prominent example, law played "a central role" in the struggle against apartheid in South Africa. not only because political constraints left "few avenues other than litigation through which to challenge the regime," but also because "South Africa repeatedly proclaimed its respect for the rule of law, to both foreign and domestic audiences," "Courts occasionally invalidated racist actions by the executive or legislature," and because "the opposition . . . embraced legality as a fundamental principle—most notably the ANC in its Freedom Charter."[115]

Another factor concerns the respective differences between the social movements that supported the efforts to secure legal change—the duration and breadth of those movements, their relationship to legal action, and their centrality in popular historical consciousness. The Supreme Court rendered its decision in *Brown* twenty-four years after the NAACP had commissioned Nathan Margold to recommend a legal strategy for challenging segregation in schools, forty-five years after the NAACP was founded, and more than half a century after activists in Louisiana brought a test case, which they lost, to contest racially separate railway carriages.[116] In short, *Brown* did not just happen. It was the product of decades of social activism, public discussion, organization-building, and mobilization—in churches, on buses, at lunch counters, on street corners, and in universities—among African Americans communities and their allies, and it followed twenty years of jurisprudence that progressively eroded the doctrine of "separate but equal" that had legitimized segregation.

By contrast, the various movements for the rights of Roma children are at a more formative stage. The year 2014 marks just twenty-five years since the fall of Communism in the countries of Central and Eastern Europe, many of which lack robust democratic traditions. This is the first period since before World War II in which free political expression for Roma or anyone else seeking to challenge discriminatory attitudes and practices has been possible. The scale, depth, and breadth of a rights-based movement among and by Roma communities, while substantial, do not approach what the movement for civil rights of African Americans had achieved by 1954, let alone by the 1960s and afterward. For a range of economic, political, and cultural reasons, the social and institutional infrastructure supporting equal rights for Roma in Europe is less well developed than was its counterpart for African Americans in the United States. Perhaps not unrelatedly, the legal cases which have challenged Roma segregation in schools were developed as much on behalf of Roma as by Roma themselves. As a result, the relatively positive jurisprudence which these cases have generated has resonated less rapidly and widely than did *Brown* and its progeny decades earlier.

Furthermore, the struggle for racial equality in the United States occupied a different place in the country's political history than does its counterpart in Europe. Ensuring equal opportunity for African Americans was not just another issue of concern, but the central unfulfilled promise of the American constitution. The slavery of African Americans was and is widely recognized as the "original sin" of the American republic. In the years during and after *Brown* was decided, rectifying and overcoming slavery's legacy—in part through ensuring equal educational opportunity for all—was considered a national responsibility. The movement for racial equality, in American schools and elsewhere, was a vehicle for national redemption.

Europe, of course, presents a different story. In contrast to the United States, no single overriding historical narrative exists—rather there are as many narratives as there are countries. Indeed, to the extent that Europe can be said to share a common approach to equality as such, it is the perspective of social welfare, rather than individual rights, which highlights the responsibility of the state—and not the identity of particular groups.[117]

Moreover, notwithstanding the gains that have been made in recent years in securing greater recognition of the historical mistreatment of the Roma (including the murder of many tens of thousands during the Nazi Holocaust), Roma occupy a less central place in European public discourse and memory.[118] Although Roma are today Europe's largest ethnic minority, their fate competes historically for attention with that of many other minority groups who have suffered at various times under discriminatory policies.[119] Even today, the condition of Roma children in Europe's schools is just one in a panoply of concerns—from the challenge of integrating immigrants in general (most Roma are nationals of the countries wherein they reside) to the situation of Muslims of North African or South Asian extraction in particular—that animate European approaches to growing ethnic diversity.

Yet another factor contributing to the different impacts of judicial decisions in the United States and Europe is the kind of segregation at issue. At the time *Brown* was decided, segregation was authorized by law in seventeen states and the District of Columbia.[120] Because in the United States, segregation was enshrined in law, when the Supreme Court spoke, it could at least make illegal what had once enjoyed legal sanction. Even if the reality on the ground would take time to change, *Brown* immediately stripped the practice of segregation of any legal authority.

By contrast, in Europe, no law required or authorized racial segregation in education at the time the cases referred to above were brought. To the contrary, segregation as practiced is a breach of legal principles that have long existed,[121] but have rarely been applied. The segregation at issue was a product of administrative practice—multiple individual decisions of school administrators, teachers, parents and psychologists—and hence not as universal as the segregation before the Supreme Court in *Brown*. Thus, in *D.H.*, 50 to 70 percent (rather than 100 percent) of Roma were sent to special schools, and a number of students in special schools were non-Roma.[122] In the schools at issue in *Oršuš*, some Roma were assigned to Roma-only classes, while others were not.[123] In *Horváth and Kiss*, "the applicants were not placed in ethnically segregated classes," though they were members of an ethnic group that was disproportionally overrepresented in such classes.[124] While the European Court's condemnation of segregation was important, it was less revolutionary than *Brown*—and may have had less immediate impact on the public consciousness—at least in part, because the law had not been so entwined with segregation in Europe as it had been in the United States.

Yet one more factor contributing to the disparate effects of court rulings on racial segregation was the international context. *Brown* was decided at a time of heightened Cold War competition between the United States and the Soviet Union. Racial segregation in American schools and in other areas of public life was widely seen as a signal failing of American democracy, which undermined U.S. claims for allegiance among African and Asian populations then emerging from colonial rule. Scholarly research has shown that the principal actors in the case—the lawyers at the NAACP; officials in the U.S. government who filed an amicus brief urging the Supreme Court to strike down segregation; and the Justices themselves—were aware of, and sensitive to, these concerns.[125] So were segments of the American public. For example, the *Pittsburgh Courier*, an African American newspaper, argued at the time that *Brown* would "stun and silence America's Communist traducers behind the Iron Curtain," for it would "effectively impress upon millions of colored people in Asia and Africa the fact that idealism and social morality can and do prevail in the Unites States, regardless of race, creed or color."[126]

By contrast, Europe today is not locked in a binary struggle for global political ascendancy, and the situation of Roma children in European schools is not of international consequence, beyond the occasional mention in U.S. State Department human rights reports. David Meyer and Michael Uyehara's chapter in this book, along with that of Erika Schlager, provide further perspective on U.S. interest in Roma in Europe. Within Europe, each government's treatment of Roma is a potential object of inquiry—by supranational organs such as the Committee of Ministers of the Council of Europe, the European Commission, or the Organization for Security and Cooperation in Europe. However, precisely because segregation of Roma children is so widespread in Europe, no government has an incentive to make an issue of another government's shortcomings, for fear of incurring reciprocal criticism.

Conclusion

Brown v. Board and the changes it portended, if only incompletely realized six decades later, have taught generations of activists in the United States and abroad that law and courts can at some times and in some places be a force for good. The experience of educational desegregation in the United States is more complicated and imperfect than *Brown*'s legend would suggest. Oversimplified accounts of *Brown*'s impact may have encouraged some to rely excessively on court-centric advocacy at the cost of other routes to change.[127] And yet, the example of the American civil rights movement and its legal struggle continue to inspire.

The still-young search for equal justice for Roma children is a reflection of that inspiration. In a short space of time, Roma rights advocates have altered the jurisprudential landscape around racial discrimination in schools. They have yet, however, to forge a movement with the power, the resources, and the stamina to change government policies and shift public attitudes. Such a movement will face many obstacles—from the hardened racism of popular stereotypes to the resistance of entrenched interests in maintaining unequal educational systems.

Much is needed. Roma communities must marshal their undervalued political potential. Historically-rooted fear of ethnic data must be overcome. Stronger ties must be forged with organizations fighting for the rights of women, persons with disabilities, the poor across all racial divides, and other ethnic, religious, and sexual minorities. Though equal schooling is a fundamental right, advocates must do better in highlighting the economic costs to European societies of continuing to condemn generation after generation of Roma children to second-class citizenship. And while litigation alone is not the answer, an increasing number of well-documented, well-argued cases must be built and filed in coming years to build on, consolidate, and translate into concrete reality the doctrinal advances already won.

If American history is any guide, the quest for equal schooling for Roma in Europe will continue for quite a while. Any assessment of progress must be mindful of Dr. King's observation that the "arc of the moral universe is long, but it bends towards justice."[128] How long? In the end, it will be Roma children, their parents, and their communities—far more than anyone else—who decide.

PART V

Looking Forward: The Imperative of Roma Community Mobilization and Leadership

Chapter 10

Making Roma Rights a Reality at the Local Level: A Spanish Case Study

Teresa Sordé Martí and Fernando Macías

Manuel says he was reborn when his elementary school shut down nine years ago, reopened, and soon earned the name La Paz (The Peace) School.[1] Now a seventeen-year-old Roma teenager, Manuel remembers how his grandmother would bid him farewell at the gate of the old school—she was not allowed to go any farther. Manuel does not have good memories of those times. He got bored in class, was often disruptive, and had difficulty learning. He remembers that his classmates' experience was much the same. Not only did Manuel feel that his teachers looked down on him and his family, but his family and neighbors did not trust the school. But when the school reopened, something important changed. All of a sudden, Manuel saw his grandmother helping his math teacher in the classroom. How could it be, Manuel thought, that instead of being angry at his grandmother, his teacher was grateful to have her assistance? (After all, his grandmother was a *Roma* woman—who had never even attended *school*.)

Last June, Manuel graduated from high school and enrolled in further vocational studies in electrical engineering. The first and only member from his extended family to earn a diploma of any kind, Manuel is clear he will not stop there. He wants "to be someone in life." Along with his grandmother, he is also a volunteer at the school, helping other Roma children pursue their education.

Manuel's story is not unique. His is one of many that illustrate the experience of Roma living in La Milagrosa, a neighborhood in the city of Albacete, and one of the poorest in Spain. Most people living in the neighborhood are of Roma descent, born into families that have been Spanish for generations, and speak a mixture of Caló (a language related to Romani, spoken by Spanish and Portuguese Roma) and Spanish. Stories like Manuel's demonstrate how it is possible to dramatically reduce poverty and provide equal opportunities for all. As this chapter will show, the strategy has combined a series of effective interventions with the creation of decision-making spaces that have encouraged meaningful and egalitarian dialogue. Egalitarian dialogue involves the full engagement of all the different stakeholders in the social change project—education professionals, local political stakeholders, affected community members and their neighbors, researchers, and government policy makers alike. Everyone participates in the conversation and discussion on equal footing. In Albacete, these spaces have been achieved thanks to the adoption of a "Dialogic Inclusion Contract," a process that has joined two key elements: inputs from experts in the international research community and contributions from local people living in the neighborhood, mostly Roma families.[2] This process has made it possible to begin to reverse situations of severe poverty and produce a positive social impact on the lives of Roma residents. This chapter describes that process through an analysis of data collected from the longitudinal case study conducted in the La Milagrosa neighborhood between 2006 and 2011 in the scope of the INCLUD-ED project.

"INCLUD-ED: Strategies for inclusion and social cohesion in Europe from education" was a research project funded by the Sixth Framework Programme for Research and Technological Development (FP6) of the European Commission. The case study described here was one of a series of six longitudinal case studies conducted in different parts of Europe. All case studies were based on local projects in highly deprived neighborhoods. The projects aimed to achieve social cohesion through education, by relying in part on strong community participation.[3] Schools wishing to be a part of the INCLUD-ED study were expected to demonstrate substantive progress in their students' performance each year.

A key component of INCLUD-ED has been its methodology. Its *communicative* research perspective has proved itself an effective tool for probing the circumstances of at-risk groups, moving beyond a mere diagnosis of social problems to identify in detail the genesis of success. From design through interpretation, the research method involves investigated subjects in all phases of the research, promoting real dialogue between users of the services and researchers.[4] This approach aims to dispel the normal social gap between researchers and participants, replacing it with knowledge generated out of the process of dialogue itself.[5] Study participants are a central part of the overall project and are involved right from the start up through the elaboration of the study's final conclusions and resolutions. For this project, these participants were Roma community members and they were the ones deciding what information about their community should be revealed. A 2010 EU conference, "Science against Poverty," commended the program for its impact on poverty reduction and included a description of the program in its final recommendations.[6]

For years, researchers at the Center for Research into Theories and Practices that Overcome Inequalities (CREA) have reflected on the extent to which research can contribute to the improvement of citizens' lives.[7] As Ramón Flecha has suggested, social impact is often confused with dissemination (making research results well known) and transference (when results are used to inform policies or civil society's initiatives). In fact, he notes that research findings are rarely used to contribute to social improvements and may even be counterproductive. But this does not have to be so. Deft communication of the results of social research can enable researchers to contribute to the realization of substantial social impact.[8]

Horizon 2020, the EU research and innovation program for the period 2014 through 2020, exemplifies this process of linking research specifically to societal goals. More than seventy-five billion euros are targeted for research and innovation projects to help the EU reach its goal of "becoming a smart, sustainable, and inclusive economy by 2020." Research and innovation projects are helping to identify policies and testing out initiatives to gain specific objectives, part of the overall Europe 2020 program. Among the targets most relevant to this chapter are reducing the number of people in or at risk of poverty and social exclusion by at least 20 million and bringing school dropout rates below 10 percent.[9] This linking of research to social impact has been well accepted; several research projects are underway throughout Europe. In what follows, this chapter probes how INCLUD-ED research findings were successfully put into practice in order to empower Roma people from La Milagrosa.[10] The chapter explores the factors that enable research to achieve a direct and clear social impact.

The Successful Action Approach

The successful action (SA) approach consists of identifying initiatives of already proven efficacy that overcome social exclusion, poverty, or other types of social problems.[11] The SA approach represents a further step than previous approaches such as good or best practices because research has already documented the transferability of these actions in a wide variety of contexts. Researchers present these "successful actions" to community members who decide how and when to recreate the actions in their own contexts, working with researchers and policy makers. This new approach was developed within the INCLUD-ED project, and then extended to other areas. Within the context of the project, different successful actions in the area of education were identified. Of these, the following five successful educational actions (SEAs) played an especially important role in the transformation process in La Paz, the reopened elementary school in La Milagrosa:

- La Paz organizes its classrooms in *interactive groups*, small heterogeneous groups which lead to success. Led by an adult facilitator, these coeducational groups usually consist of four or five students with varied levels of educational proficiency, diverse cultural backgrounds, and different language skills. The adult facilitator promotes learning through group interactions. Facilitators may be teachers, college students, volunteers, or community members. Their job is to promote "dialogical interaction" rather than particular classroom content. An SEA optimizes existing resources efficiently without separating or segregating students.[12] In addition to the academic curriculum (mathematics, language, or science), students learn how to help each other and, through this process, to avoid prejudice and misbehavior.
- La Paz invests in *family education*, another SEA. This strategy encourages family participation in educational and cultural activities, geared toward helping younger family members improve their school performance.[13] Generally, these family education programs are based on the participants' needs and interests, rather than on what professionals think they need. Programs range from literacy courses to driving lessons. The INCLUD-ED project shows it is possible to dismantle the link between low parental educational levels and children's school failure.[14] Parents' engagement in activi-

ties and training experiences may have more relevance to their children's future success than the amount of parental education.

- The initiative *increases the amount of time children spend learning.* This strategy focuses the most attention on students who need particular help. For instance, the school library hours might be extended beyond school hours, to turn it into a learning space where students and supporting volunteers can work together. The IN-CLUD-ED project demonstrated a positive correlation between increasing learning time—especially if spent on foundational subjects like math, language, and science—and students' academic performance.[15] This strategy accelerates learning for all students, while helping students at greater disadvantage obtain better results. Through this SEA, the library becomes an open community space where all people (especially children) find the resources to learn and work.

- The final SEA encourages the active participation of families and community members. This action enables family members and community members to participate in school decision-making processes, discussing key issues regarding the education of their children. Families and community members are free to express their points of view and reach consensus with others, including their children's' teachers. As the 2009 INCLUD-ED consortium report concluded: "When community members participate in decision-making, they can also monitor the school's actions and hold the school accountable for its educational results. This is important, since school autonomy in educational decisions must be accompanied by a system of accountability which ensures that the school's actions lead to good results for their students. . . . Therefore, it is important that school management bodies consider and support the decisions made by the educational community, since they play a significant role in children's learning processes."[16]

La Milagrosa: One of the Poorest Roma Neighborhoods in Spain

People in Spain refer to La Milagrosa as the Seiscientas (the Six Hundred)— the number of housing units constructed during the late 1970s and early

1980s. Over a short period of time, these subsidized housing units were inhabited by Roma families expelled from other areas of the city. Because of difficult living conditions at the outset combined with the lack of public investment for upkeep, the buildings deteriorated quickly. The neighborhood's blight manifested itself not only in the poor quality of its housing but also in the residents' poor social opportunities. For instance, in 2006 at the beginning of the project, the unemployment rate was nearly 100 percent. A serious drug problem also affected the area. The neighborhood featured regularly in national headlines because of its high levels of conflict and violence, especially between outside professionals (mainly teachers) and families. In spite of the social impact achieved thanks to the implementation of SAs, today La Milagrosa is still poor and faces many problems. In 2011, the unemployment rate was about 72 percent. In 2012, the current average wage among people from La Milagrosa who were employed was 30 percent lower than the average for the city of Albacete.[17] In 2008, more than 84 percent of those in the neighborhood had not finished their primary education.[18]

The difficulties in the neighborhood and outside interventions without consultation affected the school too; it was full of the mistrust highlighted by Manuel at the beginning of this chapter. By early 2006, the situation had become untenable. Families were increasingly alienated from school routine and critical of teachers' behavior toward the children; teachers did not have any positive expectations of the families and their children. The situation had created a climate of confrontation between families and teachers, the latter feeling themselves under attack by the community and occasionally at risk from student threats. The media reports of violence constituted only the tip of the iceberg. In reality, tensions were so extreme that teachers were asking for police protection as they entered the school and for back door access to avoid walking through the neighborhood. At times, even the police did not dare enter the neighborhood. Teachers and professionals alike viewed the community as a lost cause. At the same time, Roma families suffered from explicitly racist behavior and extreme social exclusion. For over twenty years, with conviction increasing over time, it was widely believed that the community had no future prospects.

In the face of this challenging situation, the local administration felt compelled to take action, though no clear strategy seemed at hand, particularly as previous local government investment and planning had only produced negative results. Through its education inspector, the administration consulted some of the INCLUD-ED researchers. The first meeting flagged the highly conflictual school situation as a priority for action. The researchers pointed out that successful intervention in the school would be highly dependent on mutual understanding between the many different actors involved. Proceeding from this initial vantage point, various town hall meetings including families, municipal stakeholders, researchers, and the education inspector were organized. After many conversations, all actors involved agreed to transform the school into a new educational space where SEAs could be implemented and where teachers and families might work together. Eventually, the government decided to shut down the existing school (San Juan) and open up another one in the same building, with the goal of implementing the SEAs. Teachers in the pre-existing school were relocated (with their agreement and that of the Teachers' Unions) and a selection process was called to recruit new teachers willing to work very closely with the families in the context of an educational project based on SEAs.

During preliminary discussions, several debates emerged. One concerned the teachers' qualifications: should the new teachers be specialists in remedial education or would mainstream teaching skills suffice? The community decided against hiring remedial teachers and instead supported recruitment of teachers able to start teaching English as early as kindergarten—an obvious strategy to improve the quality of education offered. From the outset, annual recruitment has taken place locally, in sharp contrast to the typically centralized process governing most Spanish public schools. The school is a popular work site, despite the long hours of work expected, so recruitment is competitive adding to the quality of teaching.

Several interesting participant reflections followed the new school launch. The school inspector noted the dramatic change in participation, from a context where teaching professionals (none of whom lived in the area or were familiar with the daily realities of life outside the school) made all the decisions with no community consultation at all, to one where family members actively participated in shaping the new curriculum and schedule. An INCLUD-ED researcher spent the night in a rudimentary Roma family apartment and then reported on this conflict-free and warm experience to participating policy makers, professionals, and police officers. Gradually perceptions shifted and the impetus to collaborate increased. It soon became clear that Roma families wanted the best education for their children, and that, given the opportunity, they would engage in decision making and other activities to contribute to the future development of their children and community. The school inspector voiced his surprise and delight at the changes: "A general school assembly was arranged and around 50 or 60 people attended it; that is, family members of all types, the full teaching team and myself. No-one could remember so many people getting together in the school. . . . Perhaps 80 or 90 percent of the families were represented, as well as neighborhood associations."[19]

But over time it became clear that to generate enduring change within the new school and the broader community, the teachers and the school board needed more than attendance at meetings: they needed robust and sustained support from the neighborhood families, including people from the neighborhood to volunteer at the school regularly. Overcoming the hostility to teachers and overall reluctance of the families took some time—many families had vivid memories of the recent confrontations.

Having experienced initial hostility, teachers too had painful recent memories to move beyond: "I cried every single day, and there was no way I could teach. However, I persisted because I felt supported by many people, and I could see how families and the same students also started to change their views and were every time more supportive, little by little. By the end of the year, I was teaching every day, and making great advancements."[20] Gradually the families realized that the teachers were committed to providing the community children with the same education they would want for their own children—an end to the long-existing educational double standard. Instead of throwing stones at the teachers, previously hostile families started to line up to sit in the classrooms, volunteer in interactive groups, and participate actively in everyday activities, including assemblies.

Families and teachers also decided to work together to renew both the external and the internal fabric of the old dilapidated school. To do this, they jointly developed a set of common rules. For many families, this was their first experience of active participation, and, since all stakeholders wanted a say in the development of the school and in the resolution of conflicts between families, teachers, and children, a "School Constitution" was then born. At this juncture, the various collaborators decided to symbolically change the name of the new school to La Paz (The Peace).

In addition to the creation of new collaborative spaces, many family members noticed another element in the school's transformation: their children were doing better in school. Rosario is a Roma mother who had five children in the school and experienced the changes there firsthand. She explained that, before the changes, she had worried that her children were not learning anything, and that their future prospects would be no better than hers. Depressed and despairing, she had neglected her children and taken to selling drugs. After a stint in prison, Rosario returned home and started to volunteer at the school. "There was a time when I was very bad, I was on drugs. I was in a center for nearly seven months. And at that time I did not take care of my children. On the contrary, they got up on their own, got dressed, and came [to school]. Later on, when I left the center and I was well, it was me and my husband. And I have not fallen back into drugs, thanks to the school, coming to school, getting involved . . . for me, it is very important, very important."[21] When the teachers of La Paz began to implement the successful actions, Rosario found herself able to engage in dialogue on an equal footing with the other participants, new teachers, researchers, and policy makers. She observed that her children were learning much more, and she herself started to attend literary groups offered by the school, where she read books such as Lorca's *La Casa de Bernarda Alba* and *The Odyssey*.[22] Rosario reports her relationship with her children drastically changed. As she says, the "changes came from the classroom to my kitchen and living room."[23]

The improvement in students' school experiences was not just Rosario's impression; it became a reality for the entire neighborhood. The statistics on absenteeism, school enrollment, and educational performance improved enormously; equally important, school-neighborhood conflicts virtually disappeared. The rate of school enrollment increased from forty-five to 114 students in the first academic year (2006–2007) and the rate of absenteeism decreased from 122 to thirteen students in the first three academic years (2006–2010). Students' performance improved in all subjects, rising two (out of ten) points for language comprehension, three points for reading and more than four points for speaking and writing.[24] Secondary school data is also very encouraging. Virtually every student who finishes primary school enrolls in and graduates from secondary school. In addition to these gains in academic results, the school atmosphere has improved enormously, with much better relationships among students, teachers, administrators, and families. This is why the local Roma associations of Castilla-La Mancha awarded La Paz school its most valued prize for people and organizations that work for Roma development: *El Quijote Gitano* (The Roma Quixote).[25] This is a very tangible symbol of the way that all parties in La Milagrosa enthusiastically supported and worked for peace. The school was deeply transformed, from a ghetto school into a radically different one.

From the School to the Whole Neighborhood

In 2009, the enormous improvement in the school inspired progress in the enhancement of other aspects of the neighborhood, such as housing, social and political participation, health, and employment. Before this period, considerable amounts of public funding had been spent on multiple projects and interventions within the community that had ultimately made no difference to the lives of resident Roma families. For example, since 1998, URBAN plans had targeted the challenging environment with the aim of improving the circumstances.[26] But these plans were not based on actions with proven success in reducing social exclusion, and they did not take into account the opinions of people living in the area, two significant limitations. Not surprisingly, the URBAN plan's impact was almost imperceptible, so that by 2001, the life conditions of the Roma families were the same or even worse than they had been before the plans started. Many families said it would have been much more useful to distribute the funding among them than spend it on the implementation of those plans.

When the municipality planned the second iteration of the URBAN plan, the city council, major stakeholders, and the grassroots community decided to work collaboratively with the INCLUD-ED researchers to implement an across-the-board successful action, following the school model, with the Dialogic Inclusion Contract.[27] Again, participants decided to create a space in which people could combine two dimensions: discussions based on researchers' presentation to the whole community of previous successful actions, and community members' opinions and interpretations about their context and the daily constraints and opportunities in their lives. Again, as in the previous dialogic spaces, decisions were taken not on the basis of the social or political status of a participant, but through mutual understanding based on the strength of the arguments put forward.[28] Through an egalitarian dialogue, all these parties made decisions about how to recreate in La Milagrosa some of the SAs.

An example of this process occurred in the area of employment. One of the actions discussed related to the creation of competitive cooperatives. Researchers presented information about competitive workers' cooperatives that had generated steady and sustainable job opportunities, thereby overcoming situations of poverty and chronic unemployment.[29] The Mondragon Cooperative Group, the tenth largest corporation in Spain, is a powerful example of the impact of worker cooperatives. As of September 2015, this group is composed of 260 institutions, of which 103 are cooperatives, 125 are subsidiary companies, and the rest are foundations, benefit societies, umbrella organizations, and international services.[30] Professionals, public administrators, and the Roma families in the area were interested in finding out more about the actions that made Mondragon a success story and in discussing ways it could be recreated in La Milagrosa. Until that point, all the services people needed in the neighborhood had been outsourced, while the people living in the community remained unemployed. The need for a cooperative able to provide those services and jobs locally and at a competitive rate seemed acute. Eventually, a competitive cooperative was established in La Milagrosa to generate new sustainable local jobs. At the beginning of 2013, it had created employment for thirteen people (ten permanent and three temporary contracts), three hundred seventeen seasonal agricultural jobs, six contracts to manage workers' professional training, and four management positions in the cooperative.[31]

Maria's story illustrates the impact this cooperative had on people's lives at that time. In her mid-forties, Maria had always worked in the informal economy, as a street vendor selling whatever she could find. But with the introduction of the cooperative, she decided to qualify as a leisure time educator and enrolled in the cooperative and in courses offered at her children's school (La Paz) under the family education program. For the first time in her life, this gave her the opportunity to work as an educator with a regular contract. Maria spoke of the importance of the experience of having a "regular" job, a turning point for her and many of her neighbors. In 2013, she and many others told us that La Milagrosa was becoming a more respectable and habitable barrio, fulfilling her own dreams and those of the community. As Maria said then, "Now, we have a future with more opportunities thanks to the school . . . every summer I can work thanks to the courses which I attended there. . . . Now, thanks to the cooperative and to the family education courses of the school, my people have more opportunities."[32]

Unfortunately, the initial success of the cooperative did not continue: at the beginning of 2014, partly from the effects of the economic crisis but also because of changes in decision-making processes, there were layoffs. The managerial model for the cooperative changed, with power and control centralized in one position. This shift resulted in Maria and many other founding members making the difficult decision to abandon the project. In informal follow-up interviews with Maria and other founding members in fall 2015, they felt that the organization had lost sight of its initial goals: to provide employment opportunities in the quarter (especially to those more in need) and to have a participatory and democratic system for decision making (that is, one person, one vote). The members who left the cooperative still believe that this has been a good experience at the personal and professional level, as it has represented a step forward in their lives.

The story of the cooperative contrasts with that of the school. During this time the school expanded to offer secondary education and continues to provide positive educational outcomes every year. With new teachers and more Roma families involved, it has become a core institution fulfilling the community's hope of a better future for themselves and their children.

The stories of Manuel, Rosario, and Maria and the case of La Milagrosa show how research can help to transform situations of poverty and social exclusion. Where planners and policy makers had previously failed to generate effective educational and employment opportunities, there is now a Roma community with students getting secondary education certification, parents receiving vocational training, and families finding themselves able to influence the economic, social, and cultural milieu in which they live.

Researchers have found that these successful actions are transferrable to a wide range of contexts. At the moment, the SA approach has been implemented in more than four hundred schools in Spain and Latin America. The approach has been scaled up by various Spanish regional governments (for example, Andalucía, Basque Country, Aragon, and Catalonia), municipalities (like Rivas Vaciamadrid), and promoted by different European institutions.[33] Thanks to agreements with trade unions, teachers' associations, and universities, successful actions are being used in more and more neighborhoods. More recently, Brazil's Instituto Natura (the nonprofit arm of the Brazilian cosmetic company Natura) is working to extend the project to the whole country and to several other Latin American countries.[34] In all cases, communities start off with the support of researchers, and very often the commitment of the public authorities, but after this initial phase, communities themselves create their own networks to support each other in the process of moving forward.

Two main lessons can be highlighted here from the La Milagrosa case study and the implementation of the successful action strategy there. First, interventions aimed at social transformation should be based on practices, initiatives, and actions which have already demonstrated their effectiveness in addressing inequalities. Second, the implementation of these actions must be the product of continuous dialogue with all the actors involved in the area, and more specifically, with those who are usually excluded from decision-making processes. If this is important in all fields, it is more urgent than ever in the case of Roma Studies to conduct research that helps address the living conditions of the majority of Roma in Europe, supports EU endeavors to promote Roma inclusion, and ultimately realizes Roma rights.

Chapter 11

Roma Mobilization and Participation:
Obstacles and Opportunities

Peter Vermeersch

Though there is a dearth of research on the political mobilization and political participation of Roma communities,[1] it is wrong to assume—as some media reports have done[2]—that Roma communities in Europe tend to avoid politics. Data from the 2011 Roma Pilot Survey conducted by the European Union Agency for Fundamental Rights (FRA) in eleven European Union member states show that in countries where Roma are a substantial minority, many take part in national elections. Over 70 percent of the respondents in Bulgaria, Greece, Slovakia, and Hungary, and over 80 percent of those in Romania reported voting in the previous national elections.[3]

The number of Roma who participate in local elections as candidates has markedly increased over the recent years. In Slovakia, for example, the number of Roma candidates increase with each local, regional or parliamentary election—the local is especially significant. According to Hrustič, in the local elections of 1998 there were 254 Roma candidates running, from whom fifty-six were elected to municipal councils and six were elected to mayoral offices. In the elections of 2002 the number of Roma candidates increased to 756, of whom 158 were elected to municipal councils. The local elections of 2006 saw the participation of more than 1,600 Roma candidates; more than 220 of them were elected to local councils. The 2013 Organization of Security and Cooperation in Europe (OSCE) *Report on the Implementation of the Action Plan on Improving the Situation of Roma and Sinti within the OSCE Area* notes that, in 2012 in Romania, 161 Roma won seats on local councils, which was a decrease compared to the 2008 local elections; in Hungary, nineteen Roma were elected to local councils; in Serbia the number was twenty-six; in Bulgaria, forty-one; and in Slovakia, twenty-eight.[4]

A growing number of Roma are involved in various forms of political and social activism, often in self-organized civil society groups. Many of these activities are supported by international donors, such as the National Democratic Institute or the Open Society Foundations. Roma organizations have also increasingly been part of a transnational advocacy network on Roma inclusion that has had some impact on the development of EU policies in this field.[5] With regard to protest, too, Roma communities are active. Throughout Europe, some of the most visible demonstrations in response to targeted expulsion and migration control strategies have been led by Roma and supporting non-Roma organizations and groups.

Yet despite evidence of such forms of mobilization and participation, and despite growing numbers of Roma who are well educated and outspoken activists seeking to engage fellow-citizens—non-Roma and Roma—as voters and activists, the archetype persists that Roma are politically more passive than other groups of citizens. Most literature about Roma discusses the scale of the Roma's socioeconomic marginalization in contemporary Europe and the problems of hate speech and anti-Roma discrimination.[6] Some of the other contributors to this volume also touch upon these issues in their chapters.[7] But more information is needed about the obstacles that hamper visible and effective Roma participation and mobilization, and new research is needed on the ways activists can successfully address problems in the field of Roma participation and mobilization. How can Roma acquire a significant presence in policy-making debates? How can they more effectively voice their claims and influence policy outcomes? To what extent can the relatively new and still emerging institutional context for consultation at the European level provide avenues for Roma political engagement? I engage with these questions in this chapter by exploring new opportunities for Roma participation and mobilization. I begin with an outline of emerging political and institutional opportunities. I reflect on obstacles to Roma social and political mobilization at the local, national, and European level and ask how these can be overcome. I conclude by highlighting recent developments in Roma youth activism, a likely arena of future Roma political mobilization.

As do the other contributors whose works are included in this volume, I use the term "Roma," which activists have promoted since the 1970s as a broad overarching label that eclipses a series of encompassing terms burdened with derogatory connotations (such as "Gypsies" or "Tsiganes").[8] On the political level the word "Roma" is now frequently used to refer to various groups, not only to those who call themselves Roma but also to groups such as Dutch *Woonwagenbewoners*, Beás (also known as Boyash) in Central Europe, or Irish Travellers (to name just a few), most of who have traditionally not viewed themselves as ethnically related to the Roma.[9] This political usage of the term is sometimes contested among scholars and activists, but it is nevertheless widespread.[10]

Institutional Change and Emerging Opportunities

Institutional changes, legal frameworks, and governance structures at the local, domestic, and European level have created new avenues for Roma participation and mobilization. With regard to national changes, development in the countries of Central and Eastern Europe, home to the largest Roma communities, has been particularly important. New policies related to the Roma were introduced in the early 1990s, when most Central and Eastern European countries gave Roma official recognition as an ethnic group or a national minority for the first time. This recognition afforded Roma cultural and linguistic rights and an opportunity to establish ethnic or national minority organizations, including, in many cases, Roma political parties. Although some countries, such as Bulgaria, forbade the formation of political parties on the basis of ethnicity, the general trend in the 1990s was toward stimulating ethnic politics as a valuable way of defending minority interests. This trend should be viewed in the context of international attempts to prevent ethnic conflict in the 1990s. As Weller writes, "It became generally accepted that what was then known as "minority governance" is an important issue for maintaining the integrity of existing states. In view of the dramatic consequences of ethnic conflict that had been observed in Europe, minority accommodation within the state became "securitized." While states had previously been very reluctant to engage with minority issues as human rights issues, they had fewer hesitations when engaging them as issues of conflict prevention or conflict transformation."[11] Some countries, in particular Hungary, developed a system for the protection of cultural autonomy through a mechanism of elected local and national minority self-governments. Other countries—a case in point is Romania—offered minorities, including Roma, special rights for political representation through reserved seats in parliament or other forms of guaranteed political representation (see David Mark's chapter in this volume for a critical assessment of these two countries' measures). In the Czech and Slovak Republics, selected Roma activists were included in governmental advisory bodies responsible for guarding state support for minorities.

During the latter half of the 1990s and the first decade of the twenty-first century, the governance-related context of Roma mobilization gradually changed. Over this period, European governments tended to focus increasingly on the specific socioeconomic and social exclusion issues facing Roma communities. A distinction was made between general minority policy programs and special policy programs for Roma. This specialized attention was, to some extent, triggered by international pressure on Central and Eastern European countries in the context of the EU enlargement process. International organizations such as the OSCE and the Council of Europe devoted attention to the human rights situation of Roma across Europe, and respect for minorities became a precondition for EU accession.[12] As Mirga elaborates in his chapter in this volume, these moves were likely also stimulated by EU governments' attempts to coordinate activities toward the Roma that, until then, had been fragmented across various ministries.

In this context, a number of governments decided to set up additional Roma institutions to aid in the design and implementation of policy programs targeted at Roma. For example, special advisors on Roma affairs were introduced in countries as diverse as the Czech Republic, Bosnia and Herzegovina, Finland, Romania, Slovakia, and Croatia.[13] Ad hoc advisory bodies that include selected Roma representatives have been introduced in countries such as the Czech Republic, Hungary, and Lithuania.

Overall, since 1989, the changing political and institutional context has increased opportunities for Roma mobilization, as Roma activists can now make use of at least three avenues of mobilization. First, they can mobilize through electoral politics. Thanks to their recognition as an ethnic or national minority, Roma now have a basis for formulating Roma interests in mainstream political parties and, in some countries, ethnically based political parties. Second, Roma can and do establish their own (ethnically defined) NGOs, sometimes on the basis of existing cultural organizations such as theater companies and music groups.[14] Third, they can fill positions in state institutions; administrative bodies responsible for implementing special Roma policies have in various cases employed Roma or engaged with activists in a dialogue about policy formation. There are examples of electoral campaigns by Roma activists that have resulted in forms of Roma political representation, especially on the local level. However, despite these measures, overall, ethnic electoral representation of Roma remains low, both in ethnic parties and in mainstream political parties.

National institutional changes have been accompanied by important Europe-wide developments, which have created alternative mobilization opportunities for Roma outside of the domain of electoral politics. Roma activists supported by international donor organizations have been able to criticize domestic governments on the basis of newly emerging Europe-wide standards on anti-discrimination and social inclusion. This dimension of political action has become increasingly salient since the enlargement of the EU toward Central and Eastern Europe.

In recent times, EU institutions have engaged in initiatives that specifically target Roma.[15] For example, in December 2007, the European Council gave its full support to the European Commission for the organization of a series of "European Roma Summits" with the first one held in September 2008 in Brussels and the second in April 2010 in Córdoba.[16]

The third summit, held in April 2014 in Brussels, is discussed in Andrzej Mirga's chapter in this volume, describing the level of EU interest in pursuing the implementation of Roma policy. These highly visible meetings gathered approximately four hundred representatives of EU institutions, national governments, regional and local public authorities, and to a certain extent civil society organizations, including some Roma.[17] Follow-up summits were then organized in cooperation with the three presidencies in office during 2010 (Spain, Belgium, and Hungary). The *Council Conclusions on Advancing Roma Inclusion* from 2010 confirmed the consolidation of this new initiative.[18]

These summits have functioned mainly as deliberative and advisory boards; they have brought together a broad range of stakeholders with the aim of increasing political awareness about the situation of Roma, especially among high-level national policy makers. Some specific outcomes have followed. The first Roma Summit, for example, concluded with the creation of a European Platform for Roma Inclusion, an initiative pushed by the European Roma Policy Coalition, among others.[19] The platform facilitates regular meetings between member state representatives, Roma activists, policymakers, and experts led by the council presidency to identify best practices and simulate cooperation and exchanges of experience on successful inclusion policies. The talks have led to several outcomes, including a document called the "10 Common Basic Principles for Roma Inclusion" (resulting from the Platform meeting in Prague on April 24, 2009, during the Czech Presidency of the EU). These principles inform policy measures and try to maintain a balance between, on the one hand, advocating special measures to support Roma and, on the other, a mainstreaming approach.[20] The suggestions are primarily meant to mobilize national governments, but close collaboration with the European Commission is also set as a goal. For example, the European Commission has issued a Commission Recommendation on the active inclusion of people excluded from the labor market (2008/867/EC). This recommendation provides a general framework for the development of national programs that focus more narrowly on unemployed Roma. The European Commission has encouraged the member state governments to provide quantifiable targets to reduce the employment gap between Roma and other sections of the population. It has, among others, suggested that member states offer Roma access to micro-credit or employ more Roma as qualified civil servants in the public sector.

In April 2011, the European Commission adopted *An EU Framework for National Roma Integration Strategies up to 2020* that confirmed this general direction. It called for "active dialogue with the Roma" both at the national and the EU level, and it demanded a clear policy commitment from EU member states. The latter were urged to draw up "national Roma integration strategies," a process that was meant to give countries the opportunity not only to compare ideas, practices, and commitments, but also to create new pathways toward more robust monitoring by independent agencies and civil society actors.[21] Although the topics of electoral representation and the participation of Roma were not directly addressed by these measures and initiatives, the European Commission repeatedly called upon member states to secure the participation of nonelected Roma civil society in the review, implementation, and monitoring of their national strategies. For its part, the European Commission, like other international organizations before it, has continued to organize dialogues with Roma NGOs. As mentioned above, it organized several EU Platform meetings on Roma inclusion, giving all stakeholders an opportunity to express their views on the national strategies and their future implementation. On one such occasion in 2012, European Commissioner Viviane Reding urged the audience to be positive about what had been achieved since 2008. But she also admitted, "Drawing up the national Roma integration strategies and sets of policy measures for Roma integration was only the first step. The next step will be even more decisive: it remains to be seen how the strategies will be implemented. This is our focus today and from now on. The assessment of the strategies has not been finalized yet. However, I can say already that there is still a lot of room for improvement, in particular when it comes to securing sufficient funding for Roma inclusion and putting monitoring mechanisms in place."[22]

How have Roma activists responded? Some have been critical not only of the national institutions for Roma representation and national policies for social inclusion, but also of the new and still developing European institutional framework and its associated European policy strategies. Although most activists and organizations are strongly supportive of the fact that there is an increasing demand from government institutions for policy attention to Roma issues across Europe, there are also rising concerns about the lack of political will to implement the agreed policies, foster real change on the ground, or address discrimination and marginalization in ways that go beyond symbolic denouncements.[23] For example, the European Roma Policy Coalition (ERPC) has welcomed the EU's Council Recommendation on effective Roma integration measures in EU member states, while at the same time cautioning groups about rising levels of discrimination and lack of progress in Roma access to government institutions. In July 2013, ERPC called for "all for the introduction of indicators for genuine Roma participation and empowerment." The then-chair of the ERPC (and director of International Programs, Fundación Secretariado Gitano), Belén Sánchez-Rubio, added, "So far, the EU Framework has not improved [the Roma's] socioeconomic situation nor visibly decreased anti-Gypsyism."[24] In the run-up to the 2014 European elections, the European Roma and Travellers' Forum, an international Roma NGO, sent out a questionnaire to the candidates for Members of the European Parliament exploring their views on Roma and the functioning of the European legal and institutional framework. It is clear from the findings that many politicians are critical of the current institutional and legal setup. In their view, there is a need for legally binding policies. They argue that Roma inclusion policies are still too dependent on the will of the member state governments. For example, there is currently no legal obligation to have Roma representatives in state institutions. The report notes: "When asked to list three things they would change in the legal Framework, a common theme seemed to emerge: according to the candidates, it lacks concrete actions, anti-gypsyism is not sufficiently addressed and monitoring and sanction mechanisms are needed to enforce the legal

Framework."[25] The section on inclusion strategies in this volume (with chapters by Mirga, Mizsei, and Matache and Oehlke) further explores this gap, in particular the dynamic between the proliferation of Roma inclusion policies and failed implementation.[26]

Obstacles for Roma Mobilization and Participation

Though Roma political activism dates back to initiatives from the 1960s and 1970s, it experienced a major boost after the fall of Communism, when the number of Roma NGOs increased significantly and the first serious attempts at forming Roma political parties took place. Yet, while currently many Roma are active political participants when it comes to voting, and while the number of Roma activists is high, the effect of Roma political activism remains limited.[27]

Following McGarry and Agarin, it is important to make a distinction between Roma presence, voice, and influence.[28] The current structures and tools for Roma mobilization and participation are mostly focused on ensuring the presence of Roma in organizations and government structures, and in some cases, providing them with a meaningful voice and some level of influence. Presence, voice, and influence are three dimensions that are crucial to participation and mobilization, and in all three spheres of action, improvements are urgently needed. What are the most important obstacles, and how can they be overcome?

First, because many Roma communities across Europe face severe forms of social and economic exclusion, they lack the necessary resources to establish ethnic organizations and political parties that are powerful, visible, and viable as competitors in the realm of mainstream party competition. As a result, dependence on international donors remains high. Roma political organizations are also dependent on the will and support of other political actors, such as mainstream political parties. For these other political actors, however, Roma participation and mobilization are often not a priority. On the contrary, they sometimes pander to anti-Roma sentiments and reinforce xenophobic political movements. Moreover, there is a complex relationship between Roma voters and mainstream political parties that are seemingly more positive about Roma; in some cases, these parties co-opt Roma organizations for no other reason than to gain Roma votes; in other cases, mainstream political parties have been known to actually buy Roma votes. What is clear is that without the necessary organizational capacity, financial means, and symbolic resources (for example, recognition by powerful politicians), Roma mobilization and participation are likely to remain unsuccessful. Comparative political science research suggests that resources are a key explanatory factor of any form of political participation. There is a positive relationship between socioeconomic level and political activity: socioeconomically weaker individuals have less freedom to organize on the group level than those with greater socioeconomic status. Without adequate resources to generate organizational strength, political participation is bound to remain weak.[29]

Second, Roma activists and politicians grapple with widely held views about who the Roma are and what they want. The marginalization of Roma is often misunderstood as a self-chosen withdrawal from mainstream society and mainstream politics. The current portrayal of Roma in the media gives the impression that they are passive objects of policy, not active subjects. Unfortunately, the current socioeconomic situation gives little hope for improvement. Most Roma continue to grapple with high levels of unemployment, especially in isolated areas where there is no access to labor market opportunity, where they often have to live in substandard housing and where they suffer from poor and/or segregated education. Lack of access to health services and dependence on social welfare benefits further reduce options for employability and increase levels of poverty. As a result of a complex constellation of economic and social trends—including economic exclusion, discrimination and racism—many Roma communities who have been historically excluded from mainstream society find themselves even more marginalized in present day European societies, particularly in Central and Eastern Europe (see the chapter by Kálmán Miszei in this volume for further elaboration of this point). Lack of effective policies for equal and inclusive citizenship for Roma has reinforced a climate of hatred against them (blame-the-victim strategies). In the context of regulatory practices that accompany modernization— such as the management of migration flows, urban planning, settlement policies, the controlling of borders and the creation of some form of European citizenship—new ways of problematizing the Roma have emerged.[30]

Third, Roma identity is not generally associated with any territorial claims. This, too, hampers the visibility and potential of Roma mobilizations. In a context still mainly defined by nation-state borders, any form of cross-border identity has limited opportunities for political mobilization. Ethnic politics are still predominantly framed in national terms, particularly in the Central and Eastern European countries: at times of elections, people are mobilized as "nations" or "national minorities." For many Roma, political participation "as Roma" is not a self-evident good because they fear it might reinforce the view that their group does not belong to the main national community, or even to the national territory, and that therefore their plight is not part of the realm of national government responsibility. Many mainstream politicians have indeed promoted such views. They have portrayed the Roma as national outsiders or migrants, even if they are not.

In order to overcome these obstacles, improvements are needed in the three dimensions crucial to participation and mobilization: presence, voice, and influence. In the area of presence, in states without effective systems in place for guaranteed representation, Roma remain underrepresented in local and national assemblies. In Central and Eastern Europe, ethnicity has often functioned as a frame for political action, but this has not been the case for Roma. Even when there are successes—in the 2014 European elections two elected MEPs claimed Roma background—the overall picture is one of only marginal political presence. Arguably the presence of minorities and vulnerable groups in representative structures is a requirement in any society committed to democratic equality; and therefore, the inclusion of Roma in government structures needs to be promoted. Such inclusion is also the first stepping-stone toward fulfilling the need to enhance the capacity of Roma politicians and activists to become equal participants in democratic policy debates and have a fair say in the making of collective decisions, especially when those decisions affect sections of the population that include many Roma.

The threat of current political rhetoric applied, among others, by right-wing populist politicians is another factor hampering Roma participation and mobilization. Over the last few years, hate speech against Roma and anti-Roma political campaigning have risen, and the number of instances of hate crime against the Roma have increased as well, both in their home countries and in the countries where Roma migrants arrive. Although Romaphobia has a long history in Europe, today Roma are more explicitly targeted than before as adversaries of the "national" population in various places. As the chapters by Guy confirms, this clearly has a strong demobilizing effect on Roma. Recent survey data presented by the EU Fundamental Rights Agency reveals the extent to which Roma feel discriminated against. For example, 46 percent of Roma respondents reported feeling discriminated against because of their ethnicity in the past twelve months, with responses from individual countries ranging from as high as 66 percent (Italy) and as low as 29 percent (Romania).[31] The focus of the political rhetoric of law and order directed toward them can only exacerbate the already pervasive feeling of being excluded.[32] According to Stewart the current populism directed against Roma is in some ways connected to the European integration project, which "paradoxically, creates the broad conditions of receptivity to xenophobic politics across the whole continent; changes in European social and economic structures which threaten traditional redistributive systems and place poor 'others' in an unflattering spotlight."[33]

As a result, the possible positive effect of the European integration process for marginalized populations is in need of critical reflection. Many Roma activists as well as external observers have had the expectation of pushing Roma inclusion progress from the European integration process. EU institutions were expected to encourage commitments among governments of member states in the field of Roma inclusion policies. For this reason, Roma activists have often addressed issues at the level of European organizations and institutions; primarily but not exclusively the European Parliament and the European Commission. This development seems indicative of the growth of a European space for Roma activism—a public space that is less state-centered, allows claims to be framed in terms of European standards, and therefore facilitates the emergence of an active European citizenship. But while this Europeanization of minority politics—and by Europeanization, I mean the fact that there are now monitoring systems related to the European integration process—has offered minority activists additional and powerful avenues of activism, it has also led to a number of important problems.

Europeanization as a dominant strategy of self-representation for minorities created the space for states lacking real willingness to develop and implement effective Roma policies to divert attention away from the responsibilities of the national state. It also created unrealistic expectations of the states about the competencies and potential impact of European institutions, and in the absence of a more general presence of European citizenship, it stimulated and objectified a trend to see minorities as bounded groups that are completely separated from the national population of a state and do not share any interests with other groups within that national population. While Europeanized actions to defend the interests of the Roma are potentially more powerful than national or local mobilizations, in practice they have problematic side effects due to limited willingness of some governments to draw the line between European and national responsibilities toward Roma inclusion.[34] In other words, there is a need for national governments to understand the problems facing Roma populations not merely as European problems but also as policy issues for which they carry national responsibility.[35]

The Avenue of Youth Activism

Although Europeanization has its risks, it has generated new opportunities for Roma mobilization. An increase in the number of cross-border contacts among Roma activists and the growth of Roma organizational networks within Europe contribute to the emergence of new viable possibilities for alternative forms of mobilization. One promising avenue is youth engagement. This development is significant, not least because of the youthfulness of the various groups routinely identified as "Roma" across Europe. Various authors have argued that the social mobility of young Roma may facilitate large-scale social change. They have suggested social mobility strategies for young Roma through new opportunities for full participation in regular educational institutions, even at a very young age or through new forms of youth activism. In attempts at creating an active political movement (or various movements), young Roma engaged in building an active political movement sometimes turn to collective action frames, ideas, and organizational platforms that differ from the older Roma movement structures.[36] The activities of such organizations as ternYpe: International Roma Youth Network and the European Roma Grassroots Organizations Network (ERGO).[37]

The success of these initiatives is a testament to the growing demand for creative new mobilizations. Desegregation in education leads to a wider variety of experiences for young Roma. These experiences are valuable, not only because they create new socioeconomic opportunities for young Roma, but also because they provide young Roma with access to diverse social networks. As a result, young Roma participants may acquire new international contacts and new skills. In the field of mobilization and participation, new ideas about how to protest against discrimination and exclusion can arise. In addition, inclusive education and inclusive youth activism may contribute to changing attitudes among co-students and fellow youth activists who are not Roma. As a result, Roma can more easily access a variety of identity groups, which in itself might be a form of social mobilization: for example, they can begin to identify not only as "Roma" but also as "youth," or become part of all kinds of networks that cut across ethnic identifications or social affiliations. Such new identifications may ultimately lead to the emergence of new collective action frames and new protest identities.

The possibility of promoting new images of Roma identity should not be underestimated.[38] Doing so might open up a new conceptual space for understanding what it means to be Roma. Very often current policies are driven by old stereotypical views and understandings of who the Roma are and the nature of the problems they face. Policy responses to Roma migration are a case in point. Often such responses have focused heavily on security and control of so-called nomadic or inherently mobile groups. These policies are usually driven by a limited analysis of the reality of Roma migration and little knowledge of the broader issue of Roma identity. The targeted and sometimes violent expulsion policies seem to have been driven by, or at least made possible through, such stereotypical pre-existing imaginaries. These widespread imaginaries are sometimes blatantly racist, but even when they seem innocent—such as the tendency to think about Roma as eternal migrants—they may be harmful. Mobilizers active in the field of antidiscrimination and social inclusion are aware of such mechanisms and may deliberately seek to engage in advancing new social understandings of Roma identity. One example of such an effort is the proposed European Roma Institute, which would highlight Roma arts and culture.[39]

Young Roma activists, therefore, can act as new reality instructors in this field. They can provide living evidence of the fluidity of group boundaries and thereby challenge entrenched associations between Roma identity and certain social problems. They make clear that the people who are routinely called Roma in fact belong to various crosscutting social groups and should not be enclosed in a discourse that premises itself on the basis of a single social attribute—such as being poor or being a victim. Roma activists can engage in recuperative identity politics as well as expose the stereotypical political identity construction practices that lead to discrimination and social exclusion.

Conclusion

In this chapter I have outlined in brief compass the opportunities and limits of Roma political participation and mobilization in the current European political and social context. I have argued that new avenues for political and social mobilization have become available to Roma activists, since new political opportunity structures have emerged on the national and European level. Yet important challenges remain, and the recent popularity of extreme right-wing populist responses to Roma mobilization and migration has created new obstacles to full participation and equal citizenship of Roma in our contemporary societies. The goal of Roma inclusion processes of political participation and mobilization should not stop with presence, voice, and influence. It should also have a broader societal impact: it should open up the public's understanding of what it means to be Roma. Current uncritical and stereotypical uses of the word Roma in the media and in political discourse should be countered by stories about Roma who are in various political arenas meaningful contributors to the ways in which European societies are governed.

Chapter 12

Roma in European Politics, Looking to the Future

David Mark

Effective political representation by Roma leaders and organizations is finally on the increase. Support for the political participation of Roma has grown across Europe; calls to empower and mobilize Roma communities are gradually becoming part of the mainstream discourse on Roma issues. These are significant developments, given the acknowledged importance of self-mobilization and leadership by marginalized communities in the process of securing social progress. Direct participation in politics, including local politics, is often effective in ways that assistance or social programs are not, even with increased funding. For Roma communities, in particular, there is evidence that elected representatives at the local level can negotiate the passage of administrative and legal measures and the distribution of resources—leading to better and more sustainable access to public services, education, and health, as well as to better infrastructure.[1]

In this chapter I focus on the political participation of Roma and argue that increased participation is essential for overall progress. First, I address criticism directed at Roma political participation, probing the accuracy of several claims related to the quality of Roma politicians. Second, I explore the legal frameworks that set the stage for Roma participation as a minority. Finally, I examine the interactions and networks established between Roma politicians and Roma constituencies. I also identify possible avenues and opportunities for intervention, especially for EU policy makers and Roma politicians, by examining existing policies, models, and programs designed to increase the participation of citizens belonging to underrepresented groups.

My work experience at the European Parliament of the European Union informs these observations and generates concrete examples of the continuing influence of political participation on policy making.

Critical Views: Ethno-Politics Versus Mainstream Political Participation

As attention to Roma political participation increases, the view that participation benefits integration efforts is coming under attack. Citing examples from Central and Eastern Europe and the Western Balkans, some critics argue that the preeminence of corrupt and professionally unfit Roma politicians has vitiated Roma political mobilization and undermined realization of positive outcomes for Roma communities. This view is widely shared by some Roma civic activists, leaders of NGOs, and professionals who hold or have held positions in intergovernmental organizations. However, such views are rarely made public.

According to these critics, this reality is particularly reflected in the abysmal track record of Roma political leaders at the national level in regard to policy making that contributes to Roma integration. Empirical evidence, they suggest, undercuts the argument that political mobilization and participation of Roma should become a priority for policy makers and civic leaders. The strongest criticism is directed against "ethno-politics," or forms of political representation that are based on ethnicity and rooted in the narrative of collective minority rights. Critics argue that this type of political representation is outdated and creates divisions between Roma and non-Roma at the societal level. In both instances, Roma politicians are portrayed as able to represent only personal and group interests, and as using their power to manipulate and control Roma communities.[2]

To unpack these arguments, it is first important to understand that the behavior of Roma elected representatives is dependent upon several variables. A Roma politician's political performance is influenced by personal choices, character, and education just as much as by ideology or political views. Of course, the same holds true for non-Roma politicians. That some politicians are corrupt, populist, or simply make inopportune decisions has nothing to do with their ethnicity. A democracy is equipped with tools and mechanisms that allow voters to replace unfit politicians during electoral cycles. Thus, the key to understanding the issue raised by the critics is linked to the efficacy of political accountability machinery—for example, whether politicians are held responsible for their actions or replaced if unfit during the next election cycle.[3]

Before delegitimizing and discouraging efforts to improve participation of Roma, critics should ask whether the instruments and processes in place to prevent abuse of power function correctly. To identify flaws preventing the emergence of a better prepared and more responsible Roma political leadership, it is imperative to consider legislative frameworks that regulate minority representation and the relationship between Roma politicians and Roma constituencies. This chapter addresses these issues by exposing some troubling realities and probing the ways in which minority politics function in the case of Roma in two countries in the Central and Eastern European (CEE) region: Romania and Hungary.

Pluralism and Free Choice: How Democracy Is Distorted Through Legislation

As some recent developments related to politics in the region show, rules and legislative measures regarding representation of Roma are often deficient, contradicting the principle of pluralism in a democratic society. Though these rules originally emerged as measures designed to enhance the representation of minorities, paradoxically they have resulted in the obstruction of free and fair electoral competition in Roma communities.

For example, in Romania, onerous requirements are imposed on organizations trying to register in electoral competitions for Parliamentary elections. In order to register for elections, current legislative regulations oblige Roma political organizations to obtain special approval in the form of status as a "public utility" conferred by the National Agency for Roma, a governmental agency.[4] As it happens, for the past eight years, the president of the National Agency for Roma has been a political appointee nominated by "the Roma Party–Pro-Europe," an incumbent organization that has represented Roma in the Romanian Parliament since the regime change in 1989. This is the only Roma organization with public utility status and, therefore, a legal entitlement to participate in national elections. Appointing a member of this organization to make such a decision—to in effect, decide whether or not other Roma organizations should gain public utility status and be able to run against it during elections—generates a clear conflict of interest and could be considered illegal under Article 253 of the Penal Code.

This unsatisfactory situation was highlighted in the report of the Organization for Security and Cooperation in Europe (OSCE) Office for Democratic Institutions and Human Rights (ODIHR), which monitored the parliamentary elections in Romania in 2012. The organization found that "the Election Law also allows for preferential treatment of organizations representing national minorities in the Council of National Minorities" contradicting "OSCE commitments, which underline the importance of pluralism with regard to political organizations and the obligation to provide necessary legal guarantees to enable competition on a basis of equal treatment before the law and by the authorities." OSCE ODIHR called for the "legislation [to be] be amended to ensure fair competition without unduly favoring the organizations represented on the Council of National Minorities or in the parliament."[5]

The Romanian Parliament has so far failed to take any steps to address this situation, an omission inconsistent with international obligations to promote political openness and a level playing field for competing organizations. This situation has had a significant impact on the Roma minority's political activity in Romania. Faced with an effective ban on participation in national elections, competing Roma organizations protested publicly against the laws that barred them from participation.[6] In an open letter addressed to Romanian state authorities, leaders demanded that they address the "abuse and discrimination found in the Electoral Law."[7] In this context, it should be noted that new entrant organizations, starting from a largely unequal position compared to the government-subsidized incumbent,[8] had boosted the participation of Roma in local elections in 2012—adding thirty-six mandates for Roma local councilors while mobilizing more than 30,000 Roma voters.[9]

Another example of deficient legislation, which has impeded effective Roma political representation, is the 2013 modification of the electoral law in Hungary that connected national elections to the system of minority representation, known as the "Minority Self Governments System." This amendment introduced the "national minority list" as a means to ensure minority representation based on a so-called "beneficial quota"—essentially a lower threshold that would allow the presence of minority representatives in parliament. The Electoral Law on the Election of Members of Parliament,

Article 7 paragraph 2, reads as follows: "A citizen who belongs to a minority can vote a) for a candidate of his electoral district and b) for the list of his own nationality" (my translations) if he or she has indicated so in the registration form for national minorities. In brief, as opposed to a non-minority citizen who can vote for both a candidate and a national party list, a citizen who registers as a member of a minority can vote only for a candidate and for the "national minority list." These legislative modifications sparked controversy, as the merits of the entire legislative system were put in question, as was the commitment of the ruling coalition to adhere to international standards.

Even before these recent changes, the Minority Self-Government System (MSG) had received ample criticism. The system allows any of the country's recognized minorities to establish local, regional, and national self-governments that can work on matters related to language and cultural heritage. The most important argument against the MSG has been that it diverts Roma from mainstream politics. In a 2006 assessment for the OSCE ODIHR, the National Democratic Institute observed:

> At the outset, advocates, scholars and policy makers expressed concern about a separate government system for deliberating "Romani issues." Procedural problems also became evident after the creation of the MSGs. . . . [The] participants identified many problems with [the] system. These included unclear competencies, the lack of differentiation between various minority needs, deficiencies in financing, and voter enfranchisement regardless of ethnic affiliation. This latter problem, combined with abuses related to candidates seeking to represent minority groups to which they did not belong, resulted in cases, such as in the community of Jazsladany, of non-Roma being elected to Romani MSGs by non-Roma voters with the aim of limiting the effectiveness of the MSG.

The report did note that 2005 changes to the law were directed at solving the latter problem.[10]

According to Paragraph 9 of the revised law, the National Minority List is determined by the National Minority Self-Government based on signatures from at least 1 percent of the citizens in the national minority register, with a maximum of 1500 signatures required for a proposed candidate. The list must include at least three candidates, and candidates must be registered in the national minority register. Clearly, the incumbent organization controlling a particular national minority exerts an important influence on how that national minority's list for parliamentary elections will be established. The incumbent organization for Roma in Hungary is Lungo Drom, the largest Roma party; it also has an alliance with the governing party in Hungary, Fidesz.

Unsurprisingly, the amended legislation came under fire from a range of stakeholders, including competing Roma political factions. Istvan Makai, head of the Roma Civic Union and president of the Budapest Roma Minority Self-Government, asserted that "the new election law forces Roma to choose between their right to vote in accordance with their political beliefs and their right to identify with their ethnicity." An article in the Hungarian daily *Népszabadság* reported suspicions that personal data on Roma public workers had been collected and used to register them as minority voters without their consent, fueling the controversy.[11]

Criticism of the amended law was not confined to political opponents. Hungarian weekly *HVG* reported that Lakatos Bela, a mayor of Roma origin affiliated with the governing party (Fidesz), suspended his membership and announced his intent to renounce it if "registered minority citizens are not able to vote on the party lists." He declared that "the new election law provides no solutions for minorities. In fact, it categorically discriminates against them and forcibly pits them against one another."[12]

At the outset of the Venice Commission,[13] the Council of Europe's advisory body on constitutional matters and the OSCE ODIHR at Hungary's invitation reviewed its constitution and more recently, several pieces of revised legislation, including the Elections Act. The Venice Commission welcomed the introduction of provisions that aimed to ensure participation of national minorities in parliament. However, both organizations recommended that voters have the right to choose between registering to vote for normal national party lists or the national minority lists and that the law should allow such registration in a reasonably short time frame before election day and on election day.[14] The issue that remained unaddressed was the exclusive right of the National Minority Self-Government, the incumbent Roma organization, to establish the "minority list" for which registered voters would eventually vote.

The most virulent reaction to the new electoral law came from the newly created Hungarian Roma Party (Magyarországi Cigány Part, MCP), which publicly called on Roma to not register on the minority roster and to refrain from voting for the "minority list."[15] Horvath Aladar, the party's spokesman and leading figure, declared that he would not vote on a list that was being established by the incumbent organization, Lungo Drom.

The cases in Romania and Hungary cast doubt on the authorities' commitment to the principle of political pluralism and fair competition. In Romania, during the last parliamentary election, only one Roma political organization was able to register. Essentially running unchallenged, the organization gained a total of 20,000 votes, a 50 percent decrease compared to the 2008 elections. In spite of this, it continues to hold the single constitutionally guaranteed seat for Roma in the Parliament and if current procedures continue, will do so for all future election cycles, irrespective of the number of votes it receives. In Hungary, the April 2014 parliamentary elections showed that the new law failed to create larger representation for Roma, although with four elected deputies, Hungary does have the highest number of Roma political representatives in Europe. Only 4048 votes, representing 0.08 percent of the national vote, were given to candidates on the "minority list." In comparison, the MCP, mentioned above, a new party organized mainly by leaders of civil organizations with candidates on a regular national party list, received more than double the votes given to the Lungo-Drom-established "minority list." Clearly Roma voters rejected the new electoral system, preferring to express their choices within the general election framework (national party lists). These results are very significant despite the fact that they have been dwarfed by majority mainstream parties.

The discrepancies in these two examples show that Roma voters do not have the opportunity for real choice, since competition within the systems of minority representation is nonexistent. Both examples also call into question whether Roma have access to accepted practices common in any democratic society. In the case of the Roma, can those who wield political power be speedily replaced by voters? Or are these provisions—meant as positive measures to ensure minority representation—a means for allowing politicians to preserve an otherwise unnatural hold on political power, irrespective of whether they are accountable to Roma communities?

A closer look at emerging legislative measures regarding minority representation in national parliaments reveals a disturbing reality in which pluralism and political accountability in Roma politics has become a victim of big political party interests. For years to come, in various forms, the current measures insure that Roma will almost always validate what majority elites have already chosen for them. This blanket validation from the Roma electorate will likely continue to be reflected by a general lack of interest and apathy in democratic processes. However, this poor track record of Roma "ethno-politics" is neither the consequence of some intrinsic corruptness manifested in Roma communities nor some Roma "authoritarian nationalist tradition" bent on oppressing the people.[16] Rather, applying a critical lens to instances where Roma representatives are elected on mainstream party lists reveals similar distortions of the principles of genuine representation and accountability. With only few exceptions, in private discussions Roma and non-Roma rights activists alike routinely expose their disappointment with Roma politicians elected on the lists of mainstream parties—opinions rarely expressed in public. Within closed circles, activists openly express frustration with politicians of Roma origin who in various contexts water down the reality of discrimination and human rights violations to gain favor with their non-Roma peers. This behavior is hardly surprising, given that these politicians' careers are rarely linked to Roma constituencies, but instead depend on the mainstream political parties that launch them.

The disconnect between Roma politicians and Roma constituencies often means that representation of Roma interests becomes secondary to the representation of party interest. For the external observer, Roma politicians are little more than tokens, or at best "poster persons," that attract the sympathies of some Roma voters. In fact, the limited or nonexistent ties to community constituencies weaken the position of Roma politicians within their ideological parties. Without establishing a robust political base, Roma politicians are unable to clearly define their contribution in terms of voters, loyal cadres, activists, or financial support. Their discourse and actions are not dictated by Roma interest but by the immediate needs of the party leadership, which may or may not converge with the plight of the Roma.

Leveling the Field: Reform of the Legislative Framework

In view of the above, electoral systems that provide mandatory minority political representation (currently Romania, Hungary, Croatia, Slovenia locally, Kosovo, and Bosnia and Herzegovina) should be critically reviewed in order to remove provisions that are undemocratic and in breach of the principle of political pluralism. Policy makers should understand that minorities do not constitute unitary blocs of consensus and that accountability, political pluralism, and the ability to elect among various programs are as important for minorities as they are for all citizens. First and foremost, legislative measures that favor incumbents over new entrants on the minority political scene should be struck down by national parliaments, constitutional courts, or the European Court of Human Rights.[17] Only then will Roma voters be able to make real choices and hold Roma politicians and their political organizations accountable. Secondly, measures that impose unreasonable administrative limitations should be eliminated, allowing ease of access to registration and participation for all political actors. This would ensure renewal of the Roma political scene and provide incumbents with pressure to perform in the interest of the community.

Apart from enacting legislative reform, efforts in the area of Roma political participation should also focus on empowering better trained and better educated Roma candidates to enter the political scene. Whether they do so by way of ethnic political platforms or through mainstream political parties is a marginal issue. What is important is that they are equipped with sufficient knowledge of community issues and are held accountable to Roma constituencies and beyond. Once elected, they should take the opportunity to promote good governance in policies related to Roma inclusion. They should develop strong relationships with Roma constituencies, strengthening their position within parties by nurturing a mobilized and politically conscious voter base. Real representation should constitute the norm rather than the exception in the Roma political world.

Mobilizing and educating Roma communities to participate in political life is still necessary despite negative examples of corrupt or subservient Roma politicians. Finally, critics should use the same yardstick when looking at processes related to Roma political participation as for assessing mainstream politics. A position that employs double standards sits on a shaky foundation.

The European Parliament: A Unique Opportunity

In spite of many setbacks, especially in national parliaments, examples of genuine representation of Roma communities at the local level and at the EU level have emerged in the last decade. Activities have included efforts to put Roma issues on the political agenda, negotiations to ensure financial resources for social inclusion programs, attempts to combat discriminatory practices in public institutions, and the adoption of strong positions against negative, repressive policies. Local political initiatives that benefit Roma communities' access to services and utilities include infrastructure developments such as the extension of paved roads, electricity grids, sewage, and water networks, as well as improved access to education, health, and employment. Efforts have ranged beyond infrastructure to cultural events that challenge commonly held prejudices to attempts to alleviate poverty. I myself have had the privilege of working on more than one such political enterprise.

In December 2004, I joined the office of newly elected Member of the European Parliament (MEP), Viktoria Mohacsi, a Hungarian liberal politician of Roma origin. Ms. Mohacsi is known for her groundbreaking role in putting together and implementing the Hungarian school de-segregation policy, which was at that time one of the most progressive and politically controversial education policies in the CEE region.[18] Upon taking office, her immediate task was to map out areas and opportunities to mainstream Roma issues into the work of the European Parliament (EP). At the same time, there was a clear need to press the European Commission, the EU's executive arm, toward adopting a more targeted approach to Roma inclusion—a goal that eluded Roma activists up until 2009.

This mapping exercise very quickly revealed the massive knowledge gap and poor track record of the European Parliament in dealing with Roma-related issues. The few official documents (resolutions, reports, opinions, and so forth) adopted by the Parliament dated back to 1995, which coincided with the last time an MEP of Roma origin served in the institution.[19] Regular documents—reports assessing the progress of Romania and Bulgaria toward accession, resolutions marking the Holocaust or Human Rights day, assessments and opinions related to the implementation of the EU anti-discrimination directives—were with some exceptions devoid of any content related to the Roma, despite the obvious challenges this twelve million strong community was facing.[20] Indeed, with a few exceptions, many MEPs concerned and otherwise active in the area of civil liberties and human rights had little or almost no knowledge of Roma-related issues.

Mohacsi's efforts were joined by the many Roma activists already working within the European Union or in other international organizations. One vivid example was our cooperation with Roma civil society and other intergovernmental institutions around the adoption of the "European Parliament Resolution on the Situation of the Roma in the European Union" in April 2005,[21] the first such document in more than a decade. The first draft included contributions from Nicolae Gheorghe, then adviser for Roma and Sinti Issues at the OSCE's ODIHR; Mr. Nicolae Valeriu, then acting director of the

European Roma Information Office; Mr. Claude Cahn, programs director of European Roma Rights Centre; and Mr. Bernard Rorke, director of the Open Society Institute's Roma Participation Program. The work on the resolution was supplemented by MEP Livia Jaroka of the European Peoples Party and MEP Els de Groen of the Greens as well as other human rights-oriented MEPs from a variety of parties. Thanks to the wide array of supporters, the resolution passed and marked the starting point of a process that has since advanced into a full-fledged EU policy.

The work of only two Roma MEPs (MEP Livia Jaroka was Roma as well as MEP Mohacsi), in close cooperation with civil society organizations and Roma activists, helped trigger the Parliament's acknowledgment of Roma-related issues, which were mainstreamed in the work of the European Parliament. As subsequent resolutions and reports attest the Parliament steered the way to the European Union becoming the leading European institution matters related to Roma inclusion. Later on, the "migration crisis" marked by the 2008 state of emergency in Italy and the 2010 French repatriation policies provided the political push factor that propelled the Roma issue from a marginal social issue to the top of the EU's agenda on inclusion questions. The groundbreaking work of the two Roma MEPs provided the institutional legitimacy that has guided and continues to guide developments related to Roma at the EU level. A close look at the European Commission's subsequent *EU Framework for National Roma Integration Strategies up to 2020*, affirmed by the Council of the European Union Conclusions, reveals a striking similarity to the political texts previously adopted by the European Parliament, although featuring more ambiguous language about alignment with national priorities.[22]

In this context, a recurrent question is whether EU Roma-related processes have translated into real outcomes for Roma families at the local level. On this debate, the jury is still out. Nevertheless, an increasing number of actors recognize the progress made in developing policy frameworks, and more importantly, in providing the bulk of the EU funds for Roma integration.[23]

Conclusion

It is important that the Roma candidates who secured seats in EP legislature cooperate in spite of ideological differences. If this is the case, the presence of Roma politicians across the aisle is a clear advantage. Roma politicians can make a significant impact on the political participation of Roma people with a special focus on participation at the local level and voter education. By focusing attention on these issues, they will not only contribute to efforts to enhance Roma participation, but also will strengthen their positions by developing relationships with a more politically conscious Roma constituency, as argued above. In practical terms, Roma MEPs can use their existing political capital to press for stronger involvement of the European Commission on issues related to Roma participation. And to make things easier, there are plenty of opportunities that can be exploited in the area of Roma voter participation.

The low participation of Roma in democratic processes has in my view a direct impact on the effectiveness of social and economic policies put in place in the past years, either in the framework of Decade of Roma Inclusion 2005–2015 or the *EU Framework for National Roma Integration Strategies*.[24] Due to the complexity of this subject, I aim to dedicate a separate analysis to it, but want to raise some possibilities for increasing that participation here. The European Union is by no means a stranger to promoting and supporting the participation of marginalized or disadvantaged groups. Examples of financial support to promote women's participation in politics abound, and there are policies being developed on the political participation of persons with disabilities.[25] At the same time, there is arguably no need for new targeted Roma-only programs or financial instruments. Calling for targeted measures for Roma remains a contentious and politically charged process. Measures that enhance Roma participation can be mainstreamed within existing programs. European Commission programs, such as "Europe for Citizens" and "Youth in Action," can provide the platforms to support voter education programs for Roma people. Similar programs under the Directorate General for Justice and the EU Agency for Fundamental Rights also touch upon the issue of electoral rights in relation to municipal elections across the European Union and participation in European Parliament elections and could see Roma-related issues being mainstreamed.

If brought to bear with effective Roma voter participation, the EU policy instruments that were launched in 2011 could make a significant change in the landscape of Roma integration by 2018, when the new European legislature will be elected. Particularly if combined with the reforms in national minority voting I suggest earlier in this chapter, EU programs could support a more organic participation of Roma people in their communities across the European Union.

Notes

Realizing Roma Rights: An Introduction

1. For the sake of coherence, we have chosen to use the term "Roma" exclusively in this text. However, some advocates and scholars use "Romani" as an adjective rather than "Roma" as both noun and adjective. Both usages are correct.

2. Sam Beck, "The Romanian Gypsy Problem," *Papers from the 4th and 5th Annual Meetings*, ed. Joanne Grumet (Cheverly, Md.: Gypsy Lore Society, 1985), 100–109, as cited in Ian Hancock, *The Pariah Syndrome: An Account of Gypsy Slavery and Persecution* (Ann Arbor, Mich.: Karoma, 1987), 1.

3. Jack Greenberg, "Report on Roma Education Today: From Slavery to Segregation and Beyond," *Columbia Law Review*, 110, no. 4 (May 2010): 919–1001, quotation 919.

4. See Council of Europe (CoE), "Roma-related texts adopted at the Council of Europe," http://www.coe.int/en/web/portal/roma-related-texts; for the specific 1969 recommendation, see CoE Parliamentary Assembly, *Situation of Gypsies and Other Travellers in Europe*, Rec 563 (Strasbourg, September 30, 1969), http://assembly.coe.int/nw/xml/XRef/Xref-XML2HTML-en.asp?fileid=14599&lang=en; for a selection of EU Roma-related texts, see EU Justice Directorate-General, "EU and Roma," http://ec.europa.eu/justice/discrimination/roma/index_en.htm.

5. For more on this topic in general, see in this volume Kálmán Mizsei, "Reconstructing Roma Integration in Central and Eastern Europe: Addressing the Failures of the Last Quarter Century"; and, for Hungary in particular, also in this volume, Will Guy, "Anti-Roma Violence, Hate Speech, and Discrimination in the New Europe: Czech Republic, Slovakia, and Hungary."

6. Claude Cahn and Elspeth Guild, *Recent Migration of Roma in Europe*, 2nd ed. (commissioned by the OSCE High Commissioner on National Minorities and CoE Commissioner for Human Rights, October 2010), 15, http://www.osce.org/hcnm/78034?download=true.

7. See, for example, the work of Isabel Fonseca, Will Guy, Ian Hancock, and Jean-Pierre Liégeois.

8. For no school, see Christian Brüggemann, *Roma Education in Comparative Perspective: Analysis of the UNDP/World Bank/EC Regional Roma Survey 2011* (Bratislava: UNDP, 2012), 38–39; for Moldova, see Dotcho Mihailov, *The Health Situation of Roma Communities: Analysis of the UNDP/World Bank/EC Regional Roma Survey 2011* (Bratislava: UNDP, 2012), 36–37, http://www.undp.org/content/dam/rbec/docs/The-health-situation-of-Roma-communities.pdf; for Romania, see World Bank, Europe and Central Asia Human Development Sector Unit, "Economic Costs of Roma Social Exclusion," Note (Washington, D.C.: World Bank, April 2010), 2,

http://siteresources.worldbank.org/. EXTROMA/Resources/Economic_Costs_Roma_Exclusion_
Note_Final.pdf.

9. Michael Mann, *The Dark Side of Democracy: Explaining Ethnic Cleansing* (Cambridge: Cambridge University Press, 2005).

10. See, for examples, Jakob Hurrle et al., *Uncertain Impact: Have Roma in Slovakia Benefitted from the European Social Fund? Findings from an Analysis of ESF Employment and Social Inclusion Projects in the 2007–2013 Programming Period* (Bratislava: UNDP, 2012), http://www.undp.org/content/dam/rbec/docs/Have-Roma-in-Slovakia-benefitted-from-the-European-Social-Fund.pdf; and "Harnessing EU Funds for Roma Inclusion," in *Beyond Rhetoric: Roma Integration Roadmap for 2020*, comp. Bernard Rorke (Budapest: Open Society Foundations, June 2011), 49.

11. *Brown v. Board of Education*, 347 U.S. 483 (1954), finding segregation in education unconstitutional, despite purportedly equal conditions.

12. As Goldston makes clear, the desegregation gains of *Brown v. Board of Education* have not been fully maintained. School segregation at the time of this writing, he shows, is as extensive as it was before the Supreme Court decided the case. Other aspects of African American discrimination also continue to plague the United States, from disproportionate rates of incarceration, to socio-economic deprivation, to lack of access to robust health care, financial services, employment and other career opportunities. For an excellent survey of the enduring legacy of slavery on the circumstances of African Americans, see Ta-Nehisi Coates, "The Case for Reparations," *The Atlantic*, June 2014.

13. Greenberg, "Report on Roma Education Today," 919.

14. James A. Goldston, "The Unfulfilled Promise of Educational Opportunity in the United States and Europe: From *Brown v. Board* to *D.H.* and Beyond," in this volume. The phrase "discrete and insular" is from the U.S. Supreme Court judgment in *United States v. Carolene Products Company*, 304 U.S. 144 (1938), footnote 4, viewed as the precursor to *Brown*.

15. Ana Bracic, "EU Accession, NGOs and Human Rights: discrimination against the Roma in Slovenia and Croatia," working paper, Center on Democracy, Development, and the Rule of Law, Stanford University, 2013, http://www.anabracic.com/uploads/1/1/3/8/11385527/bracic_roma_draft.pdf.

16. European Commission, *An EU Framework for National Roma Integration Strategies up to 2020*, Communication, COM(2011) 173 (Brussels, April 5, 2011), http://ec.europa.eu/justice/policies/discrimination/docs/com_2011_173_en.pdf.

17. Organization of Security and Cooperation in Europe (OSCE), *Action Plan on Improving the Situation of Roma and Sinti Within the OSCE Area*, MC. DEC.3/03 (Maastricht: OSCE, 2003) and also, for assessment of lack of progress, OSCE Office for Democratic Institutions and Human Rights (ODIHR), *Implementation of the Action Plan on Improving the Situation of Roma and Sinti Within the OSCE Area: Status Report 2013 (Renewed Commitments, Renewed Challenges)* (Warsaw: OSCE/ODIHR, 2013); for more on the Decade, see "The Decade of Roma Inclusion: 2005–2015," http://www.romadecade.org/; and Kálmán Mizsei's discussion of some of the factors contributing to its lack of success in "Reconstructing Roma Integration in Central and Eastern Europe."

18. European Commission, *Report on the Implementation of the EU Framework for National Roma Integration Strategies* (Brussels: EU, 2014).

19. Laura Surdu, *Monitoring the Enforcement Action Against School Segregation in Romania* (Bucharest: Romani CRISS and UNICEF, July 2008).

20. Cahn and Guild, *Recent Migration of Roma in Europe*, 7.

21. Ibid., 14.

22. EU Fundamental Rights Agency (FRA), *EU Minorities and Discrimination Survey, Data in Focus Report 1: The Roma* (Vienna: FRA, April 2009), 8.

23. Yaron Matras, *I Met Lucky People: The Story of the Romani Gypsies* (London: Allen Lane, 2014), 44–45.

24. Ibid., 212–13.

25. Nicolae Gheorghe in collaboration with Gergő Pulay, "Choices to Be Made and Prices to Be Paid: Potential Roles and Consequences in Roma Activism and Policy-Making," in *From Victimhood to Citizenship: The Path of Roma Integration—A Debate*, ed. Will Guy (Budapest: Kossuth Kiadó, distr. Central European University Press, 2013).

Chapter 1. Roma Children and Enduring Educational Exclusion in Italy

The chapter epigraph is from Italian Government, *Report to the Committee on the Elimination of Racial Discrimination*, UN Doc. No. CERD/C/ITA/15(2006) (Rome, 2006), para. 177.

1. Special Commission for the Protection and Promotion of Human Rights of the Italian Senate, *Rapporto conclusivo dell'indagine sulla condizione di Rom, Sinti e Caminanti in Italia* (Rome, 2011), 61.

2. Italian Ministry of Education (MIUR), *Gli alunni stranieri nel sistema scolastico italiano: Anno scolastico 2012–13* (Rome: MIUR, 2013), 23. Starting with the school year 2007–2008, in its annual collection of data about students of non-Italian nationality, the Ministry of Education has also collected data on "nomad" students, i.e., students belonging to the Roma minorities, irrespective of their nationality. Because in Italy ethnicity is not formally registered in censuses, the inclusion of a student in the "nomad" category is decided by the school. The ministry itself stresses that this category is very complex to define and is quite improper, since many Roma are permanently settled: see MIUR, *Gli alunni stranieri nel sistema scolastico italiano: Anno scolastico 2007–2008* (Rome: MIUR, 2009), 89.

3. The Ministry of Education estimates 36,000 Roma children of compulsory school age, but does not clarify the criteria used, see MIUR, *Alunni con cittadinanza non italiana: Anno scolastico 2007–08* (Rome: MIUR, 2009), 94. According to UNAR (the Italian National Office on Anti-Racial Discrimination), 45 percent of the estimated 140,000 Roma people living in Italy, are children under sixteen; see UNAR, *National Strategy for the Inclusion of Roma, Sinti and Caminanti Communities*, European Commission Communication No.173/2011 (Rome: UNAR, 2012), 10–11. The Roma population in Italy includes Italian citizens, EU citizens (mostly Romanian), and, originating from the former Yugoslavia, both non-EU citizens and stateless persons.

4. Many Roma children hide their identity, to avoid discrimination. Moreover, it is unclear whether most schools register all Roma children as "nomads" including those living in regular housing or only those who live in "nomad camps." If the latter is the case, the data significantly undercount the number of Roma enrolled students. Finally, students enrolled in vocational training courses are not registered.

5. The research, carried out at the Social Sciences Department of Turin University in 2009–2010 under the supervision of Prof. Adriana Luciano and Prof. Franco Prina, and funded by the Compagnia di San Paolo Foundation, was based on analysis of quantitative data and on interviews with thirty Roma children and parents, living in camps and general housing, as well as interviews with thirty teachers and social workers. The following interview excerpts referring to

Roma children and parents living in Turin are drawn from this fieldwork, conducted in cooperation with my colleague Alessandra Gallo.

6. Fondazione Casa della Carità, *EU-Inclusive: National Report on Labour and Social Inclusion of Roma People in Italy* (Milan: Fondazione Casa della Carità, 2012).

7. See, in this volume, Margareta Matache and Krista Oehlke, "A Critical Analysis of Roma Policy and Praxis: The Romanian Case"; and James A. Goldston, "The Unfulfilled Promise of Educational Opportunity in the United States and Europe: From *Brown v. Board* to *D.H.* and Beyond."

8. Commission on Culture of the Italian Chamber of Deputies, *Accoglienza studenti stranieri in Italia* (Rome, 2011), 12; my translation.

9. Italian Government, *Report to the UN CERD Committee*, 2006, para. 177.

10. John U. Ogbu and Herbert D. Simons, "Voluntary and Involuntary Minorities: A Cultural-Ecological Theory of School Performance with Some Implications for Education," *Anthropology & Education Quarterly* 29, no. 2 (1998): 155–88.

11. The provision of services for the Roma people living in "nomad camps" is mostly subcontracted by local authorities to NGOs. As Nando Sigona has pointed out, this transfer of state responsibility to NGOs makes it very difficult for them to preserve their independence and to speak with a critical voice. Moreover, NGO involvement in policy making and implementation in this field for decades raises questions as to how much their work has contributed to the situation of segregation and marginalization that the Roma minority is subjected to today; Nando Sigona, "The Governance of Romani people in Italy: Discourse, Policy and Practice," *Journal of Modern Italian Studies* 16, no. 5 (2011): 590–606, provides an excellent analysis of the historic development of the "nomad camps" in Italy.

12. For developments in nomad camps in the last decade, see Amnesty International, *The Wrong Answer: Italy's "Nomad Plan" Violates the Housing Rights of Roma in Rome* (Rome: Amnesty International, 2010); European Roma Rights Centre (ERRC) and Associazione 21 luglio, *Parallel Report to the Committee on the Rights of the Child on Italy for its Consideration at the 58th Session* (Rome: July 2011) and *Parallel Report to the Committee on the Elimination of Racial Discrimination on Italy for Its Consideration at the 80th Session* (Rome: January 2012); Thomas Hammarberg, Commissioner for Human Rights of the Council of Europe, *Report by Commissioner, following his visit to Italy from 26 to 27 May 2011*, CommDH(2011)26 (Strasbourg: September 2011); Nils Muižnieks, Commissioner for Human Rights of the Council of Europe, *Report by Commissioner, following his visit to Italy from 3 to 6 July 2012*, CommDH(2012)26 (Strasbourg: September 2012); European Commission against Racism and Intolerance (ECRI), *ECRI Fourth Report on Italy, Adopted on 6 December 2011* (Strasbourg: ECRI, 2012); Paolo Bonetti, Alessandro Simoni, and Tommaso Vitale, eds. *La condizione giuridica di Rom e Sinti in Italia* (Milan: Giuffrè, 2011).

13. The regional laws (which mostly refer to Roma as "Gypsy" or "nomad") are the only legislation that specifically protects the Roma minority in Italy because Roma are not recognized as a minority in Italian national law. Law No. 482/1999 on the protection of historical linguistic minorities recognizes twelve minorities (the Albanian, Germanic, etc.) and protects their languages through specific provisions regarding education, public offices, and the media. During the debate at the parliamentary level, however, the Roma minority was excluded from the legislation, on the grounds that they, unlike the other linguistic minorities, are not settled in a defined geographic area. Plans were made to create a separate law to recognize and protect the Roma minority, but such legislation has not been adopted yet.

14. The term "tolerated camps" is used by some municipalities to indicate those settlements that have been built without any public authorization but, unlike "unauthorized camps," are provided by the local authorities with some basic services—such as water, toilets, or even school transportation—and are protected from evictions, at least temporarily. Rome camp statistics from Amnesty International, *The Wrong Answer*, 4.

15. See notes 13, 18, 19 for information about many of those reports.

16. Since the serious consequences of these conditions on Roma children in Italy, as well as in many other European countries, have been widely analyzed and reported, I will focus on the features unique to authorized camps.

17. Interview, Associazione 21 luglio, *Rom(a) Underground: White Paper on the Condition of Roma Children in Rome* (Rome: Associazione 21 luglio, 2013), 42.

18. Ibid.

19. Ibid., 41–42.

20. Carlotta Saletti Salza, *Bambini del "campo nomadi": Romá bosniaci a Torino* (Rome: Centro Informazione Stampa Universitaria [CISU], 2003); Giorgia Peano, *Bambini rom Alunni rom: Un'etnografia della scuola* (Rome: CISU, 2013).

21. UNAR, *National Strategy for Inclusion*, 2012.

22. Berenice et al., *Segregation at a Price: The Cost of "Traveller Camps" in Naples, Rome and Milan* (Rome: Lunaria, 2013), 14–16).

23. Associazione 21 luglio, *Rom(a) Underground*, 39.

24. For Milan evictions, see ERRC and Associazione 21 luglio, *2011 Report to the Convention on the Rights of the Child (CRC) Committee*; for Rome evictions, see Associazione 21 luglio, *Rom(a) Underground*, 33.

25. Interview, Associazione 21 luglio, *Rom(a) Underground*, 35.

26. Jean-Pierre Liégeois, *Roma in Europe* (Strasbourg: Council of Europe, 2007), 160.

27. Ibid., 162.

28. For a historical analysis of the inclusion of Roma children in Italian schools, see Luca Bravi, *Tra inclusione ed esclusione: Una storia sociale dell'educazione dei rom e dei sinti in Italia* (Milan: Unicopli, 2009).

29. Saletti Salza, *Bambini del "campo nomadi"*; Leonardo Piasere, "Rom, sinti e camminanti nelle scuole italiane," in *Processi educativi nelle società multiculturali*, ed. Francesca Gobbo (Rome: CISU, 2007), 161–72, in particular 166.

30. However, not every form of "specialized schooling" is discriminatory. Fascinating analyses of the criteria that should be applied to assess whether special classes are discriminatory or not can be found in Liégeois, *Roma in Europe*, 176–85 and in European Court of Human Rights case law (see, for example, *Oršuš and Others v. Croatia*, App. no. 15766/03, ECtHR, Grand Chamber Judgment (March 16, 2010), http://hudoc.echr.coe.int/eng?i=001-97689.

31. Saletti Salza, *Bambini del "campo nomadi"*; Peano, *Bambini rom Alunni rom*.

32. Interview, unpublished field work, Turin.

33. Ibid.

34. Saletti Salza, *Bambini del "campo nomadi"*.

35. The government's approach on this issue has recently improved. See, for example, the National Project for the Inclusion of Roma, Sinti and Caminanti Children (RSC), a project of the Italian Ministry of Welfare; for more information, see the RSC project page on the Italian National Childhood and Adolescence Documentation and Analysis Centre's website, http://www.minori.it/progetti-sperimentali-285/il-progetto-rsc.

36. Commission on Culture, *Accoglienza studenti stranieri*, 12, my translation.

37. See Italian Government, *2006 Report to CERD Committee*, for example, para. 172, 173.

38. European Union Monitoring Centre (EUMC), *Roma and Travellers in Public Education: An Overview of the Situation in the EU Member States* (Vienna: EUMC, 2006), 64; Liégeois, *Roma in Europe*, 175.

39. Similar results can be found in Casa della Carità, *EU-Inclusive*, 121–22 and Massimiliano Fiorucci, ed., *Un'altra città è possibile: Percorsi di integrazione delle famiglie Rom e Sinte a Roma* (Rome: Geordie Onlus, 2010), 100–102.

40. See, for example, Consiglio Nazionale dell'Economia e del Lavoro (CNEL), *Le aspettative delle famiglie immigrate nei confronti del sistema scolastico italiano* (Rome: CNEL, 2009).

41. The following summary of Ogbu's theory is drawn from Ogbu and Simons, "Voluntary and Involuntary Minorities."

42. For instance, Mary Waters has studied the different ethnic identities adopted by the children of West-Indian black immigrants in New York City. These different identities are related to different perceptions and understandings of race relations and of opportunities in the American society. Those youngsters who identify as black Americans tend to see more racial discrimination and limits to opportunities for blacks in the United States. Those who identify as ethnic West Indians tend to see more opportunities and rewards for individual effort and initiative. Waters suggests that assimilation to America for the second-generation black immigrant is complicated by race and class and their interaction, with upwardly mobile second-generation youngsters maintaining ethnic ties to their parents' national origins and with poor inner city youngsters assimilating to the black American peer culture that surrounds them. See Mary C. Waters, "Ethnic and Racial Identities of Second-Generation Black Immigrants in New York City," *International Migration Review* 28, no. 2 (1994): 795–820. Ogbu does mention the children of West-Indian immigrants, as well as the descendants of other immigrants that are treated by the majority society like involuntary minorities, as an exception to his immigrant/nonimmigrant minority typology.

43. See, for instance, Carola Suárez-Orozco et al., "Academic Trajectories of Newcomer Immigrant Youth," *Developmental Psychology* 46, no. 3 (2010): 602–18.

44. For other discussions of the application of Ogbu's work to Europe, see Mikael Luciak, "Minority Status and Schooling—John U. Ogbu's Theory and the Schooling of Ethnic Minorities in Europe," *Intercultural Education* 15, no. 4 (2004): 359–68; Francesca Gobbo, who introduced Ogbu's theory in Italy, has also stressed its value as a theoretical framework for studies on Roma in Italy; see Gobbo, "Moving Lives: A Reflective Account of a Three Generation Travelling Attractionist Family in Italy," in *Traveller, Nomadic and Migrant Education,* ed. Patrick Alan Danaher, Máirín Kenny, and Judith Remy Leder (New York: Routledge, 2009), 13–28.

45. Leonardo Piasere, *I rom d'Europa: Una storia moderna* (Rome: Laterza, 2004).

46. See, for example, Amnesty International, *The Wrong Answer*; Associazione 21 luglio, *Rom(a) Underground*; Muižnieks, *Report: Italy, July 2012*; ECRI, *Fourth Report on Italy*; ERRC and Associazione 21 luglio, *2011 Report to the CRC Committee* and *2012 Report to the CEDAW Committee*; or any of the other reports by international organizations and NGOs mentioned in this report.

47. That is, characteristic of the minority independent of their relationship with the majority society.

48. Ogbu and Simons, "Voluntary and Involuntary Minorities," 158.

49. Ibid., 179–83.

50. Ibid., 179.

51. Liégeois, *Roma in Europe*, 194.

52. Maurizio Ambrosini, "Conclusioni: Osare l'accoglienza, Una politica oltre i pregiudizi," in *Favelas di Lombardia: La seconda indagine sugli insediamenti rom e sinti*, ed. Maurizio Ambrosini and Antonio Tosi (Milan: Fondazione Ismu, 2009), 319–42, in particular 319.

Chapter 2. Toward the Recognition of Critical Race Theory in Human Rights Law

1. World Health Organization (WHO), "Roma Health: Serbia," April 8, 2010, http://www.euro.who.int/en/where-we-work/member-states/serbia/sections/news/2010/04/roma-health.

2. Kent A. Sepkowitz, "Health of the World's Roma Population," *Lancet* 367, no. 9524 (May 27, 2006): 1707–8.

3. Ibid.

4. Glenys Parry et al., *The Heath Status of Gypsies and Travellers in the UK* (Sheffield: University of Sheffield, 2004), 6, www.shef.ac.uk/scharr/research/publications/travellers.

5. See, e.g., Marta Schaaf, *Confronting a Hidden Disease: TB in Roma Communities* (New York: Open Society Institute, 2007), http://www.soros.org/initiatives/health/focus/roma/articles_publications/publications/confronting_20070206/confronting_20070122.pdf.

6. See European Roma Rights Centre (ERRC), *Ambulance Not on the Way: The Disgrace of Healthcare for Roma in Europe* (Budapest: ERRC, 2006), http://www.errc.org/cms/upload/media/01/E6/m000001E6.pdf. The report describes "extreme human rights abuses of Roma by medical professionals" (46).

7. I have written elsewhere about the limits of this race-versus-gender approach and the opportunities presented by the theory of intersectionality in terms of its ability to present a more holistic picture of racial and gender subordination: see Alexandra Oprea, "The Erasure of Romani Women in Statistical Data: Limits of the Race Versus Gender Approach," Open Society Foundations, April 3, 2003, http://www.opensocietyfoundations.org/briefing-papers/erasure-romani-women-statistical-data-limits-race-versus-gender-approach. Since the writing of that article, some headway has been made in terms of data disaggregated by both race and gender, but the problem still persists: for example, see "ERRC Calls on States to Collect and Publish Data on Roma Health Gap," ERRC press release, November 22, 2013, http://www.errc.org/article/errc-calls-on-states-to-collect-and-publish-data-to-address-roma-health-gap/4229.

8. See Ewa Cukrowska and Angela Kóczé, *Exposing Structural Disparities of Romani Women* (Bratislava: UNDP, 2013), http://www.eurasia.undp.org/content/dam/rbec/docs/Exposing-structural-disparities-of-Romani-women.pdf; see also WHO, *Roma Health Mediation in Romania: Case Study,* Roma Health Case Study Series, no. 1 (Copenhagen: WHO Regional Office for Europe, 2013), http://www.euro.who.int/__data/assets/pdf_file/0016/235141/e96931.pdf.

9. Cukrowska and Kóczé, *Exposing Structural Disparities of Romani Women*; Niall O'Higgins, "Ethnicity and Gender in the Labour Market in Central and South East Europe," Discussion Paper No. 7667 (Bonn: Institute for the Study of Labor [IZA], October 2013), http://ftp.iza.org/dp7667.pdf; Vera Messing, "Active Labor Market Policies with an Impact Potential on Roma Employment in Five Countries of the EU," NEUJOBS Working Paper no. 19.2 (no date), http://www.neujobs.eu/sites/default/files/D19_2_final.pdf; see also also Niall O'Higgins, *Roma and Non-Roma in the Labour Market in Central and South Eastern Europe,* (Bratislava: UNDP, 2012), http://www.eurasia.undp.org/content/dam/rbec/docs/Roma-and-non-Roma-in-the-labour-market.pdf.

10. See, e.g., Alexandra Oprea, "Re-envisioning Social Justice from the Ground Up: Including the Experiences of Romani Women," *Essex Human Rights Review* 1, no. 1 (2004): 29–39; Angéla

Kóczé, *Missing Intersectionality: Race/Ethnicity, Gender, and Class in Current Research and Policies on Romani Women in Europe* (Budapest: Center for Policy Research, 2009).

11. Kimberlé Crenshaw et al., eds., *Critical Race Theory: The Key Writings That Formed the Movement* (New York: New Press, 1996). This book, including several of its articles, is referred to throughout this chapter and has informed my thinking on human and civil rights. Specific articles are cited where most relevant.

12. Luke Charles Harris was my political science professor while I was a student at Vassar College. For examples of his work, see "My Two Mothers, America, and the Million Man March" and "The Challenge and Possibility for Black Men to Embrace Feminism" in *Black Men on Race, Gender and Sexuality: A Critical Reader*, ed. Devon W. Carbado (New York: NYU Press, 1999). See also Luke Charles Harris, Kimberlé Crenshaw, and George Lipsitz, *The Race Track: Understanding and Challenging Structural Racism* (New York: New Press, 2015).

13. Crenshaw et al., *Critical Race Theory*. For a bottom-up approach, see in that volume, Mari Matsuda, "Looking to the Bottom: Critical Legal Studies and Reparations," 63–79.

14. Kimberlé Crenshaw, "Demarginalizing the Intersection of Race and Sex: A Black Feminist Critique of Antidiscrimination Doctrine, Feminist Theory and Antiracist Politics," *University of Chicago Legal Forum* 140 (1989): 139–67.

15. For basic information on intersectionality, see African American Policy Forum, "A Primer on Intersectionality," 2013, http://www.whiteprivilegeconference.com/pdf/intersectionality_primer.pdf.

16. See, e.g., Oprea, "Re-envisioning Social Justice from the Ground Up"; Kóczé, *Missing Intersectionality*.

17. Crenshaw, "Demarginalizing the Intersection of Race and Sex," 149. Although Crenshaw speaks in the context of U.S. employment litigation, her analysis easily lends itself to the context of human rights litigation.

18. See Oprea, "Re-envisioning Social Justice from the Ground Up," for a discussion of domestic violence perpetrated against Roma women; Alexandra Oprea, "Reclaiming Victimhood, Rethinking Agency," *Nevi Kali Sara, Roma Women's Journal* 3 (2011): 183–89, http://www.desire-ro.eu/wp-content/uploads/revista-NSK-3_20-07-11.pdf.

19. For gender discrimination, see e.g., *Szijjiarto v. Hungary,* Convention on the Elimination of Discrimination against Women (CEDAW) Comm., Communication No. 4, U.N. Doc. A/61/38, 366 (2006), http://www.worldcourts.com/cedaw/eng/decisions/2006.08.14_Szijjarto_v_Hungary.htm. For race discrimination, see e.g., *Nachova and Others v. Bulgaria,* App. no. 433577/98 and 43579/98, ECtHR, Grand Chamber Judgment (July 6, 2005), fatal police shooting of two Roma men, http://hudoc.echr.coe.int/eng?i=001-69630; *Karagiannopoulos v. Greece*, App. no. 27850/03, ECtHR, Judgment (First Sect.) (June 21, 2007), regarding a Roma man rendered disabled after police shot him (in French, summary in English), http://hudoc.echr.coe.int/eng?i=001-81236.

20. I have borrowed this concept of bottom-up analysis both from Crenshaw's intersectionality theory and from Mari Matsuda's "Looking to the Bottom." See also Kimberlé Crenshaw, Background Paper for the Expert Meeting on the Gender Related Aspects of Race Discrimination, World Conference Against Racism, www.wicej.addr.com/wcar_docs/crenshaw.html; Oprea, "Re-envisioning Social Justice from the Ground Up."

21. Matsuda, "Looking to the Bottom," 63.

22. Ibid., 90.

23. Crenshaw, "Demarginalizing the Intersection of Race and Sex."

24. See Rachel Kahn Best et al., "Multiple Disadvantages: An Empirical Test of Intersectionality Theory in EEO Litigation," *Law & Society Review* 45, no. 1 (December 2011): 991–1025, quotation at 992.

25. For more on political intersectionality, see Kimberlé Crenshaw, "Mapping the Margins: Intersectionality, Identity Politics and Violence Against Women of Color," *Stanford Law Review* 43, no. 6 (1991): 1241, later included in Crenshaw et al., *Critical Race Theory.*

26. An incident I describe in Oprea, "Re-envisioning Social Justice from the Ground Up."

27. This is an incident Nicoleta Bitu and I encountered at the UN Commission on the Status of Women in 2004, in New York, at a panel organized by European Women's Lobby.

28. By "dominant" white women, I am referring to women who are economically empowered and are not disabled. It is worth noting that white disabled women have also been subjected to coerced sterilization, as evidenced in *Gauer and Others v. France*, App. no 61521/08, ECtHR, Communicated Case (February 2, 2011), http://hudoc.echr.coe.int/eng?i=002-572.

29. Patricia Hill Collins, "Mammies, Matriarchs and other Controlling Images" in *Black Feminist Thought: Knowledge, Consciousness and the Politics of Empowerment* (New York: Routledge, 2000).

30. Paula Giddings, *When and Where I Enter: The Impact of Black Women on Race and Sex in America* (New York: HarperCollins, 1984).

31. Ian Hancock, "The 'Gypsy' Stereotype and the Sexualization of Romani Women," in *"Gypsies" in European Literature and Culture*, ed. Valentina Glajar and Domnica Radulescu (New York: Palgrave Macmillan, 2008), 181–92; citations are from a prepublication copy, Romani Archives and Documentation Centre, April 2007, http://www.radoc.net/radoc.php?doc=art_d_identity_sexualization&lang=en&articles=true.

32. Roma men are also viewed as sexually aggressive and a threat. Some were castrated during slavery in order to render them safe enough to drive white women around. See Hancock, "'Gypsy' Stereotype," note 35. These stereotypes of the sexually aggressive Roma male perpetrator survive today. See Shannon Woodcock, "Gender as a Catalyst for Violence in Contemporary Italy," *Patterns of Prejudice* 44, no. 5 (2010): 469.

33. Andrea Smith, *Conquest: Sexual Violence and American Indian Genocide* (New York: South End Press, 2005), 15.

34. Dorothy Roberts, *Killing the Black Body* (New York: Pantheon, 1997), 56.

35. Note here U.S. precursors to Hitler's 1933 law. Stefan Khul, *Nazi Connection: Eugencis, American Racism, and German National Socialism* (New York: Oxford University Press, 1994).

36. As quoted in Center for Reproductive Rights (CRR) and Centre for Civil and Human Rights (Poradňa), *Body and Soul: Forced and Coercive Sterilization and Other Assaults on Roma Reproductive Freedom in Slovakia, Part III* (New York: CRR, 2003), 54, http://reproductiverights.org/sites/crr.civicactions.net/files/documents/bo_slov_part3.pdf.

37. Michael Bird and Stefan Candea, "Anti-Roma Views Rampant across all Romanian Political Parties," *EU Observer*, April 29, 2014.

38. See, e.g., Andrey Ivanov with others, *The Roma in Central and Eastern Europe: Avoiding the Dependency Trap* (Bratislava: UNDP Regional Bureau, 2002), 25–26, http://www.eurasia.undp.org/content/dam/rbec/docs/Avoiding-the-dependency-trap.pdf. See also Dena Ringold, Mitchell A. Orenstein, and Erika Wilkens, *Roma in an Expanding Europe: Breaking the Poverty Cycle* (Washington, D.C.: World Bank, 2004).

39. The most prominent of these reports was CRR and Poradňa's *Body and Soul*; all four parts can be accessed at http://www.reproductiverights.org/document/body-and-soul-forced -sterilization-and-other-assaults-on-roma-reproductive-freedom.

40. See *A.S. v. Hungary*, CEDAW Comm., Communication No. 4, U.N. Doc. C/36/D (2004), http://www.un.org/womenwatch/daw/cedaw/protocol/decisions-views/Decision%204-2004%20 -%20English.pdf.

41. As quoted in CRR and Poradňa, *Body and Soul, Part III*, 53, http://reproductiverights.org /sites/crr.civicactions.net/files/documents/bo_slov_part3.pdf.

42. See in this volume, Elena Rozzi, "Roma Children and Enduring Educational Exclusion in Italy"; Teresa Sordé Martí and Fernando Macías, "Making Roma Rights a Reality at the Local Level: A Spanish Case Study"; and Margareta Matache and Krista Oehlke, "A Critical Analysis of Roma Policy and Praxis: The Romanian Case."

43. European Union Agency for Fundamental Rights, *Discrimination Against and Living Conditions of Roma Women in 11 EU Member States* (UNDP, 2012), http://fra.europa.eu/en /publication/2014/discrimination-against-and-living-conditions-roma-women-11-eu-member -states.

44. See, e.g., Network Women's Program, Open Society Institute (OSI), *Bending the Bow: Targeting Women's Human Rights and Opportunities* (New York: OSI, 2002), 48, describing an incident at 2001 World Conference on Racism in which Roma men would only allow one (compulsory sterilization) of three issues that Roma women had prepared to be addressed at the conference (the others were unemployment and violence against women).

45. Helen O'Nions, *Minority Rights Protection in International Law: The Roma of Europe* (London: Ashgate, 2007), 106, in which she frames compulsory sterilization as violating international conventions and domestic laws prohibiting genocide.

46. For anecdotal examples of the expectations around Roma women giving birth to many children, see Eniko Magyari-Vinceze, "Reproducing Inequalities Through Reproductive Control: The Case of Romani Women from Romania," *Anthropology of East Europe Review* 25, no. 2 (2007): 108, which includes descriptions of community pressure for females to have children early.

47. See e.g., O'Nions, *Minority Rights Protection*.

48. European Women's Lobby (EWL), "EWL Beijing+2 in May: A Fair and Equal Representation of Women in the Media in Europe," May 8, 2015 (claiming that only 24 percent of the news is about women and demanding that gender equality be fully mainstreamed into policies, that gender discrimination and stereotypes be prohibited in the media, and that a gender code of conduct be introduced among the media), http://www.womenlobby.org/spip.php?article7215.

49. EWL, http://www.womenlobby.org/spip.php?article1611, original at Center for Reproductive Rights, "New Report: Slovak Women Struggle to Buy Birth Control," CRR, March 11, 2011, http://www.reproductiverights.org/feature/new-report-slovak-women-struggle-to-buy-birth -control.

50. Center for Reproductive Rights; Freedom of Choice Slovakia (FOCS); and Citizen, Democracy and Accountability (CDA), *Calculated Injustice: The Slovak Republic's Failure to Ensure Access to Contraceptives* (New York: CRR, 2011), 21.

51. For a critical discussion on reproductive rights and punishment, see Priscilla A. Ocen, "Punishing Pregnancy: Race, Incarceration and the Shackling of Pregnant Prisoners," *California Law Review* 100, no. 5 (2012): 1239–311.

52. Roberts, *Killing the Black Body*, 5.

53. See also Oprea, "The Erasure of Romani Women in Statistical Data."

54. See American Law Institute (ALI), Restatement of the Law, Third, the Foreign Relations Law of the United States (St. Paul, Minn.: ALI, 1987) at sect. 102, comment d, describing implicit consent given by states that remain silent in the face of developing customary law.

55. But see *Buckley v. United Kingdom*, Case No. 23/1995/529/615 (1996), denying a Roma woman's claim of a right to park her caravan on her own property.

56. See, e.g., Johanna E. Bond, "International Intersectionality: A Theoretical and Pragmatic Exploration of Women's International Human Rights Violations," *Emory Law Journal* 52 (2003): 71–187; Lisa A. Crooms, "Indivisible Rights and Intersectional Identities or, 'What Do Women's Human Rights Have to Do with the Race Convention?'" *Howard Law Journal* 40 (1997): 619–640; Hope Lewis, "Global Intersections: Critical Race Feminist Human Rights and Inter/national Black Women," *Maine Law Review* 50 (1998): 309–26.

57. *K.H. and Others v. Slovakia,* App. no. 32881/04, ECtHR, Judgment (April 28, 2009), decision based on procedure: access to medical records, http://hudoc.echr.coe.int/eng?i=001-92418; *N.B. v. Slovakia,* App. no. 29518/10), ECtHR, Judgment (June 12, 2012), finding a violation of Article 3 and Article 8, http://hudoc.echr.coe.int/eng?i=001-111427; *I.G., M.K. and R.H. v. Slovakia,* App. no. 15966/04, ECtHR, Judgment (November 13, 2012), finding violations of Article 3 and Article 8 violations for Roma minors, http://hudoc.echr.coe.int/fre?i=001-114514.

58. ECHR, Convention for the Protection of Human Rights and Fundamental Freedoms, European Treaty Series No. 5 (1950). *V.C. v. Slovakia,* App. no. 18968/07, ECtHR, Judgment (November 8, 2011), http://hudoc.echr.coe.int/eng?i=001-107364.

59. Some cases dealt mostly with procedural violations, such as access to medical records *(K.H. v. Slovakia)*; others involved minors *(I.G., M.K. and R.H. v. Slovakia)*. *N.B. v. Slovakia* cited *V.C. v. Slovakia*: "In view of the documents available, it cannot be established that the doctors involved acted in bad faith, that the applicant's sterilisation was a part of an organised policy, or that the hospital staff's conduct was intentionally racially motivated. At the same time, the Court finds no reason for departing from its earlier finding that shortcomings in legislation and practice relating to sterilisations were liable to particularly affect members of the Roma community," para. 121.

60. See, e.g., *Hugh Jordan v. The United Kingdom,* App no. 24746/94, ECtHR, Judgment (April 8, 2001), http://hudoc.echr.coe.int/eng?i=001-59450. Where a general policy or measure has disproportionately prejudicial effects on a particular group, it is not excluded that this may be considered as discriminatory, notwithstanding that it is not specifically aimed or directed at that group."

61. See *N.B. v. Slovakia*: "it cannot be established that . . . the applicant's sterilisation was a part of an organised policy," para. 121.

62. *V.C. v. Slovakia,* para. 179. The Court found that the state failed to comply with its positive obligation under Article 8 of the Convention to secure to the applicant a sufficient measure of protection enabling her, as a member of the vulnerable Roma community, to effectively enjoy her right to respect for her private and family life in the context of her sterilization.

63. As mentioned earlier, the most prominent of these reports was CRR and Poradňa's *Body and Soul: Forced and Coercive Sterilization and Other Assaults on Roma Reproductive Freedom in Slovakia.*

64. *V.C. v. Slovakia,* para. 44: "Another study found that in 1983 approximately 26% of sterilized women in eastern Slovakia (the region where the applicant resides) were Roma, by 1907, this figure had risen to 36.6%."

65. Ibid., para. 46. In 1992 a report by Human Rights Watch noted that many Roma women were not fully aware of the irreversible nature of the procedure and were forced into it because of their poor economic situation or pressure from the authorities (para. 47): "According to other reports, in 1999 nurses working in Finnish refugee reception centres informed researchers from Amnesty International that they had noticed unusually high rates of gynecological procedures such as sterilization and removal of ovaries among female Roma asylum-seekers from eastern Slovakia."

66. Ibid., para. 44: "According to a 1979 document by Charter 77, a Czechoslovakian dissident group, a programme had been launched in Czechoslovakia offering financial incentives for Roma women to be sterilized because of earlier unsuccessful government efforts 'to control the highly unhealthy Roma population through family planning and contraception.'"

67. CRR and Poradňa, *Body and Soul, Part II*, 42, quoting a government document during communism that Human Rights Watch found, http://reproductiverights.org/sites/crr.civicactions.net/files/documents/bo_slov_part2.pdf.

68. Ibid., 44.

69. *V.C. v. Slovakia*, para. 170.

70. Ibid.

71. ECHR, Art. 14, "Prohibition of Discrimination: The enjoyment of the rights and freedoms set forth in [the] Convention shall be secured without discrimination on any ground such as sex, race, colour, language, religion, political or other opinion, national or social origin, association with a national minority, property, birth or other status."

72. *V.C. v. Slovakia*, para. 119.

73. Ibid., para. 177.

74. See Charles R. Lawrence III, "The Id, Ego & Equal Protection: Reckoning with Unconscious Bias," *Stanford Law Review*, 39, no. 2 (1987): 317–88, later included in Crenshaw et al., *Critical Race Theory*, 235–57.

75. Alvaro Gil-Robles, Commissioner for Human Rights of the Council of Europe, *Recommendation by the Commissioner for Human Rights Concerning Certain Aspects of Law and Practice Relating to Sterilization of Women in the Slovak Republic*, CommDH(2003)12, (Strasbourg, October 17, 2003), https://wcd.coe.int/ViewDoc.jsp?id=979625.

76. See Mathias Moschel, "Is the European Court of Human Rights Case Law on Anti-Roma Violence 'Beyond a Reasonable Doubt'?" *Human Rights Law Review* 12, no. 3 (2012): 479–507.

77. See the discussion of the bifurcation of race and gender in human rights treaties at the beginning of this section and the related references from Bond, "International Intersectionality"; Crooms, "Indivisible Rights and Intersectional Identities"; Lewis, *Global Intersections*. See also Crenshaw, "Demarginalizing the Intersection of Race and Sex."

78. *Mizigarova v. Slovakia*, App. no. 74832/01, ECtHR, Judgment (December 14, 2010), failing to find Art. 14 discrimination, http://hudoc.echr.coe.int/eng?i=001-102279.

79. "Greece's Mystery Girl's Mother Found: DNA Tests Confirm Bulgarian Roma Woman Is Blond Child's Parent," October 25, 2013, http://www.huffingtonpost.com/2013/10/25/greece-mystery-girl-mother_n_4163343.html reporting that brown Roma woman who lives in extreme poverty is mother of Maria and that she will be sent to jail and fined if authorities determine that she sold the child; in Ireland, the Roma parents who had custody of the child were found to be the actual biological parents. "Irish Court Orders Blonde-Haired Girl Taken from Roma Family to be Returned," *The Telegraph* (Belfast), October 23, 2013, http://www.telegraph.co.uk/news

/worldnews/europe/ireland/10400876/Irish-court-orders-blonde-haired-girl-taken-from-Roma
-family-to-be-returned.html.

80. For hypersexual, see Hancock, "The 'Gypsy' Stereotype"; Eluned Roberts-Schweitzer in collaboration with Vincent Greaney and Kreszentia Duer, *Promoting Social Cohesion Through Education: Case Studies and Tools for Using Textbooks and Curricula* (Washington, D.C.: World Bank, 2006), 6, describe a school director's contempt for/blame of a Roma mother for the inability of Roma children to succeed, since she was illiterate and could not tell time; school officials viewed the families as "oversized" and the parents as "uneducated," https://openknowledge .worldbank.org/bitstream/handle/10986/6985/354060Promotin101OFFICIAL0USE0ONLY1 .pdf?sequence=1.

81. Roberts-Schweitzer et al., *Promoting Social Cohesion Through Education*, 87.

82. For example, Roma make up roughly 10 percent of Bulgaria's population, but studies have shown that Roma children make up 63.9 percent of the children in state institutions are Roma. In the Czech Republic, Roma make up 3 percent of the population, yet Roma children make up 33 percent of the children in state custody. European Roma Rights Center, *Life Sentence: Romani Children in Institutional Care* (Budapest: ERRC, 2011), 32–33, http://www.errc.org/cms/upload /file/life-sentence-20-june-2011.pdf.

83. On the profiling of people of color in the UK, see, e.g., Ben Hayes, "A Failure to Regulate: Data Protection and Ethnic Profiling in the Police Sector in Europe," in Open Society Justice Initiatives, *Ethnic Profiling by Police in Europe*, June 2005, 32–43, https://www.opensocietyfoundations .org/sites/default/files/justiceinit_200506.pdf. See also Hungarian Helsinki Committee, "Practice of Racial Profiling Against the Roma is Acknowledged by Police," April 26, 2012 (on the profiling of Roma in Hungary) http://helsinki.hu/en/practice-of-racial-profiling-against-the -roma-community-is-acknowledged-by-the-police. European Roma Rights Center, "Ukrainian Police Must Stop Targeting Roma," October 20, 2011, http://www.errc.org/cikk.php?cikk =3937. European Roma Rights Center, "Russian Law Enforcement Officers Continue with Racial Profiling of Roma," May 20, 1007, http://www.errc.org/article/russian-law-enforcement -officers-continue-with-racial-profiling-of-roma/2783.

84. In "Greece's Mystery Girl's Mother Found," the *Huffington Post* reported that the brown Roma woman who lived in extreme poverty was mother of Maria and that she would be sent to jail and fined should authorities determine that she sold the child.

85. Quoted in *Disabled People and the Right to Life: The Protection and Violation of Disabled People's Most Basic Human Rights*, ed. Luke Clements and Janet Reed (London: Routledge, 2008), 213–14.

86. For "animalistically," see, e.g., Rachel Tritt, *Struggling for Ethnic Identity: Czechoslovakia's Endangered Gypsies* (Helsinki Watch, 1992), 29 (quoting a gynecologist's assertion that Romani women "multiply like rabbits"). Buglea is a key political figure and member of the President's National Liberal Party; for "uncontrolled," and his comparison of Roma women to cows, see Romani CRISS, "Open Letter to the National Liberal Party Requesting for a Public Position on the Statements of Rares Buglea, Regarding the Sterilization of Roma Women," http:// www.romanicriss.org/en/index.php?option=com_content&view=article&id=1747:open-letter -to-the-national-liberal-party-requesting-for-a-public-position-on-the-statements-of-rares -buglea-regarding-the-sterilization-of-roma-women&catid=315:cases.

87. World Bank, "How Gender Affects Life Choices Among Bulgarian Roma," February 12, 2014.

88. Bulgarian social worker, quoted in Clements and Reed, eds., *Disabled People and the Right to Life*, 214; the text also mentions an increase in the institutionalization of children in Bulgaria since the 1990s, 217.

89. Continuation of Buglea quote, in Romani CRISS, "Open Letter to the National Liberal Party."

90. Ibid.

91. See, e.g., Alexandra Oprea, "The Arranged Marriage of Ana Maria Cioaba," *European Journal of Women's Studies* 12 (2005): 133–48.

92. See, e.g., "Tene Bimbo Crime Family," *Investigation Discovery*, November 2013, http://www.investigationdiscovery.com/tv-shows/deadly-devotion/deadly-devotion-videos/tene-bimbo-crime-family/.

93. See Alexandra Oprea, "Psychic Charlatans, Roving Shoplifters and Traveling Con Artists: Notes on a Fraudulent Identity," *Berkeley Journal of Gender Law and Justice* 22 (2007): 31–41, discussing how this trope results in the criminalization of American Roma women in the United States.

94. Regina Austin, "Sapphire Bound," in Crenshaw et al., *Critical Race Theory*, 426–37.

95. As in the earlier Communist official quote: "Even a backward Gypsy woman is able to calculate that, from an economic point of view, it is more advantageous for her to give birth every year" (*Body and Soul, Part II*, 42).

96. For a longer discussion of the importance of reclaiming victimhood, see Oprea, "Reclaiming Victimhood." Note also the ugly stereotype in Romania of Roma women wearing long skirts for the purpose of facilitating intercourse.

97. Anne Sutherland, *Gypsies: The Hidden Americans* (Chicago: Waveland, 1986).

98. U.S. Senate Committee on Foreign Relations, Country Reports on Human Rights Practices for 2009, 1363.

99. ERRC, "Written Comments of the European Roma Rights Center Concerning Hungary: For Consideration by the UN Human Rights Committee," 98th Session (2010), 14, http://www2.ohchr.org/english/bodies/hrc/docs/ngo/ERRC.Hungary98.pdf, citing The All Hungary Media Group, September 14, 2009, http://www.politics.hu/20090914/roma-women-file-defamation-suit-against-mayor/.

Chapter 3. Policy and Practice

1. The author serves as Helsinki Commission Counsel for International Law, although the views herein are her own and are not necessarily those of the Helsinki Commission.

2. *Human Rights Abuse of the Roma, Hearing before the Subcommittee on International Security, International Organizations and Human Rights of the Committee on Foreign Affairs*, 103rd Congress, 2nd Sess. (1994).

3. See the Helsinki Final Act (also known as the Helsinki Accords), August 1, 1975, Organization for Security and Cooperation in Europe (OSCE), http://www.osce.org/mc/39501.

4. For example, CoE deputy secretary general Leurprecht resigned in 1997, reportedly in protest of the council's compromised human rights standards in admitting new members states such as Russia (where large-scale human rights violations were being committed in the context of Moscow's prosecution of the war in Chechnya) and Croatia (which was harboring indicted war criminals). Joel Blocker, "Council of Europe's 'Soft' Standards for East European Members," Radio Free Europe/Radio Liberty *Newsline* 1, no. 68 (1997).

5. Andrzej Mirga, "Roma Policy in Europe: Results and Challenges," in this volume.

6. Kálmán Mizsei, "Reconstructing Roma Integration in Central and Eastern Europe: Addressing the Failures of the Last Quarter Century," in this volume.

7. The Document of the Copenhagen Meeting of the Conference on the Human Dimension of the Conference on Security and Cooperation in Europe (CSCE), June 29, 1990, known informally as the Copenhagen Document, OSCE, http://www.osce.org/odihr/elections/14304.

8. U.S. Commission on Security and Cooperation in Europe, *The Copenhagen Meeting of the Conference on Security and Cooperation in Europe 5 June–29 June 1990,* Report (Washington, D.C.: The Commission, August 1990) (hereinafter *Report on Copenhagen 1990*).

9. Prior to the June 1989 Paris meeting, the Helsinki Commission had recommended to the Department of State two possible proposals the United States might put forward. The first proposal, on free and fair elections, was formally tabled for the United States in Paris by Helsinki Commission cochairman Congressman Steny Hoyer. It ultimately became the cornerstone for the Copenhagen Document a year later. The second proposal was for language calling for the Berlin Wall to be torn down. The Department of State declined to advance this proposal, deeming it too improbable.

10. Between 1990 and 1997, there were reportedly forty-seven pogroms carried out by ethnic Romanians or Hungarians against Roma, during which several Roma were killed and dozens burned out of their homes. See Human Rights Watch/Helsinki (HRW/H), *Lynch Law: Violence Against Roma in Romania*, Report, 6, no. 17 (HRW/H, November 1994); European Roma Rights Centre, *Sudden Rage at Dawn: Violence Against Roma in Romania* (Budapest: ERRC, September 1996); Amnesty International, *Romania: A Summary of Human Rights Concerns*, EUR 39/006/1998 (Amnesty International, March 1998). Although these mob attacks ceased in 1997, violent police raids continued.

11. "Mr. Hoyer expressed concern that Gypsies had been scapegoated, both in the Tirgu Mures and Bucharest violence." Notes on Bilateral Meeting with Romanian Head of Delegation Ion Chelebea, June 18, 1990 (archives of the Helsinki Commission).

12. OSCE terminology was crafted more narrowly than the wording of "ethnic, religious, and linguistic minorities," found in article 27 of the International Covenant on Civil and Political Rights (UN G.A. Res. 2200A [XXI] [1966], http://www2.ohchr.org/english/law/ccpr.htm). It was intended to exclude from its scope of consideration various categories peoples who did not have an ethnic kin-state, such as Croats in Yugoslavia, Slovaks in Czechoslovakia, and Ukrainians in the Soviet Union. Roma, according to this restrictive phrasing and interpretation, are not a "national minority" although some states (e.g., Hungary) now include Roma among officially recognized "national minorities."

13. Proposal Submitted by the Delegations of the Federal Republic of Germany and the German Democratic Republic, CSCE/CHDC.12, Copenhagen, June 7, 1990.

14. William Korey, *The Promises We Keep: Human Rights, the Helsinki Process, and American Foreign Policy* (New York: St. Martin's, 1994), 319–26.

15. Max Kampleman, "Plenary Remarks to the Copenhagen Meeting on the Human Dimension, June 22, 1990," in *Copenhagen CSCE Meeting on the Human Dimension, Implementation of the Helsinki Accords, Hearing Before the CSCE,* 101st Congress, 2nd Sess., July 18, 1990 (Washington, D.C.: GPO, 1990), Appendix IV, 165–75, in particular 173–74.

16. *Copenhagen CSCE Meeting on the Human Dimension 1990, Hearing* (statement of Max Kampleman, Head of the U.S. Delegation to Copenhagen CSCE Meeting on the Human Dimension), 11–12.

17. The Council of Europe Committee of Ministers had previously adopted resolutions addressing aspects of the social exclusion of "nomads" (1975), "stateless nomads and nomads of undetermined nationality" (1983), and "children of occupational travellers" (1989). While well intended, those early texts were limited in that they did not address the universal human rights of people who happened to be Roma, but rather sought to ameliorate the consequences associated with itinerant or migratory work for the fraction of Roma in western Europe who were engaged in such occupations. Roma identity was, in effect, conflated with nomadism. After 1990, when the European countries with the largest and overwhelmingly settled Roma populations joined the Council of Europe and then the European Union, there has been a push to address not only disparate economic and social conditions of Roma relative to other groups, but the human rights violations that are the source of those conditions.

18. David Meyer and Michael Uyehara, "The U.S. Department of State and International Efforts to Promote the Human Rights of Roma," in this volume.

19. Will Guy, "Anti-Roma Violence, Hate Speech, and Discrimination in the New Europe: Czech Republic, Slovakia, and Hungary," in this volume.

20. *Report of the CSCE Rapporteur Mission to the Czech Republic and the Slovak Republic, 8–12 March 1993,* CSCE Communication No. 114 (Prague: CSCE, April 19, 1993), 5–6: "The Mission found that the only minority question calling for particular attention was that of the Roma population. Indeed, this issue was the single most important problem within its mandate that the Mission encountered in the Czech Republic." The mission was dispatched as a formality for the Czech Republic to join the OSCE as a newly independent country.

21. Ina Zoon, *Report on the Czech Citizenship Law: The Effect of the Citizenship Law on the Czech Republic's Roma Community* (Prague: Tolerance Foundation, May 25, 1994); Ina Zoon, *A Need for Change in the Czech Citizenship Law: Analysis of 99 Individual Cases* (Prague: Tolerance Foundation, November 21, 1994).

22. U.S. Commission on Security and Cooperation in Europe (Helsinki Commission), *Human Rights and Democratization in the Czech Republic* (Washington, D.C.: Helsinki Commission, September 1994), 28; Helsinki Commission, *Ex Post Facto Problems of the Czech Citizenship Law* (Washington, D.C.: Helsinki Commission, September 1996), 2–3.

23. Although neutral on its face, the law was intended to make it easier to remove Roma from the Czech Republic: "the government formulated an internal document, known as the 'Catastrophic Scenario,' which dealt with many aspects of the federation's pending split. Sections leaked to the press made clear references to the 'Roma question,' including a section that said: 'We should use the process for the purpose of departure of not-needed persons from factories, especially for the reasons of structural changes, and for the departure of people of Roma nationality to the Slovak Republic.'" Human Rights Watch (HRW), *Roma in The Czech Republic: Foreigners in Their Own Land,* HRW/ Helsinki Report 8, no. 11D (New York: HRW, June 1996).

24. U.S. Department of State, *Country Report: Czech Republic Human Rights Practices,* February 1995, in *Country Reports on Human Rights Practices 1994: Europe and Canada,* http://dosfan.lib.uic.edu/ERC/democracy/1994_hrp_report/94hrp_report_eur/CzechRepublic.html.

25. "Czech Premier Attacks U.S. Human Rights Report," Reuters, February 2, 1995.

26. Concern regarding citizenship in the former Soviet Union later led the OSCE, the Council of Europe, and UNHCR to convene the 1996 Regional Conference to Address the Problems of Refugees, Displaced Persons, Other Forms of Involuntary Displacement and Returnees in the Countries of the Commonwealth of Independent States and Neighboring Countries (and subsequent follow up meetings). For a description of the conference, see Boutros Boutros-Ghali, UN

Secretary General, Report on Cooperation between the United Nations and the Organization for Security and Cooperation in Europe, General Assembly, Fifty-first session, UN Doc A/51/489 (October 14, 1996), http://www.un.org/documents/ga/docs/51/plenary/a51-489.htm, para. 10.

27. Letter to Ambassador Sam Wise, Helsinki Commission Chief of Staff, June 12, 1995 (archives of the Helsinki Commission).

28. In an effort to encourage better reporting on human rights violations relating to both religious liberties and the Roma, Helsinki Commission chairman Congressman Christopher Smith and cochairman Senator Ben Nighthorse Campbell wrote to Assistant Secretary of State for Human Rights Harold Hongju Koh on June 28, 1999, outlining suggestions for systemic improvements.

29. Notwithstanding the reticence of the U.S. embassy in Prague, the Helsinki Commission was generally successful in getting the citizenship issue raised by U.S. delegations to annual and specialized OSCE human rights meetings and in U.S.-Czech bilateral meetings in the OSCE context.

30. Ottawa Resolution of the OSCE Parliamentary Assembly, July 8, 1995, para. 33–35, 38.

31. Jane Perlez, "Czechs Use Laws to Exclude Gypsies from Gaining Citizenship and Voting," *New York Times*, December 27, 1995.

32. U.S. Commission on Security and Cooperation in Europe, *Report on Human Rights and the Process of NATO Enlargement*, (Washington, D.C.: Helsinki Commission, June 1997), testimony from the section, *Hearing Before the CSCE on Human Rights and the Process of NATO Enlargement: Czech Republic, Romania, Slovenia*, May 13, 1997, 71–73.

33. Office of the United Nations High Commissioner for Refugees (UNHCR), Regional Bureau for Europe and Division of International Protection, "The Czech and Slovak Citizenship Laws and the Problem of Statelessness," Position Paper, in *Citizenship in the Context of the Dissolution of Czechoslovakia*, European Series 2, no. 4 (Geneva: UNHCR, September 1996), 1–29, plus appendixes. Document originally prepared February 1996, made public in April 1996; published with it was the Czech reply, "Response of the Czech Republic to the UNHCR's Position Paper," in UNHCR, *Citizenship in Context*, 49–62.

34. Experts of the Council of Europe (CoE), *On the Citizenship Laws of the Czech Republic and Slovakia and Their Implementation*, Report, DIR/JUR (96) (Strasbourg: CoE, April 2, 1996), 48, para. 84.

35. European Roma Rights Centre, "Czech Government Amends Anti-Romani Citizenship Law, But the Improvements Are Cosmetic," ERRC website, October 12, 1996 (noting that "the discriminatory effects of the original citizenship law will not be abolished by the amendments approved in April").

36. "UNHCR Report Says Czech Citizenship Law Violates International Law; Council of Europe Experts Say Czechs Violate Rule of Law," *CSCE Digest* 19, no. 4 (1996): 5–6.

37. "Helsinki Commission Condemns Czech Citizenship Law: Urges Complete Revision," U.S. CSCE news release, February 20, 1996.

38. For more information, see CoE European Commission for Democracy through Law (ECDL) "Declaration on the Consequences of State Succession for the Nationality of Natural Persons," CDL-NAT(1996)007rev-e (Venice: CDL, September 14, 1996); Council of Europe, European Convention on Nationality, European Treaty Series, No. 166 (1997). The treaty, however, was not intended to have retroactive effect. Thus, while its adoption was an important political statement regarding the internationally recognized standards for citizenship, the treaty did not provide a legal remedy for those denied citizenship in the Czech Republic.

39. Alexandra Oprea, "Toward the Recognition of Critical Race Theory in Human Rights Law: Roma Women's Reproductive Rights," in this volume.

40. Dimitry Kochenov, "EU Influence on the Citizenship Policies of the Candidate Countries: The Case of the Roma Exclusion in the Czech Republic," *Journal of Contemporary European Research* 3, no. 2 (2007): 125 ("Although the citizenship story of the Czech Roma can be considered a tale from the past, it is of acute relevance to the functioning of the contemporary European Union, since it is a clear illustration of a telling failure in the pre-accession policy, which could have been avoided"); and 126 ("In the end, progress in the resolution of the statelessness issue for the Czech Roma was related to the activities of actors outside the pre-accession framework, such as the OSCE and the UK and Canadian governments").

41. Robyn Linde, "Statelessness and Roma Communities in the Czech Republic: Competing Theories of State Compliance," *International Journal on Minority and Group Rights* 13 (2006): 360.

42. The proposal was first raised at fall 1998 meetings of the OSCE Permanent Council in Vienna in advance of the December 1998 Oslo meeting of the Ministerial Council.

43. Around this time, there was some discussion of whether the burgeoning number of specialized U.S. government bodies dealing with human rights (Ambassador at Large for Religious Liberties, Special Envoy for Combatting Anti-Semitism, Ambassador at Large for War Crimes Issues, etc.) had created competing lines of authority and internal institutional competition for limited financial and political resources. See, for example, the question about the "fragmentation of the human rights agenda" raised with outgoing Assistant Secretary of State for Human Rights, Democracy, and Labor Harold Koh in discussion with Thomas Carothers and Eliot Abrams in the transcript of the event, *Advancing Democracy: The Clinton Legacy*, Carnegie Endowment for International Peace, January 12, 2002, http://carnegieendowment.org/2001/01/12/advancing-democracy-clinton-legacy/49e9.

44. Hungary faced a similar credibility problem when, as president of the European Union in 2011, it spearheaded the *EU Framework for National Roma Integration Strategies up to 2020*, Communication, COM (2011) 173 (Brussels: European Commission, April 5, 2011), followed by the Council of the EU, *Council Conclusions on an EU Framework for National Roma Integration Strategies up to 2020*, 10658/11 (Brussels, May 19, 2011). Hungary's activity on this initiative followed dozens of arson, sniper, and Molotov cocktail attacks on Roma in Hungary, resulting in multiple deaths, critical injuries, and permanent disfigurement, as well as terrorizing of whole communities.

45. Decision on enhancement of the OSCE's operational capabilities regarding Roma and Sinti issues (MC(7).DEC/5), Decisions of the Oslo Ministerial Council, December 2–3, 1998.

46. Letter to Under Secretary of State for Political Affairs Thomas R. Pickering from Helsinki Commission Chairman Senator Alfonse D'Amato, Co-Chairman Congressman Christopher Smith, and Ranking Member Steny Hoyer, December 21, 1998 (archives of the Helsinki Commission).

47. Sixth OSCE Heads of State Summit, "Istanbul Summit Declaration," in the Istanbul Document 1999 (1999), para. 31. Additional language relating to Roma was also adopted at the Summit in para. 20 of the Charter for European Security.

48. "The Racial Equality Directive (2000/43/EC) is the key piece of EU legislation for combating discrimination on the grounds of racial or ethnic origin and for giving effect to the principle of equal treatment." EU Agency for Fundamental Rights, http://fra.europa.eu/en/publication/2012/racial-equality-directive-application-and-challenges; for the directive itself, see Council of the EU, Council Directive 2000/43/EC of 29 June 2000 [Race Equality Directive] implementing

the principle of equal treatment between persons irrespective of racial or ethnic origin, *Official Journal of the EU* 180 (July 19, 2000): 22–26.

49. OSCE, *Action Plan on Improving the Situation of Roma and Sinti Within the OSCE Area,* MC.DEC/3/03 (Maastricht, the Netherlands: OSCE, 2003), http://www.osce.org/odihr/17554.

50. Charles A. Stonecipher, "One Riot, One Ambassador: Macedonia, 1999," in *Inside a U.S. Embassy: Diplomacy at Work,* 3rd ed., ed. Shawn Dorman (Herndon, Va.: Potomac Books, 2011), 184–86; Claude Cahn and Tatjana Peric, "Roma in the Kosovo Conflict: Attempted Lynching in Macedonian Refugee Camp; Romani Refugees from Kosovo," in "Roma and the Kosovo Conflict" themed issue, *Roma Rights: Journal of European Roma Rights Centre* 2 (July 15, 1999), http://www.errc.org/cikk.php?cikk=798.

Chapter 4. The U.S. Department of State and International Efforts to Promote the Human Rights of Roma

1. Hillary Clinton, U.S. Secretary of State, "Secretary Clinton's Message on International Roma Day 2009," text and video on "Dipnote," U.S. Department of State Official Blog, April 8, 2009, http://blogs.state.gov/stories/2009/04/08/secretary-clintons-message-international-roma-day.

2. Kálmán Mizsei, "Reconstructing Roma Integration in Central and Eastern Europe: Addressing the Failures of the Last Quarter Century," in this volume.

3. U.S. Department of State, Office of the Spokesperson, "Secretary of State Hillary Rodham Clinton at a Roundtable with Young Roma Professionals," Remarks, February 5, 2012, Sofia, Bulgaria, http://bulgaria.usembassy.gov/secstate_roma02052012.html.

4. Ian Hancock, "ROMA [GYPSIES]," entry in *Handbook of Texas Online* (updated version of the 1999 print edition) (Austin: Texas State Historical Association, June 15, 2010), http://www.tshaonline.org/handbook/online/articles/pxrfh.

5. Council of Europe, *Protecting the Rights of Roma* (Strasbourg: CoE, 2013).

6. See Ian Hancock, "Porrajmos: The Roma and the Holocaust," filmed lecture, part of Holocaust Living History Workshop, #28100, 57:00 (San Diego: Library Channel, University of California Television, filmed May 7, 2014, premiered June 17, 2014), http://www.uctv.tv/shows/Porrajmos-The-Romani-and-the-Holocaust-with-Ian-Hancock-Holocaust-Living-History-The-Library-Channel-28100.

7. John Kerry, U.S. Secretary of State, "Statement in Commemoration of the World War II Genocide of Roma," August 1, 2014, http://www.state.gov/secretary/remarks/2014/08/230147.htm.

8. Hancock, "ROMA [GYPSIES]."

9. Smithsonian Institution, "'Gypsies' in the United States," based on the de Wendler-Funaro archives, in online exhibit "Migrations in History" (no date), http://smithsonianeducation.org/migrations/gyp/gypstart.html.

10. In 2000, the U.S. Census Bureau made the census response form available in the Roma language for the first time. There are many dialects of the Romani language, but some three-quarters of Romani speakers speak dialects mutually intelligible to educated speakers—a situation that resembles many dialects of English. According to the U.S. Census Bureau, they chose for the census the dialect spoken by the largest population and the one most used in the United States. See Carol M. Van Horn, "Census 2000 Information Memo no. 3," January 20, 1999, https://www.census.gov/dmd/www/pdf/InfoMem.pdf.

11. See Ethel Brooks, "Remembering the Dead, Documenting Resistance, Honouring the Heroes," in Discussion Paper Series, The Holocaust and United Nations Outreach Programme (New

York: UN, January 2013), http://www.un.org/en/holocaustremembrance/docs/paper23.shtml. The paper is also the text of her remarks at the UN for the 2013 Holocaust Remembrance Ceremony, January 23, 2013; see the moving video "Rescue During the Holocaust: The Courage to Care, Holocaust Memorial Ceremony," Brooks's remarks at 48:00 of 1:37:49, United Nations Webcast, http://webtv.un.org/search/rescue-during-the-holocaust-the-courage-to-care-holocaust -memorial-ceremony/2119397922001?term=holocaust&languages=&sort=date&page=3.

12. Office of the Press Secretary, White House, "President Obama Announces More Key Administration Posts," January 11, 2016, https://www.whitehouse.gov/the-press-office/2016/01 /11/president-obama-announces-more-key-administration-posts; Office of the Press Secretary, White House, "President Clinton Names Ian Francis Hancock as Member of the United States Holocaust Memorial Council," November 26, 1997, http://clinton6.nara.gov/1997/11/1997-11-26 -ian-hancock-named-to-us-holocaust-memorial-council.html.

13. U.S. Department of State and U.S. Agency for International Development (U.S.AID), *Leading Through Civilian Power: The First Quadrennial Diplomacy and Development Review* (Washington, D.C.: U.S. State Department and U.S.AID, 2010), 10.

14. Office of the President of the United States, *National Security Strategy* (Washington, D.C.: White House, May 2010), http://www.whitehouse.gov/sites/default/files/rss_viewer/national _security_strategy.pdf; U.S. State Department and U.S.AID, *Leading Through Civilian Power*, 42.

15. Conference on Security and Co-operation in Europe, Summit of Heads of States, Final Act (Helsinki, August 1, 1975) also known as the Helsinki Act, Helsinki Final Act, or Helsinki Accords, quotation from first sentence in Principle VII, "Respect for human rights and fundamental freedoms, including the freedom of thought, conscience, religion or belief," http://www .osce.org/mc/39501?download=true.

16. Known informally as the Copenhagen Document and formally, as the Document of the Copenhagen Meeting of the Conference on the Human Dimension of the CSCE, June 29, 1990, OSCE, http://www.osce.org/odihr/elections/14304.

17. Erika Schlager, "Policy and Practice: A Case Study of U.S. Foreign Policy Regarding the Situation of Roma in Europe," in this volume.

18. Document of the Moscow Meeting of the Conference on the Human Dimension of the CSCE, October 1991, http://www.osce.org/odihr/elections/14310.

19. Organization for Security and Co-operation in Europe (OSCE), *Action Plan on Improving the Situation of Roma and Sinti Within the OSCE Area,* MC. DEC.3/03 (Maastricht: OSCE, 2003), http://www.osce.org/odihr/17554.

20. OSCE, Ministerial Council, "Enhancing OSCE Efforts to Implement the Action Plan on Improving the Situation of Roma and Sinti within the OSCE Area, with a Particular Focus on Roma and Sinti Women, Youth, and Children," MC DEC/4/13 (Kiev: OSCE, December 6, 2013), https://www.osce.org/mc/109340; see also Alexandra Oprea's discussion of the complicated nuances of race and gender for Roma women in her chapter in this volume, "Toward the Recognition of Critical Race Theory in Human Rights Law: Roma Women's Reproductive Rights."

21. Although the project ended in 2014, OSCE's Office for Democratic Institutions and Human Rights continues to maintain the Best Practices website as a resource, http://bpri-odihr.org/.

22. Council of Europe (CoE), "The Strasbourg Declaration on Roma," CM(2010)133 final (Strasbourg: CoE, October 20, 2010), https://wcd.coe.int/ViewDoc.jsp?id=1691607.

23. CoE European Commission against Racism and Intolerance (ECRI), *General Recommendation No. 3: On Combating Racism and Intolerance Against Roma/Gypsies,* CR(98)29rev.

(Strasbourg, March 6, 1998), http://www.coe.int/t/dghl/monitoring/ecri/activities/gpr/en/recommendation_n3/Recommendation_3_en.asp.

24. *Sejdić and Finci v. Bosnia and Herzegovina*, App. Nos. 27996/06 and 34836/06, ECtHR, Grand Chamber Judgment (December 22, 2009), http://hudoc.echr.coe.int/eng?i=001-96491. The ethnic requirements in question were adopted in the Constitution of Bosnia and Herzegovina resulting from the peace negotiations (the Dayton Agreement) to end the war in the former Yugoslavia.

25. European Commission, *An EU Framework for National Roma Integration Strategies up to 2020*, Communication, COM (2011) 173 (Brussels, April 5, 2011), http://ec.europa.eu/justice/policies/discrimination/docs/com_2011_173_en.pdf.

26. Will Guy, "Anti-Roma Violence, Hate Speech, and Discrimination in the New Europe: Czech Republic, Slovakia, and Hungary," in this volume.

27. Gary Robbins, Chargé d'Affaires, U.S. Mission to the OSCE, "Statement on Roma" (as delivered to the OSCE Permanent Council, Vienna, July 25, 2013), http://osce.usmission.gov/jul_25_13_roma.html; for another example, see Daniel B. Baer, Ambassador and U.S. Representative to the OSCE, "On Anti-Roma Statements in Slovakia and Anti-Roma Protests Bulgaria" (as delivered to the OSCE Permanent Council, Vienna, July 2, 2015), http://osce.usmission.gov/jul_2_15_roma.html.

28. Examples of Roma-related projects include "Support the Roma Minority Population in Effective Advocacy and Reporting," implemented in Bosnia-Herzegovina, 2007–2009; "Youth Civic Engagement & Dialogue," implemented in Moldova and Romania, 2011–2013; "Building Community Connections: Promoting Inter-Ethnic Dialogue and Civic Engagement Among Youth at the Community Level," implemented in Hungary and Slovakia, 2011–2013; and "Partnership for Roma Protection, Prevention and Promotion," implemented in Bulgaria, Kosovo, Macedonia, Romania, and Serbia, 2010–2014.

29. For example, "Leaders: Young Roma in Action," implemented in Albania, Bosnia-Herzegovina, and Kosovo, 2013–2015.

30. David Beňák, "Situation of Native Americans Similar to That of Czech Roma," trans. Gwendolyn Albert, Romea News Service, February 2, 2013, http://www.romea.cz/en/features-and-commentary/reportage/situation-of-native-americans-similar-to-that-of-czech-roma.

31. For more information, see Radu Florea et al., *Roma Education Project: Performance Evaluation Report* (Skopje, Macedonia: Foundation Open Society Macedonia [FOSM], 2013); and Suzana Pecakovska and Spomenka Lazarevska, eds., *Roma Education Program, Ten Years Later: Changes Behind the Numbers*, trans. Abakus (Skopje, Macedonia: FOSM, 2014), both available at http://www.soros.org.mk/en/Home/Publications?catID=9.

32. See, for example, Office to Monitor and Combat Trafficking in Persons, *Trafficking in Persons* (Washington, D.C.: U.S. State Department, July 2015), http://www.state.gov/j/tip/rls/tiprpt/2015/index.htm.

33. John Kerry, U.S. Secretary of State, "International Roma Day Press Statement," April 7, 2016, http://www.state.gov/secretary/remarks/2016/04/255594.htm.

Chapter 5. A Critical Analysis of Roma Policy and Praxis

1. National Council for Combating Discrimination, Ordinance no. 137 from August 31, 2000, http://www.cncd.org.ro/legislatie/Legislatie-nationala/ORDONANTA-nr-137-din-31-august-2000-15/.

2. Ministry of Education and Research, The Cabinet of the State Secretary for Pre-University Education, *Notification no. 29323/20.04.2004*, 2004, http://www.edu.ro/download/notadmrr3 .pdf.

3. European Commission, *Non-Discrimination and Equal Opportunities: A Renewed Commitment, Community Instruments and Policies for Roma Inclusion*, Commission Staff Working Document, COM(2008)420 (Brussels: European Commission, 2008), http://ec.europa.eu/justice /discrimination/files/sec_2008_2172.pdf.

4. Jose Manuel Barroso, President of the European Commission, Speech at the EU's Third European Roma Summit, Brussels, April 4, 2014, http://europa.eu/rapid/press-release_SPEECH -14-288_en.htm.

5. See, as one major example of new commitments: European Commission, *An EU Framework for National Roma Integration Strategies up to 2020*, Communication, COM(2011) 173 (Brussels, April 5, 2011), http://ec.europa.eu/justice/policies/discrimination/docs/com_2011_173_en .pdf.

6. Romanian Government, [*Decision no. 430 from April 25, 2001 Regarding the Governmental Strategy for Improving the Roma Situation*], in Romanian, http://www.mmuncii.ro/pub /imagemanager/images/file/Legislatie/HOTARARI-DE-GUVERN/HG430-2001.pdf.

7. The survey was conducted in 2011, separately but in collaboration with the UNDP/World Bank/EC survey, reports on various areas are still forthcoming. Data mentioned here are from European Union Agency for Fundamental Rights (FRA), *Roma Survey—Data in Focus, Education: The Situation of Roma in 11 EU Member States* (Vienna: FRA, 2014), 11, http://fra.europa.eu /sites/default/files/fra-2014_roma-survey_education_tk0113748enc.pdf.

8. Christian Bruggeman, *Roma Education in Comparative Perspective: Analysis of the UNDP/ World Bank/EC Regional Roma Survey 2011* (Bratislava: UNDP, 2012), 33, http://www.unesco.org /new/fileadmin/MULTIMEDIA/HQ/ED/pdf/Roma-Education-Comparative-Perspective -UNDP.pdf.

9. Eurostat statistics explained, Tertiary education attainment EU-28, 2014 http://ec.europa .eu/eurostat/statistics-explained/index.php/File:Tertiary_educational_attainment,_EU-28_Fig _7.PNG.

10. European Commission, *Report on the Implementation of the EU Framework for National Roma Integration Strategies* (Brussels: EU, 2014), 4, http://ec.europa.eu/justice/discrimination /files/roma_implement_strategies2014_en.pdf.

11. Cited in World Bank, *Diagnosis and Policy Advice for Supporting Roma Inclusion in Romania*, 2014, http://www-wds.worldbank.org/external/default/WDSContentServer/WDSP /IB/2014/04/09/000333037_20140409142900/Rendered/PDF/866710WP0P14500nal0Report00E nglish0.pdf.

12. National Statistics Institute, Population and Housing Census, 2002 and 2011, http://www .insse.ro/cms/files/RPL2002INS/vol4/tabele/t12.pdf; and http://www.recensamantromania.ro /rezultate-2/, table 18.

13. PHARE was an EU program created to help fund development in countries hoping to join the EU; Romanian Ministry of Education (RME), [*School Desegregation: Progress and Challenges: Experiences from the PHARE 2003 "Access to Education for Disadvantaged Groups" Project*], in Romanian (Bucharest: RME, 2006), http://www.edu.ro/index.php/articles/6758.

14. Catalina Ulrich, [*Programele PHARE: "Acces la educație pentru grupuri dezavantajate" Studiu de Impact*], original in Romanian; excerpted English translation, *Impact Study: Access to*

Education for Disadvantaged Groups (Bucharest: MECI, 2009), http://www.academia.edu /4316359/Impact_study_Access_to_education_for_disadvantaged_groups_PHARE_Romania. The translated text does not include most of the desegregation chapter.

15. According to a County Office report, the school has a tradition "to create socially segregated classes." *Romani CRISS v. Colegiul Național Ioniță Asan and Inspectoratul Școlar Judențean Olt* (the county school department), complaint filed Bucharest 2011 and adjudicated by Romanian National Council for Combatting Discrimination (NCCD) decision 559 in file 52-2012 (December 12, 2012); see the case description in Human European Consultancy and Migration Policy Group, *Report on Measures to Combat Discrimination Directives 2000/43/EC And 2000/78/EC, Country Report 2013: Romania* (Brussels: European Network of Legal Experts in the Non-Discrimination Field, August 2014), 14–15, http://www.equalitylaw.eu/country /romania.

16. "First grade A" Step-by-Step class enrolled twenty-eight children, two of them were Roma with a good socioeconomic situation; another "first grade A" enrolled thirty-two children, also two of them were Roma with a good socioeconomic situation. "First grade B" enrolled twelve children, ten of them Roma and two belonging to mixed Roma-Romanian families, all of them with a modest socioeconomic situation. Data collected from *Romani CRISS v. Colegiul Național Ioniță Asan.* For condition of classroom, see also Human European Consultancy and Migration Policy Group, *Report on Measures to Combat Discrimination Directives 2000/43/EC And 2000/78/ EC, Country Report 2013.*

17. European Commission, *Implementation of the EU Framework 2014*, 3.

18. In addition, when the Romanian National Council for Combatting Discrimination (NCCD) ruled against the mayor, they were overruled by the appeals court (*Cherecheș v. NCCD*), Reference no. file 1741/33/2011, decision 640 Romanian High Court of Cassation and Justice [September 27, 2013]; see case description in Human European Consultancy and Migration Policy Group, *Measures to Combat Discrimination Country Report 2013: Romania*, 13, with further comments at 11, 46, 87, and description of the original case at 166–67.

19. Romani CRISS and Euroregional Center for Public Initiatives, "Romani Children Segregation in Hospitals Challenged for the First Time in Romania," press release, December 21, 2011, http://www.romanicriss.org/PDF/Press%20release%20children%20segregation%20in%20 hospital%20Marie%20Curie%20dec%202011.pdf.

20. European Roma Rights Centre (ERRC), Romani CRISS, Sanse Egale, *Open Letter: Forced Eviction of Roma from Eforie Sud*, October 2, 2013, in Romanian, http://www.romanicriss .org/PDF/letter%20of%20concern%20evacuare%20Eforie.pdf; for an article on the situation and the letter in English, see, "Romania Eviction Leaves 100 People Homeless in Dangerous Conditions–Authorities Must Act Urgently," http://www.errc.org/article/romania-eviction -leaves-100-people-homeless-in-dangerous-conditions-%E2%80%93-authorities-must-act -urgently/4204.

21. Van Meter and Van Horn, cited in Michel Hill and Peter Hupe, *Implementing Public Policy: Governance in Theory and Practice* (London: Sage Publications, 2002).

22. Romanian Government, [*Governmental Strategy for Improving the Roma Situation 2001*], discussed throughout this chapter as the 2001 Strategy.

23. Romanian Government, [*Governmental Strategy for Improving the Roma Situation 2001*] *amended in 2006*, http://www.mmuncii.ro/pub/imagemanager/images/file/Legislatie/HOTARARI -DE-GUVERN/HG430-2001.pdf.

24. European Commission, *Romania: May 2006 Monitoring Report,* COM (2006) 214 final, Staff Working Document (Brussels, May 16, 2006), 11–12, http://ec.europa.eu/enlargement/pdf /key_documents/2006/monitoring_report_ro_en.pdf.

25. Focus Consultancy Ltd, *Assessment of the Roma Strategy Implementation Mechanism* (London: EC, July 2005), in English, http://www.anr.gov.ro/docs/rapoarte/Focus_Final_Evaluation _Report_181.pdf.

26. Romanian Government, *Strategy for the Inclusion of the Romanian Citizens Belonging to Roma Minority for the Period 2012–2020* (Bucharest, 2011), http://ec.europa.eu/justice /discrimination/files/roma_romania_strategy_en.pdf; see also the revised version, *Strategy for the Inclusion of the Romanian Citizens Belonging to Roma Minority for the Period 2015–2020* (Bucharest, 2015), http://ec.europa.eu/justice/discrimination/files/roma_romania_strategy2_en.pdf.

27. For more information, see http://www.sgg.ro/docs/File/UPP/doc/proiecte_finale /Strategia_BR_varianta_finala_aprobata_de_Guvern.pdf.

28. European Commission, *The Commission's Assessment of Romania's National Strategy,* 2012, http://ec.europa.eu/justice/discrimination/files/country_factsheets_2012/romania_en.pdf.

29. See Margareta Matache, "Ten Years to Make a Difference? Reflections on the Lacunae of the EU Roma Strategy 2020," *European Review Journal* (forthcoming 2017).

30. Romanian Government, *Strategy for the Inclusion of the Romanian Citizens Belonging to Roma Minority for the Period 2015–2020.*

31. Romani CRISS, *Brief Point to the Adoption of the Strategy for Roma Inclusion 2015–2020,* 2015, available at office@romanicriss.org.

32. UN Human Rights Office of the High Commissioner, *End-of-mission statement on Romania, by Professor Philip Alston, United Nations Human Rights Council Special Rapporteur on Extreme Poverty and Human Rights,* 2015, http://www.ohchr.org/EN/NewsEvents/Pages /DisplayNews.aspx?NewsID=16737&LangID=E.

33. Romanian Government, [*Governmental Strategy for Improving the Roma Situation 2001*].

34. Roma Education Fund (REF) and Gallup Romania, *Analysis of the Impact of Affirmative Action for Roma in High Schools, Vocational Schools and Universities* (Budapest: REF, 2009), http://www.romaeducationfund.hu/sites/default/files/publications/gallup_romania_english.pdf.

35. Ibid.

36. Anca Nedelcu and Catalina Ulrich, *Stadiul implementării strategiei privind educația timpurie și analiza practicilor promițătoare în educația timpurie din România* (The Status of Implementation of the National Strategy on Early Childhood and Analysis of Promising Practices Focusing on Early Childhood in Romania), 2015, http://www.unicef.ro/wp-content/uploads /Unicef_Stadiul-implementarii-strategiei . . . edu-timpurie_pt-site_20.07.2015.pdf.

37. Christian Bruggeman, *Roma Education in Comparative Perspective: Analysis of the UNDP/World Bank/EC Regional Roma Survey 2011* (Bratislava: UNDP, 2012), 33, http://www .unesco.org/new/fileadmin/MULTIMEDIA/HQ/ED/pdf/Roma-Education-Comparative -Perspective-UNDP.pdf.

38. Romanian Government, [*Governmental Strategy for Improving the Roma Situation 2001*].

39. Romanian Ministry of Education, the Desegregation Order, 2007, http://www.legex.ro /Ordin-1540-19.07.2007-82075.aspx.

40. Laura Surdu, *Monitoring the Implementation of the Anti-Segregation Measures in Romania* (Bucharest: Romani CRISS, 2008).

41. World Bank, Human Development and Sustainable Development Teams, Europe and Central Asia, *Diagnostics and Policy Advice for Supporting Roma Inclusion in Romania* (Wash-

ington, D.C.: World Bank, February 2014), http://www-wds.worldbank.org/external/default /WDSContentServer/WDSP/IB/2014/04/09/000333037_20140409142900/Rendered/PDF/86671 0WP0P14500nal0Report00English0.pdf.

42. European Commission, *Better Regulations-Simply Explained* (Luxembourg: EC, 2006), http://ec.europa.eu/smart-regulation/better_regulation/documents/brochure/brochure_en .pdf.

43. Margareta Matache, *Dezvolatarea timpurie a copiilor romi: idei, politici si instrumente* (Early Development of Romani Children: Ideas, Policies and Tools), PhD dissertation, University of Bucharest, 2011.

44. For the percent figure, see European Commission, *An EU Framework for National Roma Integration Strategies up to 2020*, Communication, COM(2011) 173 (Brussels, April 5, 2011), 16 http://ec.europa.eu/justice/policies/discrimination/docs/com_2011_173_en.pdf; on bilingual education, see Amare Rromentza, *Evaluation of the Educational Public Policies for Roma* (Bucharest: UNICEF Romania, 2009), http://www.unicef.ro/wp-content/uploads//evaluarea-politicilor -publice-educationale-pentru-rromi_2.pdf.

45. For more information, see http://www.amarerromentza.org/ro/; see also John Bennett, *Roma Early Childhood Inclusion* (Budapest: Open Society Foundations, Roma Education Fund, UNICEF, 2012), Box 17, 73, http://www.unicef.org/romania/RECI-Overview.pdf.

46. Gheorghe Sarau, "Roma's Education in Romania," blogpost, May 26, 2009, http:// gheorghesarau.wordpress.com/2009/10/02/romas-education-in-romania-author-gheorghe -sarau/.

47. Flavio Cunha and James J. Heckman "Investing in Our Young People," in Childhood Programs and Practices in the First Decade of Life, ed. Arthur J. Reynolds et al. (Cambridge: Cambridge University Press, 2010), 381–414.

48. Ovidiu Bărbulescu, "Ponta: ONG-urile, responsabile de 20 ani pentru integrarea romilor. Guvernul va folosi mai bine banii (Ponta: NGOs responsible for 20 years for Roma inclusion. The Government will use the money better)," quoting Prime Minister Ponta, Mediafax, Bucharest, July 11, 2013, http://www.mediafax.ro/politic/ponta-ong-urile-responsabile-de-20-ani-pentru -integrarea-romilor-guvernul-va-folosi-mai-bine-banii-11117807.

49. Ibid.

Chapter 6. Roma Policy in Europe

1. In this chapter I focus on European and EU Roma policies as formulated and realized by international and intergovernmental organizations, along with national governments. I leave out of my analysis all the ideas, initiatives, and recommendations formulated or promoted by the Roma civil sector and political organizations gathered in the so-called Roma movement, as well as non-Roma civil organizations engaged in Roma issues. These efforts could be subjects of separate inquiry and analysis.

2. Will Guy, André Liebich, and Elena Marushiakova, *Improving the Tools for the Social Inclusion and Non-Discrimination of Roma in the EU* (Luxembourg: EC, 2010).

3. For Communist countries, see David Crowe and John Kolsti, eds., *The Gypsies of Eastern Europe* (Armonk, N.Y.: M. E. Sharpe, 1991); Will Guy, ed., *Between Past and Future: The Roma of Central and Eastern Europe* (Hatfield: University of Hertfordshire Press, 2001); Zoltan Barany, *The East European Gypsies: Regime Change, Marginality and Ethnopolitics* (Cambridge: Cambridge University Press, 2002). For Western Europe, see Barbara Adams et al., eds., *Gypsies and Government Policy in England: A Study of the Travellers' Way of Life in Relation to the Policies*

and Practices of Central and Local Government (London: Heinemann, 1975); Jean-Pierre Liegeois, "Governments and Gypsies: From Rejection to Assimilation," in The Other Nomads, ed. Aparna Rao (Cologne: Böhlau Verlag, 1987).

4. Andrzej Mirga and Nicolae Gheorghe, "Roma in the Twenty-First Century: Policy Paper," (Princeton, N.J.: Project on Ethnic Relation, 1997), http://www.per-usa.org/1997-2007/21st_c .htm.

5. Dena Ringold, Roma and the Transition in Central and Eastern Europe: Trends and Challenges (Washington, D.C.: World Bank, 2000), http://siteresources.worldbank.org/EXTROMA /Resources/transition.pdf.

6. Janos Ladanyi, "The Hungarian Neo-Liberal State, Ethnic Classification and the Creation of a Roma Underclass," in Poverty, Ethnicity, and Gender in Eastern Europe During the Market Transition, ed. Rebecca Emigh and Ivan Szelenyi (Westport, Conn.: Greenwood, 2001); Huub van Baar, The European Roma: Minority Representation, Memory and the Limits of Transnational Governmentality (Amsterdam: Gravenhage, 2011); Nidhi Trehan and Nando Sigona, ed., Romani Politics in Contemporary Europe: Poverty, Ethnic Mobilization, and the Neo-Liberal Order (Houndsmill: Palgrave Macmillan, 2009).

7. Janos Ladanyi and Ivan Szelenyi, Patterns of Exclusion: Constructing Gypsy Ethnicity and the Making of an Underclass in Transition Societies in Europe, East European Monographs (New York: Columbia University Press, 2006). Some scholars objected to the concept and framework of analyzing Roma situation in terms of underclass formation; see Michael Stewart, "Deprivation, the Roma and 'the Underclass,'" in Postsocialism: Ideals, Ideologies and Practices in Eurasia, ed. Chris Hann (London: Routledge, 2001), 133–57.

8. Mirga and Gheorghe, "Roma in the Twenty-First Century."

9. Max van der Stoel, CSCE (Conference on Security and Cooperation in Europe, now Organization for SCE) High Commissioner on National Minorities (HCNM), Roma (Gypsies) in the CSCE Region: Report of the HCNM, CSCE Communication No. 240 (Prague: CSCE, September, 1993), http://www.opsce.org/hcnm/36441?download=true. See also Council of Europe Parliamentary Assembly, Gypsies in Europe, Recommendation 1203 (Strasbourg: 1993), http://assembly .coe.int/nw/xml/XRef/X2H-Xref-ViewPDF.asp?FileID=15237&lang=en.

10. For more on OSCE and Roma issues, see Andrzej Mirga, "Roma and Sinti: Status and Outlook," in OSCE Yearbook 2011, ed. Ursel Schlichting (Hamburg: Institute for Peace Research and Security Policy [IFSH], 2012), 303–19. For Council of Europe (CoE) and Roma, see CoE Assembly, Gypsies in Europe, Recommendation 1203; in 1995, soon after the adoption of that recommendation, CoE established an expert committee on Roma and Travellers (MG-S-ROM) under the Migration Division (which has since been replaced by Ad hoc Committee of Experts on Roma Issues [CAHROM]); for more on CoE and Roma, see CoE's Roma topic webpage, http:// www.coe.int/t/dg3/romatravellers/. For UN and Roma, General Recommendation 27 on Discrimination Against Roma of the Committee on the Elimination of Racial Discrimination (CERD) set out a number of measures to be followed by states, CERD (2000), Fifty-seventh Session; see also Roma Regional Working Group, United Nations Development Group, "The Role of the United Nations in Advancing Roma Inclusion," Joint Position Paper, February 2013, http:// www.europe.ohchr.org/Documents/Publications/RomaInclusion.pdf.

11. See, for example, the OSCE Office for Democratic Institutions and Human Rights (ODIHR) Good Practice Roma Integration project (http://www.osce.org/odihr/91077), WE-BLAN, a joint project with the Office of the UN High Commissioner on Refugees, for Roma without civil registration or ID documents in Western Balkans, http://www.romadecade.org

/cms/upload/file/9385_file16_weblan—presentation-on-the-networks-vision-mission-and -activities.pdf, or the CoE's Roma mediators program, http://www.romadecade.org/cms/upload /file/9469_file4_presentation-for-zagreb-romed-%255Bcompatibility-mode%255D.pdf.

12. For more on Roma and UN monitoring, see Marcia Rooker, *The International Supervision of Protection of Romani People in Europe* (Nijmegen: Nijmegen University Press, 2002); for an overview of the monitoring of the COE's Framework Convention for the Protection of National Minorities, see Council of Europe, *Filling the Frame: Five Years of Monitoring the Framework Convention for the Protection of National Minorities* (Strasbourg: CoE, 2004). For monitoring by non-treaty groups, see, for example, Max van der Stoel, OSCE High Commissioner on National Minorities, *Report on the Situation of Roma and Sinti in the OSCE Area*, (The Hague: OSCE, 2000), http://www.osce.org/hcnm/42063; Thomas Hammarberg, Commissioner for Human Rights of CoE, *Human Rights of Roma and Travellers in Europe* (Strasbourg: CoE, 2012); CoE European Commission against Racism and Intolerance (ECRI), *General Recommendation No. 3: On Combating Racism and Intolerance Against Roma/Gypsies*, CR(98)29rev. (Strasbourg, March 6, 1998), http://www.coe.int/t/dghl/monitoring/ecri/activities/gpr/en/recommendation_n3 /Recommendation_3_en.asp.

13. See in particular in this volume, James A. Goldston, "The Unfulfilled Promise of Educational Opportunity in the United States and Europe: From *Brown v. Board* to *D.H.* and Beyond"; and Alexandra Oprea, "Toward the Recognition of Critical Race Theory in Human Rights Law: Romani Women's Reproductive Rights."

14. This program was presented as "a crisis management package," see Zsuzsanna Farkas Szilagyi, and Antal Heizer, [*Report on the Situation of the Gypsy Community in Hungary*] in Hungarian (Budapest: State Secretary at the Office of the Prime Minister, 1996), 12.

15. See Project on Ethnic Relations (PER), *State Policies Towards Romani Communities in Candidate Countries to the EU: Government and Romani Participation in Policy Making*, Conference Report (Princeton, N.J., 1999); see also "Government Programmes on Roma," themed issue, *Roma Rights: Journal of European Roma Rights Centre* nos. 2–3 (August 15, 2001); also, Open Society Institute (OSI), *Monitoring of the EU Accession Process: Minority Rights Protection* (Budapest: OSI, 2002).

16. Project on Ethnic Relations (PER), *Roma and the EU Accession: Elected and Appointed Romani Representatives in an Enlarged Europe*, Conference Report (Princeton, N.J.: PER, 2003), http://www.per-usa.org/Reports/Per Brussels Report.pdf; Eva Sobotka and Peter Vermeersch, "Governing Human Rights and Roma Inclusion: Can the EU be a Catalyst for Local Social Change?" *Human Rights Quarterly* 34, no. 3 (2012): 800–822.

17. OSCE Office for Democratic Institutions and Human Rights (ODIHR), *Implementation of the Action Plan on Improving the Situation of Roma and Sinti Within the OSCE Area: Status Report 2008* (Warsaw: OSCE/ODIHR, 2008), http://www.osce.org/odihr/33500?download =true.

18. Council of the European Union, Council Directive 2000/43/EC of 29 June 2000 [Race Equality Directive] implementing the principle of equal treatment between persons irrespective of racial or ethnic origin, *Official Journal of the EU* 180 (July 19, 2000): 22–26; see also Olivier De Schutter and Annelies Verstichel, "The Role of the Union in Integrating the Roma: Present and Possible Future," *European Diversity and Autonomy Papers (EDAP)* 2 (Bozen, Italy: European Academy, 2005), http://webfolder.eurac.edu/EURAC/Publications/edap/2005_edap02.pdf.

19. For Roma decade, see, for example, World Bank, "European Leaders In Unprecedented Initiative to Fight Discrimination against Roma," Press Release, January 31, 2005, Sofia, Bulgaria,

http://go.worldbank.org/IESOEW1510; for complex structure, see OSCE ODIHR, *Roma Status Report 2008*, Appendix III, 60.

20. See, for example, European Roma Policy Coalition, "EU Social Agenda: Roma Inclusion Remains Deadlocked," press release, June 2, 2008, http://www.errc.org/cms/upload/media/03/1E /m0000031E.pdf; and subsequent statements or reports by this informal network of human rights and Roma organizations that lobbied for EU Roma policy.

21. European Council, *Presidency Conclusions of the Brussels European Council: 14 December 2007*, 16616/1/07 Rev.1 (Brussels, February 28, 2008), 14, http://www.consilium.europa.eu /ueDocs/cms_Data/docs/pressData/en/ec/97669.pdf, para. 50, both quotes.

22. EU Directorate General, Employment, Social Affairs and Equal Opportunities, *The Roma in the European Social Fund 2007–2013*, Information Pamphlet (Brussels: EU, 2010), http:// www.euromanet.eu/upload/00/75/tp_Roma_ESF_2007-2013_en.pdf.

23. Commission of the European Communities, *Non-Discrimination and Equal Opportunities: A Renewed Commitment; Community Instruments and Policies for Roma Inclusion*. Commission Staff Working Document, COM(2008) 420 (Brussels: Commission of the European Communities, 2008), http://ec.europa.eu/social/BlobServlet?docId=481&langId=en, 4.

24. Ibid., 5.

25. Ibid., 3.

26. Ibid., 29–30.

27. The proposal first was included in an analysis of the French situation from Viviane Reding, EU Vice-President and Commissioner for Justice; László Andor, EU Commissioner for Employment, Social Affairs and Inclusion, and Cecilia Malmström, EU Commissioner for Home Affairs, "The Situation of Roma in France and Europe," Joint Information Note, IP/10/407; MEMO/10/121, September 1, 2010, http://www.statewatch.org/news/2010/sep/EC-Roma-France -report.pdf; see also European Commission, "European Commission to Assess Member States' use of EU funds for Roma Integration," News Announcement, September 7, 2010, http://ec.europa .eu/social/main.jsp?catId=89&langId=en&newsId=861&furtherNews=yes.

28. See, for example, László Andor, EU Commissioner, Employment, Social Affairs and Inclusion, "Moving from Hopes and Aspirations to Concrete Action: EU Funding and the New EU Framework for National Roma Integration Strategies," Speech, High-level Event on Structural Funds' Contribution to Roma Inclusion (Sofia, June 21, 2011), http://europa.eu/rapid/press-release _SPEECH-11-464_en.htm; see also Christoph Hasselbach, "European Commission to Push Member States to Do More to Help Roma, *Deutche Welle*, October 10, 2010, http://www.dw.de/european -commission-to-push-member-states-to-do-more-to-help-roma/a-6104685-1; "EC's Laszlo Andor, on European Funds and the Roma's Inclusion," *Romanian Business News Actmedia*, April 23, 2013, http://actmedia.eu/daily/ec-s-laszlo-andor-on-european-funds-and-the-roma-s-inclusion/45646.

29. Michael Stewart, ed., *The Gypsy "Menace": Populism and the New Anti-Gypsy Politics* (London: Hurst, 2012).

30. OSCE Office for Democratic Institutions and Human Rights (ODIHR), *Addressing Violence, Promoting Integration, Field Assessment of Violent Incidents Against Roma in Hungary: Key Developments, Findings and Recommendations* (Warsaw: OSCE, June 15, 2010), http://www.osce .org/odihr/68545?download=true.

31. Jamie Bartlett et al., *Populism in Europe: Hungary* (London: DEMOS, 2012), http://www .demos.co.uk/files/Demos_Hungary_Book_web-1.pdf?1327923915.

32. For overall violence against Roma between 2008 and 2010, see European Roma Rights Centre (ERRC), "Factsheet: Roma Rights Record" (Budapest: ERRC, October 4, 2010), http://

www.errc.org/popup-article-view.php?article_id=3573. In the Czech Republic, for example, the 2008 Vitkov attack against a Roma family left a Roma girl not yet two years old with second- and third-degree burns over 80 percent of her body. For more on the Czech Republic, see ERRC, "Attacks Against Roma in the Czech Republic, January 2008–July 2012" (Budapest: ERRC, July 31, 2012), http://www.errc.org/cms/upload/file/attacks-list-in-czech-republic.pdf. In Bulgaria, see for example, coverage of the Katunitsa riots, "Ethnic Tensions Mar Bulgaria's Presidential Elections," EuraActiv.com with Bulgarian partner *Dnevnik*, September 27, 2011, http://www.euractiv .com/elections/ethnical-tensions-mar-bulgarias-election-campaign-news-507927. On violence in Slovakia, see, for example, Bernard Rorke, "Killing Time: The Lethal Force of Anti-Roma Racism," Open Society Foundations, July 18, 2012, http://www.opensocietyfoundations.org/voices /killing-time-lethal-force-anti-roma-racism.

33. These directives included the Race Equality Directive, previously mentioned on freedom of movement in the EU (https://eumovement.wordpress.com/directive-200438ec/), and on the protection of personal data (http://eur-lex.europa.eu/legal-content/EN/TXT/?uri=URISERV:l14012) , and especially, the 2008 Framework Decision on combating certain forms and expressions of racism and xenophobia by means of criminal law, http://eur-lex.europa.eu/LexUriServ/LexUriServ.do ?uri=OJ:L:2008:328:0055:0058:en:PDF. For scapegoating, see Amnesty International, *"We Ask for Justice": Europe's Failure to Protect Roma from Racist Violence* (London: Amnesty International, 2014), http://www.amnesty.eu/content/assets/Reports/08042014_Europes_failure_to _protect_Roma_from_racist_violence.pdf.

34. OSCE Office for Democratic Institutions and Human Rights and High Commissioner on National Minorities, *Assessment of the Human Rights Situation of Roma and Sinti in Italy: Report of a Fact-Finding Mission to Milan, Naples, and Rome on July 20–26, 2008* (Warsaw: OSCE, 2009), http://www.osce.org/odihr/36374; Elena Rozzi, too, discusses the situation in Italy in her chapter in this volume.

35. Sergio Carrera, "Shifting Responsibilities for EU Roma Citizens: The 2010 French Affair on Roma Evictions and Expulsions Continued," *CEPS Liberty and Security in Europe Papers* 55 (Brussels: Centre for European Policy Studies, June 2013), http://www.ceps.eu/system/files/No% 2055%20Shifting%20Responsibilities%20for%20EU%20Roma%20Citizens.pdf.

36. Ibid., 1.

37. Ibid., 2.

38. Council of the EU, *Council Conclusions on an EU Framework for National Roma Integration Strategies up to 2020,* 10658/11 (Brussels, May 19, 2011), http://ec.europa.eu/justice/policies /discrimination/docs/com_2011_173_en.pdf.

39. European Council, *Presidency Conclusions of the Brussels European Council: 23–24 June 2011,* EUCO 23/1/11 Rev.1 (Brussels: September 29, 2011), 13, http://eur-lex.europa.eu/legal -content/EN/TXT/?uri=CELEX:52011XG0902(01)&qid=1445838238551. These decisions have been complemented with three unprecedented EU Roma Summits in Brussels on September 16, 2008, in Cordoba, Spain, on April 8, 2010, and Brussels, April 4, 2014; establishment of the EU Platform for Roma Inclusion in 2008; and the Task Force on Roma in 2010 at the European Commission.

40. EU funding to support social inclusion of "disadvantaged people, including Roma," reached some 26.5 billion euro in the programming period 2007–2013, European Commission, *Roma in Europe: The Implementation of European Union Instruments and Policies for Roma Inclusion—Progress Report 2008–2010,* Commission Staff Working Document, SEC(2010) 400 final (Brussels: European Commission, April 7, 2010), 26.

41. For example, Kálmán Mizsei in a 2013 opinion piece summarizes: "despite good intentions, little has changed. In fact, the Roma's suffering has increased as a result of the euro crisis, and intolerance has intensified, especially in the countries with the largest Roma populations—Romania, Hungary, Bulgaria, Slovakia, the Czech Republic, and Greece. Despite the European Commission's call for member states to apply more European Union (EU) funds to programs aimed at integrating Roma before the close of the 2007–2013 EU budget period, none of these six countries has done so. Some of them—such as Bulgaria and Romania—are among the most laggard spenders of EU funds, particularly resources from the European Social Fund." Mizsei, "Robbing the Roma," Open Society Foundations, January 23, 2013, https://www.opensocietyfoundations .org/voices/robbing-roma.

42. Council of the EU, *Council Conclusions on an EU Framework,* 4.

43. European Commission, *Steps Forward in Implementing National Roma Strategies,* Communication, COM(2013) 454 final (Brussels: European Commission, June 26, 2013), http://ec .europa.eu/justice/discrimination/files/com_2013_454_en.pdf.

44. For examples of civil society responses, see "National Roma Integration Strategies: What Next?" themed issue, *Roma Rights: Journal of European Roma Rights Centre* 2013 (January 4, 2014), http://www.errc.org/article/roma-rights-2013-national-roma-integration-strategies-what -next/4238; Roma Initiatives Office, Open Society Foundations (OSF), *Review of EU Framework National Roma Integration Strategies (NRIS),* (Budapest: OSF, February, 2012), http://www .opensocietyfoundations.org/sites/default/files/roma-integration-strategies-20120221.pdf.

45. Bernard Rorke, "What Future for the EU Framework? What Prospects for Roma Inclusion?" in "National Roma Integration Strategies: What Next?" themed issue, *Roma Rights: Journal of European Roma Rights Centre* 2013 (January 4, 2014): 5–10, particularly 6, http://www.errc .org/article/roma-rights-2013-national-roma-integration-strategies-what-next/4238.

46. Giulano Amato (Chairman) and Judy Batt (Rapporteur),*The Long-Term Implications of EU Enlargement: The Nature of the New Border,* Final Report of the Reflection Group (Badia Fiesolana: European University Institute, 1999), 39, http://cadmus.eui.eu/bitstream/handle/1814 /14277/FinalReport.pdf?sequence=1.

47. Within the EU Roma Platform meetings, the key international organizations have been participating and sharing their experiences in Roma integration; similarly, a series of high-level conferences organized by the EU Enlargement Directorate-General with governments of the Western Balkan countries between 2010 and 2012, have been conducted at which organizations such as OSCE (and its field operations), UNHCR, UNDP, World Bank, and the Decade-for-Roma-Inclusion Secretariat shared their experiences and lessons learned with regard to Roma integration.

48. For good practices, see Guy, Liebich, and Marushiakova, *Improving the Tools for Social Inclusion;* for models, see European Commission, *What Works for Roma Inclusion in the EU: Policies and Model Approaches* (Luxembourg: European Union, 2012), http://ec.europa.eu /justice/discrimination/files/whatworksfor_romainclusion_en.pdf and Roma Education Fund (REF), "A Good Start: The EU Roma Pilot," press release, Brussels, June 4, 2012, http://www .romaeducationfund.hu/good-start-eu-roma-pilot.

49. See, for example, European Union Agency for Fundamental Rights (FRA), T*he Situation of Roma EU Citizens Moving to and Settling in Other EU Member States* (Vienna: FRA, European Commission, November 2009), http://fra.europa.eu/sites/default/files/fra_uploads/785 -ROMA-Movement-Positive-Initiatives_en.pdf; Claude Cahn and Elspeth Guild, *Recent Migration of Roma in Europe,* 2nd Edition (CoE Commissioner for Human Rights, OSCE HCNM, October 2010), http://www.osce.org/hcnm/78034?download=true; CoE's Parliamentary Assembly, *The*

Situation of Roma in Europe: Movement and Migration, Report (June 1, 2012) http://www.aedh
.eu/plugins/fckeditor/userfiles/file/Discriminations%20et%20droits%20des%20minorit%
C3%A9s/Report%20CoE%20Roms%20June%202012.pdf.

50. Editorial Board, "Europe's Populist Insurgents Turning Right," *Economist,* January 4,
2014, http://www.economist.com/news/briefing/21592666-parties-nationalist-right-are-changing
-terms-european-political-debate-does.

51. Dena Ringold, Mitchell A. Orenstein, and Erika Wilkens, *Roma in an Expanding Europe:
Breaking the Poverty Cycle* (Washington, D.C.: World Bank, 2004), http://documents.worldbank
.org/curated/en/2004/12/5518636/roma-expanding-europe-breaking-poverty-cycle; Eva Sobotka, "Human Rights and Roma Policy Formation in Czech Republic, Slovakia and Poland," in
The Roma: A Minority in Europe, Historical, Political and Social Perspectives, ed. Roni Stauber
and Raphael Vago (Budapest: Central European University Press, 2007), 135–61; OSCE ODIHR,
Roma Status Report 2008.

52. OSCE ODIHR and HCNM, *Human Rights Situation of Roma and Sinti in Italy 2009
Report.*

53. Only few so-called "old" EU member state had some sort of Roma policy in place before
that date (Finland, Spain, and Greece for their Roma populations and UK and France for traveling Roma or Gypsy populations). For the rest, adopting Roma strategies has been a new task and
experience, see European Commission, *Steps Forward,* 3–4.

54. OSCE ODIHR, *Roma Status Report 2008,* 60.

55. Ibid., 7.

56. Ibid., 9.

57. EC, *Roma in Europe: Progress Report 2008–2010,* 3.

58. Ibid.

59. Janez Lenarcic, Speech, in *Minutes from the CoE High-Level meeting on Roma of 20 October 2010,* Speaker No. 24 ROMS (2010)PV final (Strasbourg: CoE, November 22, 2010), https://
wcd.coe.int/ViewDoc.jsp?Ref=ROMS(2010)PV&Language=lanEnglish&Ver=final&Site=COE
&BackColorInternet=DBDCF2&BackColorIntranet=FDC864&BackColorLogged=FDC864; see
also in those minutes, Appendix 5, "The Strasbourg Declaration on Roma," https://wcd.coe.int
/ViewDoc.jsp?id=1691607.

60. For more on the economic costs of Roma social exclusion, see World Bank, Europe and
Central Asia Human Development Department, "Economic Costs of Roma Social Exclusion,"
Note (Washington, D.C.: World Bank, April 2010), http://siteresources.worldbank.org/EXTROMA
/Resources/Economic_Costs_Roma_Exclusion_Note_Final.pdf; see also OSF Open Society
Institute, "EU Policies for Roma Inclusion," Policy Assessment (Brussels: OSF, July 2011), https://
www.opensocietyfoundations.org/sites/default/files/2011-07%2520EU%2520Roma%2520Inclusi
on%2520Policies%2520final.pdf.

61. OSCE Office for Democratic Institutions and Human Rights (ODIHR), *Implementation
of the Action Plan on Improving the Situation of Roma and Sinti Within the OSCE Area: Status
Report 2013 (Renewed Commitments, Renewed Challenges)* (Warsaw: OSCE/ODIHR, 2013),
19–23, http://www.osce.org/odihr/107406.

62. Ibid., on education and housing, 30; on health, 35; on education programs, 46–50.

63. Ibid., 4.

64. European Commission, *Report on the Implementation of the EU Framework for National
Roma Integration Strategies* (Brussels: EU, 2014), 3, http://ec.europa.eu/justice/discrimination
/files/roma_implement_strategies2014_en.pdf.

65. Council of the European Union, *Council Recommendation on Effective Roma Integration Measures in the Member States* (Brussels: EU, December 9, 10, 2013), http://www.consilium .europa.eu/uedocs/cms_data/docs/pressdata/en/lsa/139979.pdf. Short European Commission, *Implementation of the EU Framework 2014* ("starting point," 2; "long-term . . . leadership," 13; "first ever . . . non-Roma," 1).

66. European Commission, *Implementation of the EU Framework 2014*, 10.

67. Ibid., 11.

68. Roma Initiative, Open Society Foundations (OSF), *No Data—No Progress. Country Findings. Data Collection in Countries Participating in the Decade of Roma Inclusion 2005–2015* (Budapest: OSF, August 2010), http://www.opensocietyfoundations.org/sites/default/files/no-data -no-progress-country-reports-20100628_0.pdf.

69. OSCE ODIHR, *Roma Status Report 2013*, 19–20; EC, *Implementation of the EU Framework 2014*, 3.

70. EC, *Implementation of the EU Framework 2014*, 1.

71. Ibid., 3.

72. Council of EU, *Council Recommendation on Effective Roma Integration Measures*, 13, http://www.consilium.europa.eu/uedocs/cms_data/docs/pressdata/en/lsa/139979.pdf.

73. OSCE ODIHR, *Roma Status Report 2013*, 10. For studies that show lack of data for assessing outcomes, see, as examples, EMS Consortium, *From Pre-accession to Accession: Thematic Review of the Phare Assistance to Roma Minorities,* Thematic Evaluation Report ZZ/MIN/03082 (Brussels: European Commission, December 2004); Jakob Hurrle et al., *Uncertain Impact: Have the Roma in Slovakia benefitted from the European Social Fund? Findings from an Analysis of ESF Employment and Social Inclusion Projects in the 2007–2013 Programming Period,* Roma Inclusion Working Papers (Bratislava: UNDP, 2012); Bálint-Ábel Beremenyi and Anna Mirga, *Lost in Action? Evaluating the 6 Years of the Comprehensive Plan for the Gitano Population in Catalonia* (FAGIC EMIGRA, Barcelona, 2012).

74. OSCE ODIHR, *Roma Status Report 2008*, 19–20.

75. Ibid., 67.

76. Similarly, the EU PHARE funding for Roma represented a small fraction of the 1.5 billion euros total funding under PHARE for candidate countries, see Will Guy, "Roma Inclusion at the Crossroads: Can the Lessons from PHARE be Learned?" in "Funding Roma Rights: Challenges and Prospects," themed issue, *Roma Rights: Journal of European Roma Rights Centre* 2011 (October 5, 2012).

77. European Council, *Presidency Conclusions of the Brussels European Council: 14 December 2007*(previously cited), 14, para. 50, http://www.consilium.europa.eu/ueDocs/cms_Data/docs /pressData/en/ec/97669.pdf.

78. European Commission, *The European Social Fund and Roma*, Report Summary (Brussels: EU, 2010), http://ec.europa.eu/employment_social/esf/docs/esf_roma_en.pdf, particularly 3. The report summary indicated that "11 Member States programmed activities targeting Roma (among other vulnerable groups) during the 2000–2006 programming period, in which they invested € 3 billion. The interventions took place within the framework of 81 measures in 57 Operational Programmes. A total of 3.3 million people benefited from measures targeting Roma among other vulnerable groups." Ibid., 6.

79. Viviane Reding, Laszlo Andor, and Cecilia Malmström, "The Situation of Roma in France and Europe," 17. The authors indicate in the table on 17 the total sums made available

under the European Social Fund for general social inclusion policies toward vulnerable groups, including Roma and specific budgets targeting Roma; the sums do not differ much, as these are around 10 billion EUR in the programming period 2012–2013. However, in the same table, the authors indicate that funding exclusively allocated for Roma amounts to 176 million EUR, http://www.statewatch.org/news/2010/sep/EC-Roma-France-report.pdf.

80. European Commission, *Roma in Europe: Progress Report 2008–2010*, 26.

81. Hurrle, Ivanov, Grill, Kling, and Škobla, *Uncertain Impact*.

82. OSCE, *Action Plan on Improving the Situation of Roma and Sinti in the OSCE Area*, MC. DEC.3/03 (Maastricht: OSCE, 2003), http://www.osce.org/odihr/17554?download=true.

83. OSCE ODIHR, *Roma Status Report 2008*, 19–21.

84. Guy, ed., *Between Past and Future*.

85. OSCE ODIHR, *Roma Status Report 2008*, 19–23.

86. Ibid., 22.

87. OSCE ODIHR, *Roma Status Report 2013*, 27–33.

88. Council of Europe, *The Situation of Roma in Europe: A Challenge for Local and Regional Authorities*, Resolution 333, adopted by the CoE Congress of Local and Regional Authorities, on October 19, 2011, in Strasbourg, https://wcd.coe.int/ViewDoc.jsp?id=1855297.

89. Council of EU, *Council Recommendation on Effective Roma Integration Measures*, 10, http://www.consilium.europa.eu/uedocs/cms_data/docs/pressdata/en/lsa/139979.pdf. See also Area-Based Development on Social Inclusion, UNDP, "Going Local on Roma Inclusion," in *The Place for Everyone*, UNDP Newsletter, no. 5, May 2014, http://localdevelopmentforinclusion.org/going-local-on-roma-inclusion.html.

90. EURoma network, European Network on Social Inclusion and Roma under the Structural Funds, http://www.euromanet.eu/; Open Society Foundations (OSF), "Making the Most of EU Funds for Roma," program page (Budapest: OSF, no date), http://www.opensocietyfoundations.org/about/programs/making-most-eu-funds-roma; Open Society Institute, "Mayors Making the Most of EU Funds for Roma Inclusion Network (MERI)," (Budapest: OSI, 2012), http://www.logincee.org/about_meri; and European Commission, "Awards Ceremony: Mayors Making the Most of EU Funds for Roma Inclusion," (Budapest: EC, October 11 and 12, 2012), http://ec.europa.eu/social/main.jsp?langId=en&catId=88&eventsId=610.

91. In her chapter in this volume, Elena Rozzi discusses some of the many factors keeping Roma children from the education they need. She also discusses the importance of seeing Roma as agents, as well as some approaches to this difficult conundrum.

92. Will Guy, ed., *From Victimhood to Citizenship: The Path of Roma Integration: A Debate* (Budapest: Kossuth Kiadó, distr. by Central European University Press, 2013).

Chapter 7. Reconstructing Roma Integration in Central and Eastern Europe

1. Michael Mann, *The Dark Side of Democracy: Explaining Ethnic Cleansing* (Cambridge: Cambridge University Press, 2005).

2. Valerie Bunce, *Subversive Institutions: The Design and the Destruction of Socialism and the State* (Cambridge: Cambridge University Press, 1999).

3. For the region overall, see the vivid case study in Charles King, *The Ghost of Freedom: A History of the Caucasus* (Oxford: Oxford University Press, 2008); for the former Yugoslavia, see Lenard J. Cohen and Jasna Dragović-Soso, eds., *State Collapse in South-Eastern Europe: New Perspectives on Yugoslavia's Disintegration* (Purdue, Ind.: Purdue University Press, 2008).

4. For a detailed description, see European Roma Rights Center, *Abandoned Minority: Roma Rights History in Kosovo* (Budapest: ERRC, 2011), http://www.errc.org/cms/upload/file/abandoned -minority-roma-rights-history-in-kosovo-dec-2011.pdf.

5. István Kemény and Gábor Havas, "Cigánynak lenni," in *Társadalmi riport 1996*, ed. Rudolf Andorka, Tamás Kolosi, and György Vukovich (Budapest: TÁRKI, Századvég, 1996), 352–80.

6. See *D.H. and Others v. the Czech Republic*, App. no. 57325/00, ECtHR, Grand Chamber Judgment (November 13, 2007), http://hudoc.echr.coe.int/sites/eng/pages/search.aspx?i=001 -83256; and also see, in this volume, James A. Goldston, "The Unfulfilled Promise of Educational Opportunity in the United States and Europe: From *Brown v. Board* to *D.H.* and Beyond."

7. *D.H. and Others v. the Czech Republic*.

8. Joerg Forbrig, "A Source of Democratic Legitimacy? Civil Society in East-Central Europe," (Paper presented at "Contours of Legitimacy in Central Europe Conference," European Studies Centre, Oxford, May 2002), 10–13, http://users.ox.ac.uk/~oaces/conference/papers/Joerg _Forbrig.pdf.

9. See Morten Kjaerum, Director, EU Agency for Fundamental Rights (FRA), "Exclusion and Discrimination in Education: the Case of Roma in the European Union," Speech ("Realizing Roma Rights Conference," FXB Center, Harvard University, Cambridge Mass., April 8, 2013), http://fra.europa.eu/en/speech/2013/exclusion-and-discrimination-education-case-roma -european-union. In this speech on International Roma Day, Kjaerum said: "Exclusion from education takes different forms: from blunt refusal to enroll Roma children under pressure from non-Roma parents to placement in 'special schools' or ethnically segregated classes." The same phenomenon is described in Amnesty International, *Unlock Their Future: End the Segregation of Romani Children in Slovakia's Schools* (London: Amnesty International, September 2010), http:// www.amnesty.nl/sites/default/files/public/rapport_unlocktheirfuture_roma.pdf as well as in ERRC, *Segregated Schooling of Roma* (Budapest: ERRC, 2004), 57–61, http://www.errc.org/cms /upload/media/00/04/m00000004.pdf.

10. Michael Stewart, ed., *The Gypsy "Menace": Populism and the New Anti-Gypsy Politics* (London: Hurst, 2012).

11. Will Guy, "Anti-Roma Violence, Hate Speech, and Discrimination in the New Europe," in this volume.

12. See Gábor Havas, "A Kemény-iskolától a SZETÁ-ig és tovább," *Beszélő*, February 2, 2014, http://beszelo.c3.hu/onlinecikk/a-kemeny-iskolatol-a-szeta-ig-es-tovabb.

13. The OSI effort was spearheaded on the inspirational level by George Soros himself, the founder and chairman of OSI. He has admirably pursued emancipation of Roma in East Central Europe for about two decades. The president of OSI for most of this period, Aryeh Neier, has been a preeminent defender of human and civil rights in the United States and worldwide, as has Deborah Harding, formerly the longtime director of OSI's Roma program.

14. Michael Stewart also shows how Sarkozy's action and other anti-Roma acts in Western Europe fit into a trend of appealing to and strengthening of populist racially exclusive political currents; see Stewart, ed., *The Gypsy "Menace"*.

15. For basic information, see BBC Europe page, "Q&A: France Roma Expulsions," *BBC online*, October 19, 2010, http://www.bbc.com/news/world-europe-11027288; see also Viviane Reding, EU Vice-President and Commissioner for Justice; László Andor, EU Commissioner for Employment, Social Affairs and Inclusion, and Cecilia Malmström, EU Commissioner for Home Affairs, "The Situation of Roma in France and Europe," Joint Information Note, IP/10/407;

MEMO/10/121, September 1, 2010, http://www.statewatch.org/news/2010/sep/EC-Roma-France
-report.pdf.

16. See European Commission, *The Social and Economic Integration of the Roma in Europe,*
Communication COM(2010)133 final (Brussels: EC, April 7, 2010), http://eur-lex.europa.eu/legal
-content/EN/TXT/PDF/?uri=CELEX:52010DC0133&rid=1; for the CoE, see among others, CoE
Committee of Ministers, *On Policies for Roma and/or Travelers in Europe.* Recommendation CM/
Rec(2008)5 (Strasbourg, February 20, 2008), https://wcd.coe.int/ViewDoc.jsp?id=1253509&Site
=CM&BackColorInternet=C3C3C3&BackColorIntranet=EDB021&BackColorLogged=F5D383;
for OSCE, see *Action Plan on Improving the Situation of Roma and Sinti in the OSCE Area,* MC.
DEC.3/03 (Maastricht: OSCE, 2003), http://www.osce.org/odihr/17554.

17. Andrzej Mirga, "Roma Policy in Europe: Results and Challenges."

18. Andrey Ivanov with others, *Avoiding the Dependency Trap: The Roma in Central and Eastern Europe*, A Regional Human Development Report (Bratislava: UNDP Regional Bureau, 2002),
http://www.eurasia.undp.org/content/dam/rbec/docs/Avoiding-the-dependency-trap.pdf. That research then was repeated for the Western Balkans, see Andrey Ivanov with others, *At Risk: Roma
and the Displaced in South Eastern Europe* (Bratislava: UNDP Regional Bureau, 2006), http://
www.eurasia.undp.org/content/rbec/en/home/library/roma/At-risk-Roma-displaced-Southeast
-Europe.html.

19. Roma Initiatives Office, Open Society Institute, "Governments Endorse 'Decade of Roma
Inclusion,'" press release, Budapest, July 8, 2003, http://www.opensocietyfoundations.org/press
-releases/governments-endorse-decade-roma-inclusion.

20. European Commission, *An EU Framework for National Roma Integration Strategies up
to 2020*, Communication, COM(2011) 173 (Brussels, April 5, 2011), http://ec.europa.eu/justice
/policies/discrimination/docs/com_2011_173_en.pdf, followed by Council of the EU, *Council
Conclusions on an EU Framework for National Roma Integration Strategies up to 2020,* 10658/11
(Brussels, May 19, 2011).

21. For a description of this program, including the survey methodology, see Andrey Ivanov, Jaroslav Kling, and Justin Kagin, *Integrated Household Surveys Among Roma Populations:
One Possible Approach to Sampling Used in the UNDP-World Bank-EC Regional Roma Survey
2011,* Roma Inclusion Working Papers (Bratislava: UNDP, 2012), http://www.eurasia.undp.org
/content/dam/rbec/docs/Roma-household-survey-methodology.pdf. Compared to data from
2004, the data seem to indicate some improvement in the educational levels of Roma in most
countries—with the Czech Republic, Hungary, and Slovakia showing much higher educational
levels than the rest of the countries for Roma. Poverty indicators also show improvements, but
those data are only compared for the Balkan countries, not for Hungary, the Czech Republic
and Slovakia. In any case, since the data examined socially vulnerable populations, many of
whom took advantage of the greater freedom of movement that came with EU enlargement,
comparison is difficult: we do not know many people moved in or out of a particular country
since 2004.

22. For more on the Decade, including publications and reports of events, see "The Decade
of Roma Inclusion: 2005–2015," http://www.romadecade.org/. The Decade Secretariat, the Decade's technical support unit, is located in Budapest; the presidency of the Decade has revolved
to different countries over time.

23. The Roma Education Fund, headquartered in Budapest, has branch offices in several
countries. For more information, see "Roma Education Fund, Closing the Gap in Educational
Outcomes between Roma and non-Roma," http://www.romaeducationfund.hu/.

24. World Bank, Europe and Central Asia Human Development Unit, "Economic Costs of Roma Social Exclusion," Note (Washington, D.C.: World Bank April 2010), http://siteresources .worldbank.org/EXTROMA/Resources/Economic_Costs_Roma_Exclusion_Note_Final.pdf; and in more detail, World Bank, Europe and Central Asia Human Development Unit, *Roma Inclusion: An Economic Opportunity for Bulgaria, Czech Republic, Romania and Serbia*, Policy Note, 69655 (Washington, D.C.: World Bank, September 30, 2010), https://openknowledge .worldbank.org/bitstream/handle/10986/12905/696550ESW0P1180Economic0Opportunity.pdf ?sequence=1.

25. The program offers technical assistance as well as supplementary funding. See Open Society Foundations (OSF), "Making the Most of EU Funds for Roma," program page (Budapest: OSF, no date), http://www.opensocietyfoundations.org/about/programs/making-most-eu-funds -roma.

26. European Commission, *An EU Framework for National Roma Integration*; Council of the EU, *Council Conclusions on an EU Framework for Roma Integration*, full reference in earlier note). During the adoption of the *EU Framework* of May 2011 and the *Council Conclusions* of June 2011 (affirming the *EU Framework*), Hungary was chairing the EU. The European Commission's work was fairly autonomous, but the Hungarian government organized a robust consensus for the *Council Conclusions*, a task it did well and one of the major successes of the Hungarian EU presidency.

27. Kai Consulting, *Where the Paved Road Ends: Regional Disparities and Roma Integration. Report on the Interim Results of the Most Disadvantaged Micro-Regions Program (Hungary)* (Budapest: Making the Most of EU Funds for the Roma, OSF, March 2011).

28. For a sincere, self-reflective note on this and various other NGO shortcomings, see Nicolae Gheorghe in collaboration with Gergő Pulay, "Choices to Be Made and Prices to Be Paid: Potential Roles and Consequences in Roma Activism and Policy-Making," in *From Victimhood to Citizenship: The Path of Roma Integration—A Debate*, ed. Will Guy (Budapest: Kossuth Kiadó, distr. Central European University Press, 2013).

29. Kálmán Mizsei and Ádám Kullmann, "Struggling with an Opportunity: The First 10 Years with the EU for Central Europe and the Baltics—A Few Lessons," *CEPS Essay* no. 12 (Brussels: Centre for European Policy Studies, May 2, 2014), http://www.ceps.be/book/struggling -opportunity-first-10-years-eu-central-europe-and-baltics.

30. Ibid.; Kai Consulting, *Where the Paved Road Ends*.

31. BBC Europe page, "Bulgarian Rally Links Roma to Organised Crime," *BBC online*, October 1, 2011, http://www.bbc.co.uk/news/world-europe-15140291.

32. For details on the case and the most recent loss on appeal, see Chance for Children Foundation, "The Nyíregyháza Resegregation Case," http://www.cfcf.hu/en/ny%C3%ADregyh%C3%A1za -resegregation-case; for a report on the earlier court ruling, see "Megbukott a szegregált iskola Nyíregyházán," *Index*, February 28, 2014, http://index.hu/belfold/2014/02/28/szegregalt_iskola _nyiregyhaza/; Goldston's chapter also discusses the case. See also http://budapestbeacon.com /public-policy/hungarys-highest-court-legitimizes-segregation-in-the-case-of-religious -schooling/22387 April 23, 2015, by Eszter Neuberger.

Chapter 8. Anti-Roma Violence, Hate Speech, and Discrimination in the New Europe

1. See, in this volume, Elena Rozzi, "Roma Children and Enduring Educational Exclusion in Italy"; Peter Vermeersch, "Roma Mobilization and Participation: Obstacles and Opportunities";

Teresa Sordé Martí and Fernando Macías, "Making Roma Rights a Reality at the Local Level: A Spanish Case Study"; and Margareta Matache and Krista Oehlke, "A Critical Analysis of Roma Policy and Praxis: The Romanian Case."

2. Colin Clark and Elaine Campbell, "Gypsy Invasion: A Critical Analysis of Newspaper Reaction to Czech and Slovak Romani Asylum Seekers in Britain, 1997," *Romani Studies* series 5, 10, no. 1 (2000): 23–47.

3. Dena Ringold, Mitchell A. Orenstein, and Erika Wilkens, *Roma in an Expanding Europe: Breaking the Poverty Cycle* (Washington, D.C.: World Bank, 2004), 38–41, http://siteresources .worldbank.org/EXTROMA/Resources/roma_in_expanding_europe.pdf.

4. Ringold, Orenstein, and Wilkens, *Roma in an Expanding Europe,* 13.

5. European Commission, *European Union Support for Roma Communities in Central and Eastern Europe* (Brussels: EC, 2003), 4, http://ec.europa.eu/enlargement/pdf/brochure_roma _oct2003_en.pdf.

6. Council of Europe, *Framework Convention for the Protection of National Minorities,* European Treaty Series No. 157 (1995) art. 4, para. 2, https://www.coe.int/en/web/conventions/full -list/-/conventions/rms/090000168007cdac.

7. For the directive itself, see Council of the European Union (EU), Council Directive 2000/43/EC of 29 June 2000 [Race Equality Directive] implementing the principle of equal treatment between persons irrespective of racial or ethnic origin, *Official Journal of the EU* 180 (July 19, 2000): 22–26; for an overview, see European Commission, *The Race Equality Directive: What Is the Race Equality Directive?* Memo/07/257 (Brussels: EC, 2007), http://europa.eu/rapid /press-release_MEMO-07-257_en.htm?locale=en.

8. "EU Charter of Fundamental Rights," http://ec.europa.eu/justice/fundamental-rights /charter/index_en.htm.

9. "The Treaty of Lisbon," http://eur-lex.europa.eu/legal-content/EN/TXT/?uri=URISERV :ai0033.

10. See, in this volume, Andrzej Mirga, "Roma Policy in Europe: Results and Challenges."

11. The European Roma Policy Coalition (ERPC) is a network of national and international NGOs (including Amnesty International and the European Roma Rights Center) working on aspects of discrimination against Roma people; for basic information see "European Roma Policy Coalition," December 1, 2010, at http://www.errc.org/article/european-roma-policy-coalition -erpc/3796, for examples of its advocacy around this issue, see "European Roma Policy Coalition Statement on EU Social Agenda," July 4, 2008, http://www.errc.org/cikk.php?cikk=2967; and ERPC, "Essential Elements of the 'EU Framework for National Roma Integration Strategies,'" November 2, 2010, http://www.errc.org/cms/upload/file/erpc-essential-elements-euframework -02112010.pdf; the European Roma Grassroots Organisations Network (ERGO), with offices in Brussels and in the Netherlands, is as its name suggests a coaliton of local Roma specific-country groups; current information is available at http://www.ergonetwork.org/ergo-network/.

12. European Commission, *An EU Framework for National Roma Integration Strategies up to 2020,* Communication, COM(2011) 173 (Brussels: April 5, 2011), http://ec.europa.eu/justice /policies/discrimination/docs/com_2011_173_en.pdf; for an overview, see European Commission, *Working Together for Roma Inclusion: The EU Framework Explained* (Luxembourg: European Union, 2011), http://ec.europa.eu/justice/discrimination/files/working_together_for_roma _inclusion_en.pdf.

13. Decade Watch, *Results of the 2009 Survey* (Budapest: Open Society Institute, 2009), http:// www.romadecade.org/news/decade-watch-results-of-the-2009-survey/9317.

14. Organization of Security and Cooperation in Europe (OSCE), *Action Plan on Improving the Situation of Roma and Sinti within the OSCE Area*, MC. DEC.3/03 (Maastricht, the Netherlands: OSCE, 2003), http://www.osce.org/odihr/17554.

15. European Roma Policy Coalition (ERPC), "ERPC Welcomes New Council Recommendation on Roma" (Brussels: ERPC, December 10, 2013), http://cms.horus.be/files/99935/Media Archive/2013-12-10%20ERPC%20press%20release.pdf.

16. Amnesty International, *Violent Attacks against Roma in Hungary: Time to Investigate Racial Motivation* (London: Amnesty International, 2010).

17. OSCE Office for Democratic Institutions and Human Rights (ODIHR), *Addressing Violence, Promoting Integration, Field Assessment of Violent Incidents against Roma in Hungary: Key Developments, Findings and Recommendations* (Warsaw: OSCE, June 15, 2010), http://www.osce .org/odihr/68545.

18. Czech Ministry of the Interior, "Documents on the Fight against Extremism," webpage (in English) lists links to government reports on extremism since 1999 up until the present (Prague: Czech Ministry of the Interior), http://www.mvcr.cz/mvcren/article/documents-on-the -fight-against-extremism.aspx.

19. András L. Pap, "Dogmatism, Hypocrisy and the Inadequacy of Legal and Social Responses Combating Hate Crimes and Extremism: The CEE Experience," in *The Gypsy "Menace": Populism and the New Anti-Gypsy Politics*, ed. Michael Stewart (London: Hurst, 2012), 295–311, in particular, 301–2.

20. OSCE ODIHR, *Police and Roma and Sinti: Current Challenges and Good Practices in Building Trust and Understanding,* Summary Report of the Expert Meeting (Warsaw: OSCE ODIHR, April 8, 2014), 3.

21. OSCE ODIHR, *Implementation of the Action Plan on Improving the Situation of Roma and Sinti Within the OSCE Area: Status Report 2013 (Renewed Commitments, Renewed Challenges)* (Warsaw: OSCE ODIHR, 2013), 11, http://www.osce.org/odihr/107406?download=true.

22. European Union Agency of Fundamental Rights (FRA), *EU-MIDIS Data in Focus 6: Minorities as Victims of Crime* (Vienna: FRA, 2012).

23. Council of the European Union, *Council Recommendation of 9 December 2013 on Effective Roma Integration Measures in the Member States* 2013/C 378/01, *Official Journal of the EU* 378 (December 24, 2013): 1–7, http://eur-lex.europa.eu/legal-content/EN/TXT/?uri=uriserv:OJ.C _.2013.378.01.0001.01.ENG.

24. Rachel Tritt, *Struggling for Ethnic Identity: Czechoslovakia's Endangered Gypsies* (New York: Human Rights Watch, 1993), 2–3.

25. The OSCE ODIHR-sponsored volume edited by Michael Stewart, *The Gypsy "Menace": Populism and the New Anti-Gypsy Politics* (London: Hurst, 2012), offers comprehensive coverage of these developments.

26. Pew Research Center, *Global Attitudes Project* (Washington, D.C.: Pew Research Center, 2009), http://www.pewglobal.org/files/2009/11/Pew-Global-Attitudes-2009-Pulse-of-Europe -Report-Nov-2-1030am-NOT-EMBARGOED.pdf.

27. Human Rights Watch (HRW), *Roma in the Czech Republic: Foreigners in Their Own Land,* HRW/Helsinki Report 8, no. 11D (New York: HRW, 1996), 2, 6, http://www.hrw.org/legacy /reports/1996/Czech.htm; European Roma Rights Centre (ERRC), *Time of the Skinheads: Denial and Exclusion of Roma in Slovakia* (Budapest: ERRC, 1997), http://www.errc.org/article/time-of -the-skinheads-denial-and-exclusion-of-roma-in-slovakia/3674.

28. ERRC, *Imperfect Justice: Anti-Roma Violence and Impunity* (Budapest: ERRC, March 6, 2011), http://www.errc.org/cms/upload/file/czech-hungary-slovakia-imperfect-justice-06-march -2011.pdf.

29. Gwendolyn Albert and Zdeněk Ryšavý, "Hungary: Murders of Roma People Were Planned," trans. Gwendolyn Albert, Romea News Service online (Budapest), March 25, 2011, http://www.romea.cz/en/news/world/hungary-murders-of-roma-people-were-planned.

30. John Boyd, "Lipsic Compares DNV Shooting and Brievik Massacre," The Daily.SK (Slovakia), August 31, 2011, http://www.thedaily.sk/lipsic-compares-dnv-shooting-and-brievik -massacre.

31. "Czech Republic: Crossbow Shooter Gets 10 Years for Manslaughter of Romani Man," Romea News Service, May 31, 2013.

32. Ibid.

33. Dan Bilefsky, "Killing Spree in Slovakia Taps into a Troubled Vein," *New York Times*, September 2, 2010.

34. For the Czech Republic, see Gwendolyn Albert, "Anti-Gypsyism and the Extreme Right in the Czech Republic 2008–2011," 137–65 and for Hungary, see Pap, "Dogmatism, Hypocrisy," both in Stewart, ed., *The Gypsy "Menace"*.

35. Merin Abbass et al., *Right-Wing Extremism in Central Europe: An Overview* (Berlin: Friedrich Ebert, December 2011), 1, http://library.fes.de/pdf-files/id-moe/08840.pdf.

36. Tomáš Nociar in Abbass et al., *Right-Wing Extremism*, 4; see also Pap, "Dogmatism, Hypocrisy."

37. The extremist, xenophobic and anti-Roma Ataka party has remained the fourth largest party in the Bulgarian Parliament since its founding in 2005 (see Georgia Efremova, "Integralist Narratives and Redemptive Anti-Gypsy Politics in Bulgaria," in Stewart, *The Gypsy "Menace"*, 43–66, in particular 47–50). In the 2013 parliamentary elections, Ataka won 7 percent of the vote.

38. Václav Walach in Abbass et al., *Right-Wing Extremism*, 1–2.

39. "Open Letter to the Non-Extremist Anti-Romani Demonstrators in the Czech Republic," Romea News Service, July 9, 2013, http://www.romea.cz/en/news/czech/romea-association -s-open-letter-to-the-non-extremist-anti-romani-demonstrators-in-the-czech-republic.

40. Nociar in Abbass et al., *Right-Wing Extremism*, 4.

41. Andrej Nosko, "A Victory for Extremism in Slovakia, and What It Means," Open Society Foundations, December 4, 2013, http://www.opensocietyfoundations.org/voices/victory -extremism-slovakia-and-what-it-means.

42. Beata Balogová, "Far-Right Leader Kotleba Wins in Banská Bystrica," *Slovak Spectator*, November 24, 2013, http://spectator.sme.sk/articles/view/52139/2/far_right_leader_kotleba _wins_in_banska_bystrica.html.

43. ERRC, *Written Comments of the ERRC Concerning the Slovak Republic for Consideration by the UN Committee on the Elimination of Racial Discrimination* [CERD] (Budapest: ERRC, July 30, 2004), www.errc.org/cms/upload/media/00/AF/m000000AF.doc.

44. Balogová, "Far-Right Leader Kotleba Wins."

45. Gwendolyn Albert, "Slovakia: Fascist Marian Kotleba Plans to 'Clean Up' Romani Settlement," Romea News Service, September 17, 2012, http://www.romea.cz/en/news/world/slovakia -fascist-marian-kotleba-plans-to-clean-up-romani-settlement.

46. A.L.B., "To Viktor the Spoils," Eastern Approaches, *The Economist*, April 7, 2014.

47. Ibid.

48. MTI [Hungarian News Agency], "Socialists Call for Probe into Jobbik Mayor's Talk of 'Civil War,'" Politics.HU, MTI, April 20, 2012, http://www.politics.hu/20120420/socialists-call -for-probe-into-jobbik-mayors-talk-of-civil-war/.

49. Pap, "Dogmatism, Hypocrisy," 306.

50. Ibid., 304.

51. Anikó Bernát et al., *The Roots of Radicalism and Anti-Roma Attitudes on the Far Right* (Budapest: TARKI, 2013).

52. Council of the European Union (EU), *Framework Decision 2008/913/JHA of 28 November 2008 [Framework Decision on Combating Racism and Xenophobia]* combating certain forms and expressions of racism and xenophobia by means of criminal law, *Official Journal of the EU* 328 (December 6, 2008): 55–58, http://europa.eu/legislation_summaries/justice_freedom _security/combating_discrimination/l33178_en.htm.

53. Walach, in Abbass et al., *Right-Wing Extremism*, 2.

54. Gwendolyn Albert, "On the Chopping Block," *Prague Post,* July 21, 2010, http://www .praguepost.cz/opinion/5111-on-the-chopping-block.html.

55. Dita Asiedu, "Are the Deputy Prime Minister's Offensive Remarks about the Roma Influencing Ordinary Citizens?" Letter from Prague, *Radio Prague,* April 8, 2007, http://www.radio .cz/en/section/letter/are-the-deputy-prime-ministers-offensive-remarks-about-the-roma -influencing-ordinary-citizens.

56. ČTK (Czech Television), "Czech Deputy PM Čunek Saved Millions, but Lived on Welfare," Romea News Service, October 29, 2007, http://www.romea.cz/en/news/czech/czech-deputy -pm-cunek-saved-millions-but-lived-on-welfare-ct.

57. Jarmila Balážová, "Czech Senator Čunek Chairing Senate Subcommittee on Human Rights," Romea News Service, December 10, 2012, http://www.romea.cz/en/news/czech/czech -senator-cunek-chairing-senate-subcommittee-on-human-rights.

58. Jana Baudyšová, "Czech Republic: Trafficking in Poverty on the Rise, Landlords Cashing In," Romea News Service, March 8, 2013, http://www.romea.cz/en/news/czech/czech-republic -trafficking-in-poverty-on-the-rise-landlords-cashing-in.

59. ERRC, *Written Comments Concerning the Slovak Republic for CERD 2004.*

60. Radio Free Europe/Radio Liberty, "Family Allowance Cut in Slovakia Following Racist Statements Towards Roma," May 10, 2003, http://www.errc.org/article/family-allowance-cut-in -slovakia-following-racist-statements-towards-roma/1393.

61. Counseling Center for Civil and Human Rights, "European Court for Human Rights Condemns Slovakia for Forced Sterilization of Romani Woman," Romea News Service, November 8, 2011, http://www.romea.cz/en/news/world/european-court-for-human-rights-condemns -slovakia-for-forced-sterilization-of-romani-woman.

62. Gwendolyn Albert, "Forced Sterilization and Romani Women's Resistance in Central Europe," in *Different Takes* no. 71 (Amherst, Mass.: Population and Development Program, Hampshire College, Summer 2011), http://popdev.hampshire.edu/sites/default/files/uploads /u4763/DT%2071%20Albert.pdf.

63. See Alexandra Oprea, "Toward the Recognition of Critical Race Theory in Human Rights Law: Roma Women's Reproductive Rights."

64. ERRC, *Written Comments Concerning the Slovak Republic for CERD 2004.*

65. B.C., "Walls Are Going Up Again," *The Economist,* July 25, 2013.

66. Arie Farnam, "Slovakian Roma Forced to Ghettos," *Christian Science Monitor,* January 3, 2003, http://www.csmonitor.com/2003/0103/p04s02-woeu.html.

67. Thomas Hammarberg, Commissioner for Human Rights of CoE, *Report by Commissioner Following His Visit to Slovakia, from 26 to 27 September 2011,* CommDH(2011)42 (Strasbourg: CoE, December 20, 2011), https://wcd.coe.int/ViewDoc.jsp?id=1885987.

68. Markus Salzmann, "Right-Wing Pogroms against Roma in Hungary," *World Socialist,* September 5, 2012, http://www.wsws.org/en/articles/2012/09/hung-s05.html.

69. Jenő Kaltenbach and Catherine Twigg, "Spoken Today, Committed Tomorrow," *Roma Rights: Journal of European Roma Rights Centre* 1 (July 30, 2009), http://www.errc.org/cms/upload/media/04/12/m00000412.pdf.

70. Lydia Gall, "Hungary's Alarming Climate of Intolerance," Global Public Square blog, *CNN World,* January 18, 2013, http://globalpublicsquare.blogs.cnn.com/2013/01/18/hungarys-alarming-climate-of-intolerance/.

71. *Times of Israel,* "Hungarian Jews speak up for Roma," January 11, 2013, http://www.timesofisrael.com/hungarian-jews-speak-up-for-roma.

72. Gall, "Hungary's Alarming Climate of Intolerance."

73. European Commission, *Report on the Implementation of the EU Framework for National Roma Integration Strategies* (Brussels: EU, 2014), 9, sect. 3.5, http://ec.europa.eu/justice/discrimination/files/roma_implement_strategies2014_en.pdf.

74. Council of EU, *Council Recommendation on Effective Roma Integration 2013*, para. 19.

75. Ibid.

76. Jakob Hurrle et al., *Uncertain Impact: Have the Roma in Slovakia benefitted from the European Social Fund? Findings from an Analysis of ESF Employment and Social Inclusion Projects in the 2007–2013 Programming Period,* Roma Inclusion Working Papers (Bratislava: UNDP, 2012), http://www.undp.org/content/dam/rbec/docs/Have-Roma-in-Slovakia-benefitted-from-the-European-Social-Fund.pdf.

77. European Commission, *Implementation of the EU Framework 2014,* 9, sect. 3.5.

78. Ibid., 46.

79. Amnesty International, "Roma in Europe: Demanding Justice and Protection in the Face of Violence," Amnesty International, April 8, 2014, http://www.amnesty.org/en/news/roma-europe-demanding-justice-and-protection-face-violence-2014-04-08.

80. OSCE ODIHR, *Equal Access to Quality Education for Roma Children: Field Assessment Visit to the Czech Republic* (Warsaw: OSCE, October 26, 2012), http://www.osce.org/odihr/96661?download=true.

81. European Union Agency of Fundamental Rights (FRA), *The Situation of Roma EU Citizens Moving to and Settling in Other EU Member States: Selected Positive Initiatives* (Vienna: FRA, European Commission, November 2009), 19, http://fra.europa.eu/sites/default/files/fra_uploads/707-Roma_Movement_PositiveInitiatives-final_en.pdf.

82. FRA, *Case Study: Living Together, Czech Republic* (Vienna: FRA, European Commission, October 2009), http://fra.europa.eu/sites/default/files/fra_uploads/601-ROMA_Housing_Case-final-ENCS.pdf.

83. Will Guy, André Liebich, and Elena Marushiakova, *Improving the Tools for the Social Inclusion and Non-Discrimination of Roma in the EU* (Luxembourg: European Commission, 2010), 35, http://www.errc.org/cms/upload/file/improving-the-tools-for-the-social-inclusion-and-non-discrimination-of-roma-in-the-eu-2010.pdf.

84. Council of Europe, "Good Practice 23: Issues of Inclusion and Segregation: Reorganising the System of Public Education in Hódmezővásárhely," Database of Good Practices and Policies, November 19, 2012, goodpracticeroma.ppa.coe.int/en/pdf/126.

85. FRA, *Situation of Roma EU Citizens Moving*, 6.

86. Lucie Fremlova, *From Segregation to Inclusion: Roma Pupils in the United Kingdom* (Long Medford UK: Equality and Budapest: Roma Education Fund, November 2011), http://equality.uk.com/Education_files/From%20segregation%20to%20integration_1.pdf.

87. Ringold, Orenstein, and Wilkens, *Roma in an Expanding Europe*, xxii.

88. François-Xavier Bagnoud Center for Health and Human Rights, *Accelerating Patterns of Anti-Roma Violence in Hungary* (Boston: FXB Center, Harvard University, February 4, 2014), http://fxb.harvard.edu/wp-content/uploads/sites/5/2014/02/FXB-Hungary-Report_Released-February-4-2014.pdf.

Chapter 9. The Unfulfilled Promise of Educational Opportunity in the United States and Europe

1. *Brown v. Board of Education*, 347 U.S. 483 (1954), finding segregation in education unconstitutional, despite purportedly equal conditions.

2. Maryland: *Pearson, et al. v. Murray*, 182 A. 590 (1936); *Missouri ex rel. Gaines v. Canada*, 305 U.S. 337 (1938).

3. *McLaurin v. Oklahoma State Regents*, 339 U.S. 637 (1950); Texas: *Sweatt v. Painter*, 339 U.S. 629 (1950).

4. *Plessy v. Ferguson*, 163 U.S. 537 (1896), upholding "separate but equal" facilities.

5. Gary Orfield and Chungmei Lee, *Historic Reversals, Accelerating Resegregation, and the Need for New Integration Strategies* (Los Angeles: UCLA Civil Rights Project, August 2007), 5.

6. *Green v. County School Board*, 391 U.S. 430 (1968).

7. *Swann v. Charlotte-Mecklenburg Board of Education*, 402 U.S. 1 (1970).

8. Orfield and Lee, *Historic Reversals*, 5; *Milliken v. Bradley*, 418 U.S. 717 (1974).

9. Gary Orfield and Chungmei Lee, *Racial Transformation and the Changing Nature of Segregation* (Los Angeles: UCLA Civil Rights Project, January 2006), 13.

10. See, e.g., *Board of Education of Oklahoma City v. Dowell*, 498 U.S. 237 (1991), holding that an injunction may be permanently dissolved once desegregation is achieved; *Freeman v. Pitts*, 503 U.S. 467 (1992), holding that courts may incrementally discontinue monitoring of a school district as it complies with a desegregation decree; *Missouri v. Jenkins*, 515 U.S. 70 (1995) holding that de facto interdistrict segregation is permissible.

11. Gary Orfield, John Kucsera, and Genevieve Seigel-Hawley, *E Pluribus . . . Separation: Deepening Double Segregation for More Students* (Los Angeles: UCLA Civil Rights Project, September 2012), xviii.

12. Ibid., 23. In 2009–2010, typical exposure in public schools of black students to white students was at 29.2 percent, down from 34.9 percent in 1991–1992 (table 5). The rate of exposure of Latino students to white students dropped from 31.5 to 25.2 in the same period (tables 6 and 7).

13. Orfield and Lee, *Historic Reversals*, 4, 5.

14. Kathleen Sullivan, "What Happened to *Brown*?" *New York Review of Books*, September 23, 2004, 47.

15. *Parents Involved in Community Schools v. Seattle School District No. 1*, 551 U.S. 701 (2007), invalidating municipal programs that sought to maintain school-by-school diversity by limiting transfers on the basis of race or using race as a "tiebreaker" for admission to particular schools.

16. Orfield and Lee, *Historic Reversals*, 4.

17. Ibid., 11. See also, e.g., N. Hannah-Jones, "How School Segregation Divides Ferguson— And the United States," *New York Times*, December 19, 2014. Hannah-Jones quotes Catherine Lhamon, head of the U.S. Department of Education's civil rights office: "American schools are disturbingly racially segregated—period."

18. Richard Kluger, *Simple Justice: The History of* Brown v. Board of Education *and Black America's Struggle for Equality,* rev. ed. (1976, New York: Random House, 2004), x. All citations are to this edition.

19. Ibid., 749.

20. J. Harvie Wilkinson, *From* Brown *to* Bakke: *The Supreme Court and School Integration, 1954–1978* (New York: Oxford University Press, 1979), 6.

21. Editors' Note, *Yale Law Journal* 93 (1984): 981.

22. Michael Klarman, *"Brown,* Racial Change and the Civil Rights Movement," *Virginia Law Review* 80, no. 1 (1994): 10.

23. Gerald Rosenberg, *The Hollow Hope* (Chicago: University of Chicago Press, 1991), 70–71.

24. Ibid. See also Grainne de Burca, "The Trajectories of European and American Antidiscrimination Law," *American Journal of Comparative Law* 60, no. 1 (winter 2012): 1–22, particularly 2–4 (citations omitted).

25. Martha Minow, *"Brown v. Board* in the World: How the Global Turn Matters for School Reform, Human Rights and Legal Knowledge," *San Diego Law Review* 50, no. 1 (2013): 2.

26. *Brown v. Board of Education (II),* 349 U.S. 294 (1955), "all deliberate," 757; Charles J. Ogletree, *All Deliberate Speed: Reflections on the First Half-Century of* Brown v. Board of Education (New York: W.W. Norton & Company, 2004), xiii and xv.

27. Ibid., xiv.

28. Richard J. Goldstone and Brian Ray, "The International Legacy of *Brown v. Board of Education,"* *McGeorge Law Review* 35 (2004): 105.

29. See in this volume, Elena Rozzi, "Roma Children and Enduring Educational Exclusion in Italy"; Teresa Sordé Martí and Fernando Macías, "Making Roma Rights a Reality at the Local Level: A Spanish Case Study"; and Margareta Matache and Krista Oehlke, "A Critical Analysis of Roma Policy and Praxis: The Romanian Case."

30. Laura Surdu, Enikö Vincze, and Marius Wamsiedel, *Roma School Participation, Non-Attendance and Discrimination in Romania* (Bucharest: Romani CRISS with UNICEF Romania, 2011), 64, 72–73.

31. Ian Hancock, *The Pariah Syndrome: An Account of Gypsy Slavery and Persecution* (Ann Arbor, MI: Karoma, 1987); David M. Crowe, *A History of the Gypsies of Eastern Europe and Russia* (New York: Palgrave Macmillan, 2007), 107–22.

32. See Anna Jurová, *Vývoj rómskej problematiky na Slovensku po roku 1945* (Bratislava: Goldpress Publishers, 1993), 102, as cited in Adriana Zimova, *"D.H. and Others v. The Czech Republic*: Vindicating Destabilization Rights in a Supranational Context" (Paper prepared for Harvard Law School class, 2012, on file with author).

33. Will Guy, André Liebich, and Elena Marushiakova, *Improving the Tools for the Social Inclusion and Non-discrimination of Roma in the EU* (Luxembourg: European Union, 2010), 9, referring to Rumyan Russinov, "Equal Opportunity In Education: Eliminating Discrimination Against Roma," *UN Chronicle* 44, no. 3 (September 2007).

34. Nina Pavelcikova, *Romove v Ceskych Zemlch v Letech 1945–1989* [The Roma in the Czech Lands 1945–1989] (Prague: Úřad dokumentace a vyšetřování zločinů komunismu PČR, 2004), 81, as cited in Zimova, *"D.H. and Others."*

35. See Zimova, "*D.H. and Others,*" 128; see also Czech Statistical Office (CZSO), Census Results, in particular table 37, "Czech Republic: Selected Basic Indicators in 1970–2011," https://www.czso.cz/csu/czso/home.

36. See Pavelcikova, *Romove v Ceskych Zemich*, 129.

37. Ibid.

38. Christian Bruggeman, *Roma Education in Comparative Perspective: Analysis of the UNDP/World Bank/EC Regional Roma Survey 2011* (Bratislava: UNDP, 2012), 9.

39. See, for example, Bruggeman, *Roma Education in Comparative Perspective*; Russinov, "Equal Opportunity in Education"; Surdu, Vincze, and Wamsiedel, *Roma School Participation*.

40. The European Court of Human Rights (ECtHR) adjudicates cases brought under the European Convention on Human Rights (ECHR) of the Council of Europe, a regional body established after World War II to promote human rights and cultural engagement and exchange across the continent (see the glossary in the appendix for information about other relevant organizations). The formal name for the ECHR is the Convention for the Protection of Human Rights and Fundamental Freedoms, but it is generally referred to by those initials or the short form of European Convention on Human Rights.

41. A summary of most of the cases is contained in Adél Kegye and Crina Elena Morteanu, *Handbook on Tackling the Segregation of Roma Children in Nursery and Primary Schools: From Investigation to Decision Making*, part 2 (Budapest: Chance for Children Foundation, 2013), http://cfcf.hu/images/stories/pdf/Handbook_FINAL_PART%202_2013.11.05.pdf.

42. *D.H. and Others v. the Czech Republic*, App. no. 57325/00, ECtHR, Grand Chamber Judgment (November 13, 2007), http://hudoc.echr.CoE.int/sites/eng/pages/search.aspx?i=001-83256.

43. Ibid., para. 205.

44. The court found that it "does not need to examine the[] individual cases" of each of the 18 applicants, because "it has been established that the relevant legislation as applied in practice at the material time had a disproportionately prejudicial effect on the Roma community" as such. Ibid., para. 209. For Article 14, see European Convention on Human Rights (ECHR), European Treaty Series No. 5 (1950), http://www.conventions.CoE.int/Treaty/Commun/QueVoulezVous.asp?NT=005&CM=8&DF=05/08/2015&CL=ENG.

45. UN Committee on the Elimination of Racial Discrimination (CERD), *Concluding Observations on the Czech Republic*, UN Doc. CERD/C/304/Add. 47 (CERD Committee, March 30, 1998), para. 13.

46. *D.H. and Others v. the Czech Republic*, para. 195.

47. Ibid., para. 198.

48. Council of the European Union, Council Directive 2000/43/EC of 29 June 2000 [henceforth Racial Equality Directive] Implementing the Principle of Equal Treatment Between Persons Irrespective of Racial or Ethnic Origin, *Official Journal of the EU* 180 (July 19, 2000): 22–26. Note that the Council of the European Union is different from the Council of Europe (COE): the European Union (EU) was created to promote effective trade, economic growth, and freedom of movement of services, capital, goods and people among its members' countries; it is much smaller than the forty-seven-member COE (which is oriented toward human rights and cultural exchange rather than commerce). However, one of the requirements of membership in the EU is ratification of the ECHR.

49. *Oršuš and Others v. Croatia*, App. no. 15766/03, ECtHR, Grand Chamber Judgment (March 16, 2010), http://hudoc.echr.CoE.int/eng?i=001-97689, para. 155, 156–86.

50. *Horváth and Kiss v. Hungary*, App. no. 11146/11, ECtHR, Judgment, Second Section (January 29, 2013), http://hudoc.echr.CoE.int/eng?i=001-116124, para. 110, 111.

51. Ibid., para. 104.

52. Ibid., para. 115.

53. Ibid., para. 116. See also para. 119, noting "positive obligations incumbent on the State in a situation where there is a history of discrimination against ethnic minority children."

54. Registrar of the Court, "School placements for Roma children must not amount to ethnic or racial segregation," (Press Release) ECtHR (May 30, 2013). A case description in English, along with the judgment in French, can be found in *Affaire Lavida et Autres c. Grèce*, App. no. 7973/10, ECtHR, Judgment (May 30, 2013), http://hudoc.echr.CoE.int/eng?i=001-120188.

55. *D.H. and Others v. the Czech Republic*, paras. 181, 182 (citations omitted). See also *Oršuš and Others v. Croatia*, para. 147; *Horváth and Kiss v. Hungary*, para. 102.

56. *United States v. Carolene Products Company*, 304 U.S. 144 (1938), quotations from 152–53, footnote 4.

57. See David A. Strauss, "Is *Carolene Products* Obsolete?" *University of Illinois Law Review* 2010, no. 4 (2010): 1251–1279, quotation from 1259.

58. European Union: Racial Equality Directive (Council Directive 2000/43/EC); Charter of Fundamental Rights (2000/C 364/01) (2000), Chapter III, Article 21 [Charter printed in *Official Journal of the EU* as 2012/C 326/02, 326 (October 26, 2012): 391–407]. Council of Europe: Protocol No. 12 to the Convention for the Protection of Human Rights and Fundamental Freedoms, CETS No.: 177 (Rome, 2000).

59. See, e.g., from the European Union (EU): Guy, Liebich, and Marushiakova, *Improving Tools for Social Inclusion of Roma*, 9 ("Discrimination and residential segregation have led to the segregation of Romani children in Roma-only standard schools and classes and in schools for children with mental disabilities"); European Commission, *An EU Framework for National Roma Integration Strategies up to 2020*, Communication, COM(2011) 173 (April 5, 2011), 5 ("Member States should ensure that all Roma children have access to quality education and are not subject to discrimination or segregation"); Council of the EU, *Council Conclusions on an EU Framework for National Roma Integration Strategies up to 2020*, 10658/11 (Brussels, May 19, 2011), para. 10 ("many Roma still face deep poverty, profound social exclusion, barriers in exercising fundamental rights, and discrimination, which often means limited access to quality education"). And from the Council of Europe (COE): Committee of Ministers, "Recommendation CM/Rec(2009)4 of the Committee of Ministers to member states on the education of Roma and Travellers in Europe" (June 17, 2009) ("the disadvantaged position of Roma and Travellers in European societies cannot be overcome unless access to quality education is guaranteed"); Nils Muižnieks, Commissioner for Human Rights of the COE, "States must take resolute measures to end school segregation of Roma," Commissioner's Human Rights Comment (blog post), Strasbourg: November 8, 2012. ("Segregation is one of the worst forms of discrimination and a serious violation of the rights of the children concerned.")

60. *Sampanis et Autres c. Grèce*, App. no. 32526/05, ECtHR, Judgment. Sect. 1 (June 5, 2008) para. 96–97; Legal Summary in English, http://hudoc.echr.CoE.int/eng?i=002-2052.

61. The first case had 11 applicants. The second had 140, all Greek nationals of Roma origin, belonging to 38 families who at the time of the events lived at the Psari residential site near Aspropyrgos. Ninety-eight of the applicants, some of whom were also applicants in Sampanis, were children aged between five and a half and fifteen; the other forty-two were their parents or

guardians. *Sampani and Others v. Greece,* App. no. 59608/09, ECtHR, Judgment. Sect. 1 (December 11, 2012); Legal Summary in English, http://hudoc.echr.CoE.int/eng?i=002-7332.

62. Registrar of the Court, "Failure of the authorities to integrate Roma children into the ordinary education system amounted to discrimination against them," ECtHR, press release, December 11, 2012.

63. Ibid.

64. See COE Committee of Ministers, "Execution of Judgment, *Sampanis and others v. Greece,*" Resolution CM/ResDH(2011)119 (September 14, 2011), http://hudoc.echr.CoE.int/eng?i=001-106912http://hudoc.echr.CoE.int/eng?i=001-106912.

65. Greek Helsinki Monitor, *Submission to the European Commission against Racism and Intolerance (ECRI) on Greece* (Glyke Nera, Greece, January 13, 2014), 13–14, http://www.unhcr.gr/1againstracism/en/submission-to-the-european-commission-against-racism-and-intolerance-ecri-on-greece/.

66. Ibid.; Nikos Roumpis, Jennifer Collins, and Charles McPhedran, "Roma Hope for Understanding after Mystery Girl Scandal," *USA Today,* November 4, 2013, http://www.usatoday.com/story/news/world/2013/11/02/gypsies-greece-maria-roma/3189467/.

67. European Roma Rights Centre (ERRC), "ERRC Prevails in Court against Bulgarian Ministry of Education on School Segregation of Roma," February 1, 2006, http://www.errc.org/article/errc-prevails-in-court-against-bulgarian-ministry-of-education-on-school-segregation-of-roma/2471.

68. Jon Fox and Zsuzsanna Vidra, *Applying Tolerance Indicators: Roma School Segregation* (San Domenico di Fiesole: European University Institute, 2013), 12.

69. European Commission against Racism and Intolerance, *ECRI Fourth Report on Bulgaria* (Strasbourg: February 24, 2009), para. 52.

70. Bulgarian National Council for Cooperation Ethnic and Integration Issues (NCCEII), *National Roma Integration Strategy of the Republic of Bulgaria (2012–2020)* (Sofia: NCCEII, 2012) 11–13, http://ec.europa.eu/justice/discrimination/files/roma_bulgaria_strategy_en.pdf.

71. Marko Hajdinjak and Maya Kosseva with Antonina Zhelyazkova, *Tolerance and Cultural Diversity Discourses in Bulgaria* (San Domenico di Fiesole, Italy: European University Institute, 2012), 38.

72. Kegya and Morteanu, *Tackling the Segregation of Roma Children,* Part 2, sec. 5.8.

73. Ibid., sec. 5.8.1–2.

74. Romanian Ministry of Education, Research and Youth, Order 1540/19 of July 2007, in Romanian, http://www.legex.ro/Ordin-1540-19.07.2007-82075.aspx.

75. Surdu, Vincze, and Wamsiedel, *Roma School Participation in Romania,* 95.

76. Thomas Hammarberg, Commissioner for Human Rights of the COE, "Letter from Commissioner to Mr. Emil Boc, Prime Minister of Romania," CommDH(2010)53, November 17, 2010, 4.

77. COE Advisory Committee on the Framework Convention for the Protection of National Minorities, *Third Opinion on Romania,* ACFC/OP/III(2012)001(Strasbourg, March 21, 2012), para. 27.

78. COE Committee of Ministers, "Decision at 1157th Meeting," December 3, 2012, para. 2.

79. Office for Democratic Institutions and Human Rights (ODHIR), *Equal Access to Quality Education for Roma Children: Field Assessment Visit to the Czech Republic* (Warsaw: ODHIR, May 2012), 5, http://www.osce.org/odihr/96661?download=true.

80. Czech Public Defender of Rights, *Research of the Public Defender of Rights into the Question of Ethnic Composition of Pupils of Former Special Schools* (Brno, Czech Republic, 2012), in Czech, http://www.ochrance.cz/fileadmin/user_upload/DISKRIMINACE/Vyzkum/Vyzkum _skoly-zprava.pdf as reported in English in European Roma Rights Centre (ERRC), *Written Comments Concerning Czech Republic For Consideration by the Committee on Economic, Social and Cultural Rights, 52nd Session (2–6 December 2013)*, 5.

81. European Roma Rights Centre, "Czech Government Takes Backwards Step on Inclusive Education—NGOs Sound Alarm," April 22, 2013, http://www.errc.org/article/czech-government -takes-backwards-step-on-inclusive-education-%E2%80%93-ngos-sound-alarm/4134.

82. Quoted in Henry Foy and Duncan Robinson, "Brussels Takes a Tougher Line on Roma Discrimination," *Financial Times*, April 29, 2015.

83. See, e.g., Draft Strategy Document, 2016–2019, Open Society Foundations Roma Initiatives (on file with author) (describing Open Society Foundations project encouraging Roma parents to enroll their children in the first year of mainstream education in schools in Ostrava, Czech Republic. By enrolling their children in schools that offer quality mainstream education, the parents leverage additional pressure by restricting the funding going to the practical schools and classes, which is 1.5 times higher per capita than in mainstream schools. Since 2013, two such campaigns have been implemented, resulting in a substantial reduction in the number of Roma children enrolled in segregated education).

84. Tom Bass, "What Have They Done? Oršuš and Desegregation in Medimurje County," Roma Education Fund, May 15, 2013, http://www.romaeducationfund.hu/news/.ref/news-and -events/what-have-they-done.

85. Roma Education Fund, "Back to School for Romani Children in Medimurje County," September 17, 2013, http://www.romaeducationfund.hu/news/ref/news-and-events/back-school -romani-children-medimurje-county.

86. Roma Education Fund, "Infographic: Croatia: Child by Child, Step by Step" (2013), available at http://infogr.am/croatia-child-by-child-step-by-step?src=web.

87. Roma Education Fund, "Back to School."

88. COE Committee of Ministers, "Communication form Hungary concerning the case of Horváth and Kiss against Hungary (Application No. 11146/11): Action Report and Action Plan of 29 January 2014, DH-DD(2014)186," paras. 1–2.

89. E-mail correspondence with Lilla Farkas, Chance for Children Foundation, www.cfcf .hu, March 2014.

90. Eszter Neuberger, "Hungary's Highest Court Legitimizes Segregation in the Case of Religious Schooling," *Budapest Beacon,* April 23, 2015.

91. Gábor Kertesi and Gábor Kézdi, *Roma School Segregation, School Choice, and Educational Policies In 100 Hungarian Towns* (Budapest: Roma Education Fund, 2013), http://www .romaeducationfund.hu/sites/default/files/publications/school_segregationschool_choice_and _educational_policies_-_final_2013.pdf.

92. For example, in cooperation with a civil society initiative launched in 2013 by Open Society Foundations, parents of several Roma children in Ostrava have begun organizing to defend their children's rights to attend high-quality, integrated primary schools. Correspondence on file with author.

93. Hungarian Ministry of Public Administration and Justice and State Secretariat for Social Inclusion, *National Social Inclusion Strategy* (Budapest: Ministry of Public Administration

and Justice, December 2011), 36–37, http://ec.europa.eu/justice/discrimination/files/roma _hungary_strategy_en.pdf.

94. European Union Agency for Fundamental Rights (FRA), *The Situation of Roma in 11 EU Member States: Survey Results at a Glance* (Luxembourg: FRA, 2012), 15.

95. World Bank, "Brief: Roma," February 24, 2015, http://www.worldbank.org/en/region/eca /brief/roma; see also Bruggeman, *Roma Education in Comparative Perspective*.

96. EU FRA, *The Situation of Roma in 11 EU Member States*, 12.

97. Interviews, Applicants, *D.H. and Others v. the Czech Republic*, Prague, November 2007.

98. Jonathan Birdwell et al., *Backsliders: Measuring Democracy in the EU* (London: Demos, 2013), 22. See also John Bennett, *Roma Early Childhood Inclusion* (Budapest: Open Society Foundations, Roma Education Fund, UNICEF, 2012), 29, http://www.romaeducationfund.hu/sites /default/files/publications/reci-overview-final-web.pdf.

99. Eva S. Balogh, "Openly Racist Opinion of a Hungarian Judge," *Hungarian Spectrum*, April 27, 2014, http://hungarianspectrum.wordpress.com/tag/bekes-county-court/.

100. "Romani Rappers: Avoid Czech practical primary schools," Romea News Service, February 12, 2013, http://www.romea.cz/en/news/czech/romani-rappers-avoid-czech-practical -primary-schools.

101. Ombudsperson, Czech Republic, interview with the author, Prague, February 2014.

102. See Article 20 of Act No 125 of 2003 on equal treatment and the promotion of equal opportunities, in Hungarian, http://www.egyenlobanasmod.hu/data/2003_CXXV_tv_20130701 .pdf. See also Lilla Farkas, "Limited Enforcement Possibilities under European Anti-Discrimination Legislation—A Case Study of Procedural Novelties: *Actio Popularis* Action in Hungary," *Erasmus Law Review* 3, no. 3 (2010): 186 (citations omitted).

103. *Brown v. Board of Education II*, 349 U.S. 294, 757 (1955).

104. *Green v. County School Board,* 391 U.S. 430, 442 (1968).

105. *Swann v. Charlotte-Mecklenburg*, 402 U.S. 1, 15 (1971).

106. European Convention on Human Rights, Art. 46.

107. *Marckx v. Belgium,* App. no. 6833/74, ECtHR, Judgment (Plenary Court) (June 13, 1979), http://hudoc.echr.CoE.int/eng?i=001-57534, para 58.

108. Council of Europe, "High Level Conference on the Future of the European Court of Human Rights" (Brighton Declaration), April 2012, para. 11, http://www.echr.CoE.int /Documents/2012_Brighton_FinalDeclaration_ENG.pdf.

109. "effective remedy," European Convention on Human Rights, Art. 13; "effective, proportionate," EU Racial Equality Directive, Art. 15; see generally Christa Tobler, *Remedies and Sanctions in EU Non-Discrimination Law* (Brussels: European Commission, 2005).

110. See, for example, the argument that desegregation remedies in the United States may have impeded racial progress in Derrick Bell, *Silent Covenants:* Brown v. Board of Education *and the Unfulfilled Hopes for Racial Reform* (New York: Oxford University Press, 2004), 20–25, 105, 109.

111. Kluger, *Simple Justice*, 702–3.

112. See, e.g., *Hirst v. United Kingdom*, App. no. 74025/01, ECtHR, Grand Chamber Judgment (October 6, 2005), in which the court held that a blanket ban on prisoner voting violated the convention. Subsequently, British prime minister David Cameron said that the idea of giving prisoners the right to vote made him "physically ill," as quoted by Philippe Naughton, "Cameron Sickened by Prisoner Vote," *The Times*, November 3, 2010.

113. As an obstacle, for example: *Dred Scott v. Sanford*, 60 U.S. 393 (1857), denying African Americans standing to bring constitutional claims and constraining the power of the federal

government to ban slavery; *Lochner v. New York*, 198 U.S. 45 (1905), finding New York labor protection laws in breach of the Fourteenth Amendment, beginning an era of jurisprudence that was intolerant of most government regulations. As change, for example: *West Coast Hotel Co. v. Parrish*, 300 U.S. 379 (1937), upholding the constitutionality of state minimum wage law and ending the *Lochner* era of jurisprudence; and of course, most famously *Brown v. Board of Education*, 347 U.S. 483 (1954).

114. See, e.g., Treaty of Rome (1957) (establishing the European Economic Community), art. 119 (affirming the principle that men and women should receive equal pay for equal work); European Union Treaty of Amsterdam (1997) (amending the Treaty of Rome), art. 2 (affirming the principle of equality between men and women); European Union Treaty of Lisbon (2007) (which, among other acts, renders binding the Charter of Fundamental Rights, including expansive provisions with respect to equality and non-discrimination); Racial Equality Directive (2000) (mandating equal treatment on the basis of racial or ethnic origin in all areas of EU competence).

115. Richard L. Abel, *Politics by Other Means: Law in the Struggle Against Apartheid, 1980–1994* (New York: Routledge, 1995), 2–3.

116. *Plessy v. Ferguson*, 163 U.S. 537 (1896).

117. See de Burca, "The Trajectories of European and American Antidiscrimination Law," 5.

118. Donald L. Niewyk, "The Holocaust: Jews, Gypsies, and the Handicapped," in *Centuries of Genocide: Essays and Eyewitness Accounts,* ed. Samuel Totten and William S. Parsons (New York: Routledge, 2012), 191–248, in particular, 191.

119. European Commission, "EU and Roma," European Commission website.

120. Rosenberg, *The Hollow Hope*, 42.

121. Article 14, the nondiscrimination guarantee, has been part of the European Convention on Human Rights since 1950; Article 2 of ECHR's Protocol No. 1, which secures the right to education, has been in force since 1952.

122. *Oršuš and Others v. Croatia*, para 151.

123. Ibid., para.152.

124. *Horváth and Kiss v. Hungary*, para. 113.

125. See, generally, Mary L. Dudziak, *Cold War Civil Rights: Race and the Image of American Democracy* (Princeton, N.J.: Princeton University Press, 2000); and Mary L. Dudziak, "*Brown* as a Cold War Case," *Journal of American History* 91, no. 1 (2004): 32–42.

126. *Pittsburgh Courier,* May 1954 as quoted in Dudziak, *Cold War Civil Rights*, 93; also quoted in Mary L. Dudziak, "The Global Impact of *Brown v. Board of Education*," Supreme Court of the United States Blog, February 18, 2010, http://www.scotusblog.com/2010/02/the-global-impact-of-brown-v-board-of-education/.

127. See, e.g., Rosenberg, *The Hollow Hope*.

128. King of course paraphrased Unitarian minister and noted abolitionist Theodore Parker. See J. Stiehm, "Oval Office Rug Gets History Wrong," *Washington Post*, September 4, 2010.

Chapter 10. Making Roma Rights a Reality at the Local Level

1. All personal Roma names are pseudonyms in order to ensure the anonymity and confidentiality of study participants' personal data; however, the name of the neighborhood is the actual name, La Milagrosa (Albacete, Spain). The research leading to the results presented in this chapter has received funding from the European Union's Sixth Framework Programme (FP6, 2006–2011) as "INCLUDE-ED, Strategies for Inclusion and Social Cohesion in Europe from Education," Project 28603, http://cordis.europa.eu/project/rcn/84827_en.html.

2. Maria Padrós et al., "Contrasting Scientific Knowledge with Knowledge from the Life-world: The Dialogic Inclusion Contract," *Qualitative Inquiry* 17, no. 3 (2011): 304–12.

3. For more information about the INCLUD-ED project, see http://creaub.info/included/.

4. Jesús Gómez and Ramón Flecha, "Participatory Paradigms: Researching 'with' Rather than 'On,'" in *Researching Widening Access: Issues and Approaches in an International Context*, ed. Beth Crossan, Jim Gallacher, and Michael Osborne (London: Routledge, 2004), 129–40; Jesús Gómez et al., *Metodología Comunicativa Crítica* [Critical Communicative Methodology] (Barcelona: El Roure, 2006); Aitor Gómez, Sandra Racionero, and Teresa Sordé, "Ten Years of Critical Communicative Methodology," *International Review of Qualitative Research* 3, no. 1 (2010): 17–43.

5. Jürgen Habermas, *The Theory of Communicative Action: Reason and the Rationalization of Society* (Boston: Beacon, 1984).

6. EU Spanish Presidency, *Science Against Poverty Report* (Project 268169), last updated June 11, 2012, in the European Commission's Community Research and Development Information Service (CORDIS); this activity report for the project contains the conference program for Science Against Poverty (held April 8–9, 2010, in Segovia), at which INCLUDE-ED presented results; see http://cordis.europa.eu/result/rcn/52690_en.html.

7. In 2015, CREA reorganized and is now called Community of Researchers on Excellence for All; this paper uses the name Center for Research into Theories and Practices that Overcome Inequalities, as that was the organization's name at the time of the INCLUD-ED research; for more information about the name change and the theories behind this project, see http://creaub .info/cat/.

8. Ramón Flecha, "Buenas prácticas: Cómo lograr impacto en los proyectos del Reto 6" [Good Practices: How to Achieve Impact with the Projects of Challenge 6], in *H2020: Information Session About Challenge 6*, ed. FECYT and European Commission (Bilbao: Universidad de Deusto, January 24, 2014).

9. For more on Horizon 2020 and its projects, see European Commission (EC) website, Horizon 2020 section, "The EU Framework Programme for Research and Innovation," http://ec .europa.eu/programmes/horizon2020/en; for more on Europe 2020, see the EC website section by that name; for specific targets, see "Europe 2020 in a Nutshell"; quote from "Europe 2020," front page, last updated June 23, 2015, http://ec.europa.eu/europe2020/index_en.htm.

10. Because of the social impact the INCLUD-ED project achieved, the European Commission cited it as one of ten research success stories (and the only one from the social sciences and humanities research area) in a memo making the case for research expenditures; see European Commission, "Added Value of Research, Innovation, and Science Portfolio," Memo11/520 (Brussels, July 19, 2011), http://europa.eu/rapid/press-release_MEMO-11-520_en.pdf.

11. Ramon Flecha and Marta Soler, "Communicative Methodology: Successful Actions and Dialogic Democracy," *Current Sociology* 62, no. 2 (March 2014): 232–42.

12. Rosa Valls and Leonidas Kyriakides, "The Power of Interactive Groups: How Diversity of Adults Volunteering in Classroom Groups Can Promote Inclusion and Success for Children of Vulnerable Minority Ethnic Populations," *Cambridge Journal of Education* 43, no. 1 (2013): 17–33.

13. Javier Díez, Suzanne Gatt, and Sandra Racionero, "Placing Immigrant and Minority Family and Community Members at the School's Centre: The Role of Community Participation," *European Journal of Education* 46, no. 2 (2011): 184–96.

14. INCLUD-ED Consortium, *Actions for Success in Schools in Europe* (Brussels: European Commission, October 2009).

15. Ibid.

16. Ibid., 55.

17. Ayuntamiento de Albacete, *Albacete Integra. Plan para la integración social del municipio de Albacete 2012–2014* [Integrated Albacete: Plan for Albacete's Social Integration 2012–2014] (Albacete: Ayuntamiento de Albacete, 2012).

18. European Anti-Poverty Network (EAPN), *Estudio de barrios en vulnerabilidad y/o exclusión socia* [Study of Vulnerable Barrios and Social Exclusion] (Albacete: EAPN Castilla La Mancha, 2008), http://www.eapnclm.org/upload/01/35/Albacete__Albacete.pdf.

19. Center for Research into Theories and Practices that Overcome Inequalities, University of Barcelona (CREA-UB), *Case Analysis of Local Projects Working Towards Social Cohesion—Spain,* Project 6 (2nd Round) (Brussels: European Commission, 2008).

20. Ibid.

21. Ainhoa Flecha, "Healthier Lives for European Minority Groups: School and Health Care, Lessons from the Roma," *International Journal on Environmental Research and Public Health* 10, no. 8 (2013): 3089–111, quotation at 3103.

22. CREA-UB, *Case Analysis of Local Projects Working Towards Social Cohesion—Spain,* Project 6 (2nd Round).

23. Ibid.

24. CREA-UB, *Case Analysis of Local Projects Working Towards Social Cohesion—Spain,* Project 6 (4th Round) (Brussels: European Commission, 2010).

25. *La Verdad,* "El colegio de la Paz, Quijote Gitano del 2008" [La Paz School, Quixote Gitano of 2008] *La Verdad* (Albacete) April 9, 2008, http://www.laverdad.es/albacete/20080409/albacete/colegio-quijote-gitano-2008-20080409.html.

26. URBAN was a European Union initiative to provide guidelines on the economic and social regeneration of cities and neighborhoods in crisis in order to promote sustainable urban development. The specific URBAN objectives were (1) to formulate and implement innovative strategies for sustainable economic and social regeneration of small and medium-sized towns and cities or of distressed urban neighborhoods in larger cities, and (2) to enhance and exchange knowledge and experience in relation to sustainable urban regeneration and development in the areas concerned. The city of Albacete, and particularly La Milagrosa, obtained significant funds under URBAN II plan. More information about the plan, including links to archived information, is available at Eur-Lex Europa, http://europa.eu/legislation_summaries/employment_and_social_policy/social_inclusion_fight_against_poverty/g24209_en.htm.

27. Padrós et al., "Contrasting Scientific Knowledge with Knowledge from the Lifeworld."

28. Aitor Gómez, Lidia Puigvert, and Ramon Flecha, "Critical Communicative Methodology: Informing Real Social Transformation through Research," *Qualitative Inquiry* 17, no.3 (2011): 235–45.

29. Ramon Flecha and Iñaki Santa Cruz, "Cooperation for Economic Success: The Mondragon Case," *Analyse & Kritik* 33, no. 1 (2011): 157–70.

30. Mondragon Corporation, Economic and Financial Indicators in About Us section of the company website, http://www.mondragon-corporation.com/eng/about-us/economic-and-financial-indicators/, accessed September 20, 2015; note these indicators are slightly different from those in Mondragon's 2014 Annual Report, http://www.mondragon-corporation.com/eng/about-us/economic-and-financial-indicators/annual-report/, 4.

31. Cooperative Miguel Fenollera, *Video presentación resultados Cooperativa* [Presentation Video of the Cooperative's outcomes]. (Albacete: Fenollera cooperative employment, 2013),

https://www.facebook.com/video.php?v=497959286914115; Ana Burgués, Sandra Martin, and Ignacio Santa Cruz, "La relación entre cooperativas transformadoras y desigualdades sociales en los territorios [The Relation Between Transformative Cooperatives and Social Inequalities in the Territories]," *Scripta Nova* 42, no. 17 (2013), http://www.ub.es/geocrit/sn/sn-427/sn-427-4.htm; Flecha and Soler, "Communicative Methodology."

32. Rosa Valls, *Actuaciones socioeducativas de éxito para la superación de la pobreza. Informe 2* [Successful Educational and Social Actions for the Overcoming of Poverty, Report 2], Project of the Spanish Plan of Research, Development and Innovation (Madrid: Ministry of Economy and Competitiveness, 2012–2014).

33. See, for example, Ana Contreras, *European Report 1: ROM UP! The Inclusion of Roma through Successful Quality Educational Experiences* (Barcelona: Romani Association of Women Drom Kotar Mestipen, 2012); and ROM UP, http://www.rom-up.eu/home.htm; for current activities, see the Romani Association of Women Drom Kotar Mestipen, http://www.dromkotar.org/.

34. With the help of a network of partners, Instituto Natura is implementing and supporting projects aimed at improving public education in Brazil and Latin America, guided by the effectiveness of learning outcomes, as well as the equity and social cohesion that these project can generate. Since 2012, CREA has been working with Instituto Natura to transfer the knowledge generated by INCLUD-ED regarding Successful Educational Actions to schools in Latin America. As part of this effort, Instituto Natura has launched the project, "Schools as Learning Communities," to implement SEAs in schools in six Latin American countries. For further information about this partnership, see http://www.institutonatura.org.br/projetos/pesquisa-sobre-comunidades-de-aprendizagem/.

Chapter 11. Roma Mobilization and Participation

1. Research on Roma political mobilization includes information on protests and political demands to governments, while research on political participation includes information on voting patterns. Although the literature on the political voice of the Roma is growing (see, e.g., Yaron Matras, "Scholarship and the Politics of Romani Identity: Strategic and Conceptual Issues," in *European Yearbook of Minority Issues*, ed. European Centre for Minority Issues [ECMI] and European Academy Bozen/Bolzano [EURAC] vol. 10 [for 2011] [Leiden: Brill/Nijhoff, 2013], 211–47; Aidan McGarry and Timofey Agarin, "Unpacking the Roma Participation Puzzle: Presence, Voice and Influence," *Journal of Ethnic and Migration Studies* [June 2014]: 1–19), the bulk of the current research focuses on issues of socioeconomic deprivation and discrimination.

2. See, for example, "Bottom of the Heap—Europe's Roma," *The Economist*, June 21, 2008, 35–38.

3. See the Survey Data Explorer (data search tool): Results from the 2011 Roma Survey, Discrimination and Participation section, voting in the last election, on the European Union Agency for Fundamental Rights (FRA) website, http://fra.europa.eu/DVS/DVT/roma.php.

4. See Tomáš Hrustič, "The Trends in the Participation of Romani Candidates in Elections in Slovakia," in "Challenges of Representation," themed issue, *Roma Rights: Journal of European Roma Rights Centre* 2012 (August 22, 2013): 39–47, http://www.errc.org/roma-rights-journal/roma-rights-2012-challenges-of-representation-voice-on-roma-politics-power-and-participation/4174/4; Organization of Security and Cooperation in Europe (OSCE) and Office for Democratic Institutions and Human Rights (ODIHR), *Implementation of the Action Plan on Improving the Situation of Roma and Sinti within the OSCE Area: Status Report 2013 (Renewed Commit-*

ments, Continued Challenges) (Warsaw: OSCE ODIHR 2013), 53, http://www.osce.org/odihr/107406.

5. Peter Vermeersch, "Advocacy Networks and Romani Politics in Central and Eastern Europe," *Journal on Ethnopolitics and Minority Issues in Europe* 1 (2001): 1–22; Eva Sobotka, "The Influence of Civil Society Actors on Roma Issues within the EU Framework," *International Journal on Minority and Group Rights* 18 (2010).

6. However, there is also still need for more precise data on these socioeconomic circumstances. See, for example, Christina McDonald and Katy Negrin, *No Data—No Progress* (Open Society Institute, 2010), http://www.soros.org/initiatives/roma/articles_publications/publications/no-data-no-progress-20100628; for examples of the literature I refer to, see EU Agency for Fundamental Rights (FRA), Open Society Foundations, and Czech Government, *Improving Access to Housing for Roma: Good Local Practices, Funding and Legislation* (Luxembourg: FRA, 2011); FRA, *Selected Positive Initiatives The Situation of Roma EU Citizens Moving to and Settling in Other EU Member States* (Vienna: FRA, 2009), http://fra.europa.eu/fraWebsite/attachments/Roma_Movement_PositiveInitiatives-final_en.pdf; FRA, *The Situation of Roma EU Citizens Moving to and Settling in Other EU Member States* (Luxembourg: EC, FRA, 2009); FRA, *The Situation of Roma in 11 EU Member States* (Vienna: FRA, 2012); Bernard Rorke, *Review of EU Framework National Roma Integration Strategies (NRIS): Open Society Foundations (OSF) Review of NRIS Submitted by Bulgaria, the Czech Republic, Hungary, Romania and Slovakia* (OSF, 2012), http://www.soros.org/sites/default/files/roma-integration-strategies-20120221.pdf; UNICEF, *Towards Roma Inclusion: A Review of Roma Education Initiatives in Central and South-Eastern Europe* (Geneva: UNICEF, 2010), http://www.unicef.org/ceecis/ROMA_PAPER_FINAL_LAST.pdf; for discussion, see Michael Stewart, "Introduction" in *Multi-Disciplinary Approaches to Romany Studies*, ed. Michael Stewart and Marton Rövid (Budapest: Central European University, 2010), 1–9.

7. See, for example, in this volume, Elena Rozzi, "Roma Children and Enduring Educational Exclusion in Italy"; and Will Guy, "Anti-Roma Violence, Hate Speech, and Discrimination in the New Europe: Czech Republic, Slovakia, and Hungary."

8. On the activist use of Roma, see Peter Vermeersch, *The Romani Movement: Minority Politics and Ethnic Mobilization in Contemporary Central Europe* (Oxford: Berghahn, 2006).

9. See, e.g., Thomas Acton, "Categorising Irish Travellers," in *Irish Travellers: Culture and Ethnicity*, ed. M. McCann, S. O Siochain, and J. Ruane (Belfast: Institute of Irish Studies, Queen's University of Belfast, 1994), 36–53.

10. See, for example, Nicolae Gheorghe, "The Social Construction of Romani Identity," in *Gypsy Politics and Traveller Identity*, ed. Thomas Acton (Hertfordshire: University of Hertfordshire Press, 1997), 153–63; Matras, "Scholarship and the Politics of Romani Identity"; and Michael Stewart, *The Time of the Gypsies* (Boulder, Colo.: Westview Press, 1997), 28.

11. Marc Weller, "Democratic Governance and Minority Political Participation: Emerging Legal Standards and Practice," in *Political Participation of Minorities: A Commentary on International Standards and Practice*, ed. Marc Weller and Katherine Nobbs (Oxford: Oxford University Press, 2010), lvii–lxiii.

12. Peter Vermeersch and Melanie Ram, "The Roma," in *Minority Rights in Central and Eastern Europe*, ed. Bernd Rechel (New York: BASEES/Routledge, 2009), 61–73.

13. For more details, see Eva Sobotka, "Special Contact Mechanisms for Roma," in *Political Participation of Minorities*, ed. Marc Weller and Katherine Nobbs (Oxford: Oxford University Press, 2010), 503–23.

14. See, e.g., Alaina Lemon, *Between Two Fires: Gypsy Performance and Romani Memory from Pushkin to Postsocialism* (Durham, N.C.: Duke University Press, 2000).

15. Peter Vermeersch, "The European Union and the Roma: An Analysis of Recent Institutional and Policy Developments," in *European Yearbook of Minority Issues*, vol. 10, 341–58.

16. European Commission (EC), "Instruments and Policies for Roma Inclusion," press release, MEMO/08/462, Brussels, July 2, 2008, http://europa.eu/rapid/press-release_MEMO-08 -462_en.htm?locale=en; about the EC Communication *Non-discrimination and Equal Opportunities: A Renewed Commitment*, and the accompanying report *Non-Discrimination and Equal Opportunities: A Renewed Commitment, Community Instruments and Policies for Roma Inclusion*, Commission Staff Working Document, COM(2008)420 (Brussels: European Commission, July 2, 2008), http://ec.europa.eu/justice/discrimination/files/sec_2008_2172.pdf.

17. See Roma activist Valeriu Nicolae's criticism of the limited Roma participation in these summits in his satirical blog post "The Amazing and 'Extensive Work' on Roma of the European Commission," March 14, 2014, http://valeriucnicolae.wordpress.com/2014/03/10/the-amazing -and-extensive-work-on-roma-of-the-european-commission/comment-page-1/.

18. Council of the European Union, *Council Conclusions on Advancing Roma Inclusion*, 1058/10 (Draft: Brussels, May 27, 2010; Final Correction, Luxembourg: June 7, 2010).

19. The European Roma Policy Coalition (ERPC) is a network (including Amnesty International and the European Roma Rights Center) of NGOs operating at EU level on issues of human rights, antidiscrimination, antiracism, social inclusion, and Roma and Travellers' rights. For basic information see "European Roma Policy Coalition," December 1, 2010, European Roma Rights Centre, http://www.errc.org/article/european-roma-policy-coalition-erpc/3796.

20. Principle no. 2 is "explicit but not exclusive targeting." The principles were also attached as an annex to conclusions from the Council of the EU (Social Affairs) in June 8, 2009. See EU Directorate-General for Employment, Social Affairs and Inclusion, *Vademecum: The 10 Common Basic Principles on Roma Inclusion* (Brussels: European Commission, 2010), http://bookshop .europa.eu/en/the-10-common-basic-principles-on-roma-inclusion-pbKE3010317/.

21. European Commission, *An EU Framework for National Roma Integration Strategies up to 2020*, Communication, COM(2011) 173 (Brussels, April 5, 2011) http://ec.europa.eu/justice /policies/discrimination/docs/com_2011_173_en.pdf.

22. Viviane Reding, Vice-President of the European Commission and EU Justice Commissioner, "Roma Integration: Are National Governments Ready to Live Up [to] Their Commitments?" Speech 12/215: Extraordinary Meeting of the European Platform for Roma Inclusion, Brussels, March 22, 2012, http://europa.eu/rapid/press-release_SPEECH-12-215_en.htm?locale =FR).

23. See also, in this volume, Margareta Matache and Krista Oehlke, "A Critical Analysis of Roma Policy and Praxis: The Romanian Case."

24. European Roma Policy Coalition (ERPC), "Roma Exclusion: It's Time for Member States to Tackle This European 'Scandal' Seriously," European Roma Grassroots Organisations Network, July 8, 2013, http://www.ergonetwork.org/ergo-network/news/123/000000/Roma-exclusion -it-s-time-for-Member-States-to-tackle-this-European-scandal-seriously.

25. See European Roma and Travellers Forum (ERTF), *Do We Roma Matter? Survey 2014: EP Candidates and Roma* (Strasbourg: ERTF, 2014), 29–30, http://www.ertf.org/images/Reports /ERTF_Survey_Do_we_Roma_Matter_EN_web_version.pdf. Sometimes Roma activists play a crucial role in bringing to the fore specific Roma problems. The European Roma Information Office (ERIO), for example, a Brussels-based NGO that gives voice to concerns of Roma organ-

izations across Europe, pointed out in April 2014 that current European initiatives have largely ignored the plight of elderly Roma, whose socioeconomic exclusion presents a particular challenge. See ERIO and AGE Platform Europe (ERIO-AGE), "The Socio-Economic Discrimination of Older Roma Should Be Included in Roma Integration Strategies," ERIO-AGE, 2014, http://www.erionet.eu/doc-joint-statement_age-erio_080414.

26. See, in this volume, Andrzej Mirga, "Roma Policy in Europe: Results and Challenges"; Kálmán Mizsei, "Reconstructing Roma Integration in Central and Eastern Europe: Addressing the Failures of the Last Quarter Century"; and Margareta Matache and Krista Oehlke, "A Critical Analysis of Roma Policy and Praxis: The Romanian Case."

27. This part of the chapter draws on my earlier work; see Peter Vermeersch, "Roma and Mobility in the European Union" in *Roma and Traveller Inclusion in Europe*, ed. Kati Pietarinen (Belgium: Green European Foundation, 2011), 91–97; "The European Union and the Roma: An Analysis of Recent Institutional and Policy Developments," in ECMI and Eurac, *European Yearbook of Minority Issues*, vol. 10, 341–58.

28. McGarry and Agarin, "Unpacking the Roma Participation Puzzle."

29. James D. Wright, "Review of Sidney Verba and Norman H. Nie, *Participation in America: Political Democracy and Social Equality*," *Contemporary Sociology* 4 (May 1975): 272–73.

30. Huub van Baar, "Socio-Economic Mobility and Neo-Liberal Governmentality in Post-Socialist Europe: Activation and the Dehumanisation of the Roma," *Journal of Ethnic and Migration Studies* 38, no. 8 (2012): 1289–304.

31. See "Survey Data Explorer: Results from the 2011 Roma Survey," Discrimination and Participation section, "Feeling Discriminated Against Because of Ethnicity," EU Agency for Fundamental Rights, http://fra.europa.eu/DVS/DVT/roma.php.

32. Documented, for example, in Michael Stewart, ed., *The Gypsy "Menace": Populism and the New Anti-Gypsy Politics* (London: Hurst, 2012).

33. Ibid., 3.

34. Peter Vermeersch, "Reframing the Roma: EU Initiatives and the Politics of Reinterpretation," *Journal of Ethnic and Migration Studies* 38, no. 8 (2012): 1195–212.

35. In this volume, Erika Schlager provides some perspective from the late 1990s on the issue of governments regarding Roma as the responsibility of international organizations ("Policy and Practice: A Case Study of US Foreign Policy Regarding the Situation of Roma in Europe").

36. UNICEF, *Towards Roma Inclusion*; UNICEF, European Social Observatory (OSE), and the Belgian Federal Planning Service for Social Integration, "Preventing Social Exclusion through the EUROPE 2020 STRATEGY: Early Childhood Development and the Inclusion of Roma Families," Discussion Paper prepared at the request of the Belgian EU presidency for the Fourth European Roma Platform, Brussels, December 2010, and finalized at a meeting in Budapest, February, 2011.

37. TernYpe: International Roma Youth Network "unites different Roma youth organizations from Albania, Bulgaria, Germany, Hungary, Italy, Macedonia, Slovakia, Spain and Poland" and has an office in Berlin; see http://www.ternype.eu; the European Roma Grassroots Organisations Network (ERGO), with offices in Brussels and in the Netherlands, is as its name suggests a coaliton of local Roma specific-country groups; for current information, see http://www.ergonetwork.org.

38. See, for example, the activities of the Romedia Foundation, which "works towards contributing to a positive perception of Romani ethnic identity, combating anti-Roma prejudice, and providing alternative information to policy makers on Roma through the production of films and videos," and more, http://www.romediafoundation.org/aboutus.

39. See Open Society Foundations, Roma Initiatives Office, "European Roma Institute," May 2015, https://www.opensocietyfoundations.org/publications/european-roma-institute.

Chapter 12. Roma in European Politics, Looking to the Future

1. David Mark, "Roma at Crossroads: Politics and Empowerment," in *Recycling Hatred: Racism(s) in Europe Today: A Dialogue Between Academics, Equality Experts and Civil Society Activists* (Brussels: European Network Against Racism [ENAR], 2013), 132–41.

2. One of the strongest critics of Roma "ethno-politics" is Dr. Martin Kovats, who argues that "Roma nationalism does not represent the emancipation of a suppressed people in the tradition of anti-colonial struggles, but the promotion of an authoritarian nationalist tradition in which a political community is constructed through the manipulation of vulnerable people, to secure the interests of an unaccountable elite" ("The Politics of Roma Identity: Between Nationalism and Destitution," July 30, 2003, https://www.opendemocracy.net/people-migrationeurope/article_1399.jsp).

3. Of course, political accountability is not always adequate to limit the use and abuse of power by those entrusted with it. That is why modern democracies are reinforced by constitutions, the rule of law, and the separation of powers among governing institutions.

4. 2008 Law for the Election to the Chamber of Deputies and the Senate (henceforth Election Law), Law no. 35/2008, Article 9, Paragraph 3, with subsequent amendments and modification, stipulates that: "Other legally constituted organizations of citizens belonging to national minorities, that are of public utility and that present to the Central Electoral Bureau, no further than 30 days after the announcement of the date of election, a list of members comprising a minimum of 15% of the number of citizens who at the last census have declared as belonging to that minority, can advance candidatures" (my translation from the Romanian).

5. Organization for Security and Cooperation in Europe (OSCE) Office for Democratic Institutions and Human Rights (ODIHR) Election Expert Team, *Romania: Parliamentary Elections 9 December 2012*, Final Report (Warsaw: OSCE ODIHR, January 16, 2013), 18–20, http://www.osce.org/odihr/98757?download=true. The registration of candidates was rejected for the following organizations because they did not have a public utility status: the Democratic Union of Croats in Romania, the Vox Mentis Foundation, Masaryk Youth Organization, Democratic Union of Turk-Muslim Roma in Romania, League of Italian Communities, Tartar Democratic Union (Decisions 11/11.10.2012, 12/11.10.2012, 13/11.10.2012, 28/18.10.2012, 38/29.10.2012, and 41/31.10.2012 of the Central Electoral Bureau).

6. "Romii protestează la uşa lui Băsescu: Vrem să muncim, nu vrem să cerşim!" *Jurnalul National*, September 12, 2012, http://jurnalul.ro/stiri/observator/romii-protesteaza-la-usa-lui-basescu-vrem-sa-muncim-nu-vrem-sa-cersim-623441.html.

7. Florin Cioaba, Marian Daragiu, and Florin Motoi, "Abuzul si discriminarea din Legea electorala 35/2008," Uniunea Nationala a Comunitatilor de Romi, September 17, 2013, http://www.uncr.ro/stire.php?id=10.

8. Minority organizations that are members of the Council of National Minorities and are represented in the Romanian Parliament are subsidized by the state. In 2014 the Roma Party received 2,700,000 euro in subsidies. See Romanian Government Decision No. 52/2014, http://lege5.ro/Gratuit/gm4tambqha/hotararea-nr-52-2014-pentru-aprobarea-modului-de-repartizare-si-de-utilizare-a-sumelor-prevazute-la-lit-a-si-b-din-anexa-nr-3-13-02a-la-bugetul-secretariatului-general-al-guvernului-aprobat-prin-legea/1.

9. Romanian Central Election Bureau, [Summary of Results of the Local Council Elections of June 10 and 24, 2012] (in Romanian), www.beclocale2012.ro/DOCUMENTE%20BEC/REZULTATE%20FINALE/PV%20SCANATE/Consilii%20Locale%20anexa%206a.pdf.

10. National Democratic Institute, *The Hungarian Minority Self-Government System as a Means of Increasing Romani Political Participation*, Assessment Report (Warsaw: OSCE ODIHR, 2007), quotation on 5, http://www.osce.org/odihr/25974.

11. "Választási csalásra készülnek roma közmunkások adataival?" *Népszabadság* (NOL), January 8, 2014, http://nol.hu/belfold/20140108-roma_nevjegyzek__csalasveszely-1436525.

12. "Felfüggesztette Fidesz-tagságát egy roma polgármester," *HVG*, December 17, 2013, http://hvg.hu/itthon/20131217_Felfuggesztette_Fidesztagsagat_egy_roma.

13. The European Commission for Democracy through Law (ECDL), better known as the Venice Commission, is the Council of Europe's advisory body on constitutional matters. For more information, see www.venice.coe.int/WebForms/pages/?p=01_Presentation.

14. Venice Commission (ECDL) and OSCE ODIHR, Joint Opinion on the Act on the Elections of Members of Parliament of Hungary, CDL-AD(2012)012, Opinion No. 662 / 2012 (Strasbourg, June 18, 2012), www.osce.org/odihr/91534?download=true.

15. György Kerényi, "A kisebbségi regisztráció ellen lép fel a Magyarországi Cigány Párt," December 24, 2013, http://vs.hu/24-en-delutanra-kisebbsegi-regisztracio-ellen-lep-fel-magyarorszagi-cigany-part-1224.

16. Quotations from Kovats, "The Politics of Roma Identity."

17. The European Court of Human Rights (ECtHR) can rule on such matters if all national legal options are exhausted. A recent ECtHR case, *Danis and Association of Ethnic Turks v. Romania* found reason to consider if the rights of a Turkish minority organization were violated by exactly the type of regulation I discuss above; see *Danis et Asociația Etnicilor Turci c. Roumanie*, App. no. 16632/09, ECtHR, Section 3, Communicated Case (March 11, 2013) (in French), http://hudoc.echr.coe.int/eng?i=001-118361.

18. Viktória Mohácsi, "Government Initiatives: Hungary's School Integration Program," in *Separate and Unequal, Combating Discrimination Against Roma in Education*, ed. Edwin Rekosh and Maxine Sleeper (Budapest: Public Interest Law Initiative, 2004), 239–54.

19. European Parliament, Resolution on Discrimination against the Roma, adopted 13 July 1995, *Official Journal of the EU* 249 (September, 25, 1995): 156. The mandate of Roma MEP, Mr. Juan De Dios Ramirez-Heredia (Spain, Socialist), started in 1994 and ended in 1999.

20. See European Parliament, Resolution on the Accession of Romania to the European Union, adopted 30 November 2006 (2006/2115(INI)) *Official Journal of the EU* 316E (December 22, 2006): 121–24, http://eur-lex.europa.eu/legal-content/EN/TXT/?qid=1441082670129&uri=CELEX:52006IP0512; European Parliament, Resolution on the Accession of Bulgaria to the European Union, adopted 30 November 2006 (2006/2114(INI)) *Official Journal of the EU* 316E (December 22, 2006): 117–21, http://eur-lex.europa.eu/legal-content/EN/TXT/?qid=1441083380399&uri=CELEX:52006IP0511.

21. European Parliament Resolution on the situation of the Roma in the European Union, adopted 28 April 2005 (P6_TA(2005)0151) *Official Journal of the EU* 45E (February 23, 2006): 129–33, http://eur-lex.europa.eu/legal-content/EN/TXT/?uri=CELEX:52005IP0151&qid=1441083795675.

22. European Commission, *An EU Framework for National Roma Integration Strategies up to 2020*, Communication, COM(2011) 173 (Brussels, April 5, 2011), http://ec.europa.eu/justice

/policies/discrimination/docs/com_2011_173_en.pdf; Council of the European Union, *Council Conclusions on an EU Framework for National Roma Integration Strategies up to 2020,* 10658/11 (Brussels, May 19, 2011), http://ec.europa.eu/justice/policies/discrimination/docs/com_2011_173 _en.pdf.

23. OSCE Office for Democratic Institutions and Human Rights (ODIHR), *Implementation of the Action Plan on Improving the Situation of Roma and Sinti Within the OSCE Area: Status Report 2013 (Renewed Commitments, Renewed Challenges)* (Warsaw: OSCE/ODIHR, 2013), 19–23, http://www.osce.org/odihr/107406.

24. For more on the Decade, including publications and reports of events, see "The Decade of Roma Inclusion: 2005–2015," http://www.romadecade.org/.

25. See, for example, European Commission, "Contribute to Change—Young Women in Political Careers," July 7, 2012, project description available at http://ec.europa.eu/citizenship /sharing-experiences/support-to-projects-initiated-by-civil-society-organisations/02072012_en .htm; European Union Agency for Fundamental Rights (FRA), "Political Participation of Persons with Disabilities," http://fra.europa.eu/en/project/2013/political-participation-persons-disabilities; the site includes links to several reports.

Contributors

Jacqueline Bhabha is FXB Director of Research, Professor of the Practice of Health and Human Rights at the Harvard School of Public Health; the Jeremiah Smith Jr. Lecturer in Law at Harvard Law School; and an Adjunct Lecturer in Public Policy at the Harvard Kennedy School. She received a first class honors degree and an M.Sc. from Oxford University, and a J.D. from the College of Law in London. She has published extensively on issues of transnational child migration, refugee protection, children's rights, and citizenship. She is editor of *Children Without a State*, author of *Child Migration & Human Rights in a Global Age*, and editor of *Human Rights and Adolescence* (University of Pennsylvania Press, 2014).

James A. Goldston is executive director of the Open Society Justice Initiative, which advances the rule of law and legal protection of rights worldwide. A leading practitioner of international human rights and criminal law, he has litigated several groundbreaking cases before the European Court of Human Rights and UN treaty bodies, including on issues of torture, counterterrorism, and racial discrimination. He has previously served as coordinator of prosecutions and senior trial attorney in the Office of the Prosecutor at the International Criminal Court, and as an Assistant United States Attorney in the Southern District of New York.

Will Guy is a research fellow at the Centre for the Study of Ethnicity and Citizenship at the University of Bristol, UK. After completing a Ph.D. on Communist policy for Czechoslovak Roma, he researched Roma issues in Europe, editing four books and writing extensively. From 2000 onward he evaluated Roma integration programs in Bulgaria, Croatia, the Czech Republic, Greece, Hungary, Slovakia, and Spain for the European Commission and was joint author reviewing EU assistance to Roma in Central and Eastern Europe. Recently he was lead author of a study of Roma-related policies and best practices in eighteen EU member states.

Fernando Macías is a Ph.D. candidate at Universitat de Barcelona (UB). He holds B.A. and M.A. degrees in education. He received a Special Master Award in 2013 for his research, "Roma Family Participation in the Schools." He is a Roma researcher at the Centre of Research in Theories and Practices That Overcome Inequalities at the UB (CREA-UB) and also a member of the Roma Studies Centre there. He has participated in the FP6 European research "INCLUD-ED: Strategies for Inclusion and Social Cohesion in Europe from Education" (2006–2011).

David Mark, born in Timisoara, Romania, completed his M.A. in international relations and European studies at the West University of Hungary. He is a Roma activist and was previously a Roma Initiatives fellow for the Open Society Foundations. He was also the coordinator of the European Roma Policy Coalition (ERPC), and informal coalition of nongovernmental organizations operating at the EU level on issues of human rights, antidiscrimination, antiracism, social inclusion, and Roma rights. Previously, he held the position of Executive Director of the Roma Civil Alliance of Romania (ACRR) and was a member of the staff in the cabinet of Member of the European Parliament Viktória Mohácsi. He is a Ph.D. candidate in political sciences at the University of Bucharest.

Margareta Matache is a Roma rights activist from Romania. In 2012 she was awarded a Hauser research fellowship at the FXB Center for Health and Human Rights, Harvard University, where she is currently an instructor. From 2005 to 2012 she was the executive director of Romani CRISS, a leading NGO that defends and promotes the rights of Roma. During her tenure at Romani CRISS she took a stand against discrimination in landmark cases targeting the president, prime minister, and foreign minister of Romania. The organization's advocacy and litigation efforts also contributed to the approval of the domestic School Desegregation Bill. She completed her Ph.D. at the University of Bucharest magna cum laude. Her publications and research have covered the rights and agency of Roma children and adolescents, anti-Roma sentiments and violence, segregation in education, and participatory action research.

David Meyer is a foreign affairs officer in the U.S. Department of State's Bureau of Democracy, Human Rights and Labor Office of European Affairs. He manages the State Department's human rights and democracy policies in Eurasia and the Western Balkans in addition to covering regional Roma issues. David joined the Department as a Presidential Management Fellow and completed assignments in USAID's Office of Conflict Management and Mitigation and at the U.S. embassy in Warsaw. He holds an M.Sc. in comparative politics from the London School of Economics and Political Science and a bachelor's degree in international affairs from George Washington University.

Andrzej Mirga is Polish Roma, an ethnologist, analyst, activist, and the first Roma to study at the Jagiellonian University in Cracow. He taught at various universities, led the Polish Roma association, served as an expert to the Council of Europe's Specialist Group on Roma/Gypsies and to the European Commission's High-Level Group on the labor market and ethnic minorities under Vladimir Spidla, and as Roma representative to the Poland's Common Commission of the Government and National Ethnic Minorities. He is a long-term associate of the Project on Ethnic Relations, a U.S.-based organization. He served as Senior Adviser on Roma and Sinti Issues at OSCE ODIHR (2006–2013). Recently, he joined the Roma Education Fund's board. He is the author of many publications.

Kálmán Mizsei is currently Head of Mission for the European Union Advisory Mission on Civilian Security Sector Reform in Ukraine. Between 2011 and 2013 he served as chairman of the Making the Most of EU Funds for Roma Integration at the Open Society Foundations, supporting George Soros's effort for Roma integration in Central and Southeastern Europe. He is also adjunct professor at the Central European University in Budapest. He served as EU Special Representative for Moldova, negotiating over the Transnistrian "frozen conflict" and contributing to the solving of the Moldovan political crisis in 2009. Previously he was United Nations Development Programme Regional Director for Europe and the CIS. He holds a Ph.D. in economics from the Budapest University of Economics and advised numerous governments in Central and Eastern Europe on their economic transitions.

Krista Oehlke is a program coordinator at the FXB Center for Health and Human Rights at Harvard University, where she coordinates the center's

Child Protection curriculum, a joint venture with UNICEF, and previously served as editorial assistant for the *Health and Human Rights Journal*. She supports a range of human rights projects at the center through research, writing, and reporting; and her emerging interest in Roma rights has been bolstered by some of this work. She holds a B.A. in comparative literature from Dartmouth College, with concentrations in Spanish and philosophy.

Alexandra Oprea is a Romanian Romani attorney, author, and activist who lives in the United States. Under the tutelage of Kimberlé Crenshaw at both Columbia University and UCLA, she has pioneered the application of intersectionality theory to Romani women. She has worked with Romani asylum seekers for over a decade and has worked with Romani grassroots organizations, as well as with the African American Policy Forum on affirmative action campaigns. She has published in the areas of racism, intersectionality, domestic violence, child marriages, exclusionary discourses, and reproductive rights. She received a B.A. from Vassar College, a J.D. from UCLA School of Law, and an M.I.A. from Columbia University, School of International and Public Affairs, where she focused on human rights in the context of race and gender discrimination.

Elena Rozzi is an Italian activist engaged in promoting Roma and migrant children's rights through advocacy, research, and legal empowerment. She serves on the board of the Association for Legal Studies on Migration, a leading NGO that promotes the rights of discriminated minorities in Italy, where she coordinates several projects on migrant children and Roma rights. Since 2013, she has been a member of the Scientific Committee of the Italian Ministry of Welfare's National Project for the Inclusion of Roma Children. She has conducted research on Roma integration policies at the Turin University Social Sciences Department and the Association of Italian Municipalities. From 2001 to 2007, she was coordinator of Save the Children Italy's Migrant Children Programme at the national and EU level. She has published several articles and reports.

Erika Schlager is Counsel for International Law for the U.S. Commission on Security and Cooperation in Europe (also known as the Helsinki Commission), a congressionally created agency mandated to monitor the implementation of agreements of the Organization on Security and Cooperation in Europe. She reports on a broad range of human rights concerns, with a particular focus on Central Europe, the human rights situation of the Romani minority, U.S. human rights practices raised in the OSCE context, and international legal issues. Her publications include "A Hard Look at Compliance with 'Soft' Law: The Case of the OSCE," in *Commitment and Compliance*, ed. Dinah Shelton (Oxford University Press, 2003); and "The Roma—Europe's Largest Minority," in Encyclopædia Britannica's 2006 Book of the Year (Special Report). She was educated at the University of North Carolina at Greensboro and holds an A.M. degree in Soviet Union Area Studies from Harvard University and a J.D. degree from the George Washington University Law School. She studied at Warsaw University as a Fulbright Fellow and received a Diploma from the International Institute of Human Rights Law in Strasbourg, France.

Teresa Sordé Martí holds doctorates from Universitat de Barcelona and from Harvard University, both focused on the overcoming of Roma exclusion. She is Serra Húnter Professor of Sociology at the Universitat Autònoma de Barcelona. She has been actively involved in both the European Framework Programme FP5 WORKALÓ, FP6 INCLUD-ED and the FP7 IMPACT-EV, and has directed three researches on Roma migration in Spain (funded by OSCE and the Spanish Ministry of Science). She has published three books in the cultural and Romani studies fields as well as articles in publications including the *Journal of Mixed Methods*, *Qualitative Inquiry*, *Ethnicities*, and the *Journal of Migration and Ethnic Studies*.

Michael Uyehara is currently deputy head of the Mission in Serbia of the Organization for Security and Cooperation in Europe (OSCE). Prior to his Belgrade assignment, he had responsibility at the U.S. Department of State for human rights policy in Europe and Eurasia. From 2009 to 2012, he worked at the U.S. Mission to International Organizations in Vienna. He has also been a U.S. diplomat in Iraq (2008–2009), Ukraine (2005–2008), Indonesia (2000–2002), Japan (1995–1998), and the Philippines (1991–1993). At the State Department, he has been responsible for U.S. policy for Belarus (2002–2004) and the Pacific Islands (1989–1991). He served a consular tour in the UK. His wife, Margaret, is U.S. ambassador to Montenegro; they have five children.

Peter Vermeersch is a professor of politics at the University of Leuven in Belgium, where he is research coordinator of the LINES Institute (Leuven

International and European Studies). He was previously researcher-in-residence at the OSCE Secretariat in Prague (2001) and visiting scholar at the Minda de Gunzburg Center for European Studies, Harvard University (2007–2008). His research covers topics such as minority politics, nationalism, everyday citizenship, and democratization. He is author of a broad range of articles on these topics, published in journals such as *East European Politics and Societies*, *Journal of Ethnic and Migration Studies*, and *Human Rights Quarterly*. His main contribution to Romani studies is a widely cited book on Roma and activism, *The Romani Movement: Minority Politics and Ethnic Mobilization in Contemporary Central Europe* (Berghahn, 2006).

Index

Page numbers in **bold** indicate tables or figures.

Acknowledgments

This book would not have been possible without the support and encouragement of the François-Xavier Bagnoud Center for Health and Human Rights at Harvard University (Harvard FXB). *Realizing Roma Rights* is the brainchild of the FXB Center's Roma Program team and its dedicated engagement with activist and scholarly efforts to seek equality for Europe's Roma citizens.

While anti-Roma violence was spreading in Hungary, and explicitly racist pronouncements were proliferating in Greece, France, and Italy, the FXB Center developed Harvard University's first Roma Program in 2011. Since then, the Center has built its program teaching, research and publications, executive training, and interdisciplinary dialogue. *Realizing Roma Rights* is an important milestone in Harvard FXB's efforts to encourage reflection on historical and contemporary Roma marginalization and address the invisibility of Roma issues in current social and political theory. These efforts have been supported by much advice and encouragement from FXB colleagues along the way. We extend our deepest gratitude to Jennifer Leaning, Arlan Fuller, Bonnie Shnayerson, Cynthia Gomez, and Tezeta Tulloch. Without Krista Oehlke's skillful management of the publication process and manuscript completion, this volume would not have seen the light of day. Special thanks also go to Susan Lloyd McGarry for her superb editorial skills.

In April 2013, a range of Harvard centers, including the FXB Center, the Mahindra Humanities Center, and the Center for European Studies, collaborated with the Office of Democratic Institutions and Human Rights (ODIHR) of the Organization for Security and Cooperation in Europe (OSCE) to organize Harvard's first Roma conference. Entitled *Realizing Roma Rights: Addressing Violence, Discrimination and Segregation in Europe*, the conference brought together a stellar line up of experts from the academy, government, and civil society. This jointly edited book, a collaboration between

FXB and the OSCE/ODIHR Contact Point for Roma and Sinti Issues, reflects the collective endeavor spearheaded by the conference. We are grateful to all the conference partners, participants, and attendees. Particular thanks are due to Elaine Papoulias, Steven Biel, and Sarah Razor for their generous contributions. We are also grateful to Mirjam Karoly, the OSCE/ODIHR Senior Advisor on Roma and Sinti Issues, for her support.

Our publisher, Peter Agree, has been a source of inspiration and support since the outset. It was he who recognized the importance of a volume on Roma rights issues, who entrusted this project to us, and supported its progress throughout. We owe him a huge debt of thanks. We are also grateful to the technical and anonymous reviewers, whose careful advice strengthened our arguments and refined our thinking.

Finally, no image could better reflect our hope for the book and the hard work that went into its production than *A Moment of Change* (*Moment Promène*), the cover painting by renowned Roma Serbian artist Zoran Tairovic. His work honors the struggles of the Roma movement to realize rights, and we are grateful to him for giving us permission to use the image.